CLOSE REA

THE READER

Edited by FRANK LENTRICCHIA

and ANDREW DUBOIS

DUKE UNIVERSITY PRESS   *Durham and London 2003*

© 2003 Duke University Press
All rights reserved
Printed in the United States of America on acid-free paper ⊚
Typeset in Trump Mediaeval by Tseng Information Systems, Inc.
Library of Congress Cataloging-in-Publication Data
appear on the last printed page of this book.
Acknowledgment of copyrights begins on page 385.

Close Reading

To Tom Ferraro

CONTENTS

PREFACE

T HIS ANTHOLOGY IS INTENDED to represent and undercut what we take to be the major clash in the practice of literary criticism in the past century: that between so-called formalist and so-called nonformalist (especially "political") modes of reading. The headings of the two major sections are meant to suggest that formalist critics are always interested in the vast world which lies outside literature and that the nonformalists who have dominated literary criticism and theory over the last decades of the twentieth century do their most persuasive work by attending closely to the artistic character of the text before them. The common ground, then, is a commitment to close attention to literary texture and what is embodied there. We emphasize the continuity, not the clash of critical schools—this is the implicit polemical point of the book—though we believe it important to remain on high alert to the major differences. We like to imagine an ideal literary critic as one who commands and seamlessly integrates both styles of reading.

It is our hope for students who might use this book, but have no desire to become literary critics—that is to say, most students—that they will emerge better equipped as close readers to deal critically with the messages, linguistically and visually encoded, that flood and threaten to drown us daily. By dealing "critically" we mean "independently": persons who wish to preserve and sustain their independence are good close readers.

Thanks to Grant Farred who made an important suggestion regarding the selections, and to Jason Puskar and Helen Vendler for their generous critical readings of a draft of the introduction. Caleb Smith compiled the index, and Charles Del Dotto acquired the permissions; finally, thanks to Ken Wissoker for his long-standing support of the project.

The introduction is the work of Andrew DuBois, for which his older collaborator is grateful.

CLOSE READING

Close Reading: An Introduction
ANDREW DuBois

THE THEMATIC FOCUS of this anthology is on reading and critical response. But since reading and responding to what one reads is an ancient practice, of which there exists a library of examples ecclesiastical, ecstatic, pedantic, dogmatic, incidental, and so on, the book before you confines itself to essays of literary speculation in the twentieth century that have a more or less direct bearing on the question of how to read a text.

More specifically, the selections in this volume (beginning with an essay by John Crowe Ransom published in *The World's Body* in 1938) range from the formalist work of the New Critics—though among the writers here, only Ransom (and only then by implication) gives himself that name—to work of the later twentieth century concerned more with matters in essence political. The arrangement of these selections is not meant to make claims about critical progress or regress; it is, however, meant to assert that a genuine (perhaps the central) debate in twentieth-century literary criticism is a debate between formalist and nonformalist methods of response. Conversely, the selections themselves are meant subtly to obscure the assumed clarity of these categories; for wherever there is deep engagement with art, there can likely be no methodological purity, nor programmatic effacement of the fact of multivalence. (The two headings under which these essays are arranged—"Formalism (Plus)" and "After Formalism?"—are in their willful diffidence meant both to acknowledge and to question the aforementioned categories.)

The selections here have two things in common. First, as has been suggested above, they all respond directly to objects of literary (and sometimes cinematic) art, from *Hamlet* to "Lycidas" to "The Rape of the Lock," from *Ulysses* to *Invisible Man* to *Beloved*, with clusters around the writings of

Austen, Keats, and Stevens in between. Second, they are all meant to be engaging to read. Such is also the intention of the following introduction. By responding with care to the objects of literary critical art reprinted below, this introduction hopes to offer a succinct story of the issue of reading in modern literary criticism. Like all stories, what falls within its compass is partial; and yet within its compass, the story is complete.

Paying attention: almost anyone can do it; and it's not requisite for reading, but for reading well? At any rate, attention, properly paid, will, over time, with personally productive tendencies or habits of focus and repetitions of thought remembered into generally applicable patterns, beget method.

We have now reached close reading good and proper. As a term, *close reading* hardly seems to leave the realm of so-called common sense, where it would appear to mean something understandable and vague like "reading with special attention"; but it is also jargon, albeit jargon of a not uninviting variety. The term *close reading* is associated in critical history with the New Criticism, a mode of Anglo-American scholarship that began between the World Wars and flourished into an institutional dominance that would not be relinquished until sometime during the war in Vietnam. The New Criticism had its theoretical side, but critical practice was what finally distinguished it most successfully from other modes of scholarly work. It benefited from being eminently teachable, and the entrenchment of its methods, first in universities and then in secondary schools, attests to the amenability of that practice to practitioners of varying sophistication. Paul de Man, not exactly the great defender of this practice, but who nevertheless wrote on it with eloquence and respectful clarity, gives a good sense of what it entails in recounting his graduate student experience as a teaching assistant for "The Interpretation of Literature," a course taught by Ruben Brower at Harvard in the 1950s. "Students," writes de Man,

> were not to say anything that was not derived from the text they were considering. They were not to make any statements that they could not support by a specific use of language that actually occurred in the text. They were asked, in other words, to begin by reading texts closely as texts and not to move at once into the general context of human experience or history. Much more humbly or modestly, they were to start out from the bafflement that such singular turns of tone, phrase, and figure were bound to produce in readers attentive enough to notice them and honest enough not

to hide their non-understanding behind the screen of received ideas that often passes, in literary instruction, for humanistic knowledge.[1]

Still today, with the supposed decline of New Criticism as institutional practice, it is not uncommon at even the highest levels of undergraduate education that students be asked to "do a close reading," if only as a sort of hors d'oeuvre to the final extratextual platter.

How did the seemingly nonspecific concept of close reading become a "thing" that it is possible to "do"? Again, we must insist on actual practice and its influence, since, for instance, there is no *single* influential manifesto or statement of purpose that insists on the term itself as the sole name for a particular practice. In *The New Criticism* (1941), which gave a name to the critics, and gave chapter by chapter accounts of I. A. Richards and William Empson, T. S. Eliot, Yvor Winters, and, essentially, himself, John Crowe Ransom used the term, but not in a very specific sense. Of course, the same could be said for the term "New Criticism," which has been hypostatized into a capital-letter entity despite, for instance, appearing in that form in Ransom's book only in the title (admittedly, a fine place for it, in terms of nominal promotion). Title notwithstanding, and despite the term's constant use by Ransom, the manner of its usage does not necessarily announce its importance as terminology. Its first occurrence comes, in fact, with a sideways caveat against generalizing the practice of a range of writers under any single designation (the critic being discussed is R. P. Blackmur): "though he is distinct, and repels the tag of any common category, he is nevertheless a 'new' critic in the sense of this book."[2] In this case, however, Ransom's simplicity and repetition proved a virtue for subsequent recognition, as he employs just a simple subject, an even simpler adjective, and now-jettisoned inverted commas: "Critical writing like [Blackmur's] is done in our time. In depth and precision at once it is beyond all earlier criticism in our language. It is a new criticism, and it has already some unity of method. . . . It is new, and I have tried to exhibit it for what it is worth. . . . But criticism is an extraordinarily difficult thing to get right, and this is a new criticism. What is new is unsure, inconsistent, perhaps raw; even this new criticism"[3]; "Discussion of the new criticism must start with Mr. Richards. The new criticism very nearly began with him"[4]; and, skipping ahead: "Writings as acute and at the same time as patient as this have not existed in English criticism, I think, before Richards and Empson. They become frequent now; Richards and Empson have spread quickly. That is a principal reason why I think it is time to identify a powerful intellectual movement that deserves to be called a new criticism."[5] As to the mystery of how names take hold, guesses are perhaps better left unhazarded, or better made by historians, philologists, and social anthropologists. At any rate, a critical designation it became, naming critics marked, as we have already heard from Ransom, by depth, precision, acuity, and patience, by their giving of a special kind of attention in relation to literary art; special enough to be called new, these critics veered less far from the literary objects of art than did their immediate predecessors, and their diverse methods, appropriately enough, became known as close reading.

From our current vantage, paying attention to the literary text in and of itself may or may not seem a given; at any rate, it is a notion which, whether or not necessary in the collective mind of our critical era, seems nonetheless natural to scholarship. Yet it was not always so. The New Criticism was in fact a radical response to arcane Indo-European philology on the one hand, and on the other to a body of historical scholarship that seemed more deeply interested in sociology and biography than in literature. A classic example of work of the latter kind is Hippolyte Taine's *History of English Literature* (1864). Though in certain senses comprehensive, this French scholar's study favored a method of the sort that appalled the New Critics, so far did they consider it to be from what was essential in studying literature. Taine laid this method bare in the book's introduction: "The discovery has been made that a literary work is not a mere play of the imagination, . . . but a transcript of contemporary manners and customs and the sign of a particular state of intellect. The conclusion derived from this is that, through literary monuments, we can retrace the way in which men felt and thought many centuries ago."[6] Elsewhere Taine compresses his sociological drive into one succinct sentence: "I have undertaken to write the history of a literature and to ascertain the psychology of a people."[7] Yet to get grandly to the people required first to get to the person ("Nothing exists except through the individual; it is necessary to know the individual himself."); and what better way to get to the person, in a history of literature, than through the literary work? This is just where Taine goes, though the turnaround from work to worker is so quick that one is strained to remember the work:

> What revelations do we find in the calendared leaves of a modern poem? A modern poet, a man like De Musset, Victor Hugo, Larmartine, or Heine, graduated from a college and traveled, wearing a dress-coat and gloves, favored by ladies, bowing fifty times and uttering a dozen witticisms in an evening, reading daily newspapers, generally occupying an apartment on the second story, not overcheerful on account of his nerves, and especially because, in this dense democracy in which we stifle each other, the discredit of official rank exaggerates his pretensions by raising his importance,

and, owing to the delicacy of his personal sensations, leading him to regard himself as a Deity. Such is what we detect behind modern *meditations* and *sonnets.*[8]

Taine's vigorous, amusing writing cannot obscure the absence of a certain kind of reading. The New Critics reacted against a criticism of such flippant over-determination; and using our own meaning of the literary "modern," we might well ask: How do you ascertain from reading *The Waste Land* what floor of his apartment building Eliot occupied, if he occupied an apartment at all, and what does it have to do with the poem?

Criticism would eventually become more sophisticated and (in some cases) more subtle in using biographical material to elucidate the literary work, just as it has supposedly become more sophisticated in its methods for moving from a commitment to the text to engagement with the world. Yet it seems in retrospect that any advances that occurred depended in part on New Critical lessons. For otherwise, these moves towards extrinsic contexts ran the risk of disregarding the literary work that was ostensibly the object of inquiry. This strain of disregard in the old criticism is particularly grating to certain sensibilities, suggesting as it does that the literary work itself is extraneous, a hindrance to what is truly important: as Taine asks, "Why do you study the shell unless to form some idea of the animal? In the same way do you study the document in order to comprehend the man; both shell and document are dead fragments and of value only as indications of the complete living being. The aim is to reach this being; this is what you strive to reconstruct. It is a mistake to study the document as if it existed alone by itself."[9] The New Critics combated an approach such as Taine's with a simple negation, saying, in effect: It is a mistake *not* to study the document as if it existed alone.

But this position initiates its own problems, for it is not so simple to know what should be studied in a work. The New Critics focused on what de Man (in the earlier citation) calls "turns of tone, phrase, and figure," but even this does not hint at the specificity of the critical vocabulary that developed out of their practice. As a specialized vocabulary it proved to be widely accessible, and indeed many of their favorite terms have been "naturalized" into the institutional equivalent of rock formations. The terms were not neologisms, but instead were common enough, though perhaps not in wide critical circulation. One such term can be found in the title of William Empson's first book, *Seven Types of Ambiguity* (1929). Now, few readers would contest that poetic language is laden with ambiguity; the fullness of meaning the term implies is indeed a mainstay of our recognizing the richness of writing. Yet in 1941, even a critic as astute as Ransom registers, with a humility perhaps not proven by his work, a bit of mild surprise at the term: "Ambiguity will occur if a poem invites two different readings of its meanings . . . and does not decide conclusively between them. It is rather a commoner thing than the dull readers—with whom I concede my own affiliations—have supposed."[10] Empson is typical of the New Critics in his extensive elaboration of his primary term, in what amounts, as the title of his book suggests, to a critical taxonomy.

Empson's "ambiguity" is also telling as jargon because it suggests a general New Critical concern with *tension* in the poem. Ambiguity for Empson registers the tension produced in a poem by competing meanings in a word (a concept he investigated more fully in *The Structure of Complex Words* [1951]). Poetic tension and its resolution was central to New Critical interest—which is a boon to the criticism, insofar as the active mind, somewhat belying its contemplative aspect, apparently is drawn toward energy and motion, however metaphorical that motion may be. A fine vigorous mind like Taine's would not stay put with an object he ultimately found staid, but made an extrinsic move to maintain interest. The New Critics instead made central the tropic, imagistic and thematic motion they saw as intrinsic to the poem, thus satisfying what seems to be an unspoken law of the intellect: It needs some *action*.

The writer who probably did the most to promote this aspect of the New Criticism was Cleanth Brooks. Much of his influence is due to the didactic strength of two widely adopted textbooks cowritten with his fellow southerner Robert Penn Warren, *Understanding Poetry* (1938) and *Understanding Fiction* (1943). But it is finally in his essays that Brooks established most powerfully his own soon-to-be-standard terms in a series of brilliant readings that showed everyone how best to use them. In "Irony as a Principle of Structure," first published in 1948, Brooks proves his title with explications of a well-chosen, wide range of work by Gray, Arnold, Shakespeare, Wordsworth, and Randall Jarrell. (While the New Critics have been charged with bias in favor of the metaphysicals and moderns, whom they admittedly promoted, their work shows surprising catholicity.) *Irony*, first and foremost, is a quality of tension between a statement and its context. Brooks elaborates the term beyond this primary meaning, but like Empson's *ambiguity* it has some form of tension in its signifying background.

A term achieving like prominence is *paradox*, which Brooks elaborates most memorably in the first chapter of *The Well Wrought Urn* (1947). The book's title, which suggests the New Critics' high valuation of finish of construction, is drawn from Donne's "The Canonization," and Brooks's explication of that poem in chapter one ("The Language of Paradox") is in all likelihood the paradigmatic New Critical reading. Again, *paradox* is a term signifying a certain kind of tension (this time, a tension of logic), and again, Brooks leads readers to an understanding of the term by leading them through some poems. He begins with Wordsworth's sonnets "It is a Beauteous Evening, Calm and Free" and "Composed upon Westminster Bridge"; for although Wordsworth "usually prefers thc direct attack" in his poetry, which "would not appear to promise many examples of the language of paradox,"[11] Brooks asserts that the power of these poems does not arise from their use of poetic language and figures *per se* (indeed, he considers the latter sonnet to contain "some very flat writing and some well-worn comparisons,"[12] but springs instead from the paradoxical situation out of which that language arises. Having shown that even a poet he charges with "timid[ity]" resorts to this basic aspect of the "normal language of poetry," Brooks characteristically "refer[s] the reader to a concrete case" in which a poet "consciously employ[s]" paradox "to gain a compression and precision otherwise unobtainable"[13]:

> Donne's "Canonization" ought to provide a sufficiently extreme instance. The basic metaphor which underlies the poem (and which is reflected in the title) involves a sort of paradox. For the poet daringly treats profane love as if it were divine love. The canonization is not that of a pair of holy anchorites who have renounced the world and the flesh. The hermitage of each is the other's body; but they do renounce the world, and so their title to sainthood is cunningly argued. The poem then is a parody of Christian sainthood; but it is an intensely serious parody of a sort that modern man, habituated as he is to an easy yes or no, can hardly understand. He refuses to accept the paradox as a serious rhetorical device; and since he is able to accept it only as a cheap trick, he is forced into this dilemma. Either: Donne does not take love seriously; here he is merely sharpening his wit as a sort of mechanical exercise. Or: Donne does not take sainthood seriously; here he is merely indulging in a cynical and bawdy parody.
>
> Neither account is true; a reading of the poem will show that Donne takes both love and religion seriously; it will show, further, that the paradox is here his inevitable instrument. But to see this plainly will require a closer reading than most of us give to poetry.[14]

Brooks launches from this model of clarity into an almost line by line explication of the poem that is as "cunningly argued" as the poem itself. The intellectual force of the argument is provided by Brooks's running perception of Donne's "development of the theme" and "modulation of tone," a perception made possible and manageable by his close tracking of "the dominant meta-

phor"—the world of the lovers is like the world of holy anchorites in their respective relation to the secular world—which all along contains and supports
the paradox between the sacred and the profane. The rhetorical force of the argument is provided by the lucid, authoritative, decorous (not stodgy) style that
Brooks shares with most of his New Critical *confrères*. No band of critics can
touch them as writers.

Ambiguity, paradox, irony, tone—all these terms make an appearance in
"Keats's Sylvan Historian: History Without Footnotes," Brooks's masterful reading of "Ode on a Grecian Urn." So does another term, the importance of which
was already inherent in the critical elevation of *irony* and *ambiguity*. That term,
context, would return in a different incarnation to haunt the New Critics, used
by later critics who argued that the formalist readings of the earlier school
did not take into account factors of history, race, gender, and sexuality that
would necessarily complicate any interpretation. This claim is true enough,
and Brooks perhaps would not argue with it (though he might amend "complicate" to "muddle"); he makes clear that he has no intention of establishing a context extrinsic to the poem, a decision that must itself be historicized.
We have already seen something of the tradition of reductive sociology against
which these formalist critics were working; and the seeming irrelevance of such
extrinsic investigation is parodied in Brooks's citation of an ironic question
from Browning: " 'What porridge had John Keats?' "

Still, political critics today might find themselves sympathetic to the question Brooks asks of the "Ode," namely, "What is the relation of the beauty (the
goodness, the perfection) of a poem to the truth or falsity of what it seems to
assert?" Their sympathy would probably end where his method for finding an
answer begins, which is with the "organic context" or inner coherence of the
poem. It probably needs to be noted that there is nothing inherent in Brooks's
method that makes it politically dubious. On the contrary, it seems that the *literary* critic must necessarily first establish the intrinsic context of the literary
object; otherwise, all extrinsic moves (which are also "contextual" work) are
themselves suspicious. As Brooks writes, there are "claims to be made upon the
reader"; it only seems fair to honor these claims before making claims upon
the poem. Of what they consist, of course, is neither self-evident nor timeless.
Brooks certainly has a special terminology in which he voices those claims:
"If the urn has been properly dramatized, if we have followed the development of the metaphors, if we have been alive to the paradoxes which work
throughout the poem, perhaps then, we shall be prepared for the enigmatic,
final paradox which the 'silent form' utters" (this volume). But beneath that terminological specificity is a notion being virtually preached to us, the notion of

the reader's responsibility to the text: *if we have followed, if we have been alive, then we shall be prepared.* This responsibility, as we will see, takes many forms, and carries with it many questions, not the least pressing of which have come in recent years from such political critics as we earlier invoked. The essence of responsibility in Brooks is revealed in the recurrence of a certain kind of transitional statement ("If one attends closely . . . ," "Attended to with care . . .") that hints at the love the critic has for the object of art under study. Responsibility as love: it may be naïve, maybe not, but it's decent.

Kenneth Burke complicates everything. Associated until recently with the New Critics, Burke is essentially an intellectual free agent, clearly so in "Symbolic Action in a Poem by Keats." The essay has much in common with Brooks's "Sylvan Historian." First and obviously, both critics give readings of the "Ode on a Grecian Urn." Second and strangely, their readings work in the same direction and share the same purpose: moving through the poem, and registering its developments and transformations, they reach the famous final oracular statement, which they then can justify, Brooks in terms of "dramatic propriety," Burke "dramatistically."

But with reading, the differences start to show. "Suppose," writes Burke, "that we had but this one poem by Keats, and knew nothing of its author or its period, so that we could treat it only in itself, as a series of internal transformations to be studied in their development from a certain point, and without reference to any motives outside the Ode" (this volume). It is an enviably brief summary of what would come to be called New Critical method, with which Burke must have some affinity, since he can so gracefully name it. And yet (with what Burke calls "the inestimable advantage that goes with having looked ahead") one might predict that his initial "suppose" is pointing up the fact that the sentence that follows it is pure supposition, and as such, is impossible to sustain given the facts of an impure world. Or not impossible, perhaps, but (as far as Burke is concerned) undesirable and irresponsible, since an idealistic criticism that disallows any external knowledge is unable to account for the true human work a poem does. Still, for Burke, a consideration of material outside the text is not a license to forego close reading in a New Critical sense:

> Our primary concern is to follow the transformations of the poem itself. But to understand its full nature as a symbolic act, we should use whatever knowledge is available. In the case of Keats, not only do we know the place of this poem in his work and its time, but also we have material to guide our speculations as regards correlations between poem and poet. I grant that

such speculations interfere with the symmetry of criticism as a game. . . . But linguistic analysis has opened up new possibilities in the correlating of producer and product—and these concerns have such important bearing upon matters of culture and conduct in general that no sheer conventions or ideals of criticism should be allowed to interfere with their development (this volume).

The passage points in several ways to the uniqueness of Burke in the New Critical milieu. First, there is his drive to historicize—his wish to place the poem in relation to both the career of its author and to the literary era in which it was written. (This approach is hardly wholly absent from the work of other critics, but Burke is more insistent on its inclusion.) Second, there is his admission of biographical "material"—in this case, Keats's letters. Third, there is his recourse to "new possibilities" in "linguistic analysis," which we might take here as shorthand for Marxist and Freudian critical method: the former is manifest in Burke's argument for the "relation between private property and the love-death equation"; the latter shows through in his noticing moves "from purely dialectical considerations into psychological ones," as well as in his emphasis on the "correlation between the state of agitation in the poems and the physical condition of the poet" (this volume). Fourth, and most Burkean of all, is his conception of the poem as "symbolic act."

Human beings are symbol makers, symbol users. Burke contends that the use of language in the creation of a linguistic structure or object of art is itself an act, a symbolic act the purpose of which goes beyond (or lies behind) the mere creation of that structure. This purpose tends toward psychic purgation, assuagement, or transcendence. In the case of the "Ode," Burke asserts that the purpose achieved by the poem is the symbolic transcendence by the romantic poet Keats of romantic philosophy, a purpose Burke renders all the more poignant by showing how the spiritual nature of that transcendence is dialectically connected to the sad physical facts of Keats's grave disease. Burke's Aristotelian strategy is to analyze such linguistic structures "dramatistically," a move less obscure than it sounds. Remember that the essential fact of drama is the conflict of forces. Beginning with the poem and moving to relevant outside sources, Burke recreates the dramatic process that led to the poem itself. His standard terms for the forces in conflict are the aforementioned *purpose*; *agency* (in this case, writing); *agent* (Keats); *scene* (specifically, Keats's life; generally, nineteenth-century Romanticism); and *act* ("Ode on a Grecian Urn"). These forces combine in any number of ways ("ratios"). In the course of divining, through his dramatistic method, the manner in which these ratios make themselves felt, Burke shows how the poet, through his poem, acts on himself and the culture at large.

This backbone of Burkean analysis is a far stone's throw from anything allowable in the radical, radically circumscribed formalist world of the New Critics; yet Burke can go toe-to-formalist-toe with any critic you want to match him with. Although he, too, tracks metaphor and the development of paradox, makes visible irony's structure and clarifies verbal ambiguity, Burke is just as likely in his formalism to sound less like a New Critic than like a classical rhetorician. To notice "the sweeping periodic sentence" beginning the poem, the "periodic structure" of the rhetorical questions that follow, and the "unheard tonal felicity" served by the return to rhetorical questions in the fourth stanza; to register formal order, as manifest in the third stanza, which as "the central stanza of the Ode" marks the proper "fulcrum of its swing": these are the critical marks of a genuine formalist. Burke's example for current critics is, surprisingly, as a methodological conciliator. In our peaceable post-Burkean critical kingdom, the lion may henceforth lie down with the lamb, the formalist and cultural critic be one. And yet the end of his essay is an admonition in waiting to any critic applying too vulgar a version of cause and effect, to any criticism reducing the text solely to a symptom of cultural disease; which reduction, as you will see when you read his finale, runs the risk of being deeply inessential.

A pattern emerges from the essays inaugurating this collection, representative of the days of their creation, and returns us to the question of what is essential. This pattern as sign of the times is the recurring problem of science. Nowadays, literary critics have their own problems on this score—primarily (and see especially in this regard Eve Kosofsky Sedgwick's "Jane Austen and the Masturbating Girl"), they question scientific "objectivity," under the aegis of which human beings have done some pretty nasty things. The New Critics' problem with science lay elsewhere, and was made manifest not by a revisionary ethics, but by written anxieties. They fought science not by questioning its discursive status as truth, but by proposing an alternative truth of art that was not merely complementary, but better (or so it was asserted).

Burke, again, is somewhat the exception: he lets the "truth" of science stand, for what it is worth, without overt critique, by letting Keats's poem and its final motto do whatever alternative proposing is done; and "anxiety" is too weak a word for Burke, who, given what he has written elsewhere, fears that the meeting of science and ideological system has apocalyptic potential—hence the value of symbolic action, which (among its other virtues) serves as potential diffuser, as (it is hoped) a temporary stopgap against annihilation. Nevertheless, Burke's decision to run his argument through the byways of science suggests the existence of the problem, insofar as the "relief" or "liberating quality" of the Urn's counter-assertion can be understood as resulting from psychic circumstances not limited to the world of nineteenth-century romantic poets. These circumstances may be shared, for instance, by American literary critics of the twentieth century, like Cleanth Brooks, who finds as much relief in Keats's ode as Burke assumes did Keats himself: "[T]he 'truth' which the sylvan historian gives is the only kind of truth which we are likely to get on this earth, and, furthermore, it is the only kind that we *have* to have. The names, dates, and special circumstances, the wealth of data—these the sylvan historian quietly ignores. But we shall never get all the facts anyway—there is no end to the accumulation of facts. Moreover, mere accumulations of facts—a point our own generation is only beginning to realize—are meaningless. The sylvan historian does better than that: it takes a few details and so orders them that we have not only beauty but insight into essential truth" (this volume). The tonal shifts between a vague fatalism and humanist recuperation are rich in this passage, which seems to be addressed against what Brooks earlier in his essay calls "formal history." It is also addressed against science in all its anti-artistic forms. And just as the final statement of the Urn gains its power and validity only through its dramatic context, so does the interpretive work of Brooks, as he sees it, achieve validity only by remaining in its tight formalist orbit; for such work is not "meant to march out of its context to compete with the scientific and philosophical generalizations which dominate our world" (this volume). You cannot compete with that which dominates the world, unless competition means engaging in the inevitable process of being defeated. You can, though, make pointed verbal sideswipes, as Brooks does in a question in his essay on the language of paradox: "What happens to Donne's lovers if we consider them 'scientifically,' without the benefit of the supernaturalism which the poet confers upon them?"[15] Nothing worth while, we can be sure of that.

The critical point here—framed by Brooks in terms of science and history versus literature—is that whatever else it is about, and it is usually about a lot of things, literary criticism is about (or responds to) whatever is going on around it (if only by avoiding it). Criticism, then, is just a more institutionally embedded version of reading in general. Because if you are a reader in this world, sooner or later you will be asked to justify yourself: *what are you doing? what is it good for?* The pressure is real—not life-threatening, maybe, but life-lessening, if reading is part of your life—and it comes not only from some real or imagined flock of heathens. Response to this pressure can take many forms. One that might have appealed to the by now widely reported religious side of some New Critics (but apparently did not) is the refusal to dignify such questions of justification with a direct response, save *Thou sayest,* a position assumed by Jesus before Pilate; or again, when the Pharisees asked Jesus to condemn the adulteress, whereupon he wrote on the ground with his finger, *as though he heard them not.* Nonresponse, it must be added, both among fellow critics and hostile accusers, will usually be labeled quietism, and thus considered a loss in whatever competition is ostensibly occurring; but we must decide for ourselves what is real and what is false response and to what is worth responding.

More satisfactory, or at least potentially more successful, from a worldly point of view, is to match the essence of your own side against the essence of the other—the meat of the matter approach. This strategy has the virtue of bypassing the charge of superficiality implicit in the initial set of questions (veiled accusations), while rhetorically returning the favor. It is an approach taken by John Crowe Ransom in "Poetry: A Note on Ontology." For though the ostensible project there, and one successfully achieved, is the distinguishing of one ideal of poetry from another, Ransom's success would not be so complete did he not distinguish poetry (or art) from science: "*Science gratifies a rational or practical impulse and exhibits the minimum of perception. Art gratifies a perceptual impulse and exhibits the minimum of reason*" (italics are Ransom's). One can agree or disagree with these lines, but their rhetorical balance is obvious—that is, the game is given away neither to science nor to art. But these lines, as we have been taught to read them, are preceded by plenty of "context": "[S]cience at work is always *a science,* and committed to a special interest. It is not by refutation but by abstraction that science destroys the image. It means to get its 'value' out of the image, and we may be sure that it has no use for the image in its original state of freedom. People who are engrossed in their pet 'values' become habitual killers" (this volume); and elsewhere: "Nothing can darken perception better than a repetitive moral earnestness, based on the reputed superiority and higher destiny of the human species. If morality is the code by which we expect the race to achieve the more perfect possession of nature, it is an incitement to a more heroic science, but not to aesthetic experience, nor religious; if it is the code of humility, by which we intend to know nature as nature is, that is another matter; but in an age of science morality is inevitably for the general public the former; and so transcendent a morality as the latter is now unheard of" (this volume). Finally, almost directly before the italicized formula cited above, Ransom wonders, "What will come next? Perhaps poetry, if the gigantic effort of science begins to seem disproportionate to the reward, according to a sense of diminishing returns" (this volume). So, by the arrival of the rhetorically balanced assessment of science and art, its meaning is thoroughly tilted in favor of art; and whatever its application to a general cultural problem, it is also a statement by one man stemming from his values and his own perception of the world.

This, for many of us, is a reason to enjoy criticism: not only because it explains to us or helps us better understand a particular text, but also because loving to read ourselves, we enjoy watching other people read. Criticism, seen in this light, implies a community of readers (perhaps it is really a fictional community, mutually believed in but actually constructed out of a solitary practice). As in any community there is likely to be as much irritation as love (they seem often enough to be parceled together). This friction contributes to the enjoyment produced by critics, for they revise and chastise each other (and sometimes their earlier selves), often in entertaining fashion, usually out of some sense of loyalty to this community of readers (or *their* vision of it, what it *should* be). Almost every major critic has made a written *cri de coeur*, ranging in tone from the recent popular melodrama of Harold Bloom, lamenting in question-begging, self-professed Falstaffian fashion the moral outrage that no one, save he, remembers how to value true literature; to the late Northrop Frye, lamenting in 1951 critical valuation itself, and suggesting (against certain New Critical mores) that "there is surely no reason why criticism, as a systematic and organized study, should not be, at least partly, a science."[16] Dissension, disagreement, lament as potential corrective: all are primary critical facts.

Ransom, as we saw, had something to say about both science and evaluation ("value" and "pet values"), not to mention morality and art. Such a scatter-shot topical approach is not unique. The topics are, however, brought together into coherence through a dialectical argument that finds the scientific poetry of ideas and the imagistic poetry of things synthesized in metaphysical poetry, a synthesis effected primarily through formalist means, exemplified by, but hardly limited to, Ransom's naming and discussion of the technical devices of meter, fiction, and trope.

The poetry of things Ransom calls "Physical Poetry," and since it is poetry, after all, the "things" therein, as the critic makes clear, are not real physical "things," but descriptive representations of things, called "images." Ransom cites the work of the Imagist Amy Lowell as an example of Physical Poetry (here in "Thompson's Lunch Room, Grand Central Station"):

Jagged greenwhite bowls of pressed glass
Rearing snow-peaks of chipped sugar
Above the lighthouse-shaped castors
Of gray pepper and gray-white salt.

Of poetry such as this (he also cites a Shakespearean selection from George Moore's anthology *Pure Poetry*), Ransom remarks that its "visible content is a thing-content," and that it exhibits "the faculty of presenting images so whole and clean that they resist the catalysis of thought." Yet there is counterresistance in a poetry of ideas which Ransom terms Platonic Poetry, the poetic "elaboration of ideas as such." Ransom has little sympathy for such work, seeing in it a Victorian tendency toward the falsification of reality, especially noxious in those moralizing homiletics that trot out the "soul" alongside the "natural" world in "an imitation of Physical Poetry," a "bogus poetry" practiced "in order to show that an image will prove an idea," but one which "does not contain real images but illustrations." Finally, Ransom recognizes that there is in poetry neither a total purity of thing nor of thought. This "impurity" of poetry is not corruption, however, for the aesthetic moment is "a curious moment of suspension; between the Platonism in us, which is militant, always sciencing and devouring, and a starved inhibited aspiration towards innocence which, if it could only be free, would like to respect and know the object as it might of its own accord reveal itself." The critic finds his essential exhibits of these impure but innocent moments of suspension in metaphysical poetry, which Ransom calls "the most original and exciting, and intellectually perhaps the most seasoned, that we know in our literature," and one which he elucidates deftly through formalist means in service of ontological concerns.

It was a special criticism then, and seems even more so now, a fact best attested by citing another cri de coeur, of recent vintage, from Helen Vendler, a critic well known for her formalist work. It will have to serve as our only outside evidence that the kind of work once done by the best New Critics is currently undervalued. The setting is the introduction to a book of essays looking at the changing elements of style in three poets: prosody in terms of its existential meaning in Gerard Manley Hopkins; grammar and its production of atmosphere in Seamus Heaney; and lineation and its connection to the aesthetic and moral character of the volumes of Jorie Graham. Vendler's focus on these "microlevels" of lyric occasions a pensive reflection, which the age, perhaps, demands: "It is distressing, to anyone who cares for and respects the concentrated intellectual and imaginative work that goes into a successful poem, to see how rarely that intense (if instinctive) labor is perceived, remarked on, and appreciated. It is even more distressing—given the human perceptual, aesthetic, and moral signals conveyed (as I hope to show) by such elements as prosody, grammar, and lineation—that most contemporary interpretations of poetry never mention such things, or, if they do, it is to register them factually rather than to deduce their human import."[17] To read Ransom is to follow Vendler in distress, if indeed such work is no longer being frequently done; for astute examination of the most basic materials of a poem, in the process of understanding the reality of a poetry's being, gives us at the very least more material on which to base that decision essential for any reader, the ongoing decision regarding how much, exactly, writing has to do with *our* being, how individually, humanly important reading really, ontologically, is.

The kind of claims made by Ransom, and the work of critical distinction they entail and make explicit, need not come only from the critic, though critics may provide the necessary service of clarifying what is otherwise obscure. The essays in this collection by Murray Krieger, R. P. Blackmur, Frank Lentricchia, and Helen Vendler offer evidence that the literary object itself is already doing critical work, that reading is not just what one does *to* a poem, but that it is often already happening *inside* the poem. It is evidence presented, respectively, in the study of a genre, an author, a poem, and a poetic relationship. We will begin with Murray Krieger's "The Ekphrastic Principle and the Still Movement of Poetry; or *Laokoön* Revisited," since its argument depends on Keats's poem on the Urn, with which we are now so familiar, and on a little poem about a jar, with which we will soon become more intimate.

Krieger's immediate claim is that "the poem, in the very act of becoming successfully poetic . . . implicitly constitutes its own poetic." That is to say, a successful poem is *meta*poetic, insofar as it reveals, through a kind of internal criticism, its own process of becoming a poem. In a time-honored rhetorical ploy preparing the way for a defense, Krieger acknowledges that this is an "extravagant proposal."[18] Most extravagant is probably his ostensible dispute with a classic text of aesthetics, Gotthold Lessing's *Laocoön* (1766), subtitled "An Essay on the Limits of Painting and Poetry." Krieger's essay attempts to relax certain limits between the arts asserted by Lessing, while maintaining all the while the latter's "good sense" in "keeping distinct among the arts what belonged to Peter and what to Paul, what to space and what to time." Space, here, belongs to visual art; time belongs to literature. Noting first that the "spatial metaphor inevitably becomes the critic's language for form" in discussing literary texts, Krieger then asserts a similar phenomenon in literature itself by remarking on the common "use of an object of spatial and plastic art to symbolize the spatiality and plasticity of literature's temporality." Here the argument for a meta-poetics becomes a genre study, for, as Krieger writes, "a classic genre was formulated that, in effect, institutionalized this tactic: the *ekphrasis*, or the imitation in literature of a work of plastic art. The object of imitation, as spatial work, becomes the metaphor for the temporal work which seeks to capture it in that temporality. The spatial work freezes the temporal work even as the latter seeks to free it from space. *Ekphrasis* concerns me here, then, to the extent that I see it introduced in order to use a plastic object as a symbol of the frozen, stilled world of plastic relationships which must be superimposed upon literature's turning world to 'still' it" (this volume). From this follows an investigation calling on a wide range of work across centuries. A litany of the writers discussed— Sir Thomas Browne, Coleridge, Eliot, Faulkner, Herrick, Keats, Marvell, Pope, Wordsworth, and Yeats, among others, not to mention the critics—can easily suggest that range, but the subtlety of the argument, centered in its citations around "the urn as the ekphrastic object par excellence," must be read to be appreciated; suffice it to say (as Krieger says) that by the essay's end, "*Ekphrasis*, no longer a narrow kind of poem defined by its object of imitation, broadens to become a general principle of poetics, asserted by every poem in the assertion of its integrity" (this volume). Out of a formalist study of generic convention, a study of discrete but related works, is thus born a theory applicable across genre.

One measure of the success of the theoretical rubric Krieger offers is that once it has been assimilated, it seems to apply to almost everything one reads when one attends to matters of form. This is the danger of any powerful theory, for such range of application cannot assure a theory's truth, though it may appear to. In fact, range of application may be a point at which to critique a theory, since it points to potential evidence of that theory's effacement of contingency and particularity in the service of a more generalizing, abstracting project; a strong theory tends to produce plenty of such work, since the theory can be overlaid onto any text without that text's having been read properly on its own terms, or, more accurately, with that text's having been pre-read according only to the terms of the applied theory. There is also a body of literary criticism (and no small amount of it) that is neither "theoretical" nor "practical" only, but instead modulates between these (perhaps imaginary, because pure) points on the critical continuum. Such is the case with Krieger, for despite the strength of his theory, it comes (at least in the essay) out of a practical examination of literary genre and lyric form; and when it comes, in its most explicit expression, a few pages from the end, it remains to be argued with and amended. There is, then, a measure of discretion peeking through Krieger's mass of so-called "extravagance," which he might well have been led to by his respectfully regarded historical antagonist; for Lessing, in prefacing his great aesthetic work, warns precisely against critical indiscretion. The critic who compares poetry and painting must take care that his observations are exact:

> The principal value of [the critic's] observations depends on their correct application to the individual case. And since for every one really discerning critic there have always been fifty clever ones, it would have been a miracle if this application had always been made with the caution necessary to maintain a proper balance between the two arts.[19]

Let us say, using Lessing's words, that a chief problem of literary criticism has been and will be the maintaining of a proper balance between two arts; that is, between practical and theoretical criticism, between formal explanation generated from close attention to specific texts and a more general explanation generated from a process of abstraction. Neither art can be dispensed with, and their balancing act is always tenuous at best; but no matter how the critical pendulum of an era swings, there will likely always be critics who have nothing more to prove than their attentive relationship to the object of art, a true reader's relationship, which will always be both general and specific.

Structurally, the distinction between theory and particularity is one we have seen before, in Ransom's distinction between Platonic poetry and Physical poetry; and again we must stress that these distinctions are exploratory matter for both critics and creative writers. One poet whose corpus addresses these issues as relentlessly as any critic's is Wallace Stevens. Long mistakenly accused by some readers of being merely a soulless "poet of ideas," Stevens has over time attracted the attention of a host of discerning critics capable of showing the humanity reflected in his thoughtful, rigorous, lyrical lines. The title of the poem concluding his *Collected Poems*, "Not Ideas About the Thing But the Thing Itself," might serve here to suggest how concerned Stevens was with the distinctions made implicitly in Krieger's and explicitly in Ransom's essays, and the poet's *oeuvre* goes a way toward proving the latter critic's conclusion: namely, that categorical purity is a fact of our desire, and in writing, where the purity of idea or thing can be hazarded, idea and thing will also always meet again, as human fact, against desire. It is a difficult enough matter when rendered by Ransom in expository prose; and in the poetry of a poet of generally agreed-upon difficulty? A guide can come in handy.

Such is the service performed by R. P. Blackmur in his still unsurpassed essay of introduction, "Examples of Wallace Stevens." It is a service the more remarkable for being performed on the basis of the 1931 revised edition of Stevens's first volume, *Harmonium* (1923), and five years before his second volume would appear. (Imagine a critic today expending so much acuity on a poet whose worth was proven only by a first book.) Blackmur's choice of object of inquiry is doubly indicative—of the Modernist era in general, when the soon-to-be major writers were showing their precocity, and the major critics were attending to them; and of Blackmur's judgment in particular, for *Harmonium* has not suffered through the years, and Stevens went on to fulfill his early promise.

Such prescient judgment is almost always recommendation enough, but we will supplement that prescience by noting that Blackmur's name is the first thing we read in the preface to Ransom's *The New Criticism*, followed by accurate praise:

> Mr. R. P. Blackmur is a distinguished critic, and no other living critic is less apt to take unassimilated the formulas of the profession and apply them hastily to the poem. His critical writing gives us the sense of materials turned over a great many times, and carried into the light of the usual illuminations. (I do not mean that they are not exposed also to some illuminations made at home.) The writing is close, and a little difficult, rather than simple and systematic as it might be if the critic had been shallower and more obliging. . . . Intelligent readers when they make acquaintance with him will know that they read what could not possibly have been written earlier than a few years ago. After what I have said, it is no discredit to Mr. Blackmur to observe that he has mastered some or all of the critical systems treated in this book; those of Richards (and his pupil Empson), Eliot, and Winters.[20]

This passage shows in its composition the preeminence accorded Blackmur, but more important for our present purpose is the hint it gives regarding the essay printed here. For Blackmur has indeed assimilated the formulas of the profession and mastered the critical systems of his time. This achievement shows itself in the range of local observation; in the critic's being obviously unbeholden to any specific critical system; and in the eschewing of an overvigorous, overingenious line of argument in favor of a loosely argued essay allowing for recognition of linguistic particularity that has the benefit of coverage (the word "examples" in its title is apt).

Strictly speaking, there is in Blackmur's essay an argument: that the mode of Stevens is rhetorical, designated thus "because it is not lyric or dramatic or epic, because it does not transcend its substance, but is a reflection upon a hard surface, a shining mirror of rhetoric." (It should probably be noted that this argument, made here in relation to *Harmonium*, would not necessarily hold true for the rest of Stevens's work, and that, of course, it was not, could not have been, intended to.) Yet as an argument it coalesces only at the essay's end, and seems generated by, rather than generative of, the observations that precede it. The impression is one of a reader in the act of reading and thinking through a series of recognized but unresolved issues, who then attempts to make the foregoing work graspable in a final generalizing move that has the virtue of having not strictly limited the inquiry before it began: a risky but appealing way of structuring an essay, which with Blackmur's skill turns out to be a success.

Readerly astuteness of the kind we encounter in Blackmur will often manifest itself in its recognition of what is, or might be, obvious, which as a rule of public reading seems counterintuitive. But what is obvious is often in need of recognition, not only because it marks a sensible starting place, but because it is always imperiled by criticism: imperiled, on the one hand, because nothing is more easily obscured than the obvious, nor more likely to be obscured, given the critical ego, which is often eager to prove itself in th'empyrean of thought, not the slough of what everybody ought to know already; on the other hand imperiled, because what is obvious becomes the goes-without-saying, and thus is easily falsified or forgotten. Here, then, is something obvious: what most separates the great poets from the rest of us is neither the depth of their intellect nor the breadth of their experience; neither a deeper alienation nor its better sublimation through the discipline of writing; neither knowledge of their own minds nor their insight into humanity (though they may, and in most cases undoubtedly do, outdo us in all these things). What *most* separates them from us is their practical vocabulary, or how they use the words they know.

This obvious fact is Blackmur's entrée into Stevens. What follows is an analysis suggesting both that Stevens knows more words (which is half the battle) and uses them better than most (the other half). Along the way are many useful observations made: on the difference between precise and imprecise ambiguity (the difference between Stevens and Cummings); on "the approach of language, through the magic of elegance, to nonsense"; on etymology and context, understanding and understatement, and the turning of conviction into feeling via words. It is work that, in addition to its local educational rewards, prepares the way for a comparative exegesis of tropes in three major Modernists (which is required reading for the light it still sheds on the persistent problem of Modernist difficulty). Moving from examples of Stevens alone to examples of Stevens, Eliot, and Pound, Blackmur, after close examination of the texts at hand, levies his critical judgment:

> It should be clear that whereas the obscurities of Eliot and Pound are intrinsic difficulties of the poems, to which the reader must come well armed

with specific sorts of external knowledge and belief, the obscurities of Mr. Stevens clarify themselves to the intelligence alone. Mode and value are different—not more or less valuable, but different. And all result from the concentrated language which is the medium of poetry. The three poets load their words with the maximum content; naturally, the poems remain obscure until the reader takes out what the poet puts in. What still remains will be the essential impenetrability of words, the bottomlessness of knowledge. To these the reader, like the poet, must submit. (this volume)

So culminates Blackmur's comparative work, and he then returns to Stevens alone, giving a welcome reading of the poet's first long poem, "The Comedian as the Letter C." But let us linger briefly on the passage above, especially on Blackmur's invocation of the variety—the "specific sorts," the "bottomlessness"—of knowledge, as preparatory to discussing Frank Lentricchia's "How to Do Things with Wallace Stevens." For that essay, on Stevens's "Anecdote of the Jar," is a debate about such variety, about what sorts of knowledge will help us locate meaning, pleasure, and truth; in short, it is a literal object-lesson in how many resources we must call upon when we are reading.

A poem, Stevens once wrote (he called it a "hymn"), is nothing less than the "organic centre of responses," and Lentricchia in his essay is true to the poet's poetics. Always centered on "Anecdote of the Jar," his responses range widely, range with conviction (and convincingly) *because* they are centered: responses ranging from performance to theorization of the anecdote itself, as personal and social knowledge; to responses formalist, structuralist, romantic, and political, as well as responses critical (and self-critical) of the limits of these forms of response; to responses related to other experiences of reading (William James, Michael Herr, Don DeLillo, Michel Foucault); to responses, most deeply, of love for the text and for its creator, the maker of responses. To read Lentricchia's essay, with its synthesizing impulse predicated on attention, full of care, to the texture, tone, and particularities (down to the syllabic level) of Stevens's poem is to be reminded of Ransom's assertion in *The New Criticism* that "the texture of poetry is one of incessant particularity, and each fresh particular is capable of enlisting emotions and attitudes. And when we analyze poetry in cognitive terms we allow, incidentally, for all that can find their excuse, or their chance, in the text."[21] Part of the critic's responsibility is to act not only as generator of, but as evaluator of and discriminator among those chances. Lentricchia thematizes this sometimes hidden aspect of criticism by writing through it, as it were, by exposing the scaffolding of thought and decision-making, the accepting and discarding, that precedes and allows for the "values" usually found expressed, as if they had fallen unbelatedly from the turnip truck, in a finished piece of criticism.

Lentricchia can produce this essay on the discriminating mind, without neglecting or merely "using" Stevens's poem, because Stevens's poem is itself a parable-as-anecdote on the related theme of writerly decision-making (or at least it begins as such, after which it becomes a study in writerly observation). In "Stevens and Keats's 'To Autumn,'" Helen Vendler also considers the compositional decisions of the writer, in this case decisions related to Stevens's reading of a major poem by a major predecessor. Vendler, who in her essay moves us past *Harmonium* and into Stevens's later work, shows with precision the critical or readerly side of the poet, while also showing just how deeply a poem can be impressed upon a receptive mind: "For Stevens, Keats's ode offered an irresistible antecedent model; Stevens hovered over the ode repeatedly in his musings. He became, to my way of thinking, the best reader of the ode, the most subtle interpreter of its rich meanings. Our understanding of latent significance in the older poem broadens when the ode is seen refracted through Stevens' lines. At the same time we may perceive, in Stevens' departures from the ode, implicit critiques of its stance." Such understanding and perception are vital to any accurate account of what we read, an accounting made difficult not only by the object of art but also by our vexed and shifting relationship to it (the same sort of relationship writers tend to have to their own work and to the work of those they read).

In the final essay of our first section, "'Lycidas': A Poem Finally Anonymous," Stanley Fish offers one of his finest essays in a career-long effort to examine observation and decision-making from the perspective of the reader. He, too, writes on a poem that seems (like "Anecdote of the Jar") to emphasize an underlying interest. For Milton's great pastoral elegy, in ways perhaps different from those of other canonical lyrics, is so dense and shape-shifting that a reader is forced to make choices even to render the poem readable. These choices, Fish argues, are often made pragmatically and promote conclusions that are untrue to an observation that, unblind, nevertheless denies what is seen in its avidity for coherence. It may seem strange to include Fish under a formalist heading. But our heading is loose, and the critical times since the height of New Criticism have become looser still. Even now it seems clear that Fish in his essay is handling texture, tension, and meaning in the reading of a poem in a way essentially consistent with the formalist writers of the twenties, thirties, forties, and fifties; he is concerned with the reader—and so, it should be asserted, was the New Criticism—and he is, in a manner not inconsistent with a definition never definitively elaborated, "close reading." The organic center of responses holds; in our own time, the poem, the novel, the play is still a magnet for our attention. The periphery, though, the minds and thoughts of readers—the periphery becomes increasingly diffuse, its gravitation toward its centralizing object hectic.

History wants to escape, on the one hand; or, it escapes, and is called the past, that which has already happened. Yet it is we who want to escape, since whatever can be remembered or felt has presence, and that is called History. Its presence obscures our present, so that we are never really there.

We dream, in dreaming of a pure eternal present, communally possessed, of universality, that seemingly deathless spatiotemporal category which is in time but not of it. Universality is simultaneity of value, of which any critic, any reader, may be skeptical. Why, because it effaces history? No, history is not the be-all end-all (though it is, in a sense, everything), and has no inherent value. Readers may be skeptical of universality for altogether different reasons. Criticism, especially, might resist universality because universality, if it existed (or was assumed to exist) in art, would risk making interpretive reading impossible, and would render the reader superfluous. That the critic, the reader of distinction, may resist this situation not only from political commitment, but also from a readerly and writerly commitment, is an option raised glancingly by Roland Barthes in his little essay on a photo exhibition called "The Great Family of Man": "Birth, death? Yes, these are facts of nature, universal facts. But if one removes History from them, there is nothing more to be said about them; any comment about them becomes purely tautological" (this volume). That thing, of course, about which nothing more can be said is what the critic, the reader-as-writer, must reject.

Now in confronting what he calls "a class of assertions which escape History," Barthes is doubtless involved in a political project: to show that certain concepts are not "natural" but have been *naturalized*, and are thus the product of a historical writing, which must be subjected to critical reading because (as he fears) this writing and the story it tells is a deception which "only make[s] the gestures of man look eternal the better to defuse them." Is historicizing the only way to give the lie to this universalization, this eternalization? It is certainly effective; at any rate, the mere invocation of History here becomes something almost compositional in its application, compositional in the way a splotch of bright yellow dabbed in the corner of an otherwise all-orange painting shows how much yellow was peeking through that painting all along. Such is the effect of this Barthesian parenthesis tossed off in the midst of more "subtle" analysis: "(but why not ask the parents of Emmet Till, the young Negro assassinated by the Whites what *they* think of *The Great Family of Man?*)"

Of course, one may wonder, why rehearse again this old story, this critique of universality? Certain terms by now surely raise red flags and demand some sensible qualification: *universal, objective, inherent?* We learn to attack the terms but must learn too that the job is effectively done only when we alter for the better the structures, systems, and beliefs that have generated the terms themselves. Barthes, who knows this, early attacks the core of The Great Family of Man's myth of the universal human community. "This myth," he writes, "functions in two stages: first the difference between human morphologies is asserted, exoticism is insistently stressed, the infinite variations of the species, the diversity in skins, skulls and customs are made manifest, the image of Babel is complacently projected over that of the world. Then, from this pluralism, a type of unity is magically produced: man is born, works, laughs and dies everywhere in the same way; and if there still remains in these actions some ethnic peculiarity, at least one hints that there is underlying each one an identical 'nature,' that their diversity is only formal and does not belie the existence of a common mold. Of course this means postulating a human essence" (this volume).

Barthes attacks a target the intellectually spurious tendencies of which are manifest less obviously, but quite often, elsewhere in our critical milieu. As he sees it, The Great Family of Man admits diversity, contingency, and variation (how could it do otherwise, as these photographed facts stare the viewer in the face?); "then, from this pluralism, a type of unity is magically produced;" this "diversity . . . does not belie the existence of a common mold"; "this means postulating a human essence." Such postulation as Barthes points out also happens often in criticism, even if in different terms. For example, in his essay on "Lycidas," Stanley Fish offers a litany of the crazy familiar contingency of the poem's shifts of style, diction, pose, tense, mood, and tone. He then writes:

> Together and individually, these characterizations constitute a challenge to the poem's unity, and it is as an assertion of unity that the case for the defense is always presented.
>
> Typically, that defense proceeds by first acknowledging and then domesticating the discontinuities that provoke it. . . . ['Lycidas' criticism] is, in short, an effort to put the poem together, and the form that effort almost always takes is the putting together of an integrated and consistent first-person voice. Indeed it is the assumption that the poem is . . . the expression

of a unified consciousness that generates the pressure to discover a continuity in the narrative. The unity in relation to which the felt discontinuities must be brought into line is therefore a *psychological* unity; the drama
whose coherence everyone is in the business of demonstrating is mental.
(this volume)

Structurally, the maneuvers described by Barthes and those described by Fish
are similar, moving from an admitted contingency into its effacement, then
into its replacement by some unity. The important difference is that whereas
in Barthes's account we ended with the exhibition's ideological postulation of
"a human essence," in Fish's essay we end with "a psychological unity."

The rub here is that in criticism on, say, lyric poetry, "a psychological unity"
can do, and does do with regularity, much the same work as "a human essence."
The unity posited in the case of each poem may be different (it is this difference that critics of lyric most celebrate), but the fact of a psychological unity
is in effect assumed across the board for each given lyric. In relation to lyric,
to the ostensible expression of a particular consciousness, the possibility of a
psychological unity is essential: it is the possibility of a critical universal, a lyrical essence.

If the way in which contingency is effaced by psychological unity in the
criticism of lyric is indeed structurally similar to the way contingency is effaced
by the idea of "universality," it seems (following the success of Barthes) that it
is necessary to historicize these moves. But historicize what, and where, and
how? Fredric Jameson suggests in "Nostalgia for the Present" "that at an outer
limit, the sense people have of themselves and their own moment of history
may ultimately have *nothing* whatsoever to do with its reality: that the existential may be absolutely distinct, as some ultimate 'false consciousness,' from the
structural and social significance of a collective phenomenon" (this volume).
This possibility is widely known in relation to historicizing the subject, that is,
historicizing ourselves and our methods. (We know *of* it, though we may forget
it on purpose to be better able to get work done.) But what holds for the subject
also holds for the object, especially when the object, the written object, is as
close to the "existential" as readers can usually imagine.

If the existential as an ultimate false consciousness were a fact, there is no
reason it should be any more true for one writer than for any other. Sometimes,
though, the fact, or its possibility, seems more often apparently found in particular people's writing, which is one reason to attend to certain writers. John
Ashbery gave a reading in Iowa a few years back, where he read his poem with
the last line: "My wife thinks I'm in Oslo—Oslo, France, that is." During the

question and answer session somebody asked him if there really was an Oslo, France, and instead of answering the question, Ashbery replied: "Why don't you ask me if I have a wife?"

It's a socratic parable, with which Ashbery hints at the sticky relationship between the "existential" and "reality" (and "history"), between personal and collective information, between the subject who writes the work and who may or may not be in the work, or may be to whatever degree, and the subject who reads the work and the subjects in and of the work, and, of course, between the work and everything else. To even begin to pretend to know how to historicize such a situation, our situation, seems deluded. It is here that the work of Stephen Greenblatt should be introduced, because it seems sometimes able to admit history at this very point of confusion, and also to allow history to insinuate certain relationships to both the subject and the work without settling on some apparently objective interpretation or asserting a strict causal narrative that erases the confusions that are, after all, a primary indicator of history itself. Greenblatt speaks to these confusions in the introduction to his collection of essays *Learning to Curse,* calling them instead "elusiveness," and asserting the relation between this elusiveness and aesthetic pleasure.[22] He then writes: "Virtually every form of aesthetic pleasure . . . is located in an intermediate zone of social transaction, a betwixt and between." This he calls "mobility, a mobility that includes the power of ready mutation." His own criticism enacts a similar mobility, as against the apparent disinterestedness or stability which he compares unfavorably to that mobility.

An example: "The Mousetrap," an essay written by Catherine Gallagher and Greenblatt, emphasizes the mobility of aesthetic pleasure and loosely allegorizes its own critical mobility. The authors begin by relating a midrash of four sons and their father which is part of the Passover Seder; three pages in, we learn that the performative eating of matzoh and drinking of wine is "closely related to the symbolic logic of the Eucharist"; evidence for the relationship is given; Eucharistic controversies of the sixteenth and seventeenth centuries are explored at some length; and these controversies are brought to bear on *Hamlet.* The historical material expands one's understanding of Shakespeare's play, but another effect of the essay is lodged in its opening gambit, the story of the four sons and their father, and what it has to say about the pragmatics of historicizing criticism.

When "The Mousetrap" says, "The issue here and throughout the Seder is a Jew's relation to historical memory," a corollary assertion can be heard regarding the critic's relation to historical memory. If that corollary is taken seriously, the relation proves to be various in exciting ways. Imagine, for instance, the critic as the father *and* the four sons, the critic asking questions and then attempting to answer them. There is first the son who does not know how to ask, which those will find poignant who have tried to work on something that confounds the understanding. In the face of this silent son, the father begins by personalizing the explanation: "This is because of that which the Lord did for me when I came forth from Egypt." One sees in this beginning a clue pointing to so many of Greenblatt's own beginnings, the anecdotes which inaugurate much of his work: when you don't know how to ask, tell a personal story (or at least a story containing "the personal"). To the simple son, who asks "What is this?" the father "moves from the personal to the collective." This, too, many readers of New Historical work will recognize as a familiar maneuver.

The wise son is probably the formalist side of the critic, here wishing to imbue literary forms with historical meaning: "What mean the testimonies, and the statutes and the ordinances, which the Lord our God hath commanded you?" (He is also the casuist, the pedant, and the geek.) Finally, there is the wicked son, who asks, "What do you mean by this service?" As the essay notes, although the question does not fundamentally differ from the earlier question of the simple son, "the midrash chooses to hear in the wicked son's question a failure of identification." He refuses to experience the events as though they were his own. What is interesting and moving here is the implication that even if our questions remain essentially the same, we ourselves are contingent: our intentions shift, or our moods; motivations change; and what began as an inquiry in the simplicity of genuine and open interest can become an exercise in bad faith, carried on grammatically but not spiritually.

Of course, one sometimes cannot help being simple, or not knowing how to ask; and while we aspire to be wise, we are sometimes bound to be wicked. There can be integrity even there (as well as excitement and fun). Yet as Greenblatt and Gallagher write: "This integrity is purchased by a refusal of an ambiguous injunction: to regard yourself *as though* means in part to pretend to be something you are not—the term acknowledges some distance between your actual and your imagined identity—but it also means to accept something that you are, something that you may not have understood about yourself and your origin and your destiny" (this volume). This critical allegory escapes the positing of some psychological unity, some stable identity, while establishing active and transformative identification as a positive critical value; at the same time, it admits the occasional inevitability of a failure of identification; it can view failure as a form of integrity, and perhaps even admit it as a necessary step on the path to wisdom.

The critical mobility allegorized here is one that shuttles between the per-

sonal present and collective past, makes history contemporary through identification, and makes the personal historical through the well-told anecdote. In
"Literary History and Literary Modernity," another critic, Paul de Man, makes
the case that modern literature is modern, and is literature, precisely because
it cannot shake off history, cannot as it wishes it could "fulfill itself in a single
moment.... The distinctive character of literature thus becomes manifest as an
inability to escape from a condition that is felt to be unbearable.... As soon as
[modern man] can feel appeased in this situation he ceases to be a writer" (this
volume). Gallagher and Greenblatt are not appeased, and thus their shuttling
from time to document, from then to now, from document to time. That they
locate and produce pleasure in this mobility makes the historical condition as
defined by de Man somewhat (slightly) more bearable.

More bearable for some, at least—but for others? Eve Kosofsky Sedgwick, in
her controversial study of *Sense and Sensibility*, "Jane Austen and the Masturbating Girl" (the title of which, writes Sedgwick, serves "as the Q.E.D. of phobic
narratives about the degeneracy of academic discourse in the humanities"), is
skeptical of one aspect of the method, such as she sees it, of the New Historicism, with which Gallagher and Greenblatt are generally associated. She criticizes "the New Historicists' positivist alibi for perpetuating and disseminating the shock of the violent narratives in which they trade," their "spread[ing]
around to a group of other readers, as if that would ground or diffuse it, the in-
admissably, inabsorbably complex shock" (this volume) of certain off-putting
historical documents. It is an interestingly defensive criticism, willfully defensive, even, given the shocking document Sedgwick exhibits in her essay, fully
equal in inadmissibility to any New Historicist citation.

Sedgwick's off-hand critique is useful for our purpose in emphasizing a feature held in common by "Jane Austen and the Masturbating Girl," "The Mousetrap," and several other essays in this collection's second section besides: reading by juxtaposition. To juxtapose, as Sedgwick does, a late nineteenth-century
document of medical science studying (with great brutality) masturbation and
psychological problems in two young girls to an eighteenth-century novel of
(seemingly) utmost decorum, whose main characters are also two young girls,
is, "through the frame" of the former (and unexpected) document, "to see how
most of the love story of *Sense and Sensibility*, no simple one, has been rendered all but invisible to most readers" (this volume). We have seen a similar
process at work in Gallagher and Greenblatt's essay, where the juxtaposition of
Hamlet and documents of Eucharistic controversy is meant to make visible a
once easily noticeable, now underemphasized aspect of the play.

In both cases, this decision to juxtapose historical and literary texts serves a purpose perhaps greater than the need of any local, practical exegesis; or rather, in addition to its exegetical function, such juxtaposition makes with great efficacy a larger theoretical point. That point, important for recent literary criticism, is that reading for meaning is a process of considerable relativity, and that reaching an understanding of what one reads is a highly contingent affair. "Contingency," and its more politically charged cousin "relativity," have of course never been absent from reading or from reading's more sophisticated literary-critical manifestations, even when purity, scientificity, or objectivity are strongly asserted against them. But essays such as Gallagher and Greenblatt's and Sedgwick's emphasize to a sea-changing degree the reality of relativity in the readerly process, not only by their citational practices, which formally spatialize and thus make intellectually concrete the abstraction that is contingency, but also in their outright critiques of objectivity.

Paradoxically, objectivity is critiqued most effectively via a critique of the reading or writing subject, or of a staid concept of the subject's identity. In Sedgwick's essay, it is a critique well suited to the literary object of study, since Austen, with characteristic subtlety, thematizes in *Sense and Sensibility* the notion of a fluctuating subject that renders objective analysis difficult. (There is, for instance, the chapter-ending moment when the Dashwood sisters have been coerced into accepting yet another dinner invitation from the overly gracious Sir John and his social companion Lady Middleton: " 'Why should they ask us?' said Marianne, as soon as they were gone. 'The rent of this cottage is said to be low; but we have it on very hard terms, if we are to dine at the Park whenever anyone is staying either with them or with us.' 'They mean no less to be civil and kind to us now,' said Elinor, 'by these frequent invitations than by those which we received from them a few weeks ago. The alteration is not in them, if their parties are grown tedious and dull. We must look for the change elsewhere.' ")

Sedgwick's method in her best-known essay asserts its strongest meaning through the blurring of outlines. This takes different forms, one of which is the simple strategy of not reducing complexities into a categorical either/or impasse: "Is this, then, a hetero- or a homoerotic novel (or moment in a novel)? No doubt it must be said to be both." (Such judiciousness surreptitiously tempers the ostensible outrageousness of Sedgwick's work, as it does in her assertion of a "homosocial" continuum in *Between Men*.) Also powerful and structurally compelling are the blurred boundaries effected by the essay's dense network of analogy, in which masturbation, inattention, addiction, writing, and reading stand variously one for the other. Categorical diffusion not only helps prove the essay's larger point about the multiple strains making up "any presumptive understanding of the relation of 'hetero' to 'homo' as modern sexual identities," but also (and paradoxically, given the analogical terms) calls the reader to attention, insofar as the network, to produce its full argumentative effect, must be held whole in the mind and still remain available to local discrimination. A case in point occurs when Sedgwick writes slyly of the character Edward Ferrars's "servitude to an erotic habit formed in the idleness of an improperly supervised youth," which habit would certainly seem, in the context of the essay, to be masturbation. In the context of *Sense and Sensibility*, however, this "habit" is the distasteful Miss Lucy Steele, and it is we who are being "improperly supervised."

Bad faith, purposeful decorum-busting, both, or what? The question might be responsibly asked of politically motivated criticism in general (under which rubric Sedgwick, as a leader in Queer Studies, stands). Moral and ethical stakes are raised by such criticism, and no one wants to be on the sharp end of the stake. More often than not, there is a battle in such work between drawing meaning out of a text (in a New Critical exegetical sense) and reading meaning into a text (with the interpretive spuriousness implied by the latter cliché being exacerbated by the long accepted idealism implied by the former). Work polemical in its essence, as a politically motivated criticism must be, is itself bound to engender polemics, and recent years have seen their share of them. Still, the general academic shift from "close reading" to a political "reading against" various putative sins (sexism, patriarchy, racism, capitalism, homophobia, imperialism) did not, despite hearsay to the contrary, kill reading.

Reading in the service of a political agenda does not, in fact, necessarily mean failing to read also in the service of the work of art. In "Nostalgia for the Present," Fredric Jameson's Marxism brings him after all very close to J. G. Ballard's novel *Time Out of Joint* and to the movies *Something Wild* and *Blue Velvet*, just as in "Jane Austen's Cover Story (and Its Secret Agents)," Sandra Gilbert and Susan Gubar are able, as politically and critically active feminists, to approach intimately the novels of Austen: "Authorship for Austen is an escape from the very restraints she imposes on her female characters. And in this respect she seems typical, for women may have contributed so significantly to narrative fiction precisely because it effectively objectifies, even as it sustains and hides, the subjectivity of the author. Put another way, in the novels Austen questions and criticizes her own aesthetic and ironic sensibilities, noting the limits and asserting the dangers of an imagination undisciplined by the rigors of art" (this volume). Such imaginative sympathy with the work and its creator can be one of the benefits of a political drive in reading, as can the practical expansion of the general field of inquiry that results from bringing into the critical arena perspectives previously underemployed. (Gilbert and Gubar's politics may now seem part of the academic "mainstream," but they were less so in 1979, when *The Madwoman in the Attic*, from which the present essay comes, was published.) The expansion of literary criticism can obviously be theoretical, marked by a flourishing of new ideas, but it can also involve, more simply, the promotion of relevant but mostly forgotten writers as once-again readable commodities. Thus "Jane Austen's Cover Story" introduces its less informed readers to Maria Edgeworth, "possibly one of the most popular and influential novelists of her time," in an effort to bring a realistic perspective to the study of her iconic contemporary Austen.

Political reading is also capable of fulfilling the humanist promise of reading as self-education, as a tutorial on the self (perhaps paradoxically so, insofar as politics is essentially interpersonal. Reading itself, with or without an explicit politics, is paradoxical in the same way). In reading politically, the reader may find a more elaborate or compelling articulation of what was otherwise only felt. This process can make the initial felt politics more effective, since what is felt needs articulation to allow for practical collective action. Such seems to be the case when Gilbert and Gubar register "Austen's self-division—her fascination with the imagination and her anxiety that it is unfeminine—[which] is part of her consciousness of the unique dilemma of all women, who must acquiesce in their status as objects after an adolescence in which they experience themselves as free agents" (this volume). The "requisite sense of doubleness" that these critics articulate via Austen's fiction finds in another critic's essay a parallel suggesting how psychological, how therapeutic, our readerly politics are. In "The World and the Home," his postcolonialist study of Nadine Gordimer's *My Son's Story* and Toni Morrison's *Beloved*, Homi Bhabha writes of "the moment of aesthetic distance that provides the narrative with a double-edge which like the colored South African subject represents a hybridity, a difference 'within.'" He comments on "the freak displacements of these novels, [in which] the profound divisions of an enslaved or apartheid society—negrification, denigration, classification, violence, incarceration—are relocated in the midst of the ambivalence of psychic identification—that space where love and hate can be projected or inverted; where the relation of 'object' to identity is always split and doubled" (this volume). Trying to diagnose and cure the problems of the world through reading, we diagnose the problems of our selves, a diagnosis that is also exacerbation; for when we read politically, we purposefully take on an "ambivalence of psychic identification," doubly splitting ourselves: first, into what we are outside of the book and what we are, through identification, within it; second, into politically active selves in our reaction to the world via the book, and as political escapists in turning to the book and away from the world in the first place.

Bhabha knows that doing politics through literature, though by no means impossible or futile, is a tenuous task, for the medium, the materials out of which literature is made, register the already tenuous connection between the world and its parts:

> If we are seeking a "worlding" of literature, then perhaps it lies in a critical act that attempts to grasp the sleight of hand with which literature conjures with historical specificity, using the medium of *psychic uncertainty, aesthetic distancing, or the obscure signs of the spirit-world, the sublime and the subliminal.* As literary creatures and political animals we ought to concern ourselves with the understanding of human action and the social world as a moment when *something is beyond control, but it is not beyond accommodation.* This act of writing the world, of taking the measure of its dwelling, is magically caught in Morrison's description of her house of fiction—art as "the fully realized presence of a haunting" of history. Read as an image that describes the relation of art to social reality, my translation of Morrison's phrase becomes a statement on the political responsibility of the critic. For the critic must attempt to fully realize, and take responsibility for, the un-spoken, unrepresented pasts that haunt the historical present. (this volume)

Difficult, no doubt, "to fully realize" what is being asked here of readers; and indeed, anyone reading with a politics in tow will find that positive effects, if they come, come slowly. But it is nevertheless a way of reading that can bring the reader closer to what is being read. It is a concept of reading that makes its existence felt. As a foundational force it solidifies more slowly than cold concrete dries, but it constructs a foundation as solid as concrete when dry it eventually does. Reading, whether done "closely" or politically, is in its finest manifestation capable of examining evil, or whatever else we call the bad, sad self-inflicted things of this world, capable of turning the spotlight on it in an attempt to freeze it, so as better to bag it. The reader hungers for human aesthetic truth, a complex worthy of our desire. The reader says to the book, like Molly once to Poldy Bloom, "Give us a touch." We're dying for it.

One response to the phenomenon known as "the turn to theory" which dominated post–New Critical academic discourse was to see in it the cessation of a certain kind of reading, or, by some accounts, the cessation of the reading of literature itself. Always Paul de Man is asserting otherwise: "It turns out that the resistance to theory is in fact a resistance to reading . . . a straightforward *report* on the present state of literary theory in the United States would have to stress the emphasis on reading, a direction which is already present, moreover, in the New Critical tradition of the forties and fifties."[23] De Man not only stresses reading in relation to theory, but also emphasizes a historical continuity between the New Criticism and theory; de Man will insist on this connection even to the rhetorical detriment of theory (though no doubt aiming at a later rhetorical recuperation): "Mere reading, it turns out, prior to any theory, is able to transform critical discourse in a manner that would appear deeply subversive to those who think of the teaching of literature as a substitute for the teaching of theology, ethics, psychology, or intellectual history. Close reading accomplishes this often in spite of itself because it cannot fail to respond to structures of language which it is the more or less secret aim of literary teaching to keep hidden."[24] It is an interesting response to the critics of theory to claim that at the level of *reading,* the subversive movement associated with a theoretical influx had actually been initiated earlier, in New Critical practice.

What definition of reading allows for the meeting of critical practices which have been usually spoken of as either oppositional or distinct? The mild paranoia expressed in phraseology such as "hidden" "secret aim[s]" is characteristic in strange ways of contemporary theoretical discourse. It points toward the base of a new definition of reading (though perhaps only coincidentally); for where there is paranoia, there is bound to be a search for structure. To read, de Man says, is "to respond to structures of language," to "the structure of language prior to the meaning it produces." At this level of structure, New Criticism does not merely meet theory, but is theory, "if by theory one understands the rooting of literary exegesis and of critical evaluation in a system of some conceptual generality."[25] "Theory," then, gains in definitional complexity (as is typical in de Man's writing), picking up additions, variations, and eventually a chronology: "Literary theory can be said to come into being when the approach to literary texts is no longer based on nonlinguistic, that is to say historical and aesthetic, considerations or, to put it somewhat less crudely, when the object of discussion is no longer the meaning or the value but the modalities of production and of reception of meaning and of value prior to their establishment—the implication being that this establishment is problematic enough to require an autonomous discipline of critical investigation to consider its possibility and its status."[26] Here the drift of theory is away from New Criticism, though not far away, since New Criticism did deal with "modalities of production and of reception." (Granted, it considered different modalities; and the reception of an ideal reader was assumed rather than theorized, with the partial exception of Richards's psychological work.) The real difference in de Man's account of reading seems to be terminological and, one might say, disciplinary. Its difference from earlier accounts involves a paradox: for though the difficulty of discussing meaning prior to its establishment necessitates "an autonomous discipline of critical investigation," the move to theory proper is a move into interdisciplinarity, a vexed autonomy:

> The advent of theory, the break that is now so often being deplored and that sets it aside from literary history and from literary criticism, occurs with the introduction of linguistic terminology in the metalanguage about literature. By linguistic terminology is meant a terminology that designates reference prior to designating the referent and takes into account, in the consideration of the world, the referential function of language or, to be somewhat more specific, that considers reference as a function of language and not necessarily as an intuition. Intuition implies perception, consciousness, experience, and leads at once into the world of logic and of understanding with all its correlatives, among which aesthetics occupies a prominent place. The assumption that there can be a science of language which is not necessarily a logic leads to the development of a terminology which is not necessarily aesthetic. Contemporary literary theory comes into its own in such events as the application of Saussurian linguistics to literary texts.[27]

So the break from New Criticism (a practice not devoid of theory) and the move into theory proper is marked by a move into linguistics and a break from aesthetics. This may be why so many critics considered theory detrimental to the reading of literature, since "reading" and "literature" are intertwined not only with aesthetics but with aesthetic *appreciation*. To remove this as a grounding critical consideration was by some accounts tantamount to the annihilation of reading as we had known it.

It is in part to be believed; a critique of anything, especially anything in language, *as we had known it* was always part of the point of doing theory. Michel Foucault was the master of this skeptical investigative mode, working so successfully in working thematically, exposing the history (and thus the contingency) of received and supposedly fixed ideas related to, among other topics, sex, discipline, and madness. Essentially a macrocriticism, Foucault's work will perhaps stand a tenuous binarized grouping with the more micro-practice of Jacques Derrida, exemplified by the opening of his classic essay "Différance":

> I will speak, therefore, of a letter.
>
> Of the first letter, if the alphabet, and most of the speculations which have ventured into it, are to be believed.
>
> I will speak, therefore, of the letter *a*, this initial letter which it apparently has been necessary to insinuate, here and there, into the writing of the word *difference*; and to do so in the course of a writing on writing, and also of a writing within writing whose different trajectories thereby find themselves, at certain very determined points, intersecting with a kind of gross spelling mistake, a lapse in the discipline and law which regulate writing and keep it seemly. One can always, de facto or de jure, erase or reduce this lapse in spelling, and find it (according to situations to be analyzed each time, although amounting to the same), grave or unseemly, that is, to follow the most ingenuous hypothesis, amusing. Thus, even if one seeks to pass over such an infraction in silence, the interest that one takes in it can be recognized and situated in advance as prescribed by the mute irony, the inaudible misplacement, of this literal permutation. One can always act as if it made no difference. And I must state here and now that today's discourse will be less a justification of, and even less an apology for, this silent lapse in spelling, than a kind of insistent intensification of its play.[28]

Citing this passage does not, perhaps, reveal much about Derrida's philosophy, strictly speaking, but it may say something about the post–New Critical literary criticism that stems from this French *philosophe:* no moment, no mark (grapheme) is too small for examination; prior speculations, even the most naturalized grounds for these speculations (such as the alphabet), are not necessarily reliable; contingency is asserted (there are "situations to be analyzed each time"); conflicts between speaking and writing are insinuated; (some idea of) scholarly decorum is willfully broken with; legalistic (about laws and their prescription) and casuistic, such writing lapses into irrationality at about the same rate as it lapses into (almost a spoof of) reason; it uses its own specialized words; and (probably most importantly for reading recent literary critical history) "justification," "apology," and "play" are clustered together.

Derrida insists on *play,* as in both "flexibility" and "performance," and the insistence itself filters into criticism as both an increase in the number of ways of getting into the text and in the number of star-making critical performances (a culture of academic celebrity). Another side of theory is its turn to the political, which, while it cannot be seen as a justificatory move merely, can in part be seen as such, responding precisely to the perception, exacerbated by increasingly obscure theoretical work, of literary criticism as "mere" play. An apology for theory can likewise take a political turn. Yet in what amounts to his apology, de Man always returns instead to *reading* as the basis of the theoretical critical project: "To stress the by no means self-evident necessity of reading implies at least two things. First of all, it implies that literature is not a transparent message in which it can be taken for granted that the distinction between the message and the means of communication is clearly established. Second, and more problematically, it implies that the grammatical decoding of a text leaves a residue of indetermination that has to be, but cannot be, resolved by grammatical means, however extensively conceived."[29] This sums up fairly two basic points of the deconstructive theoretical program with which de Man's work is associated: communicative transparency does not exist; and texts are profoundly indeterminate. The clarity with which these often obtusely rendered points are communicated maybe masks the fact that such points are hardly "implied" in de Man's stress on the "necessity of reading." His argumentative move, however, identifies poststructuralist inquiry with reading itself, or, more accurately, de Man's critical inquiry with reading itself. The two become equivalent, an effective defense of any literary critical practice: What *I'm* doing is *reading*; and *you*?

It is strange to find de Man denying that Roland Barthes reads "in the full theoretical sense of the term" ("Up till very recently, French critics never bothered to read at all, or never considered the problem worthy of their attention . . . The same is still by and large the case for Barthes and his continuators; the only French theoretician who actually *reads* texts, in the full theoretical sense of the term, is Jacques Derrida"), but it probably best attests to the strictness of de Man's use of "reading" as a term. He does, however, give credit to Barthes, if not by name than by naming a methodology: "The replacement of a hermeneutic by a semiotic model, of interpretation by decoding, would represent, in view of the baffling historical instability of textual meanings (including, of course, those of canonical texts), a considerable progress. Much of the hesitation associated with 'reading' could thus be dispelled."[30] We can call such "decoding" reading, an especially revealing kind of reading when practiced by Barthes (a real genius of reading and writing both). The short essays reprinted here are from his *Mythologies* (1957), a book whose final long essay "initiated," wrote Barthes, "at least as far as I am concerned," semiological analysis. In that essay, "Myth Today," Barthes systematically outlines an approach to "this vast science of signs which

Saussure postulated some forty years ago under the name of *semiology*," a science that has "not yet come into being."[31] What are the characteristics of this nonexistent science which Barthes is helping to bring into existence? By way of partial explanation, Barthes writes:

> Any semiology postulates a relation between two terms, a signifier and a signified. This relation concerns objects which belong to different categories, and this is why it is not one of equality but one of equivalence. We must here be on our guard for despite common parlance which simply says that the signifier *expresses* the signified, we are dealing, in any semiological system, not with two, but with three different terms. For what we grasp is not at all one term after the other, but the correlation which unites them: there are, therefore, the signifier, the signified and the sign, which is the associative total of the first two terms. Take a bunch of roses: I use it to *signify* my passion. Do we have here, then, only a signifier and a signified, the roses and my passion? Not even that: to put it accurately, there are here only "passionified" roses. But on the plane of analysis, we do have three terms; for these roses weighted with passion perfectly and correctly allow themselves to be decomposed into roses and passion: the former and the latter existed before uniting and forming this third object, which is the sign. It is as true to say that on the plane of experience I cannot dissociate the roses from the message they carry, as to say that on the plane of analysis I cannot confuse the roses as signifier and the roses as sign: the signifier is empty, the sign is full, it is a meaning. Or take a black pebble: I can make it signify in several ways, it is a mere signifier; but if I weigh it with a definite signified (a death sentence, for instance, in an anonymous vote), it will become a sign.[32]

So the search in Barthes's essays printed here is for the sign, which must be distinguished from that which is signified, since "it is both reprehensible and deceitful to confuse the sign with what is signified." That pronouncement comes at the end of an "ethic of signs" in "The Romans in Films," an essay about the 1953 movie version of *Julius Caesar*; rather, the essay is about two of the movie's signs: hair on the forehead and sweat on the face. The search here is different from New Critical or post-structuralist inquiry, which both seem to "go inside" the text, either to illuminate internal obscurities through explication or to expose internal indeterminacy. Here Barthes (and this represents only one aspect of this wide-ranging critic) is dealing with things on the surface, as hair and sweat suggest with some literality. Discussing the former he writes of "the mainspring of the Spectacle—the *sign*—operating in the open;" of the latter, that "the sign is ambiguous: it remains on the surface, yet does not for all that give up the attempt to pass itself off as depth."

Semiological analysis such as this brought cultural studies into being. It is obviously indispensable for reading the mass of stuff we call popular culture, and as a "science" its methods are widely applicable. See, for example, its application to the study of popular culture and periodization in the service of a political formalism (in this case, a Marxist one) in Jameson's "Nostalgia for the Present," where a specifically postmodern "formal possibility" of allegorically mobilizing "a vision of the past" is explained in large part by showing the "semic organization" of a Melanie Griffith movie; or in "To Move Without Moving: An Analysis of Creativity and Commerce in Ralph Ellison's Trueblood Episode," Houston A. Baker Jr.'s reading of *Invisible Man*, in which he inaugurates his thesis by "suggesting that the Trueblood episode, like other systematic symbolic phenomena, gains and generates its meanings in a dialogic relation with various systems of signs" (this volume).

Baker's and Jameson's essays share an intellectually foundational notion "that there is always a historical, or ideological, subtext in a literary work of art" (Baker, in fact, cites Jameson on this point). They also, of course, discuss both popular culture and its relation to a particular novel. But in Baker's essay we see a telling difference, which perhaps will suggest why the study of popular culture cannot afford to be considered a mere contemporary plaything of conventional literary study. The difference is this: in Baker's essay, popular culture and literature *per se* are located at the same site (with popular culture present not as theme, but as content), within the novel *Invisible Man*. The most interesting aspect of the novel as a form, after all, is that it potentially lets everything in, and Ellison's novel exploits this formal possibility. The (venerable) popular cultural forms Baker examines as central to his study are Afro-American folklore and the blues; and what he argues, in a way especially meaningful for a profession of reading that is always discriminating and canonizing, is that "the distinction between folklore and literary art evident in Ellison's critical practice collapses in his creative practice" (this volume). To understand the literary work, one must understand the cultural forms that help constitute it.

Ellison's novel, with its reach, its range, its unboundedness, presents special problems for the reader attempting to place it properly. In this respect, *Invisible Man* has much in common with work as diverse as Goethe's *Faust*, Melville's *Moby Dick*, and Joyce's *Ulysses*. It is an example of what Franco Moretti calls (in his book of the same name) "Modern Epic," that "work of transition, technically revolutionary, [that] *cannot avoid being internally discontinuous. . . . The final product may well, if fortune smiles, be a masterpiece:

but under no circumstances can it be a consistent, well-amalgamated master-piece."[33] In the selection printed here, Moretti makes an argument for the generic reclassification of Joyce's novel, an argument predicated on the conviction that existing historical and generic categories are sometimes inadequate to the task of literary understanding; that in special, radical cases, the literary work itself forces those categories into obsolescence. As Paul de Man writes in "Literary History and Literary Modernity," his close theoretical reading of that conviction, literature, "with respect to its own specificity (that is, as an existing entity susceptible to historical description) . . . exists at the same time in the modes of error and truth; it both betrays and obeys its own mode of being" (this volume). And so do we all, so we find ourselves reading.

NOTES

1   Paul de Man, *The Resistance to Theory* (Minneapolis: University of Minnesota Press, 1986), 23.
2   John Crowe Ransom, *The New Criticism* (Norfolk, Conn.: New Directions, 1941), viii.
3   Ransom, *The New Criticism*, x.
4   Ibid., 3.
5   Ibid., 111.
6   Hippolyte Taine, *History of English Literature.* Translated by H. Van Laun (New York: Henry Holt, 1896), 1. For a portrait of Taine more sympathetic than the one offered here, see chapter 1 of Marshall Brown's *Turning Points: Essays in the History of Cultural Expressions* (Stanford, Calif.: Stanford University Press, 1997).
7   Ibid., 25.
8   Ibid., 4.
9   Ibid., 1–2.
10   Ransom, *The New Criticism*, 102–3.
11   Cleanth Brooks, *The Well Wrought Urn: Studies in the Structure of Poetry* (New York: Harcourt Brace, 1947), 3.
12   Ibid., 5.
13   Ibid., 10.
14   Ibid., 10–11.
15   Ibid., 16–17.
16   Northrop Frye, "The Archetypes of Literature" in *The Kenyon Review*, vol. 13, winter 1951, 93.
17   Helen Vendler, *The Breaking of Style* (Cambridge: Harvard University Press, 1995), 6.
18   Perhaps it seemed more extravagant in 1965, when the essay was written, than it does today. The post-Modernist period is often preoccupied with work that calls attention to its own processes. Such work has always existed, of course, and in abundance, as Krieger's essay shows; but (to offer paradigmatic examples from drama, prose, and poetry) the assimilation into the culture at large of Brechtian "alienation effects," metafiction as exemplified

by Barth, Barthelme, and Borges, and the self-referential lyric of Ashbery, seems almost complete.

19 Gotthold Lessing, *Laocoön: An Essay on the Limits of Painting and Poetry.* Translated by Edward McCormick (Baltimore, Md.: Johns Hopkins University Press, 1984), 3.

20 Ransom, *The New Criticism,* vii–viii.

21 Ibid., 25.

22 Stephen Greenblatt, *Learning to Curse* (NY: Routledge, 1990), 11.

23 de Man, *Resistance to Theory,* 15–17.

24 Ibid., 24.

25 Ibid., 5.

26 Ibid., 7.

27 Ibid., 8.

28 Jacques Derrida, *Margins of Philosophy.* Translated by Alan Bass (Chicago: University of Chicago Press, 1982), 3.

29 de Man, *Resistance to Theory,* 15.

30 Ibid., 15.

31 Roland Barthes, *Mythologies,* 1957. Translated by Annette Lavers (New York: Hill and Wang, 1972), 111.

32 Ibid., 112–13.

33 Franco Moretti, *Modern Epic.* Translated by Quintin Hoare (London: Verso, 1996), 120.

FORMALISM (PLUS)

1. Poetry: A Note on Ontology

JOHN CROWE RANSOM

A POETRY MAY BE distinguished from a poetry by virtue of subject-matter, and subject-matter may be differentiated with respect to its ontology, or the reality of its being. An excellent variety of critical doctrine arises recently out of this differentiation, and thus perhaps criticism leans again upon ontological analysis as it was meant to do by Kant. The recent critics remark in effect that some poetry deals with things, while some other poetry deals with ideas. The two poetries will differ from each other as radically as a thing differs from an idea.

The distinction in the hands of critics is a fruitful one. There is apt to go along with it a principle of valuation, which is the consequence of a temperament, and therefore basic. The critic likes things and intends that his poet shall offer them: or likes ideas and intends that he shall offer them: and approves him as he does the one or the other. Criticism cannot well go much deeper than this. The critic has carried to the last terms his analysis of the stuff of which poetry is made, and valued it frankly as his temperament or his need requires him to value it.

So philosophical a critic seems to be highly modern. He is; but this critic as a matter of fact is peculiarly on one side of the question. (The implication is unfavourable to the other side of the question.) He is in revolt against the tyranny of ideas, and against the poetry which celebrates ideas, and which may be identified—so far as his usual generalization may be trusted—with the hateful poetry of the Victorians. His bias is in favour of the things. On the other hand the critic who likes Victorian verse, or the poetry of ideas, has probably not thought of anything of so grand a simplicity as electing between the things and the ideas, being apparently not quite capable of the ontological distinction. Therefore he does not know the real or constitutional ground of his liking, and may somewhat ingenuously claim that his predilection is for those poets who give him inspiration, or comfort, or truth, or honest meters, or something else equally "worthwhile." But Plato, who was not a modern, was just as clear as we are about the basic distinction between the ideas and the things, and yet stands far apart from the aforesaid conscious modern in passionately preferring the ideas over the things. The weight of Plato's testimony would certainly fall on the side of the Victorians, though they may scarcely have thought of calling him as their witness. But this consideration need not conclude the hearing.

I. PHYSICAL POETRY

The poetry which deals with things was much in favour a few years ago with the resolute body of critics. And the critics affected the poets. If necessary, they became the poets, and triumphantly illustrated the new mode. The Imagists were important figures in the history of our poetry, and they were both theorists and creators. It was their intention to present things in their thinginess, or *Dinge* in their *Dinglichkeit;* and to such an extent had the public lost its sense of Dinglichkeit that their redirection was wholesome. What the public was inclined to seek in poetry was ideas, whether large ones or small ones, grand ones or pretty ones, certainly ideas to live by and die by, but what the Imagists identified with the stuff of poetry was, simply, things.

Their application of their own principle was sufficiently heroic, though they scarcely consented to be as extreme in the practice as in the theory. They had artistic talent, every one of the original group, and it was impossible that they should make of poetry so simple an exercise as in doctrine they seemed to think it was. Yet Miss Lowell wrote a poem on *Thompson's Lunch Room, Grand Central Station;* it is admirable if its intention is to show the whole reach of her courage. Its detail goes like this:

> Jagged greenwhite bowls of pressed glass
> Rearing snow-peaks of chipped sugar
> Above the lighthouse-shaped castors
> Of gray pepper and gray-white salt.

For most of us as for the public idealist, with his "values," this is inconsequential. Unhappily it seems that the things as things do not necessarily interest us, and that in fact we are not quite constructed with the capacity for a disinterested interest. But it must be noted even here that the things are on their good behaviour, looking rather well, and arranged by lines into something approaching a military formation. More technically, there is cross-imagery in the snow-peaks of sugar, and in the lighthouse-shaped castors, and cross-imagery involves association, and will presently involve dissociation and thinking. The meter is but a vestige, but even so it means something, for meter is a powerful intellectual determinant marshalling the words and, inevitably, the things. The Dinglichkeit of this Imagist specimen, or the realism, was therefore not pure. But it was nearer pure than the world was used to in poetry, and the exhibit was astonishing.

For the purpose of this note I shall give to such poetry, dwelling as exclusively as it dares upon physical things, the name Physical Poetry. It is to stand opposite to that poetry which dwells as firmly as it dares upon ideas.

But perhaps thing *versus* idea does not seem to name an opposition precisely. Then we might phrase it a little differently: image *versus* idea. The idealistic philosophies are not sure that things exist, but they mean the equivalent when they refer to images. (Or they may consent to perceptions; or to impressions, following Hume, and following Croce, who remarks that they are pre-intellectual and independent of concepts. It is all the same, unless we are extremely technical.) It is sufficient if they concede that image is the raw material of idea. Though it may be an unwieldy and useless affair for the idealist as it stands, much needing to be licked into shape, nevertheless its relation to idea is that of a material cause, and it cannot be dispossessed of its priority.

It cannot be dispossessed of a primordial freshness, which idea can never claim. An idea is derivative and tamed. The image is in the natural or wild state, and it has to be discovered there, not put there, obeying its own law and none of ours. We think we can lay hold of image and take it captive, but the docile captive is not the real image but only the idea, which is the image with its character beaten out of it.

But we must be very careful: idealists are nothing if not dialectical. They object that an image in an original state of innocence is a delusion and cannot exist, that no image ever comes to us which does not imply the world of ideas, there is "no percept without a concept." There is something in it. Every property discovered in the image is a universal property, and nothing discovered in the image is marvellous in kind though it may be pinned down historically or statistically as a single instance. But there is this to be understood too: the image which is not remarkable in any particular property is marvellous in its assemblage of many properties, a manifold of properties, like a mine or a field, something to be explored for the properties; yet science can manage the image, which is infinite in properties, only by equating it to the one property with which the science is concerned: for science at work is always *a science,* and committed to a special interest. It is not by refutation but by abstraction that science destroys the image. It means to get its "value" out of the image, and we may be sure that it has no use for the image in its original state of freedom. People who are engrossed with their pet "values" become habitual killers. Their game is the images, or the things, and they acquire the ability to shoot them as far off as they can be seen, and do. It is thus that we lose the power of imagination, or whatever faculty it is by which we are able to contemplate things as they are in their rich and contingent materiality. But our dreams reproach us, for in dreams they come alive again. Likewise our memory; which makes light of our science by recalling the images in their panoply of circumstance and with their morning freshness upon them.

It is the dream, the recollection, which compels us to poetry, and to deliberate aesthetic experience. It can hardly be argued, I think, that the arts are constituted automatically out of original images, and arise in some early age of innocence. (Though Croce seems to support this view, and to make art a pre-adult stage of experience.) Art is based on second love, not first love. In it we make a return to something which we had wilfully alienated. The child is occupied mostly with things, but it is because he is still unfurnished with systematic ideas, not because he is a ripe citizen by nature and comes along already trailing clouds of glory. Images are clouds of glory for the man who has discovered that ideas are a sort of darkness. Imagism, that is, the recent historical movement, may resemble a naïve poetry of mere things, but we can read the theoretical pronouncements of Imagists, and we can learn that Imagism is motivated by a distaste for the systematic abstractedness of thought. It presupposes acquaintance with science; that famous activity which is "constructive" with respect to the tools of our economic role in this world, and destructive with respect to nature. Imagists wish to escape from science by immersing themselves in images.

Not far off the simplicity of Imagism was, a little later, the subtler simplicity of Mr. George Moore's project shared with several others, in behalf of "pure poetry." In Moore's house on Ebury Street they talked about poetry, with an after-dinner warmth if not an early-morning discretion, and their tastes agreed almost perfectly and reinforced one another. The fruit of these conversations was the volume *Pure Poetry.* It must have been the most exclusive anthology of English poetry that had yet appeared, since its room was closed to all the poems that dallied visibly with ideas, so that many poems that had been coveted by all other anthologists do not appear there. Nevertheless the book is delicious, and something more deserves to be said for it.

First, that "pure poetry" is a kind of Physical Poetry. Its visible content is a thing-content. Technically, I suppose, it is effective in this character if it can exhibit its material in such a way that an image or set of images and not an idea must occupy the foreground of the reader's attention. Thus:

> Full fathom five thy father lies
> Of his bones are coral made.

Here it is difficult for anybody (except the perfect idealist who is always theoretically possible and who would expect to take a return from anything whatever) to receive any experience except that of a very distinct image, or set of images. It has the configuration of image, which consists in being sharp of edges, and the modality of image, which consists in being given and nonnegotiable, and the density, which consists in being full, a plenum of qualities. What is to be done with it? It is pure exhibit; it is to be contemplated; perhaps it is to be enjoyed. The art of poetry depends more frequently on this faculty than on any other in its repertory; the faculty of presenting images so whole and clean that they resist the catalysis of thought.

And something else must be said, going in the opposite direction. "Pure poetry," all the same, is not as pure as it is claimed to be, though on the whole it is Physical Poetry. (All true poetry is a phase of Physical Poetry.) It is not as pure as Imagism is, or at least it is not as pure as Imagism would be if it lived up to its principles; and in fact it is significant that the volume does not contain any Imagist poems, which argues a difference in taste somewhere. Imagism may take trifling things for its material; presumably it will take the first things the poet encounters, since "importance" and "interest" are not primary qualities which a thing possesses but secondary or tertiary ones which the idealist attributes to it by virtue of his own requirements. "Pure poetry" as Moore conceives it, and as the lyrics of Poe and Shakespeare offer it, deals with the more dramatic materials, and here dramatic means human, or at least capable of being referred to the critical set of human interests. Employing this sort of material the poet cannot exactly intend to set the human economists in us actually into motion, but perhaps he does intend to comfort us with the fleeting sense that it is potentially our kind of material.

In the same way "pure poetry" is nicely metered, where Imagism was free. Technique is written on it. And by the way the anthology contains no rugged anonymous Scottish ballad either, and probably for a like reason: because it would not be technically finished. Now both Moore and de la Mare are accomplished conservative artists, and what they do or what they approve may be of limited range but it is sure to be technically admirable, and it is certain that they understand what technique in poetry is though they do not define it. Technique takes the thing-content and meters and orders it. Meter is not an original property of things. It is artificial, and conveys the sense of human control, even if it does not wish to impair the thinginess of the things. Metric is a science, and so far as we attend to it we are within the scientific atmosphere. Order is the logical arrangement of things. It involves the dramatic "form" which selects the things, and brings out their appropriate qualities, and carries them through a systematic course of predication until the total impression is a unit of logic and not merely a solid lump of thing-content. The "pure poems" which Moore admires are studied, though it would be fatal if they looked studious. A sustained effort of ideation effected these compositions. It is covered up, and communicates itself only on a subliminal plane of consciousness. But experienced readers are quite aware of it; they know at once what is the matter when they encounter a realism shamelessly passing for poetry, or a well-planned but blundering poetry.

As critics we should have every good will toward Physical Poetry: it is the basic constituent of any poetry. But the product is always something short of a pure or absolute existence, and it cannot quite be said that it consists of nothing but physical objects. The fact is that when we are more than usually satisfied with a Physical Poetry our analysis will probably disclose that it is more than usually impure.

II. PLATONIC POETRY

The poetry of ideas I shall denominate: Platonic Poetry. This also has grades of purity. A discourse which employed only abstract ideas with no images would be a scientific document and not a poem at all, not even a Platonic poem. Platonic Poetry dips heavily into the physical. If Physical Poetry tends to employ some ideation surreptitiously while still looking innocent of idea, Platonic Poetry more than returns the compliment, for it tries as hard as it can to look like Physical Poetry, as if it proposed to conceal its medicine, which is the idea to be propagated, within the sugar candy of objectivity and Dinglichkeit. As an instance, it is almost inevitable that I quote a famous Victorian utterance:

> The year's at the spring
> And day's at the morn;
> Morning's at seven;
> The hill-side's dew-pearled;
> The lark's on the wing;

> The snail's on the thorn:
> God's in his heaven—
> All's right with the world!

which is a piece of transparent homiletics; for in it six pretty, coordinate images are marched, like six little lambs to the slaughter, to a colon and a powerful text. Now the exhibits of this poetry in the physical kind are always large, and may take more of the attention of the reader than is desired, but they are meant mostly to be illustrative of the ideas. It is on this ground that idealists like Hegel detect something unworthy, like a pedagogical trick, in poetry after all, and consider that the race will abandon it when it has outgrown its childishness and is enlightened.

The ablest arraignment of Platonic Poetry that I have seen, as an exercise which is really science but masquerades as poetry by affecting a concern for physical objects, is that of Mr. Allen Tate in a series of studies recently in the *New Republic*.[1] I will summarize, Platonic Poetry is allegory, a discourse in things, but on the understanding that they are translatable at every point into ideas. (The usual ideas are those which constitute the popular causes, patriotic, religious, moral, or social.) Or Platonic Poetry is the elaboration of ideas as such, but in proceeding introduces for ornament some physical properties after the style of Physical Poetry; which is rhetoric. It is positive when the poet believes in the efficacy of the ideas. It is negative when he despairs of their efficacy, because they have conspicuously failed to take care of him, and utters his personal wail: "I fall upon the thorns of life! I bleed!" This is "Romantic Irony," which comes at occasional periods to interrupt the march of scientific optimism. But it still falls under the category of Platonism; it generally proposes some other ideas to take the place of those which are in vogue.

But why Platonism? To define Platonism we must remember that it is not the property of the historical person who reports dialogues about it in an Academy, any more than "pure poetry" is the property of the talkers who describe it from a house on Ebury Street. Platonism, in the sense I mean, is the name of an impulse that is native to us all, frequent, tending to take a too complete possession of our minds. Why should the spirit of mortal be proud? The chief explanation is that modern mortal is probably a Platonist. We are led to believe that nature is rational and that by the force of reasoning we shall possess it. I have read upon high authority: "Two great forces are persistent in Plato: the love of truth and zeal for human improvement." The forces are one force. We love to view the world under universal or scientific ideas to which we give the name truth; and this is because the ideas seem to make not for righteousness but for mastery. The Platonic view of the world is ultimately the predatory, for it reduces to the scientific, which we know. The Platonic Idea becomes the Logos which science worships, which is the Occidental God, whose minions we are, and whose children, claiming a large share in His powers for patrimony.

Now the fine Platonic world of ideas fails to coincide with the original world of perception, which is the world populated by the stubborn and contingent objects, and to which as artists we fly in shame. The sensibility manifested by artists makes fools of scientists, if the latter are inclined to take their special and quite useful form of truth as the whole and comprehensive article. A dandified pagan worldling like Moore can always defeat Platonism; he does it every hour; he can exhibit the savour of his fish and wines, the fragrance of his coffee and cigars, and the solidity of the images in his favourite verse. These are objects which have to be experienced, and cannot be reported, for what is their simple essence that the Platonist can abstract? Moore may sound mystical but he is within the literal truth when he defends "pure poetry" on the ground that the things are constant, and it is the ideas which change—changing according to the latest mode under which the species indulges its grandiose expectation of subjugating nature. The things are constant in the sense that the ideas are never emancipated from the necessity of referring back to them as their original; and the sense that they are not altered nor diminished no matter which ideas may take off from them as a point of departure. The way to obtain the true Dinglichkeit of a formal dinner or a landscape or a beloved person is to approach the object as such, and in humility; then it unfolds a nature which we are unprepared for if we have put our trust in the simple idea which attempted to represent it.

The special antipathy of Moore is to the ideas as they put on their moral complexion, the ideas that relate everything to that insignificant centre of action, the human "soul" in its most Platonic and Pharisaic aspect. Nothing can darken perception better than a repetitive moral earnestness, based on the reputed superiority and higher destiny of the human species. If morality is the code by which we expect the race to achieve the more perfect possession of nature, it is an incitement to a more heroic science, but not to aesthetic experience, nor religious; if it is the code of humility, by which we intend to know nature as nature is, that is another matter; but in an age of science morality is inevitably for the general public the former; and so transcendent a morality as the latter is now unheard of. And therefore:

> O love, *they* die in yon rich sky,
>   *They* faint on hill or field or river;

> *Our* echoes roll from soul to soul,
> And grow forever and forever.

(The italics are mine.) These lines conclude an otherwise innocent poem, a candidate for the anthology, upon which Moore remarks: "The Victorian could never reconcile himself to finishing a poem without speaking about the soul, and the lines are particularly vindictive." Vindictive is just. By what right did the Laureate exult in the death of the physical echoes and call upon his love to witness it, but out of the imperiousness of his savage Platonism? Plato himself would have admired this ending, and considered that it redeemed an otherwise vicious poem.

Why do persons who have ideas to promulgate risk the trial by poetry? If the poets are hired to do it, which is the polite conception of some Hegelians, why do their employers think it worth the money, which they hold in public trust for the cause? Does a science have to become a poetry too? A science is the less effective as a science when it muddies its clear waters with irrelevance, a sermon becomes less cogent when it begins to quote the poets. The moralist, the scientist, and the prophet of idealism think evidently that they must establish their conclusions in poetry, though they reach these conclusions upon quite other evidence. The poetry is likely to destroy the conclusions with a sort of death by drowning, if it is a free poetry.

When that happens the Platonists may be cured of Platonism. There are probably two cures, of which this is the better. One cure is by adversity, by the failure of the ideas to work, on account of treachery or violence, or the contingencies of weather, constitution, love, and economics; leaving the Platonist defeated and bewildered, possibly humbled, but on the other hand possibly turned cynical and worthless. Very much preferable is the cure which comes by education in the fine arts, erasing his Platonism more gently, leading him to feel that that is not a becoming habit of mind which dulls the perceptions.

The definition which some writers have given to art is: the reference of the idea to the image. The implication is that the act is not for the purpose of honest comparison so much as for the purpose of proving the idea by image. But in the event the idea is not disproved so much as it is made to look ineffective and therefore foolish. The ideas will not cover the objects upon which they are imposed, they are too attenuated and threadlike; for ideas have extension and objects have intension, but extension is thin while intension is thick.

There must be a great deal of genuine poetry which started in the poet's mind as a thesis to be developed, but in which the characters and the situations have developed faster than the thesis, and of their own accord. The thesis disappears; or it is recaptured here and there and at the end, and lodged sententiously with the reader, where every successive reading of the poem will dislodge it again. Like this must be some plays, even some play out of Shakespeare, whose thesis would probably be disentangled with difficulty out of the crowded pageant; or some narrative poem with a moral plot but much pure detail; perhaps some "occasional" piece by a Laureate or official person, whose purpose is compromised but whose personal integrity is saved by his wavering between the sentiment which is a public duty and the experience which he has in his own right; even some proclaimed allegory, like Spenser's, unlikely as that may seem, which does not remain transparent and everywhere translatable into idea but makes excursions into the territory of objectivity. These are hybrid performances. They cannot possess beauty of design, though there may be a beauty in detailed passages. But it is common enough, and we should be grateful. The mind is a versatile agent, and unexpectedly stubborn in its determination not really to be hardened in Platonism. Even in an age of science like the nineteenth century the poetic talents are not so loyal to its apostolic zeal as they and it suppose, and do not deserve the unqualified scorn which it is fashionable to offer them, now that the tide has turned, for their performance is qualified.

But this may be not stern enough for concluding a note on Platonic Poetry. I refer again to that whose Platonism is steady and malignant. This poetry is an imitation of Physical Poetry, and not really a poetry. Platonists practice their bogus poetry in order to show that an image will prove an idea, but the literature which succeeds in this delicate mission does not contain real images but illustrations.

III. METAPHYSICAL POETRY

"Most men," Mr. Moore observes, "read and write poetry between fifteen and thirty and afterwards very seldom, for in youth we are attracted by ideas, and modern theory being concerned almost exclusively with ideas we live on duty, liberty, and fraternity as chameleons are said to live on light and air, till at last we turn from ideas to things, thinking that we have lost our taste for poetry, unless, perchance, we are classical scholars."

Much is conveyed in this characteristic sentence, even in proportion to its length. As for the indicated chronology, the cart is put after the horse, which is its proper sequence. And it is pleasant to be confirmed in the belief that many men do recant from their Platonism and turn back to things. But it cannot be exactly a *volte-face,* for there are qualifications. If pure ideas were what these men turn from, they would have had no poetry at all in the first period, and if pure things were what they turn to, they would be having not a classical poetry but a pure imagism, if such a thing is possible, in the second.

The mind does not come unscathed and virginal out of Platonism. Ontological interest would have to develop curiously, or wastefully and discontinuously, if men through their youth must cultivate the ideas so passionately that upon its expiration they are done with ideas forever and ready to become as little (and pre-logical) children. Because of the foolishness of idealists are ideas to be taboo for the adult mind? And, as critics, what are we to do with those poems (like "The Canonization" and "Lycidas") which could not obtain admission by Moore into the anthology but which very likely are the poems we cherish beyond others?

The reputed "innocence" of the aesthetic moment, the "knowledge without desire" which Schopenhauer praises, must submit to a little scrutiny, like anything else that looks too good to be true. We come into this world as aliens come into a land which they must conquer if they are to live. For native endowment we have an exacting "biological" constitution which knows precisely what it needs and determines for us our inevitable desires. There can be no certainty that any other impulses are there, for why should they be? They scarcely belong in the biological picture. Perhaps we are simply an efficient animal species, running smoothly, working fast, finding the formula of life only too easy, and after a certain apprenticeship piling up power and wealth far beyond the capacity of our appetites to use. What will come next? Perhaps poetry, if the gigantic effort of science begins to seem disproportionate to the reward, according to a sense of diminishing returns. But before this pretty event can come to pass, it is possible that every act of attention which is allowed us is conditioned by a gross and selfish interest.

Where is innocence then? The aesthetic moment appears as a curious moment of suspension; between the Platonism in us, which is militant, always sciencing and devouring, and a starved inhibited aspiration towards innocence which, if it could only be free, would like to respect and know the object as it might of its own accord reveal itself.

The poetic impulse is not free, yet it holds out stubbornly against science for the enjoyment of its images. It means to reconstitute the world of perceptions. Finally there is suggested some such formula as the following:

Science gratifies a rational or practical impulse and exhibits the minimum of perception. Art gratifies a perceptual impulse and exhibits the minimum of reason.

Now it would be strange if poets did not develop many technical devices for the sake of increasing the volume of the percipienda or sensibilia. I will name some of them.

First Device: meter. Meter is the most obvious device. A formal meter impresses us as a way of regulating very drastically the material, and we do not stop to remark (that is, as readers) that it has no particular aim except some nominal sort of regimentation. It symbolizes the predatory method, like a sawmill which intends to reduce all the trees to fixed unit timbers, and as business men we require some sign of our business. But to the Platonic censor in us it gives a false security, for so long as the poet appears to be working faithfully at his metrical engine he is left comparatively free to attend lovingly to the things that are being metered, and metering them need not really hurt them. Meter is the gentlest violence he can do them, if he is expected to do some violence.

Second Device: fiction. The device of the fiction is probably no less important and universal in poetry. Over every poem which looks like a poem is a sign which reads: This road does not go through to action: fictitious. Art always sets out to create an "aesthetic distance" between the object and the subject, and art takes pains to announce that it is not history. The situation treated is not quite an actual situation, for science is likely to have claimed that field, and exiled art; but a fictive or hypothetical one, so that science is less greedy and perception may take hold of it. Kant asserted that the aesthetic judgment is not concerned with the existence or nonexistence of the object, and may be interpreted as asserting that it is so far from depending on the object's existence that it really depends on the object's nonexistence. Sometimes we have a certain melancholy experience. We enjoy a scene which we receive by report only, or dream, or meet with in art; but subsequently find ourselves in the presence of an actual one that seems the very same scene; only to discover that we have not now the power to enjoy it, or to receive it aesthetically, because the economic tension is upon us and will not indulge us in the proper mood. And it is generally easier to obtain our aesthetic experience from art than from nature, because nature is actual, and communication is forbidden. But in being called fictive or hypothetical the art-object suffers no disparagement. It cannot be true in the sense of being actual, and therefore it may be despised by science. But it is true in the sense of being fair or representative, in permitting the "illusion of reality"; just as Schopenhauer discovered that music may symbolize all the modes of existence in the world; and in keeping with the customary demand of the readers of fiction proper, that it shall be "true to life." The defenders of art must require for it from its practitioners this sort of truth, and must assert of it before the world this dignity. If jealous science succeeds in keeping the field of history for its own exclusive use, it does not therefore annihilate the arts, for they reappear in a field which may be called real though one degree removed from actuality. There the arts perform their function with much less interference, and at the same time with about as much fidelity to the phenomenal world as history has.

Third Device: tropes. I have named two important devices; I am not prepared to offer the exhaustive list. I mention but one other kind, the device which comprises the figures of speech. A proper scientific discourse has no intention of employing figurative language for its definitive sort of utterance. Figures of speech twist accidence away from the straight course, as if to intimate astonishing lapses of rationality beneath the smooth surface of discourse, inviting perceptual attention, and weakening the tyranny of science over the senses. But I skip the several easier and earlier figures, which are timid, and stop on the climactic figure, which is the metaphor: with special reference to its consequence, a poetry which once in our history it produced in a beautiful and abundant exhibit, called Metaphysical Poetry.

And what is Metaphysical Poetry? The term was added to the official vocabulary of criticism by Johnson, who probably took it from Pope, who probably took it from Dryden, who used it to describe the poetry of a certain school of poets, thus: "He [John Donne] affects the metaphysics, not only in his satires, but in his amorous verses, where nature only should reign. . . . In this Mr. Cowley has copied him to a fault." But the meaning of metaphysical which was common in Dryden's time, having come down from the Middle Ages through Shakespeare, was simply: supernatural; *miraculous.* The context of the Dryden passage indicates it.

Dryden, then, noted a miraculism in poetry and repudiated it; except where it was employed for satire, where it was not seriously intended and had the effect of wit. Dryden himself employs miraculism wittily, but seems rather to avoid it if he will be really committed by it; he may employ it in his translations of Ovid, where the responsibility is Ovid's and not Dryden's, and in an occasional classical piece where he is making polite use of myths well known to be pagan errors. In his "amorous" pieces he finds the reign of nature sufficient, and it is often the worse for his amorous pieces. He is not many removes from a naturalist. (A naturalist is a person who studies nature not because he loves it but because he wants to use it, approaches it from the standpoint of common sense, and sees it thin and not thick.) Dryden might have remarked that Donne himself had a change of heart and confined his miraculism at last to the privileged field of a more or less scriptural revelation. Perhaps Dryden found his way to accepting Milton because Milton's miraculism was mostly not a contemporary sort but classical and scriptural, pitched in a time when the age of miracles had not given way to the age of science. He knew too that Cowley had shamefully recanted from his petty miraculism, which formed the conceits, and turned to the scriptural or large order of miraculism to write his heroic (but empty) verses about David; and had written a Pindaric ode in extravagant praise of "Mr. Hobs," whose naturalistic account of nature seemed to render any other account fantastic if not contrary to the social welfare.

Incidentally, we know how much Mr. Hobbes affected Dryden too, and the whole of Restoration literature. What Bacon with his disparagement of poetry had begun, in the cause of science and protestantism, Hobbes completed. The name of Hobbes is critical in any history that would account for the chill which settled upon the poets at the very moment that English poetry was attaining magnificently to the fullness of its powers. The name stood for common sense and naturalism, and the monopoly of the scientific spirit over the mind. Hobbes was the adversary, the Satan, when the latter first intimidated the English poets. After Hobbes his name is legion.

"Metaphysics," or miraculism, informs a poetry which is the most original and exciting, and intellectually perhaps the most seasoned, that we know in our literature, and very probably it has few equivalents in other literatures. But it is evident that the metaphysical effects may be large-scale or they may be small-scale. (I believe that generically, or ontologically, no distinction is to be made between them.) If Donne and Cowley illustrate the small-scale effects, Milton will illustrate the large-scale ones, probably as a consequence of the fact that he wrote major poems. Milton, in the *Paradise Lost*, told a story which was heroic and miraculous in the first place. In telling it he dramatized it, and allowed the scenes and characters to develop of their own native energy. The virtue of a long poem on a "metaphysical" subject will consist in the dramatization or substantiation of all the parts, the poet not being required to devise fresh miracles on every page so much as to establish the perfect "naturalism" of the material upon which the grand miracle is imposed. The *Paradise Lost* possesses this virtue nearly everywhere:

> Thus *Adam* to himself lamented loud
> Through the still Night, not now, as ere man fell,
> Wholsom and cool, and mild, but with black Air
> Accompanied, with damps and dreadful gloom,
> Which to his evil Conscience represented
> All things with double terror: On the ground
> Outstrecht he lay, on the cold ground, and oft

Curs'd his Creation, Death as oft accus'd
Of tardie execution, since denounc't
The day of his offence. Why comes not Death,
Said hee, with one thrice acceptable stroke
To end me?

This is exactly the sort of detail for a large-scale metaphysical work, but it would hardly serve the purpose with a slighter and more naturalistic subject: with "amorous" verses. For the critical mind Metaphysical Poetry refers perhaps almost entirely to the so-called "conceits" that constitute its staple. To define the conceit is to define small-scale Metaphysical Poetry.

It is easily defined, upon a little citation. Donne exhibits two conceits, or two branches of one conceit in the familiar lines:

Our hands were firmly cemented
By a fast balm which thence did spring;
Our eye-beams twisted, and did thread
Our eyes upon one double string.

The poem which follows sticks to the topic; it represents the lovers in precisely that mode of union and no other. Cowley is more conventional yet still bold in the lines:

Oh take my Heart, and by that means you'll prove
    Within, too stor'd enough of love:
Give me but yours, I'll by that change so thrive
    That Love in all my parts shall live.
So powerful is this my change, it render can,
My outside Woman, and your inside Man.

A conceit originates in a metaphor; and in fact the conceit is but a metaphor if the metaphor is meant; that is, if it is developed so literally that it must be meant, or predicated so baldly that nothing else can be meant. Perhaps this will do for a definition.

Clearly the seventeenth century had the courage of its metaphors, and imposed them imperially on the nearest things, and just as clearly the nineteenth century lacked this courage, and was half-heartedly metaphorical, or content with similes. The difference between the literary qualities of the two periods is the difference between the metaphor and the simile. (It must be admitted that this like other generalizations will not hold without its exceptions.) One period was pithy and original in its poetic utterance, the other was prolix and predictable. It would not quite commit itself to the metaphor even if it came upon one. Shelley is about as vigorous as usual when he says in *Adonais:*

> Thou young Dawn,
> Turn all thy dew to splendour . . .

But splendour is not the correlative of dew, it has the flat tone of a Platonic idea, while physically it scarcely means more than dew with sunshine upon it. The seventeenth century would have said: "Turn thy dew, which is water, into fire, and accomplish the transmutation of the elements." Tennyson in his boldest lyric sings:

> Come into the garden, Maud,
> For the black bat, night, has flown.

and leaves us unpersuaded of the bat. The predication would be complete without the bat, "The black night has flown," and a flying night is not very remarkable. Tennyson is only affecting a metaphor. But later in the same poem he writes:

> The red rose cries, "She is near, she is near";
>   And the white rose weeps, "She is late";
> The larkspur listens, "I hear, I hear";
>   And the lily whispers, "I wait."

and this is a technical conceit. But it is too complicated for this author, having a plurality of images which do not sustain themselves individually. The flowers stand for the lover's thoughts, and have been prepared for carefully in an earlier stanza, but their distinctness is too arbitrary, and these are like a schoolgirl's made-up metaphors. The passage will not compare with one on a very similar situation in "Green Candles," by Mr. Humbert Wolfe:

> "I know her little foot," gray carpet said:
> "Who but I should know her light tread?"
> "She shall come in," answered the open door,
> "And not," said the room, "go out any more."

Wolfe's conceit works and Tennyson's does not, and though Wolfe's performance seems not very daring or important, and only pleasant, he employs the technique of the conceit correctly: he knows that the miracle must have a basis of verisimilitude.

Such is Metaphysical Poetry; the extension of a rhetorical device; as one of the most brilliant successes in our poetry, entitled to long and thorough examination; and even here demanding somewhat by way of a more ontological criticism. I conclude with it.

We may consult the dictionary, and discover that there is a miraculism or supernaturalism in a metaphorical assertion if we are ready to mean what we say, or believe what we hear. Or we may read Mr. Hobbes, the naturalist, who was very clear upon it: "II. The second cause of absurd assertions I ascribe to the giving of names of 'bodies' to 'accidents,' or of 'accidents' to 'bodies,'" as they do that say 'faith is infused' or 'inspired,' when nothing can be 'poured' or 'breathed' into anything but body . . . and that 'phantasms' are 'spirits,' etc." Translated into our present terms, Hobbes is condemning the confusion of single qualities with whole things; or the substitution of concrete images for simple ideas.

Specifically, the miraculism arises when the poet discovers by analogy an identity between objects which is partial, though it should be considerable, and proceeds to an identification which is complete. It is to be contrasted with the simile, which says "as if" or "like," and is scrupulous to keep the identification partial. In Cowley's passage above, the lover is saying, not for the first time in this literature: "She and I have exchanged our hearts." What has actually been exchanged is affections, and affections are only in a limited sense the same as hearts. Hearts are unlike affections in being engines that pump blood and form body; and it is a miracle if the poet represents the lady's affection as rendering her inside into man. But he succeeds, with this mixture, in depositing with us the image of a very powerful affection.

From the strict point of view of literary criticism it must be insisted that the miraculism which produces the humblest conceit is the same miraculism which supplies to religions their substantive content. (This is said to assert the dignity not of the conceits but of the religions.) It is the poet and nobody else who gives to the God a nature, a form, faculties, and a history; to the God, most comprehensive of all terms, which, if there were no poetic impulse to actualize or "find" Him, would remain the driest and deadest among Platonic ideas, with all intension sacrificed to infinite extension. The myths are conceits, born of metaphors. Religions are periodically produced by poets and destroyed by naturalists. Religion depends for its ontological validity upon a literary understanding, and that is why it is frequently misunderstood. The metaphysical poets, perhaps like their spiritual fathers the mediaeval Schoolmen, were under no illusions about this. They recognized myth, as they recognized the conceits, as a device of expression; its sanctity as the consequence of its public or social importance.

But whether the topics be Gods or amorous experiences, why do poets resort to miraculism? Hardly for the purpose of controverting natural fact or scientific theory. Religion pronounces about God only where science and philosophy is negative; for a positive is wanted, that is, a God who has his being in the physical world as well as in the world of principles and abstractions. Likewise with the little secular enterprises of poetry. Not now are the poets so brave, not for a very long time have they been so brave, as to dispute the scientists on what they call their "truth"; though it is a pity that the statement cannot be turned round. Poets will concede that every act of science is legitimate, and has its efficacy. The metaphysical poets of the seventeenth century particularly admired the methodology of science, and in fact they copied it, and their phrasing is often technical, spare, and polysyllabic, though they are not repeating actual science but making those metaphorical substitutions that are so arresting.

The intention of Metaphysical Poetry is to complement science, and improve discourse. Naturalistic discourse is incomplete, for either of two reasons. It has the minimum of physical content and starves the sensibility, or it has the maximum, as if to avoid the appearance of evil, but is laborious and pointless. Platonic Poetry is too idealistic, but Physical Poetry is too realistic and realism is tedious and does not maintain interest. The poets therefore introduce the psychological device of the miracle. The predication which it permits is clean and quick but it is not a scientific predication. For scientific predication concludes an act of attention but miraculism initiates one. It leaves us looking, marvelling, and revelling in the thick *dinglich* substance that has just received its strange representation.

Let me suggest as a last word, in deference to a common Puritan scruple, that the predication of Metaphysical Poetry is true enough. It is not true like history, but no poetry is true in that sense, and only a part of science. It is true in the pragmatic sense in which some of the generalizations of science are true: it accomplishes precisely the sort of representation that it means to. It suggests to us that the object is perceptually or physically remarkable, and we had better attend to it.

NOTE

1   "Three Types of Poetry." Reprinted in *Reactionary Essays* (1936). Reprinted in *On the Limits of Poetry* (1948). [*Editor's note.*]

2. Keats's Sylvan Historian: History Without Footnotes

CLEANTH BROOKS

T HERE IS MUCH in the poetry of Keats which suggests that he would have approved of Archibald MacLeish's dictum, "A poem should not mean / But be." There is even some warrant for thinking that the Grecian urn (real or imagined) which inspired the famous ode was, for Keats, just such a poem, "palpable and mute," a poem in stone. Hence it is the more remarkable that the "Ode" itself differs from Keats's other odes by culminating in a statement—a statement even of some sententiousness in which the urn itself is made to say that beauty is truth, and—more sententious still—that this bit of wisdom sums up the whole of mortal knowledge.

This is "to mean" with a vengeance—to violate the doctrine of the objective correlative, not only by stating truths, but by defining the limits of truth. Small wonder that some critics have felt that the unravished bride of quietness protests too much.

T. S. Eliot, for example, says that "this line ["Beauty is truth," etc.] strikes me as a serious blemish on a beautiful poem; and the reason must be either that I fail to understand it, or that it is a statement which is untrue." But even for persons who feel that they do understand it, the line may still constitute a blemish. Middleton Murry, who, after a discussion of Keats's other poems and his letters, feels that he knows what Keats meant by "beauty" and what he meant by "truth," and that Keats used them in senses which allowed them to be properly bracketed together, still, is forced to conclude: "My own opinion concerning the value of these two lines *in the context of the poem itself* is not very different from Mr. T. S. Eliot's." The troubling assertion is apparently an intrusion upon the poem—does not grow out of it—is not dramatically accommodated to it.

This is essentially Garrod's objection, and the fact that Garrod does object indicates that a distaste for the ending of the "Ode" is by no means limited to critics of notoriously "modern" sympathies.

But the question of real importance is not whether Eliot, Murry, and Garrod are right in thinking that "Beauty is truth, truth beauty" injures the poem. The question of real importance concerns beauty and truth in a much more general way: what is the relation of the beauty (the goodness, the perfection) of a poem to the truth or falsity of what it seems to assert? It is a question which has particularly vexed our own generation—to give it I. A. Richards's phrasing, it is the problem of belief.

The "Ode," by its bold equation of beauty and truth, raises this question in its sharpest form—the more so when it becomes apparent that the poem itself is obviously intended to be a parable on the nature of poetry, and of art in general. The "Ode" has apparently been an enigmatic parable, to be sure: one can emphasize *beauty* is truth and throw Keats into the pure-art camp, the usual procedure. But it is only fair to point out that one could stress *truth* is beauty, and argue with the Marxist critics of the thirties for a propaganda art. The very ambiguity of the statement, "Beauty is truth, truth beauty" ought to warn us against insisting very much on the statement in isolation, and to drive us back to a consideration of the context in which the statement is set.

It will not be sufficient, however, if it merely drives us back to a study of Keats's reading, his conversation, his letters. We shall not find our answer there even if scholarship does prefer on principle investigations of Browning's ironic question, "What porridge had John Keats?" For even if we knew just what porridge he had, physical and mental, we should still not be able to settle the problem of the "Ode." The reason should be clear: our specific question is not what did Keats the man perhaps want to assert here about the relation of beauty and truth; it is rather: was Keats the poet able to exemplify that relation in this particular poem? Middleton Murry is right: the relation of the final statement in the poem to the total context is all-important.

Indeed, Eliot, in the very passage in which he attacks the "Ode" has indicated the general line which we are to take in its defense. In that passage, Eliot goes on to contrast the closing lines of the "Ode" with a line from *King Lear*, "Ripeness is all." Keats's lines strike him as false; Shakespeare's, on the other hand, as not clearly false, and as possibly quite true. Shakespeare's generalization, in other words, avoids raising the question of truth. But is it really a question of truth and falsity? One is tempted to account for the difference of effect which Eliot feels in this way: "Ripeness is all" is a statement put in the mouth of a dramatic character and a statement which is governed and qualified by the whole context of the play. It does not directly challenge an examination into its truth because its relevance is pointed up and modified by the dramatic context.

Now, suppose that one could show that Keats's lines, *in quite the same way*, constitute a speech, a consciously riddling paradox, put in the mouth of a particular character, and modified by the total context of the poem. If we could demonstrate that the speech was "in character," was dramatically appropriate, was properly prepared for—then would not the lines have all the justification of "Ripeness is all"? In such case, should we not have waived the question of the scientific or philosophic truth of the lines in favor of the application of a principle curiously like that of dramatic propriety? I suggest that some such principle is the only one legitimately to be invoked in any case. Be this as it may, the "Ode on a Grecian Urn" provides us with as neat an instance as one could wish in order to test the implications of such a maneuver.

It has seemed best to be perfectly frank about procedure: the poem is to be read in order to see whether the last lines of the poem are not, after all, dramatically prepared for. Yet there are some claims to be made upon the reader too, claims which he, for his part, will have to be prepared to honor. He must not be allowed to dismiss the early characterizations of the urn as merely so much vaguely beautiful description. He must not be too much surprised if "mere decoration" turns out to be meaningful symbolism—or if ironies develop where he has been taught to expect only sensuous pictures. Most of all, if the teasing riddle spoken finally by the urn is not to strike him as a bewildering break in tone, he must not be too much disturbed to have the element of paradox latent in the poem emphasized, even in those parts of the poem which have none of the energetic crackle of wit with which he usually associates paradox. This is surely not too much to ask of the reader—namely, to assume that Keats meant what he said and that he chose his words with care. After all, the poem begins on a note of paradox, though a mild one: for we ordinarily do not expect an urn to speak at all; and yet, Keats does more than this: he begins his poem by emphasizing the apparent contradiction.

The silence of the urn is stressed—it is a "bride of quietness"; it is a "foster-child of silence," but the urn is a "historian" too. Historians tell the truth, or are at least expected to tell the truth. What is a "Sylvan historian"? A historian who is like the forest rustic, a woodlander? Or, a historian who writes histories of the forest? Presumably, the urn is sylvan in both senses. True, the latter meaning is uppermost: the urn can "express / A flowery tale more sweetly than our rhyme," and what the urn goes on to express is a "leaf-fring'd legend" of "Tempe or the dales of Arcady." But the urn, like the "leaf-fring'd legend" which it tells, is covered with emblems of the fields and forests: "Overwrought, / With forest branches and the trodden weed." When we consider the way in which the urn utters its history, the fact that it must be sylvan in both senses is seen as inevitable. Perhaps too the fact that it is a rural historian, a rustic, a peasant historian, qualifies in our minds the dignity and the "truth" of the histories which it recites. Its histories, Keats has already conceded, may be characterized as "tales"—not formal history at all.

The sylvan historian certainly supplies no names and dates—"What men or gods are these?" the poet asks. What it does give is action—of men *or* gods, of godlike men or of superhuman (though not daemonic) gods—action, which is not the less intense for all that the urn is cool marble. The words "mad" and "ecstasy" occur, but it is the quiet, rigid urn which gives the dynamic picture. And the paradox goes further: the scene is one of violent love-making, a Bacchanalian scene, but the urn itself is like a "still unravish'd bride," or like a child, a child "of silence and slow time." It is not merely like a child, but like a "foster-child." The exactness of the term can be defended. "Silence and slow time," it is suggested, are not the true parents, but foster-parents. They are too old, one feels, to have borne the child themselves. Moreover, they dote upon the "child" as grandparents do. The urn is fresh and unblemished; it is still young, for all its antiquity, and time which destroys so much has "fostered" it.

With Stanza II we move into the world presented by the urn, into an examination, not of the urn as a whole—as an entity with its own form—but of the details which overlay it. But as we enter that world, the paradox of silent speech is carried on, this time in terms of the objects portrayed on the vase.

The first lines of the stanza state a rather bold paradox—even the dulling effect of many readings has hardly blunted it. At least we can easily revive its sharpness. Attended to with care, it is a statement which is preposterous, and yet true—true on the same level on which the original metaphor of the speaking urn is true. The unheard music is sweeter than any audible music. The poet has rather cunningly enforced his conceit by using the phrase, "ye soft pipes." Actually, we might accept the poet's metaphor without being forced to accept the adjective "soft." The pipes might, although "unheard," be shrill, just as the action which is frozen in the figures on the urn can be violent and ecstatic as in Stanza I and slow and dignified as in Stanza IV (the procession to the sacrifice). Yet, by characterizing the pipes as "soft," the poet has provided a sort of realistic basis for his metaphor: the pipes, it is suggested, are playing very softly; if we listen carefully, we can hear them; their music is just below the threshold of normal sound.

This general paradox runs through the stanza: action goes on though the actors are motionless; the song will not cease; the lover cannot leave his song;

the maiden, always to be kissed, never actually kissed, will remain changelessly beautiful. The maiden is, indeed, like the urn itself, a "still unravished bride of quietness"—not even ravished by a kiss; and it is implied, perhaps, that her changeless beauty, like that of the urn, springs from this fact.

The poet is obviously stressing the fresh, unwearied charm of the scene itself which can defy time and is deathless. But, at the same time, the poet is being perfectly fair to the terms of his metaphor. The beauty portrayed is death-less because it is lifeless. And it would be possible to shift the tone easily and ever so slightly by insisting more heavily on some of the phrasings so as to give them a darker implication. Thus, in the case of "thou canst not leave / Thy song," one could interpret: the musician cannot leave the song even if he would: he is fettered to it, a prisoner. In the same way, one could enlarge on the hint that the lover is not wholly satisfied and content: "never canst thou kiss, / . . . *yet, do not grieve.*" These items are mentioned here, not because one wishes to maintain that the poet is bitterly ironical, but because it is important for us to see that even here the paradox is being used fairly, particularly in view of the shift in tone which comes in the next stanza.

This third stanza represents, as various critics have pointed out, a recapitulation of earlier motifs. The boughs which cannot shed their leaves, the un-wearied melodist, and the ever ardent lover reappear. Indeed, I am not sure that this stanza can altogether be defended against the charge that it represents a falling-off from the delicate but firm precision of the earlier stanzas. There is a tendency to linger over the scene sentimentally: the repetition of the word "happy" is perhaps symptomatic of what is occurring. Here, if anywhere, in my opinion, is to be found the blemish on the ode—not in the last two lines. Yet, if we are to attempt a defense of the third stanza, we shall come nearest success by emphasizing the paradoxical implications of the repeated items; for what-ever development there is in the stanza inheres in the increased stress on the paradoxical element. For example, the boughs cannot "bid the Spring adieu," a phrase which repeats "nor ever can those trees be bare," but the new line strengthens the implications of speaking: the falling leaves are a gesture, a word of farewell to the joy of spring. The melodist of Stanza II played sweeter music because unheard, but here, in the third stanza, it is implied that he does not tire of his song for the same reason that the lover does not tire of his love—neither song nor love is consummated. The songs are "for ever new" because they cannot be completed.

The paradox is carried further in the case of the lover whose love is "For ever warm and still to be enjoy'd." We are really dealing with an ambiguity here, for we can take "still to be enjoy'd" as an adjectival phrase on the same level as "warm"—that is, "still virginal and warm." But the tenor of the whole poem suggests that the warmth of the love depends upon the fact that it has not been enjoyed—that is, "warm and still to be enjoy'd" may mean also "warm *because* still to be enjoy'd."

But though the poet has developed and extended his metaphors furthest here in this third stanza, the ironic counterpoise is developed furthest too. The love which a line earlier was "warm" and "panting" becomes suddenly in the next line, "All breathing human passion far above." But if it is *above* all breathing passion, it is, after all, outside the realm of breathing passion, and therefore, not human passion at all.

(If one argues that we are to take "All breathing human passion" as qualified by "That leaves a heart high-sorrowful and cloy'd"—that is, if one argues that Keats is saying that the love depicted on the urn is above only that human passion which leaves one cloyed and not above human passion in general, he misses the point. For Keats in the "Ode" is stressing the ironic fact that all human passion *does* leave one cloyed; hence the superiority of art.)

The purpose in emphasizing the ironic undercurrent in the foregoing lines is not at all to disparage Keats—to point up implications of his poem of which he was himself unaware. Far from it: the poet knows precisely what he is doing. The point is to be made simply in order to make sure that we are completely aware of what he *is* doing. Garrod, sensing this ironic undercurrent, seems to interpret it as an element over which Keats was not able to exercise full control. He says:

> Truth to his main theme [the fixity given by art to forms which in life are impermanent] has taken Keats farther than he meant to go. The pure and ideal art of this "cold Pastoral," this "silent form," *has* a cold silentness which in some degree saddens him. In the last lines of the fourth stanza, especially the last three lines . . . every reader is conscious, I should suppose, of an undertone of sadness, of disappointment.

The undertone is there, but Keats has not been taken "farther than he meant to go." Keats's attitude, even in the early stanzas, is more complex than Garrod would allow: it is more complex and more ironic, and a recognition of this is important if we are to be able to relate the last stanza to the rest of the "Ode." Keats is perfectly aware that the frozen moment of loveliness is more dynamic than is the fluid world of reality *only* because it is frozen. The love depicted on the urn remains warm and young because it is not human flesh at all but cold, ancient marble.

With Stanza IV, we are still within the world depicted by the urn, but the scene presented in this stanza forms a contrast to the earlier scenes. It emphasizes, not individual aspiration and desire, but communal life. It constitutes another chapter in the history that the "Sylvan historian" has to tell. And again, names and dates have been omitted. We are not told to what god's altar the procession moves, nor the occasion of the sacrifice.

Moreover, the little town from which the celebrants come is unknown; and the poet rather goes out of his way to leave us the widest possible option in locating it. It may be a mountain town, or a river town, or a tiny seaport. Yet, of course, there is a sense in which the nature of the town—the essential character of the town—is actually suggested by the figured urn. But it is not given explicitly. The poet is willing to leave much to our imaginations; and yet the stanza in its organization of imagery and rhythm does describe the town clearly enough; it is small, it is quiet, its people are knit together as an organic whole, and on a "pious morn" such as this, its whole population has turned out to take part in the ritual.

The stanza has been justly admired. Its magic of effect defies reduction to any formula. Yet, without pretending to "account" for the effect in any mechanical fashion, one can point to some of the elements active in securing the effect: there is the suggestiveness of the word "green" in "green altar"—something natural, spontaneous, living; there is the suggestion that the little town is caught in a curve of the seashore, or nestled in a fold of the mountains—at any rate, is something secluded and something naturally related to its terrain; there is the effect of the phrase "peaceful citadel," a phrase which involves a clash between the ideas of war and peace and resolves it in the sense of stability and independence without imperialistic ambition—the sense of stable repose.

But to return to the larger pattern of the poem: Keats does something in this fourth stanza which is highly interesting in itself and thoroughly relevant to the sense in which the urn is a historian. One of the most moving passages in the poem is that in which the poet speculates on the strange emptiness of the little town which, of course, has not been pictured on the urn at all.

The little town which has been merely implied by the procession portrayed on the urn is endowed with a poignance beyond anything else in the poem. Its streets "for evermore / Will silent be," its desolation forever shrouded in a mystery. No one in the figured procession will ever be able to go back to the town to break the silence there, not even one to tell the stranger there why the town remains desolate.

If one attends closely to what Keats is doing here, he may easily come to feel that the poet is indulging himself in an ingenious fancy, an indulgence, however, which is gratuitous and finally silly; that is, the poet has created in his own imagination the town implied by the procession of worshipers, has given it a special character of desolation and loneliness, and then has gone on to treat it as if it were a real town to which a stranger might actually come and be puzzled by its emptiness. (I can see no other interpretation of the lines, "and not a soul to tell / Why thou art desolate can e'er return.") But, actually, of course, no one will ever discover the town except by the very same process by which Keats has discovered it: namely, through the figured urn, and then, of course, he will not need to ask why it is empty. One can well imagine what a typical eighteenth-century critic would have made of this flaw in logic.

It will not be too difficult, however, to show that Keats's extension of the fancy is not irrelevant to the poem as a whole. The "reality" of the little town has a very close relation to the urn's character as a historian. If the earlier stanzas have been concerned with such paradoxes as the ability of static carving to convey dynamic action, of the soundless pipes to play music sweeter than that of the heard melody, of the figured lover to have a love more warm and panting than that of breathing flesh and blood, so in the same way the town implied by the urn comes to have a richer and more important history than that of actual cities. Indeed, the imagined town is to the figured procession as the unheard melody is to the carved pipes of the unwearied melodist. And the poet, by pretending to take the town as real—so real that he can imagine the effect of its silent streets upon the stranger who chances to come into it—has suggested in the most powerful way possible its essential reality for him—and for us. It is a case of the doctor's taking his own medicine: the poet is prepared to stand by the illusion of his own making.

With Stanza V we move back out of the enchanted world portrayed by the urn to consider the urn itself once more as a whole, as an object. The shift in point of view is marked with the first line of the stanza by the apostrophe, "O Attic shape . . ." It is the urn itself as a formed thing, as an autonomous world, to which the poet addresses these last words. And the rich, almost breathing world which the poet has conjured up for us contracts and hardens into the decorated motifs on the urn itself: "with brede / Of marble men and maidens overwrought." The beings who have a life above life—"All breathing human passion far above"—are marble, after all.

This last is a matter which, of course, the poet has never denied. The recognition that the men and maidens are frozen, fixed, arrested, has, as we have already seen, run through the second, third, and fourth stanzas as an ironic undercurrent. The central paradox of the poem, thus, comes to conclusion in the phrase, "Cold Pastoral." The word "pastoral" suggests warmth, spontaneity, the natural and the informal as well as the idyllic, the simple, and the informally charming. What the urn tells is a "flowery tale," a "leaf-fring'd legend," but the "sylvan historian" works in terms of marble. The urn itself is cold, and the life beyond life which it expresses is life which has been formed, arranged. The urn itself is a "silent form," and it speaks, not by means of statement, but by "teasing us out of thought." It is as enigmatic as eternity is, for, like eternity, its history is beyond time, outside time, and for this very reason bewilders our time-ridden minds: it teases us.

The marble men and maidens of the urn will not age as flesh-and-blood men and women will: "When old age shall this generation waste." (The word "generation," by the way, is very rich. It means on one level "that which is generated"—that which springs from human loins—Adam's breed; and yet, so intimately is death wedded to men, the word "generation" itself has become, as here, a measure of time.) The marble men and women lie outside time. The urn which they adorn will remain. The "Sylvan historian" will recite its history to other generations.

What will it say to them? Presumably, what it says to the poet now: that "formed experience," imaginative insight, embodies the basic and fundamental perception of man and nature. The urn is beautiful, and yet its beauty is based—what else is the poem concerned with?—on an imaginative perception of essentials. Such a vision is beautiful but it is also true. The sylvan historian presents us with beautiful histories, but they are true histories, and it is a good historian.

Moreover, the "truth" which the sylvan historian gives is the only kind of truth which we are likely to get on this earth, and, furthermore, it is the only kind that we *have* to have. The names, dates, and special circumstances, the wealth of data—these the sylvan historian quietly ignores. But we shall never get all the facts anyway—there is no end to the accumulation of facts. Moreover, mere accumulations of facts—a point our own generation is only beginning to realize—are meaningless. The sylvan historian does better than that: it takes a few details and so orders them that we have not only beauty but insight into essential truth. Its "history," in short, is a history without footnotes. It has the validity of myth—not myth as a pretty but irrelevant make-belief, an idle fancy, but myth as a valid perception into reality.

So much for the "meaning" of the last lines of the "Ode." It is an interpretation which differs little from past interpretations. It is put forward here with no pretension to novelty. What is important is the fact that it can be derived from the context of the "Ode" itself.

And now, what of the objection that the final lines break the tone of the poem with a display of misplaced sententiousness? One can summarize the answer already implied thus: throughout the poem the poet has stressed the paradox of the speaking urn. First, the urn itself can tell a story, can give a history. Then, the various figures depicted upon the urn play music or speak or sing. If we have been alive to these items, we shall not, perhaps, be too much surprised to have the urn speak once more, not in the sense in which it tells a story—a metaphor which is rather easy to accept—but, to have it speak on a higher level, to have it make a commentary on its own nature. If the urn has been properly dramatized, if we have followed the development of the metaphors, if we have been alive to the paradoxes which work throughout the poem, perhaps then, we shall be prepared for the enigmatic, final paradox which the "silent form" utters. But in that case, we shall not feel that the generalization, unqualified and to be taken literally, is meant to march out of its context to compete with the scientific and philosophical generalizations which dominate our world.

"Beauty is truth, truth beauty" has precisely the same status, and the same justification as Shakespeare's "Ripeness is all." It is a speech "in character" and supported by a dramatic context.

To conclude thus may seem to weight the principle of dramatic propriety with more than it can bear. This would not be fair to the complexity of the problem of truth in art nor fair to Keats's little parable. Granted; and yet the principle of dramatic propriety may take us further than would first appear. Respect for it may at least insure our dealing with the problem of truth at the level on which it is really relevant to literature. If we can see that the assertions made in a poem are to be taken as part of an organic context, if we can resist the temptation to deal with them in isolation, then we may be willing to go on to deal with the world-view, or "philosophy," or "truth" of the *poem as a whole* in terms of its dramatic wholeness: that is, we shall not neglect the maturity of attitude, the dramatic tension, the emotional *and* intellectual coherence in favor of some statement of theme abstracted from it by paraphrase. Perhaps, best of all, we might learn to distrust our ability to represent any poem adequately by paraphrase. Such a distrust is healthy. Keats's sylvan historian, who is not above "teasing" us, exhibits such a distrust, and perhaps the point of what the sylvan historian "says" is to confirm us in our distrust.

NOTES

This essay had been finished some months before I came upon Kenneth Burke's brilliant essay on Keats's "Ode" ("Symbolic Action in a Poem by Keats," *Accent* [autumn 1943]). I have decided not to make any alterations, though I have been tempted to adopt some of Burke's insights, and, in at least one case, his essay has convinced me of a point which I had considered but rejected—the pun on "breed" and "Brede."

I am happy to find that two critics with methods and purposes so different should agree so thoroughly as we do on the poem. I am pleased, for my part, therefore, to acknowledge the amount of duplication which exists between the two essays, counting it as rather important corroboration of a view of the poem which will probably seem to some critics overingenious. In spite of the common elements, however, I feel that the emphasis of my essay is sufficiently different from Burke's to justify my going on with its publication.

3. Symbolic Action in a Poem by Keats

KENNETH BURKE

W̲E̲ ̲A̲R̲E̲ ̲H̲E̲R̲E̲ ̲S̲E̲T̲ to analyze the "Ode on a Grecian Urn" as a viaticum that leads, by a series of transformations, into the oracle, "Beauty is truth, truth beauty." We shall analyze the Ode "dramatistically," in terms of symbolic action.

To consider language as a means of *information* or *knowledge* is to consider it epistemologically, semantically, in terms of "science." To consider it as a mode of *action* is to consider it in terms of "poetry." For a poem is an act, the symbolic act of the poet who made it—an act of such a nature that, in surviving as a structure or object, it enables us as readers to reenact it.

"Truth" being the essential word of knowledge (science) and "beauty" being the essential word of art or poetry, we might substitute accordingly. The oracle would then assert, "Poetry is science, science poetry." It would be particularly exhilarating to proclaim them one if there were a strong suspicion that they were at odds (as the assertion that "God's in his heaven, all's right with the world" is really a *counter*assertion to doubts about God's existence and suspicions that much is wrong). It was the dialectical opposition between the "aesthetic" and the "practical," with "poetry" on one side and utility (business and applied science) on the other that was being ecstatically denied. The *relief* in this denial was grounded in the romantic philosophy itself, a philosophy which gave strong recognition to precisely the *contrast* between "beauty" and "truth."

Perhaps we might put it this way: If the oracle were to have been uttered in the first stanza of the poem rather than the last, its phrasing proper to that place would have been: "Beauty is *not* truth, truth *not* beauty." The five stanzas of successive transformation were necessary for the romantic philosophy of a romantic poet to transcend itself (raising its romanticism to a new order, or new dimension). An abolishing of romanticism through romanticism! (To transcend romanticism through romanticism is, when all is over, to restore in one way what is removed in another.)

But to the poem, step by step through the five stanzas.

As a "way in," we begin with the sweeping periodic sentence that, before the stanza is over, has swiftly but imperceptibly been transmuted in quality from the periodic to the breathless, a cross between interrogation and exclamation:

> Thou still unravish'd bride of quietness,
>   Thou foster-child of silence and slow time,
> Sylvan historian, who canst thus express
>   A flowery tale more sweetly than our rhyme:
> What leaf-fring'd legend haunts about thy shape
>   Of deities or mortals, or of both,
>   In Tempe or the dales of Arcady?
> What men or gods are these? What maidens loth?
>   What mad pursuit? What struggle to escape?
>   What pipes and timbrels? What wild ecstasy?

Even the last quick outcries retain somewhat the quality of the periodic structure with which the stanza began. The final line introduces the subject of "pipes and timbrels," which is developed and then surpassed in Stanza II:

> Heard melodies are sweet, but those unheard
>   Are sweeter; therefore, ye soft pipes, play on;
> Not to the sensual ear, but, more endear'd,
>   Pipe to the spirit ditties of no tone:
> Fair youth, beneath the trees, thou canst not leave
>   Thy song, nor ever can those trees be bare;
>   Bold Lover, never, never canst thou kiss,
> Though winning near the goal—yet, do not grieve;
>   She cannot fade, though thou hast not thy bliss,
>   Forever wilt thou love, and she be fair!

If we had only the first stanza of this Ode, and were speculating upon it from the standpoint of motivation, we could detect there tentative indications of two motivational levels. For the lines express a doubt whether the figures on the urn are "deities or mortals"—and the motives of gods are of a different order from the motives of men. This bare hint of such a possibility emerges with something of certainty in the second stanza's development of the "pipes and timbrels" theme. For we explicitly consider a contrast between body and mind (in the contrast between "heard melodies," addressed "to the sensual ear," and "ditties of no tone," addressed "to the spirit").

Also, of course, the notion of inaudible sound brings us into the region of the mystic oxymoron (the term in rhetoric for "the figure in which an epithet of a contrary significance is added to a word: e.g., *cruel kindness; laborious idleness*"). And it clearly suggests a concern with the level of motives-behind-motives, as with the paradox of the prime mover that is itself at rest, being the unmoved ground of all motion and action. Here the poet whose sounds are the richest in our language is meditating upon *absolute* sound, the *essence* of sound, which would be soundless as the prime mover is motionless, or as the "principle" of sweetness would not be sweet, having transcended sweetness, or as the sub-atomic particles of the sun are each, in their isolate purity, said to be devoid of temperature.

Contrast Keats's unheard melodies with those of Shelley:

> Music, when soft voices die,
> Vibrates in the memory—
> Odours, when sweet violets sicken,
> Live within the sense they quicken.
>
> Rose leaves, when the rose is dead,
> Are heaped for the beloved's bed;
> And so thy thoughts, when thou art gone,
> Love itself shall slumber on.

Here the futuristic Shelley is anticipating retrospection; he is looking forward to looking back. The form of thought is naturalistic and temporalistic in terms of *past* and *future.* But the form of thought in Keats is mystical, in terms of an *eternal present.* The Ode is striving to move beyond the region of becoming into the realm of *being.* (This is another way of saying that we are here concerned with two levels of motivation.)

In the last four lines of the second stanza, the state of immediacy is conveyed by a development peculiarly Keatsian. I refer not simply to translation into terms of the erotic, but rather to a quality of *suspension* in the erotic imagery, defining an eternal prolongation of the state just prior to fulfillment— not exactly arrested ecstasy, but rather an arrested preecstasy.[1]

Suppose that we had but this one poem by Keats, and knew nothing of its author or its period, so that we could treat it only in itself, as a series of internal transformations to be studied in their development from a certain point, and without reference to any motives outside the Ode. Under such conditions, I think, we should require no further observations to characterize (from the standpoint of symbolic action) the main argument in the second stanza. We might go on to make an infinity of observations about the details of the stanza; but as regards major deployments we should deem it enough to note that the theme of "pipes and timbrels" is developed by the use of mystic oxymoron, and then surpassed (or given a development-atop-the-development) by the stressing of erotic imagery (that had been ambiguously adumbrated in the references to "maidens loth" and "mad pursuit" of Stanza I). And we could note the quality of *incipience* in this imagery, its state of arrest not at fulfillment, but at the point just prior to fulfillment.

Add, now, our knowledge of the poem's place as an enactment in a particular cultural scene, and we likewise note in this second stanza a variant of the identification between death and sexual love that was so typical of nineteenth-century romanticism and was to attain its musical monument in the Wagnerian *Liebestod*. On a purely dialectical basis, to die in love would be to be born to love (the lovers dying as individual identities that they might be transformed into a common identity). Adding historical factors, one can note the part that capitalist individualism plays in sharpening this consummation (since a property structure that heightens the sense of individual identity would thus make it more imperiously a "death" for the individual to take on the new identity made by a union of two). We can thus see why the love-death equation would be particularly representative of a romanticism that was the reflex of business.

Fortunately, the relation between private property and the love-death equation is attested on unimpeachable authority, concerning the effect of consumption and consummation in a "mutual flame":

> So between them love did shine,
> That the turtle saw his right
> Flaming in the phoenix' sight;
> Either was the other's mine.
>
> Property was thus appall'd,
> That the self was not the same;
> Single nature's double name
> Neither two nor one was called.

The addition of fire to the equation, with its pun on sexual burning, moves us from purely dialectical considerations into psychological ones. In the lines of Shakespeare, fire is the third term, the ground term for the other two (the synthesis that ends the lovers' roles as thesis and antithesis). Less obviously, the same movement from the purely dialectical to the psychological is implicit in any imagery of a *dying* or a *falling* in common, which when woven with sexual imagery signalizes a "transcendent" sexual consummation. The figure appears in a lover's compliment when Keats writes to Fanny Brawne, thus: "I never knew before, what such a love as you have made me feel, was; I did not believe in it; my Fancy was afraid of it lest it should burn me up. But if you will fully love me, though there may be some fire, 'twill not be more than we can bear when moistened and bedewed with pleasures." Our primary concern is to follow the transformations of the poem itself. But to understand its full nature as a symbolic act, we should use whatever knowledge is available. In the case of Keats, not only do we know the place of this poem in his work and its time, but also we have material to guide our speculations as regards correlations between poem and poet. I grant that such speculations interfere with the symmetry of criticism as a game. (Criticism as a game is best to watch, I guess, when one confines himself to the single unit, and reports on its movements like a radio commentator broadcasting the blow-by-blow description of a prize-fight.) But linguistic analysis has opened up new possibilities in the correlating of producer and product—and these concerns have such important bearing upon matters of culture and conduct in general that no sheer conventions or ideals of criticism should be allowed to interfere with their development.

From what we know of Keats's illness, with the peculiar inclination to erotic imaginings that accompany its fever (as with the writings of D. H. Lawrence) we can glimpse a particular bodily motive expanding and intensifying the lyric state in Keats's case. Whatever the intense *activity* of his thoughts, there was the material *pathos* of his physical condition. Whatever transformations of mind or body he experienced, his illness was there as a kind of constitutional substrate, whereby all aspects of the illness would be imbued with their derivation from a common ground (the phthisic fever thus being at one with the phthisic chill, for whatever the clear contrast between fever and chill, they are but modes of the same illness, the common underlying substance).

The correlation between the state of agitation in the poems and the physical condition of the poet is made quite clear in the poignant letters Keats wrote during his last illness. In 1819 he complains that he is "scarcely content to write the best verses for the fever they leave behind." And he continues: "I want to compose without this fever." But a few months later he confesses, "I am recommended not even to read poetry, much less write it." Or: "I must say that for 6 Months before I was taken ill I had not passed a tranquil day. Either that gloom overspread me or I was suffering under some passionate feeling, or if I turn'd to versify that exacerbated the poison of either sensation." Keats was "like a sick eagle looking at the sky," as he wrote of his mortality in a kindred poem, "On Seeing the Elgin Marbles."

But though the poet's body was a *patient*, the poet's mind was an *agent*. Thus, as a practitioner of poetry, he could *use* his fever, even perhaps encouraging, though not deliberately, esthetic habits that, in making for the perfection of his lines, would exact payment in the ravages of his body (somewhat as Hart Crane could write poetry only by modes of living that made for the cessation of his poetry and so led to his dissolution).

Speaking of agents, patients, and action here, we might pause to glance back over the centuries thus: in the Aristotelian grammar of motives, action has its reciprocal in passion, hence *passion* is the property of a *patient*. But by the Christian paradox, (which made the martyr's action identical with his passion, as the accounts of the martyrs were called both Acts and Passionals) *patience* is the property of a moral *agent*. And this Christian view, as secularized in the philosophy of romanticism, with its stress upon creativeness, leads us to the possibility of a bodily suffering redeemed by a poetic act.

In the third stanza, the central stanza of the Ode (hence properly the fulcrum of its swing) we see the two motives, the action and the passion, in the process of being separated. The possibility raised in the first stanza (which was dubious whether the level of motives was to be human or divine), and developed in the second stanza (which contrasts the "sensual" and the "spirit"), becomes definitive in Stanza III:

> Ah, happy, happy boughs! that cannot shed
>   Your leaves, nor ever bid the Spring adieu;
> And, happy melodist, unwearied,
>   For ever piping songs for ever new;
> More happy love! more happy, happy love!
>   For ever warm and still to be enjoy'd,
>   For ever panting, and for ever young;
> All breathing human passion far above,
>   That leaves a heart high-sorrowful and cloy'd,
>   A burning forehead, and a parching tongue.

The poem as a whole makes permanent, or fixes in a state of arrest, a peculiar agitation. But within this fixity, by the nature of poetry as a progressive medium, there must be development. Hence, the agitation that is maintained throughout (as a mood absolutized so that it fills the entire universe of discourse) will at the same time undergo internal transformations. In the third stanza, these are manifested as a clear division into two distinct and contrasted realms. There is a transcendental fever, which is felicitous, divinely above "all breathing human passion." And this "leaves" the other level, the level of earthly fever, "a burning forehead and a parching tongue." From the bodily fever, which is a passion, and malign, there has split off a spiritual activity, a wholly benign aspect of the total agitation.

Clearly, a movement has been finished. The poem must, if it is well-formed, take a new direction, growing out of and surpassing the curve that has by now been clearly established by the successive stages from "Is there the possibility of two motivational levels?" through "there are two motivational levels" to "the 'active' motivational level 'leaves' the 'passive' level."

Prophesying, with the inestimable advantage that goes with having looked ahead, what should we expect the new direction to be? First, let us survey the situation. Originally, before the two strands of the fever had been definitely drawn apart, the bodily passion could serve as the scene or ground of the spiritual action. But at the end of the third stanza, we abandon the level of bodily passion. The action is "far above" the passion, it "leaves" the fever. What then would this transcendent act require, to complete it?

It would require a scene of the same quality as itself. An act and a scene belong together. The nature of the one must be a fit with the nature of the other. (I like to call this the "act-scene ratio," or "dramatic ratio.") Hence, the act having now transcended its bodily setting, it will require, as its new setting, a transcendent scene. Hence, prophesying *posteventum,* we should ask that, in Stanza IV, the poem *embody* the transcendental act by endowing it with an appropriate scene.

There is a passage in *Hamlet* that well illustrates the "act-scene ratio." When Hamlet is about to follow the ghost, Horatio warns:

> What if it tempt you toward the flood, my lord,
> Or to the dreadful summit of the cliff
> That beetles o'er his base into the sea,
> And there assume some other horrible form,
> Which might deprive your sovereignty of reason
> And draw you into madness? think of it;
> The very place puts toys of desperation,
> Without more motive, into every brain
> That looks so many fathoms to the sea
> And hears it roar beneath.

In the last four lines of this speech, Horatio is saying that a scene itself might be enough to provide a man with a motive for an act as desperate and absolute as suicide. This idea (of natural scene as sufficient motivation for an act) was to reappear, in many transformations, during the subsequent centuries. We find a notable variant of it in the novels of Thomas Hardy. We find less obvious variants of it in the many philosophies of materialistic science according to which behavior and development are explained in terms of the "environmental." Theories of "geopolitics" would be a contemporary variant.

It involves primarily the law of dramatic consistency whereby the quality of the act shares the quality of the scene in which it is enacted (the synecdochic relation of container and thing contained). Its grandest variant was in supernatural cosmogonies wherein mankind took on the attributes of gods by acting in cosmic scenes that were themselves imbued with the presence of godhead.[2]

Or we may discern the logic of the act-scene ratio behind the old controversy as to whether "God willed the good because it is good," or "the good is good because God willed it." This strictly theological controversy had political implications. For if the pattern were carried into theories of secular government, the thesis corresponding to the second of these theological doctrines might run somewhat like this: "Acts are legal because the monarch decrees them to be." Such a formula would obviously provide a much stronger sanction for legal innovation on the part of a central monarch than would a doctrine that the monarch's decrees should merely put into legal code traditional concepts of the lawful. For this theory, analogue of the doctrine that "God willed the good because it is good," served in effect to limit the powers of monarchs by upholding traditional rights that the king's legal innovations would abrogate or modify. Psychologically, you will note, the doctrine that "the good is good because God willed it" was more "voluntaristic," more in keeping with the rising bourgeois stress upon the "subjective" (the idealistic way of locating the centre of motivation in the *agent*).[3]

If even theology thus responded to the pressure for dramatic symmetry by endowing God, as the transcendent act, with a transcendent scene of like quality, we should certainly expect to find analogous tactics in this Ode. For as we have noted that the romantic passion is the secular equivalent of the Christian passion, so we may recall Coleridge's notion that poetic action itself is a "dim analogue of Creation." Keats in his way confronting the same dramatistic requirement that the theologians confronted in theirs, when he has arrived at his transcendent act at the end of Stanza III (that is, when the benign fever has split away from the malign bodily counterpart, as a divorcing of spiritual action from sensual passion), he is ready in the next stanza for the imagining of a scene that would correspond in quality to the quality of the action as so transformed. His fourth stanza will concretize, or "materialize," the act, by dwelling upon its appropriate ground.

> Who are these coming to the sacrifice?
>   To what green altar, O mysterious priest,
> Lead'st thou that heifer lowing at the skies.
>   And all her silken flanks with garlands drest?
> What little town, by river or sea shore,
>   Or mountain built with peaceful citadel,
>   Is emptied of this folk, this pious morn?
> And, little town, thy streets for evermore
>   Will silent be; and not a soul to tell
>   Why thou art desolate, can e'er return.

It is a vision, as you prefer, of "death" or of "immortality." "Immortality," we might say, is the "good" word for "death," and must necessarily be conceived in terms of death (the necessity that Donne touches upon when he writes, ". . . but thinke that I / Am, by being dead, immortall"). This is why, when discussing the second stanza, I felt justified in speaking of the variations of the love-death equation, though the poem spoke not of love and *death*, but of love *for ever*. We have a deathy-deathless scene as the corresponding ground of our transcendent act. The Urn itself, as with the scene upon it, is not merely an immortal act in our present mortal scene; it was originally an immortal act in a mortal scene quite different. The imagery, of sacrifice, piety, silence, desolation, is that of communication with the immortal or the dead.[4]

Incidentally, we might note that the return to the use of rhetorical questions in the fourth stanza serves well, on a purely technical level, to keep our contact with the mood of the opening stanza, a music that now but vibrates in the memory. Indeed, one even gets the impression that the form of the rhetorical question had never been abandoned; that the poet's questings had been couched as questions throughout. This is tonal felicity at its best, and something much like unheard tonal felicity. For the actual persistence of the rhetorical questions through these stanzas would have been wearisome, whereas their return now gives us an inaudible variation, by making us feel that the exclamations in the second and third stanzas had been questions, as the questions in the first stanza had been exclamations.

But though a lyric greatly profits by so strong a sense of continuousness, or perpetuity, I am trying to stress the fact that in the fourth stanza we *come upon* something. Indeed, this fourth stanza is related to the three foregoing stanzas quite as the sestet is related to the octave in Keats's sonnet, "On First Looking Into Chapman's Homer":

> Much have I travell'd in the realms of gold,
>   And many goodly states and kingdoms seen;
>   Round many western islands have I been
> Which bards in fealty to Apollo hold.
> Oft of one wide expanse had I been told
>   That deep-brow'd Homer ruled as his demesne;
>   Yet did I never breathe its pure serene
> Till I heard Chapman speak out loud and bold;
>
> Then felt I like some watcher of the skies
>   When a new planet swims into his ken;
> Or like stout Cortez when with eagle eyes
>   He stared at the Pacific—and all his men
> Look'd at each other with a wild surmise—
>   Silent, upon a peak in Darien.

I am suggesting that, just as the sestet in this sonnet, *comes upon a scene*, so it is with the fourth stanza of the Ode. In both likewise we end on the theme of silence; and is not the Ode's reference to the thing that "not a soul can tell" quite the same in quality as the sonnet's reference to a "wild surmise"?

Thus, with the Urn as viaticum (or rather, with the *poem* as viaticum, and *in the name* of the Urn), having symbolically enacted a kind of act that transcends our mortality, we round out the process by coming to dwell upon the transcendental ground of this act. The dead world of ancient Greece, as immortalized on an Urn surviving from this period, is the vessel of this deathy-deathless ambiguity. And we have gone dialectically from the "human" to the "divine" and thence to the "ground of the divine" (here tracing in poetic imagery the kind of "dramatistic" course we have considered, on the purely conceptual plane, in the theological speculations about the "grounds" for God's creative act). Necessarily, there must be certain inadequacies in the conception of this ground, precisely because of the fact that immortality can only be conceived in terms of death. Hence the reference to the "desolate" in a scene otherwise possessing the benignity of the eternal.

The imagery of pious sacrifice, besides its fitness for such thoughts of departure as when the spiritual act splits from the sensual pathos, suggests also a bond of communication between the levels (because of its immortal character in a mortal scene). And finally, the poem, in the name of the Urn, or under the aegis of the Urn, is such a bond. For we readers, by reenacting it in the reading, use it as a viaticum to transport us into the quality of the scene which it depicts on its face (the scene containing as a fixity what the poem as act extends into a process). The scene *on* the Urn is really the scene *behind* the Urn; the Urn is literally the ground of this scene, but transcendentally the scene is the ground of the Urn. The Urn contains the scene out of which it arose.

We turn now to the closing stanza:

> O Attic shape! Fair attitude! with brede
>   Of marble men and maidens overwrought,
> With forest branches and the trodden weed;
>   Thou, silent form, dost tease us out of thought
> As doth eternity: Cold Pastoral!
>   When old age shall this generation waste,
>   Thou shalt remain, in midst of other woe
> Than ours, a friend to man, to whom thou say'st,
>   'Beauty is truth, truth beauty,'—that is all
>   Ye know on earth, and all ye need to know.

In the third stanza we were at a moment of heat, emphatically sharing an imagery of love's "panting" and "for ever warm" that was, in the transcendental order, companionate to "a burning forehead, and a parching tongue" in the order of the passions. But in the last stanza, as signalized in the marmorean utterance, "Cold Pastoral!" we have gone from transcendental fever to transcendental chill. Perhaps, were we to complete our exegesis, we should need reference to some physical step from phthisic fever to phthisic chill, that we might detect here a final correlation between bodily passion and mental action. In any event we may note that, the mental action having departed from the bodily passion, the change from fever to chill is not a sufferance. For, as only the *benign* aspects of the fever had been left after the split, so it is a wholly benign chill on which the poem ends.[5]

I wonder whether anyone can read the reference to "brede of marble men and maidens overwrought" without thinking of "breed" for "brede" and "excited" for "overwrought." (Both expressions would thus merge notions of sexuality and craftsmanship, the erotic and the poetic.) As for the designating of the Urn as an "Attitude," it fits in admirably with our stress upon symbolic action. For an attitude is an arrested, or incipient *act*—not just an *object*, or *thing*.

Yeats, in *A Vision*, speaks of "the diagrams in Law's *Boehme*, where one lifts a paper to discover both the human entrails and the starry heavens." This equating of the deeply without and the deeply within (as also with Kant's famous remark) might well be remembered when we think of the sky that stout Cortez saw in Keats's sonnet. It is an internal sky, attained through meditations induced by the reading of a book. And so the oracle, whereby truth and beauty are proclaimed as one, would seem to derive from a profound inwardness.

Otherwise, without these introductory mysteries, "truth" and "beauty" were at odds. For whereas "beauty" had its fulfillment in romantic poetry, "truth" was coming to have its fulfillment in science, technological accuracy, accountancy, statistics, actuarial tables, and the like. Hence, without benefit of the rites which one enacts in a sympathetic reading of the Ode (rites that remove the discussion to a different level), the enjoyment of "beauty" would involve an esthetic kind of awareness radically in conflict with the kind of awareness deriving from the practical "truth." And as regards the tactics of the poem, this conflict would seem to be solved by "estheticizing" the true rather than by "verifying" the beautiful.

Earlier in our essay, we suggested reading "poetry" for "beauty" and "science" for "truth," with the oracle deriving its *liberating* quality from the fact that it is uttered at a time when the poem has taken us to a level where earthly contradictions do not operate. But we might also, in purely conceptual terms, attain a level where "poetry" and "science" cease to be at odds; namely: by translating the two terms into the "grammar" that lies behind them. That is: we could generalize the term "poetry" by widening it to the point where we could substitute for it the term "act." And we could widen "science" to the point where we could substitute "scene." Thus we have:

"beauty" equals "poetry" equals "act"
"truth" equals "science" equals "scene"

We would equate "beauty" with "act," because it is not merely a decorative thing, but an assertion, an affirmative, a creation, hence in the fullest sense an act. And we would equate "truth" or "science" with the "scenic" because science is a knowledge of *what is*—and *all that is* comprises the overall universal *scene*. Our corresponding transcendence, then, got by "translation" into purely grammatical terms, would be: "Act is scene, scene act." We have got to this point by a kind of purely conceptual transformation that would correspond, I think, to the transformations of imagery leading to the oracle in the Ode.

"Act is scene, scene act." Unfortunately, I must break the symmetry a little. For poetry, as conceived in idealism (romanticism) could not quite be equated with *act*, but rather with *attitude*. For idealistic philosophies, with their stress upon the subjective, place primary stress upon the *agent* (the individual, the ego, the will, etc.). It was medieval scholasticism that placed primary stress upon the *act*. And in the Ode the Urn (which is the vessel or representative of poetry) is called an "attitude," which is not outright an act, but an incipient or arrested act, a *state of mind*, the property of an *agent*. Keats, in calling the Urn an attitude, is *personifying* it. Or we might use the italicizing resources of dialectic by saying that for Keats, beauty (poetry) was not so much "the *act* of an agent" as it was "the act of an *agent*."

Perhaps we can reenforce this interpretation by examining kindred strategies in Yeats, whose poetry similarly derives from idealistic, romantic sources. Indeed, as we have noted elsewhere,[6] Yeats's vision of immortality in his Byzantium poems but carries one step further the Keatsian identification with the Grecian Urn:

> Once out of nature I shall never take
> My bodily form from any natural thing,
> But such a form as Grecian goldsmiths make
> Of hammered gold and gold enamelling . . .

Here certainly the poet envisions immortality as "esthetically" as Keats. For he will have mortality as a golden bird, a fabricated thing, a work of Grecian goldsmiths. Here we go in the same direction as the "overwrought" Urn, but farther along in that direction.

The ending of Yeats's poem, "Among School Children," helps us to make still clearer the idealistic stress upon agent:

> Labour is blossoming or dancing where
> The body is not bruised to pleasure soul,
> Nor beauty torn out of its own despair,
> Nor blear-eyed wisdom out of midnight oil.
> O chestnut tree, great rooted blossomer,
> Are you the leaf, the blossom or the bole?
> O body swayed to music, O brightening glance,
> How can we know the dancer from the dance?

Here the chestnut tree (as personified agent) is the ground of unity or continuity for all its scenic manifestations; and with the agent (dancer) is merged the act (dance). True, we seem to have here a commingling of act, scene, and agent, all three. Yet it is the *agent* that is "foremost among the equals." Both Yeats and Keats, of course, were much more "dramatistic" in their thinking than romantic poets generally, who usually center their efforts upon the translation of *scene* into terms of *agent* (as the materialistic science that was the dialectical counterpart of romantic idealism preferred conversely to translate *agent* into terms of *scene,* or in other words, to treat "consciousness" in terms of "matter," the "mental" in terms of the "physical," "people" in terms of "environment").

To review briefly: The poem begins with an ambiguous fever which in the course of the further development is "separated out," splitting into a bodily fever and a spiritual counterpart. The bodily passion is the malign aspect of the fever, the mental action its benign aspect. In the course of the development, the malign passion is transcended and the benign active partner, the intellectual exhilaration, takes over. At the beginning, where the two aspects were ambiguously one, the bodily passion would be the "scene" of the mental action (the "objective symptoms" of the body would be paralleled by the "subjective symptoms" of the mind, the bodily state thus being the other or ground of the mental state). But as the two become separated out, the mental action transcends the bodily passion. It becomes an act in its own right, making discoveries and assertions not grounded in the bodily passion. And this quality of action, in transcending the merely physical symptoms of the fever, would thus require a different ground or scene, one more suited in quality to the quality of the transcendent act.

The transcendent act is concretized, or "materialized," in the vision of the "immortal" scene, the reference in Stanza IV to the original scene of the Urn, the "heavenly" scene of a dead, or immortal, Greece (the scene in which the Urn was originally enacted and which is also fixed on its face). To indicate the internality of this vision, we referred to a passage in Yeats relating the "depths" of the sky without to the depths of the mind within; and we showed a similar pattern in Keats's account of the vision that followed his reading of Chapman's Homer. We suggested that the poet is here coming upon a new internal sky, through identification with the Urn as act, the same sky that he came upon through identification with the enactments of Chapman's translation.

This transcendent scene is the level at which the earthly laws of contradiction no longer prevail. Hence, in the terms of this scene, he can proclaim the unity of truth and beauty (of science and art), a proclamation which he needs to make precisely because here was the basic split responsible for the romantic agitation (in both poetic and philosophic idealism). That is, it was gratifying to have the oracle proclaim the unity of poetry and science because the values of technology and business were causing them to be at odds. And from the perspective of a "higher level" (the perspective of a deed or immortal scene transcending the world of temporal contradictions) the split could be proclaimed once more a unity.

At this point, at this stage of exaltation, the fever has been replaced by chill. But the bodily passion has completely dropped out of account. All is now mental action. Hence, the chill (as in the ecstatic exclamation, "Cold Pastoral!") is proclaimed only in its benign aspect.

We may contrast this discussion with explanations such as a materialist of the Kretschmer school might offer. I refer to accounts of motivation that might treat disease as cause and poem as effect. In such accounts, the disease would not be "passive," but wholly active; and what we have called the mental action would be wholly passive, hardly more than an epiphenomenon, a mere symptom of the disease quite as are the fever and the chill themselves. Such accounts would give us no conception of the essential matter here, the intense linguistic activity.

NOTES

1 G. Wilson Knight, in *The Starlit Dome* (London: Methuen, 1959), refers to "that recurring tendency in Keats to image a poised form, a stillness suggesting motion, what might be called a 'tiptoe' effect."

2 In an article by Leo Spitzer, "*Milieu* and *Ambiance:* An Essay in Historical Semantics," *Philosophy and Phenomenological Research* (September and December 1942), one will find a wealth of material that can be read as illustrative of "dramatic ratio."

3 This stress is usually, in practice, exemplified by what I call the "lyric" or "scene-agent" ratio, involving a likeness of quality in person and place. In typical nineteenth-century writing, one can find instances of the scene-agent ratio almost at random. Here is one in Carlyle's *Heroes and Hero Worship:*

> These Arabs Mohammed was born among are certainly a notable people. Their country itself is notable; the fit habitation for such a race. Savage inaccessible rock-mountains, great grim deserts, alternating with beautiful strips of verdure: wherever water is, there is greenness, beauty; odoriferous balm shrubs, date-trees, frankincense-trees. Consider that wide waste horizon of sand, empty, silent, like a sand-sea, dividing habitable place from habitable. You are all alone there, left alone with the universe: by day a fierce sun blazing down on it with intolerable radiance; by night the great deep heaven with its stars. Such country is fit for a swift-handed, deep-hearted race of men.

4 In imagery there is no negation, or disjunction. Linguistically we can say, "this *or* that," "this, *not* that." In imagery we can but say "this *and* that," "this *with* that," "this-that," etc. Thus, imagistically considered, a commandment cannot be simply a proscription, but is also latently a provocation (a state of affairs that figures in the kind of stylistic scrupulosity and / or curiosity to which Gide's heroes have been particularly sensitive, as "thou shalt not . . ." becomes imaginatively transformed into "what would happen if . . ."). In the light of what we have said about the deathiness of immortality, and the relation between the erotic and the thought of a "dying," perhaps we might be justified in reading the last line of the great "Bright Star!" sonnet as naming states not simply alternative but also synonymous: "And so live ever—or else swoon to death." This use of the love-death equation is as startlingly paralleled in a letter to Fanny Brawne: "I have two luxuries to brood over in my

walks, your loveliness and the hour of my death. O that I could take possession of them both in the same moment."

5   In a letter to Fanny Brawne, Keats touches upon the fever-chill contrast in a passage that also touches upon the love-death equation, though here the chill figures in an untransfigured state: "I fear that I am too prudent for a dying kind of Lover. Yet, there is a great difference between going off in warm blood like Romeo; and making one's exit like a frog in a frost."

6   "On Motivation in Yeats," *The Southern Review* (winter 1942).

4. The Ekphrastic Principle and the Still Movement of Poetry; or Laokoön Revisited

Murray Krieger

LET ME INTERPRET THE proposed subject for these papers, "The Poet as Critic,"[1] as referring to the poet as critic in his poem, the poet as critic in the act of being poet; which is, in effect, to rephrase the title to read, the poetic in the poem. It would seem extravagant to suggest that the poem, in the very act of becoming successfully poetic—that is, in constituting itself poetry—implicitly constitutes its own poetic. But I would like here to entertain such an extravagant proposal.

Central to a poem's becoming successfully poetic, as I have tautologically put it, is the poem's achieving a formal and linguistic self-sufficiency. I could go on to claim, as I have elsewhere, that this formal and linguistic self-sufficiency involves the poem's coming to terms with itself, its creating the sense of roundedness. That is, through all sorts of repetitions, echoes, complexes of internal relations, it converts its chronological progression into simultaneity, its temporally unrepeatable flow into eternal recurrence; through a metaphorical bending under the pressure of aesthetic tension, it converts its linear movement into circle. But in making these claims, I am being pressed to metaphors of space to account for miracles performed in time, even if—thanks to the powers of poetic discourse—in a specially frozen sort of aesthetic time. The spatial metaphor inevitably becomes the critic's language for form. Many a self-conscious literary critic has been aware of the debt he owes to the language of the plastic arts—perhaps sculpture most of all—in his need to find a language to account for poetry's formal movements, its plasticity, if I may use the very word that most gives the temporal game away to space.

Very likely it was just this self-conscious necessity that created the tradition of *ut pictura poesis* from Simonides to Winckelmann, the tradition that drove Lessing to the classical good sense of his *Laokoön* and its insistence on keeping distinct among the arts what belonged to Peter and what to Paul, what to space and what to time. It is surely too easy to try to make poetry and sculpture meet and even fuse (as John Dewey, for example, tried to do anew in *Art as Experience*) by seeing the poem's transcending of mere movement through circular form as being one with the statue's transcending of mere stasis through its unending movement. But still the language of space persists as our inevitable metaphor to account for the poem's special temporality, its circularizing of its linear movement.[2]

I would take as my model statement Eliot's words in "Burnt Norton" about words and their relation to "the still point of the turning world":

> Words move, music moves
> Only in time; but that which is only living
> Can only die. Words, after speech, reach
> Into the silence. Only by the form, the pattern,
> Can words or music reach
> The stillness, as a Chinese jar still
> Moves perpetually in its stillness.[3]

These words, in turn, are an echo of the words of the Fourth Tempter in *Murder in the Cathedral*, themselves echoes of Thomas' earlier words about the Women of Canterbury:

> You know and do not know, what it is to act or suffer.
> You know and do not know, that acting is suffering,
> And suffering action. Neither does the actor suffer
> Nor the patient act. But both are fixed
> In an eternal action, an eternal patience
> To which all must consent that it may be willed
> And which all must suffer that they may will it,
> That the pattern may subsist, that the wheel may turn and still
> Be forever still.

I mean to take from Eliot's words about the still movement—like the Chinese jar—of verbal form the suggestion that the poet himself, in seeking to find an eloquence to account for the forms his words seek to turn themselves into, has done well to turn to metaphors from the spatial arts. Thus the poem that in the very act of becoming successfully poetic implicitly constitutes its own

poetic may do so, as Eliot suggests, by turning itself into the Chinese jar. It vio-
lates Lessing's injunction most strenuously by claiming for itself another order
than its own, by substituting the Platonic claim to oneness for the Aristotelian
theory of well-policed classes of Peter's and Paul's, with mutual appropriation
prohibited.

I use, then, as the most obvious sort of poetic within the poem this anti-
Lessing claim: the claim to form, to circular repetitiveness within the discretely
linear, and this by the use of an object of spatial and plastic art to symbolize the
spatiality and plasticity of literature's temporality. Actually, of course, a classic
genre was formulated that, in effect, institutionalized this tactic: the *ekphrasis*,
or the imitation in literature of a work of plastic art. The object of imitation,
as spatial work, becomes the metaphor for the temporal work which seeks to
capture it in that temporality. The spatial work freezes the temporal work even
as the latter seeks to free it from space. *Ekphrasis* concerns me here, then, to
the extent that I see it introduced in order to use a plastic object as a symbol of
the frozen, stilled world of plastic relationships which must be superimposed
upon literature's turning world to "still" it.

There are, of course, many less explicit ways for the poem to proclaim
as its poetic what I might term its ekphrastic principle, if I may broaden the
ekphrastic dimension beyond its narrowest and most literal employment—as
I must confess I intend eventually to do. For I would like finally to claim that
the ekphrastic dimension of literature reveals itself wherever the poem takes
on the "still" elements of plastic form which we normally attribute to the spatial arts. In so doing, the poem proclaims as its own poetic its formal necessity,
thus making more than just loosely metaphorical the use of spatial language to
describe—and thus to arrest—its movements.

A critic like Sigurd Burckhardt goes so far, in attributing plasticity to
poetry, as to insist—and persuasively—that the poem must convert the transparency of its verbal medium into the physical solidity of the medium of the
spatial arts:

> . . . whether [a painter] paints trees or triangles, they are corporeally there
> for us to respond to. . . . The painter's tree *is* an image; but if the poet
> writes "tree," he does not create an image. He *uses* one; the poetic "image"
> is one only in a metaphorical sense. Actually it is something that evokes
> an image, a sign pointing to a certain pre-established configuration in our
> visual memory. . . . The so-called poetic image achieves its effect only by
> denying its essence; it *is* a word, but it functions by making us aware of
> something other than it is. If many key terms of literary analysis—"color,"

"texture" and "image," for example—are in fact metaphors borrowed from the other arts, this is the reason: poetry has no material cause. Words already have what the artist first wants to give them—body.

I propose that the nature and primary function of the most important poetic devices—especially rhyme, meter and metaphor—is to release words in some measure from their bondage to meaning, their purely referential role, and to give or restore to them the corporeality which a true medium needs.[4]

Thus, by calling attention to the poetic function of words as substantive entities, one might extend the ekphrastic impulse to every poet in search of the sculptor's fully plastic medium.

But, as I have said, it is most useful to begin with the literally and narrowly ekphrastic, the poems which, in imitating a plastic object in language and time, make that object in its spatial simultaneity a true emblem of itself—and of poetry's ekphrastic principle. Jean H. Hagstrum, in his pioneering work *The Sister Arts*, finds his prime example of this mastery of space in time in Homer's description, in Book xviii of the *Iliad*, of the shield of Achilles wrought by Hephaestus. Hagstrum acknowledges Homer to be a painter, but only as a poet could be: "The passage remains faithful to the demands of verbal art and is by no means only an enumerative description. The shield becomes an emblem of the life of man: of nature and society, of the seasons of the year, and of cities at war and in peace; of agricultural scenes and the diversions of the rural day. There is obviously much that is non-pictorial: sound, motion, and sociological detail all "appear" on the surface of Hephaestus' masterpiece."[5] In this total mastery of moving life, the capturing of it in a "still" pattern, do we not seem to have the whole of Homer's world? In this emblem all is at an instant, though it is only in time and language that its simultaneity is created. The emblem is the constitutive symbol, the part that seems to contain the dynamic whole.

From the start, as in my title, following the example of Eliot in the quotations I have cited, I have been openly dependent upon the pun on the word *still* and the fusion in it of the opposed meanings, never and always, as applied to motion.[6] Having, like Eliot, borrowed it from Keats, I have freely used it as adjective, adverb, and verb; as still movement, still moving, and more forcefully, the stilling of movement: so "still" movement as quiet, unmoving movement; "still" moving as a forever-now movement, always in process, unending; and the union of these meanings at once twin and opposed in the "stilling" of movement, an action that is at once the quieting of movement and the perpetuation of it, the making of it, like Eliot's wheel and Chinese jar, a movement that is still and that is still with us, that is—in his words—"forever still." Thus my rendering and free borrowing of the "still" of Keats's "still unravish'd bride of quietness" in the poem which Leo Spitzer taught us profitably to view as a most splendid example of *ekphrasis*.[7] Further, Spitzer taught us to view the ekphrastic and imitative element in the poem not merely as its object but also as its formal cause. In keeping with the circular, "leaf-fring'd" frieze of the urn it describes, Spitzer tells us, ". . . the poem is circular or 'perfectly symmetrical' . . . thereby reproducing symbolically the form of the *objet d'art* which is its model."[8] In a footnote to this passage Spitzer generalizes on this practice:

> Since already in antiquity the poetic *ekphrasis* was often devoted to circular objects (shields, cups, etc.), it was tempting for poets to imitate verbally this constructive principle in their *ekphraseis*. Mörike's poem on an ancient lamp shows the same formal circularity motivated by the form of the model as does Keats's ode on the urn. . . .

So the spatial metaphor about the "shape" of the poem is not quite metaphorical, is in a sense literal. Only a little less immediately iconic than George Herbert's poems of imitative graphic form, the poem seeks to attain the "shape" of the urn. In this iconic attempt to shape itself in the form of its content, the poem seeks to perform in a way similar to the way the urns themselves, as sepulchral receptacles, sometimes sought to perform, if we can sense them as Sir Thomas Browne momentarily does in his *Urne-Buriall*. For the urn, container of ashes of the dead, seems to take on the form taken by its contents in life, thus becoming a still remaining form of a form that is no more. Browne's description is magnificently far-reaching:

> While many have handles, ears, and long necks, but more imitate a circular figure, in a spherical and round composure; whether from any mystery, best duration or capacity, were but a conjecture. But the common form with necks was a proper figure, making our last bed like our first; nor much unlike the Urnes of our Nativity, while we lay in the nether part of the earth, and inward vault of our Microcosme.[9]

In "the Urnes of our Nativity" we see a further circularity, a further reaching toward stillness (in both major senses): we see at once the end and the beginning, the receptacle of death simultaneously as the receptacle and womb of life, even while, as tomb, it takes on a spatial permanence in its circular imitation of the living form. This added circularity introduces new possibilities for temporal complexity in the use of the urn as the object of *ekphrasis*, a raising of it beyond the linear chronology of life's transience. These are possibilities that Cleanth Brooks seems to have foreseen in *The Well Wrought Urn*,[10] in which he assembles several complex uses of *urn* in poems, some of which I shall be referring to; although, interested primarily in single interpretations, he does not press their ekphrastic implications.

There is a climactic couplet in Alexander Pope's "Eloisa to Abelard" that serves at once to summarize and to symbolize this poem's studied futility. Eloisa, now denied sexual satisfaction with her lover not only by edict and by physical separation but even more irrevocably by the fact of his emasculation, becomes increasingly and more bitterly conscious of the tragic irony in the underlying sexual meaning of her repeated imperative to him: "Come!" She reaches the bitterness of the lines

> Come, Abelard! for what hast thou to dread?
> The Torch of Venus burns not for the dead.
> (lines 257–58)

He is the walking dead, deprived of all flame. If he defies Church and even the laws of space, his coldness yet prevents all or anything. And as his beloved, Eloisa is doubly cursed since *her* heat has not been subdued: ". . . yet Eloisa loves." And then the masterful couplet to which I want to call attention:

> Ah hopeless, lasting flames! like those that burn
> To light the dead, and warm th' unfruitful urn.
> (lines 261–62)

Here "urn," in its simultaneous relations to flame and death and fruit, becomes in an instant the constitutive symbol for the multiple agonies of the speaker of this monologue. As both tomb and womb, the urn is the receptacle at once of death and of love, of the remnants of the flame and of its height, of the congealing of life and the flowing of life. And a few lines later, in as daring an image, Pope adds the needed liquid element, derived of course from her tears:

> In seas of flame my plunging soul is drown'd,
> While altars blaze, and angels tremble round.
> (lines 275–76)

What is left but for her to direct her flames toward God, as Abelard's rival, in the questionable frenzy of religious ecstasy?

My point is that it is the urn of line 262 that, if I may pun myself, *receives* these meanings, at once preserves and gives life to them, as it gives life to the poem. Receiver of death as it is not permitted to be the vessel of life, it is warmed by the "hopeless, lasting flames" of a desire that dare not—indeed cannot—feed it. And the flames are at once of heat and of cold: at once agent of sexuality, of the life that is its consequence, and agent of the ashes, cold residue of life's flames and death's. The enforced, permanent chastity, this death in the midst of life, is of course reminiscent of the double-edged "stillness," the always-in-motion but never-to-be-completed action that, as with Keats' urn, accompanies the introduction, in accordance with the ekphrastic principle, of spatial forms within literature's temporality.

How different at all is Shakespeare's introduction of the urn, at the close of "The Phoenix and the Turtle," to be at once the repository of the separate ashes of the ideal lovers and the guarantor of their resurrection in the "mutual flame" of their new-born union, in accordance with the Phoenix riddle? Or Donne's introduction of the "well wrought urn" in "The Canonization" as the equivalent of his poem, an ever self-renewed memorial to his true lovers? Both these uses have been properly exploited by Cleanth Brooks in his appropriately titled book.[11] Or we may move forward in time, across the centuries to William Faulkner's *Light in August*, to see the urn crucially, and similarly, functioning. It has been pointed out[12] that each of the three major strands of the novel derives its symbolic characterization in metaphorical and ekphrastic descriptions that by now should sound familiar to us. Let me cite the three passages.

The indomitable Lena Grove, in her endless and endlessly routine—even automatic—movements is, properly enough, given an ekphrastic symbol:

> . . . backrolling now behind her a long monotonous succession of peaceful and undeviating changes from day to dark and dark to day again, through which she advanced in identical and anonymous and deliberate wagons as though through a succession of creakwheeled and limpeared avatars, like something moving forever and without progress across an urn.[13]

Continual, deliberate advance, a "succession," yet a forever movement, "without progress." The rolling wheels of all the interchangeable wagons are not finally very different from the wheel spoken of by Becket and the Fourth Tempter in Eliot's *Murder in the Cathedral*; for, like that wheel, these are fixed in an eternal motion, at once action and patience, action and the suffering of action (with the appropriate puns on *patience* and *suffering*). The eternal circularity of Lena's urn and the wagon wheels that bear her round it is further enhanced by the transcendent notion of the "avatars": the god in an ever reappearing, ever indestructible, ever freshly embodied movement, continually in touch with the world and yet remaining intact.

There are similarly definitive passages for Joe Christmas and the Reverend Hightower. First, the young Joe Christmas's vision after his discovery of the uglier facts about female physiology: "In the notseeing and the hardknowing as though in a cave he seemed to see a diminishing row of suavely shaped urns in moonlight, blanched. And not one was perfect. Each one was cracked and from each crack there issued something liquid, deathcolored, and foul. He touched a tree, leaning his propped arms against it, seeing the ranked and moonlit urns. He vomited" (165). Then Hightower's vision of the "seminary," that etymologically shrewd word, as the protected retreat from living, as the tomb of the seed killed within him:

> When he believed that he had heard the call it seemed to him that he could see his future, his life, intact and on all sides complete and inviolable, like a classic and serene vase, where the spirit could be born anew sheltered from the harsh gale of living and die so, peacefully, with only the far sound of the circumvented wind, with scarce even a handful of rotting dust to be disposed of. That was what the word seminary meant: quiet and safe walls within which the hampered and garmentworried spirit could learn anew serenity to contemplate without horror or alarm its own nakedness (419).

We should note, first, that while Joe Christmas's urn and Hightower's classic vase exist as metaphorical definitions of their visions, Lena is an actual figure on an urn of our narrator's envisioning. Christmas's vision, distorted by the ugliness of human perversity, sees the foulness of death flowing from what should be the vessel of life and love. Hightower's vision, rendered bloodless by his withdrawal from the living, sees the vacancy of purity in the aesthetic containment and noncommitment of the "classic and serene vase." (And how appropriate that what Hightower sees is a vase—devoid of contents—rather than an urn, a vase as the aesthetic equivalent of the urn while resisting that latter's involvement with either life or death.) But Lena, the creature of the endlessly repetitive, generative fertility principle, is seen as an actual figure partaking of the still movement of the life on the urn. And how different an urn from those of Christmas's vision, one that holds death as part of the ongoing life process, one that—as Sir Thomas Browne saw it—holds the body of death as the womb holds the body of life, and in the symbol that recalls the womb. So there is Christmas's death-dealing vision; there is Hightower's vision that, in desperate retreat from that of Christmas, denies life as well; and there is Lena's, the vision of wholeness under the aegis of a primal sanctity. Lena's naiveté of course does not permit *her* to have this vision, as Christmas and Hightower have theirs. Instead, all existing rather than envisioning, she must live it unself-consciously, herself crawl round the urn's surface, and be made part of the narrator's vision—and ours.

I have already suggested that the shift from urn to vase, as we get to Hightower's life metaphor, is a significant one, confirming in this sterile symbol the shift from the pulsing, dark and deathly existential concern of Joe Christmas and the Apollonian living grace of Lena's procreative innocence to the pulseless aesthetic distance of Hightower's nonliving purity. If we view the vase symbol generally as the aesthetic equivalent of the urn, the resistance to the urn's involvement with death and life—whether death-as-life (Lena) or life-as-death (Christmas)—then we can move easily to Eliot's Chinese jar and think of the latter as an echo of the "frail China jar" of Pope's "The Rape of the Lock," itself an echo of the china vases Pope speaks of elsewhere in this poem.

In "The Rape of the Lock" there would surely seem to be no place for the urns, if we take seriously their ritual involvement with the actualities and consequences of flesh-and-blood existence. Better, in this supercilious celebration of the airiness of the world of play that resists flesh and blood, to replace them with vases and jars, *objets d'art* in the toyshop unreality of Belinda's artworld. We have just seen Hightower's more serious and less successful attempt to withdraw from the consequential world-winds lead to a similar conversion from the urn to its life-free aesthetic equivalent, the vase, whose cognate term, vessel, perhaps better reminds us that it is but an extension of the urn. For, as I have elsewhere argued at length,[14] Pope's poem is created out of a wistful idolatry of the disengaged and—in terms of flesh-and-blood reality—the inconsequential, pure if fragile world of social play. Finally, I claim, the mock-heroic world of the lock, where empty symbols rather than bodies are the objects of rape and battle, becomes a metaphor for the poem itself, even as the "frail China jar," *objet d'art*, becomes the toyshop substitute for our blood-filled vessels of breathing life. The recurrent use of china as symbol of honor's empty equivalent for chastity was commented upon earlier by Cleanth Brooks.[15] This use is indicative enough of the transformation of the world of bodies to the wrought world of empty objects:

> Whether the Nymph shall break Diana's Law,
> Or some frail China Jar receive a Flaw . . .
> (Canto II, lines 105–6)

> Or when rich China vessels, fall'n from high,
> In glitt'ring dust and painted fragments lie!
> (III, 159–60)

'Twas this, the morning omens seem'd to tell,
Thrice from my trembling hand the Patch-box fell;
The tott'ring China shook without a Wind . . .
(IV, 161–63)

We may note that this very use of china as a generic term for ceramic objects is a metonym made in the spirit of Pope. Pope himself extends the significance of this metonymy in yet another passage in the poem, one whose brilliance sustains the others. It occurs in his description of the pouring of coffee:

From silver spouts the grateful liquors glide,
While China's earth receives the smoking tide . . .
(III, 109–10)

Here in this wrought ceramic world we have the transformation of earth into art; indeed, in these earthen objects is the only earth that is admitted in this poem. China is, after all, the aesthetic form of China's earth, the aesthetic reduction of China for this social company. Again we are reminded of Sir Thomas Browne, this time his relating the purgative crematory fire to man's "earth":

But all flies and sinks before fire almost in all bodies. . . . Where fire taketh leave, corruption slowly enters; In bones well burnt, fire makes a wall against it self. . . . What the Sun compoundeth, fire analyseth, not transmuteth. That devouring agent leaves almost always a morsel for the Earth, whereof all things are but a colony; and which, if time permits, the mother Element will have in their primitive mass again (*Urne-Buriall*, 30–31).

The jars and vases and cups of Pope's airy world, vessels subject only to the smoking tides of coffee poured from silver spouts, are the real China of that world, from which all other earth has—by the transmuting ceramic fire—been purged. Browne helps remind us of that more destructive purgation of earth in the fire of cremation. And the remnants of this cremation, we remember, have as their container that which also is fired out of earth. But the urn, as a created form, is one created—as Browne has already told us—in imitation of the living form as an echo of the womb which forms life. As a fired, earthen icon of what its contents had been—the earthly form consumed by fire—as holder of life and death, the urn transcends both. For it has attained the pure and permanent circularity of form and, in its frieze, has the forms of life eternally captured as, like Keats's figures or Lena Grove, they trace a still movement around it.

The sepulchral urn's aesthetic equivalent of breathing life, an equivalent that at once captures life's movement and perpetuates it, accounts for the suspended purity we have seen in the figures of Pope and Keats and Faulkner. To appropriate the term from Eloisa, we might say the "unfruitful urn" in one sense leads to a fruitful urn—the fruitful poem—in another. There is an enforced chastity binding Eloisa and Abelard, not altogether unlike the aesthetically enforced chastity binding Keats's figures on the urn. We can see this enforced chastity in Eloisa's description of Abelard, which precedes her hopeless and bitter invocation to him ("Come, Abelard!") which we witnessed earlier:

> For thee the Fates, severely kind, ordain
> A cool suspense from pleasure and from pain;
> Thy life a long dead calm of fix'd repose;
> No pulse that riots, and no blood that glows.
> (lines 249–52)

It is just this being "fix'd" in a "cool suspense" from the rioting pulse and glowing blood that lends the creatures of Pope's world of artifice in the "Rape" and the creatures trapped on Keats's urn their precious transcendence—and their unworldly incompleteness, their dance that denies the very notion of consequence. Belinda's "purer blush," Keats's "maidens loth," the mock love-battle at the end of the "Rape," the unanswered factual questions in Keats's "Ode"— these testify to the inconsequential, unbound, free nature of the chaste aesthetic transmutation of breathing existence.

There are, then, three kinds of earth and three ways of its being fired— all finally expressive of the circular tradition that moves from earth to earth. There is, first, man's living earth—his flesh—that, fired by sexual desire, fills the earthly vessel with the flowing fruit of life, of more earth; there is, secondly, as timely consequence of the first, man's dying earth that, fired by the funeral rite, is reduced to the ashes that, in urn burial, fill the third kind: the earthen vessel, an artifact that, transmuted by the ceramic fire of human craft, becomes a permanent form. The latter is at once unfruitful and still-moving, the transcendence of earth in the earthen, the transcendence of flesh in the artifice of eternity; and—where it is urn, too—it is also the receptacle of the remnants of that other earth, the flesh, that is conceived in fire and consumed by fire. Further, the urn may, as Browne describes, imitate the shape of the human conceiving urn; still further, it may have the figures of life as a frieze forever running round it, either in pursuit of desire (the first kind of firing of man's earth which I have spoken of) or in celebration of death (the second kind of the firing of earth)—the two very actions captured on Keats's urn. And, as in the case of Keats's urn, these are captured on the object that, as the third sort of the firing of earth, is in its shape the icon of the others and their container, holding them at once within it and on its circular surface. Thus it celebrates both time past (the ashes within) and time forever now (the circular pattern of scenes that is the frieze), even as, in its shape, the container of death mimics the container of life, tomb as womb. No wonder an amazing multiple pattern is projected by the purified metonymy of sexual meanings ceramically purged and yet insisted upon in "The Rape of the Lock," where "China's earth receives the smoking tide" pouring from the "silver spouts," well heated since "the fiery spirits blaze." Here is a ceramic masque, an earthen playing out of that most earthly action. Can we resist expanding these meanings to include those which range about the china vases and jars of this poem as they relate to frail sexual purity? Or, if we can consider also the "unfruitful urn" in the abortive firing of Eloisa's desires, can we resist seeing vase as the vessel that is related, without sexual consequences, to the urn, with the jar as the semantic generalizing of the ceramic impulse? And we must marvel at the resuscitation of the urn, so unpromising an object of death, into a symbol of life in death: of art. We must marvel at the choice of the urn as the ekphrastic object *par excellence* to unite the stilled and the still-now movement by concentrating within and upon itself the several sorts of earth and the several manners and consequences of their being fired.

But all, even the most aesthetically transcendent, still remain literally movements from earth to earth, from living-dying time to time both affirmed and arrested. This is reason enough to deny that one other kind of the firing of earth as a possible fourth kind: the religious firing that is to transform man's earth to pure spirit. Eloisa, her earth now fired so unfruitfully by Abelard, claims this different kind of firing by God: "But let Heav'n seize it [the soul], all at once 'tis fir'd: / Not touch'd, but rapt; not waken'd but inspir'd!" (lines 201–2). Nevertheless, this is a figurative firing only: it can move her toward the "flames refin'd" that "in breasts seraphic glow" (line 320) only by denying her literal earth, her earthly status as creature. Which is why Eloisa remains so ambivalent, why in seeing God as Abelard's rival and successor (". . . for he / Alone can rival, can succeed to thee" [line 206]), she must involve her sexuality in her religious impulse. She must confound the firing of her earth with the smothering of earthly fires which constitutes the religious metaphorical firing that she seeks. This denial of all kinds of earth and of earthly fires, sexual and aesthetic, replaces the movement from earth to earth with the Platonic movement from earth to heaven as the last movement, the permanent stilling of movement. It is destructive of the aesthetic, of the earthen, of the ekphrastic principle; is a fraudulent alternative and, for her, a false resolution. Time is merely stilled in the simple sense, the sense of "still life"; it is killed in the sense of the French translation of still life, *nature morte*. And the brilliant multiplicity of time's possibilities for running free and yet running around, repeating circularly, the brilliant revelations of the ekphrasis, of the urn at once fruitful and unfruitful—these are forever sacrificed. To alter Horace and defy Lessing, as with the urn, so with poetry.

Keats's urn, a pure ekphrasis, is an object especially created to celebrate the teasing doctrine of circularity. If this doctrine is aesthetically complete in creating, through enforced chastity, a fruitful urn of the aesthetic sort out of the unfruitful urn of the empirically human sort, in its chaste circularity it touches the empirically human only fitfully. In its freedom from what Yeats called "the fury and the mire of human veins," in its purging—at once Yeatsian and Aristotelian—of "complexities of fury," it asserts the transformation of the empirical into the archetypal ("the artifice of eternity"), in this way obeying the Hegelian injunction to move from the concrete to the concrete-universal. In the drama of poetry we recognize the creatures as creatures like us, like us most of all in their intense individuality, their here-and-now unique concreteness. But the motions they make—rituals of love and death—through aesthetic pattern and thus through the principle of echo, of repetition, become forever-now motions. This principle frees these motions from the singleness of chronology's linearity and of the empirical sort of finitude. Thus though concrete, the characters in this sense attain universality. They are converted from the merely individual to the casuistic; their motions achieve formal finality even if they never merely finish. Theirs is the finality-without-end, if I may so adapt Kant's definition of aesthetic experience. As creatures fixed on Eliot's wheel or Keats's urn, they show us the movements we all are and have been eternally fixed upon making, though we each make them but once, in singleness, and without awareness of our fixed turning.

To the usual notion of poetry's archetypal nature that moves too quickly from the particular to the universal, indeed that merely universalizes the particular, I would prefer this sense of the archetypal dimension of each poem as it struggles to capture the empirical in all its movement.[16] It must be at once as movement and as movement overcome, as movement joined and mastered, that the individual poem can make its movement eternal and still significant to us in our empirical singleness.

Yeats's Byzantium poems, as I have shown in my quoting from them, at once enunciate this aesthetic and create the ekphrastic symbol, the golden bird, that embodies it. The bird has been placed—indeed "hammered"—into these poems to continue with them their manufactured, artificial perfection forever. Purged, as the "images of day" with their "complexities of mire and blood" are "unpurged," the well-wrought object is both bird and golden handiwork even as, through miracle, it can be both at once, so that it is indeed "More miracle than bird or handiwork." Like the earthen urn or Pope's china, it is the product of the transmuting and purifying fires, alchemical medium of eternal creation, so different from the destructive fire that reduces the aged man's earth to ash. As "God's holy fire," it partakes—like "the gold mosaic of a wall"—of "the artifice of eternity" and can so transubstantiate the "aged man," the "dying animal," into the golden creature—both in and out of nature—of wise and eternal song.

Without this express insertion of the ekphrastic object, there are other birds that turn legendary under the pressure of their poetic contexts; indeed there is a chain of them leading to Yeats's golden bird that may be seen as their appropriate embodiment. And always it is this Platonic opposition between empirical singleness and archetypal inclusiveness that stirs the movement toward the golden incarnation.

In Wordsworth's treatment of his cuckoo, the poet must make a judgment about this very duality in the bird: it is a "wandering voice" even as it remains "bird," it is "far off" even as it is "near," it brings the poet "a tale / Of visionary hours" even as his sense of reality recognizes that it is only "babbling." This duality has the experiential basis we find in many of Wordsworth's poems: the moment celebrated is a conjunction of two occasions, one far past with one present. The recurrence of experience, of identical stimulus, modified by the severe changes time has wrought in the experiencing subject, permits the simultaneous perception of motion and stasis that has been my concern. As his most acute commentators have pointed out,[17] Wordsworth has himself provided just the metaphor to express this trapping of temporal change: those moments, laden with "a renovating virtue," he terms "spots of time" ("The Prelude," XII, 208)—precisely the union of spatiality and temporality I have been trying to demonstrate. The very word "spot," related as it is here to time's movement, yet brings us to stasis, the arresting of time, by seeming to refer to a place, a permanently defined spatial entity. This notion accounts, in "To the Cuckoo," for the poet's capacity to transcend the limitations of literal reality in order, through a double exposure, to blur time's movements to an identical spot. Conscious, then, of his animistic delusion, he chooses to see the cuckoo as "No bird, but an invisible thing, / A voice, a mystery. . . ." As in other bird poems by Romantic poets, the poet moves from the fact that he hears but cannot see the bird to the self-deceptive synecdoche that the voice *is* the bird, so that the bird becomes a disembodied voice, free of the mortality that attends a single finite bodily existence. Once he has thus transcended the bird as earthly animal, Wordsworth is able to return to his childhood with the claim that this is the very bird he then heard and could not find: "The same whom in my schoolboy days / I lis-tened to . . . / And I can listen to thee yet. . . ." Now, listening still, he must—by the conscious choice of self-deception—willfully create ("beget") that "golden time" which, in his boyhood, he shared instinctively. In this conscious deci-sion to ignore the reality of the babbling bird for the visionary voice, he has created for the now "blessed Bird" the "unsubstantial, faery place" that is its "fit home." Dare we think the place to be his Byzantium and the recreated bird of the mature poet's imagination his golden bird? We could, if it were not that his awareness of the self-induced state of delusion leads him to remember its "unsubstantial" nature. The delusion is not firm enough to construct an object that would perpetuate itself, *realize* itself.

The poet in Keats's "Ode to a Nightingale" also undergoes the fanciful transformation of reality induced by the song of the bird. He is, even more than Wordsworth's poet, the captive of his trance, so that his fairyland demands the firm denial of the bird's material reality: "Thou wast not born for death, immor-tal bird!" He so uncritically accepts the magic of the synecdoche as to allow the identity of the sound of the voice to lead to the undoubted identity of occasion: "The voice I hear this passing night was heard / In ancient days by emperor and clown: / Perhaps the self-same song that found a path / Through the sad heart of Ruth . . . The same that oft-times hath / Charm'd magic casements. . . ." Yet even here the reality principle naggingly remains. It reminds the poet that the suspension of chronological time is, for humanity, not an attribute of an aesthetic never-never land, a Byzantium, but an attribute of death's nothing-ness: "Now more than ever seems it rich to die . . . / Still wouldst thou sing, and I have ears in vain—/ To thy high requiem become a sod." Further, the im-mortality conferred, by contrast, upon the bird is in effect withdrawn when the poet, awakening from the spell, admits his return to empirical singleness, tolled as he is back to his "sole self." He acknowledges the final failure of the delusion sponsored by the song of the bird, now wistfully referred to as "deceiving elf," the failure of his own fancy ("the fancy cannot cheat so well"). And the song is now permitted to depart with the departure of the physical bird:

> Adieu! adieu! thy plaintive anthem fades
> Past the near meadows, over the still stream,
>> Up the hill-side; and now 'tis buried deep
>> In the next valley-glades. . . .

Beyond the "still stream," for the poet it is nothing less than "buried." Keats's poet, aware of man's need for time's movement as well as his need to capture it, has—more than Wordsworth's poet—overdone the extravagance of his earlier

Platonic delusions. But he has not managed to find a material object that can contain the still perfection in an earthly form (or an earthen form, if we dare fancy Keats to be searching for an ekphrastic equivalent to his urn). Since he cannot travel to Byzantium and convert his bird to hammered gold, both he and the bird return to time-bound reality to proceed with the complexities of aging. Only the moment, but that moment memorialized, preserved, stilled—and distilled—in the poem, remains. In this well-wrought residue, the ekphrastic principle asserts itself even in the turning aside from an ekphrastic object.

How different are these experiments in synecdoche, with their attempts to hold the turning world as it turns, from the simple postulation by Shelley of the other-than-material nature of his skylark. He begins at once with the flat disembodiment of the "blithe spirit": "Bird thou never wert." But the liveliness of motion is denied together with its status as bird. Its existence in human time is by fiat transcended, so that the collision of movement with movement captured is evaded. All is stilled, and there is no living movement. One thinks, by contrast, of the urging of movement in the pleas to the mistress in "Corinna's Going A-Maying"; the conflict between moving and staying is the very principle of form in the poem. The poet warns against the dangers of staying movement, culminating in the penultimate line, "while time serves, and we are but decaying." Here movement can *seem* to arrest decay and *seem* to make us the master of time, rather than—in decaying stasis—its slave, as the "while" of "while time serves" assures we shall be. This is the foretaste of that masterpoem about time, "To His Coy Mistress" ("Had we but world enough, and time"), and Marvell's invocation to action as the subduer of time, leading to the ekphrastic introduction of the physical, spatial object which is the emblem of his mastery over time even as time works its destructive power:

> Rather at once our time devour,
> Than languish in his slow-chapped power.
> Let us roll all our strength, and all
> Our sweetness, up into one ball . . .
> Thus, though we cannot make our sun
> Stand still, yet we will make him run.
> (lines 39–42, 45–46)

Discussion of earthly birds turned legendary, of poems concerning birds that are at once temporal and supernal, must lead to the albatross of Coleridge's "Ancient Mariner." In few other places in literature is the opposition between stillness and motion more central to the structure, and their relation is controlled by the bird as it turns sacramental. The poem swings between the movement sponsored by the breeze and the calm, the curse resulting from its being withdrawn. We are likely to agree with the first judgment of the mariner's shipmates: that he "had killed the bird / That made the breeze to blow." Everywhere descriptions of movement in its varied paces, and of calm as the dread alternative, direct the poem's own pace. The poem moves with and among its movements and calms. The gratuitous murder of the albatross marks the fall that is to stop all movement. And the mariner becalmed finds his appropriate emblem: the albatross instead of the cross is hung about his neck. It is this static, uncreative, decaying state that characterizes the poet of Coleridge's "Dejection: An Ode." The poet, in effect the cursed, becalmed mariner, asks for the airy impulse that "might startle this dull pain, and make it move and live!" (line 20). "Dejection" is a poem that laments the becalming of spirit, that claims failure, the failure of movement, as its subject. Herrick's "Corinna" showed us forcefully the implication of decay in stillness. Far more graphically in the "Ancient Mariner," total stillness is accompanied by decay, the decay that motionlessness permits to set in: "The very deep did rot" (line 123), "the rotting sea," "the rotting deck" (lines 240, 242). The mariner's becalmed life-in-death is a surrealistic paralysis, seven days and seven nights of the unblinking curse in the eyes of his struck-dead shipmates. In his suspended state he yearns for the effortless motion of "the moving moon" (line 263), a still movement not unlike the movement we have marked in a Lena Grove. The gloss to the poem at this point furnishes a moving statement of such a natural, a routine motion as the mariner requires: "In his loneliness and fixedness he yearneth towards the journeying Moon, and the stars that still sojourn, yet still move onward; and every where the blue sky belongs to them, and is their appointed rest, and their native country and their own natural homes, which they enter unannounced, as lords that are certainly expected and yet there is a silent joy at their arrival." Later, after the partial penance by the mariner and the partial forgiveness bestowed upon him, the return of the beloved breeze and his eventual return are not of this sublime order; he is returned to his native country and to man, but as a wandering stranger among them. And, still doing penance, he must move in ever-recurrent circles among them, ever retelling his tale.

His tale, the poem proper, has movement even in the face of calm; further, as "Dejection" does not, it succeeds at last in conquering—in moving beyond—the state of being becalmed; nevertheless, it remains a "still," even-now movement. For it is framed by a repetitious, unendingly repetitious, ritual action, as the mariner must tell his tale again and again, wandering continually in search of a listener—still, even now as I talk. Thus the archetypal nature of the singular, integral poetic action in its transcendence of the empirical—and thus our assurance of its casuistry, an assurance that permits our aesthetic pleasure in response to what in life would be unendurably painful. The "Ancient Mariner," in its emphasis on the necessity of the endless retelling of the tale, is a paradigm of this aspect in our greatest works. In its rounded completeness, in its coming to terms with itself—in short, through pattern, that which is bent on destroying its simple, linear temporality—the work guarantees its special, its other-than-empirical realm of being. Our despair at tragedy, for example, while preserved as despair, is yet transfigured to comfort in our knowledge and assurance of its still and inevitable movement, of how it has been and will always be—how it must be. Oedipus must pursue his stubborn ignorance identically to the identical catastrophe; Hamlet must make his always identical way to the absurd indiscriminacy of the final sword play; Lear must prance *his* always identical way to the wretched loveliness of the reconciliation scene that ironically lulls him and Cordelia to their deaths. And still they make their inevitable movements, even now as we talk—if I may stick at this point.

This is the final meaning of aesthetic inevitability or circularity—even as the urn demonstrates it; this is the final meaning of Aristotle's probability and necessity that bring poetry and its casuistry beyond history and the empirical world's possibility. The poem as total object has, despite its entrancing *movement*, become the fixed—or rather transfixed—object, its own urn, Yeats's golden bird that has been placed inside the poem to prove that the latter must breathe in its manufactured, artificial perfection forever. But, as the casuistic principle insists, it is always in its unique, contextual singleness that the poem so functions, not as a sign to the universal; in its finitude, its discrete discontinuity from all other poems, from poetry or from language as ideal forms, not as an opening to these.[18] Ekphrasis, no longer a narrow kind of poem defined by its object of imitation, broadens to become a general principle of poetics, asserted by every poem in the assertion of its integrity. Is it too much to say that essentially the same principle lies behind the employment of the poetic refrain, indeed behind the employment of meter itself? Such is largely the ground for Wordsworth's and Coleridge's justification of meter: the reduction to the sameness of repetition of that which is disparate, varied, progressive, in motion; the identity of recurrence together with the unceasing change of movement. It is the lack of such minute but systematic guarantees of recurrence that creates some of the handicaps prose fiction has in proclaiming itself a rounded object and that accounts for many of the ad hoc devices it invents to make itself into an aesthetic, a still moving, entity.

Every poem's problem as its own aesthetician, and every critic's problem after it, is essentially the problem of Keats with his Grecian urn: how to make it hold still when the poem must move. And the critic's final desperation is an echo of the outburst, at once absolute and equivocal, of the last two lines of the poem. There are unanswered factual questions asked through the course of the "Ode" ("What men or gods are these? What maidens loth? . . . Who are these coming to the sacrifice? To what green altar . . . ? What little town . . . ?"). These have guaranteed the poet's exasperation at the inadequacy of empirical data before beauty's archetypal perfection, the inadequacy of fact before arti-fact. The final two lines confer universal absolution in that they absolve in abso-lute terms (to press the redundancy) the poet's need to ask such merely informa-tional questions. We are reminded of Sir Thomas Browne's dismissal of a similar series of questions concerning the historical data surrounding his urns, "the proprietaries of these bones, or what bodies these ashes made up," questions fur-ther beyond man's resolution than those that ask "what Song the Syrens sang, or what name Achilles assumed when he hid himself among women."[19] The aesthetic of Keats's final lines, then, is the only culmination of still motion's transcendence of unarrested progression.

And so it is with the critic's desperate struggle to wrestle his slippery ob-ject to earth. It is the problem of defying the Lessing tradition, with its neat separateness of the mutually delimiting arts, and seeing the time-space break-through in the plasticity of the language of poetry. This language, in taking on Burckhardt's "corporeality," tries to become an object with as much substance as the medium of the plastic arts, the words thus establishing a plastic aesthetic for themselves, sometimes—but not necessarily—using the ekphrastic object as their emblem.

But in one sense the tradition from Edmund Burke and Lessing which sees a uniqueness in the literary medium *is* affirmed. For literature retains its essen-tial nature as a time-art even as its words, by reaching the stillness by way of pattern, seek to appropriate sculpture's plasticity as well. There is after all, then, a sense in which literature, as a time-art, does have special time-space powers. Through pattern, through context, it has the unique power to celebrate time's movement as well as to arrest it, to arrest it in the very act of celebrating it. Its involvement with progression, with empirical movement, always accom-panies its archetypal principle of repetition, of eternal return. The poem can uniquely order spatial stasis within its temporal dynamics because through its echoes and its texture it can produce—together with the illusion of progressive movement—the illusion of an organized simultaneity.

My earlier unfavorable claims about Eloisa's religious firing, like my few words on Shelley's "Skylark," were meant to serve as warning against the Platonic denial of the empirical, the mere stilling of movement. In resistance to the ekphrastic impulse, it cannot too often be urged that the aesthetic desire for pure and eternal form must not be allowed merely to freeze the entity-denying chronological flow of experience in its unrepeatable variety. The remarkable nature of Eliot's "Four Quartets," we must remember, is that the shaping of their musical form into the Chinese jar never deprives existence of its confused multiplicity. For, if we may shift to his other key metaphor, life at the periphery of the wheel never stops moving, even as it radiates from the extraordinary dance at the still center of that turning world. Yet "The Rape of the Lock" reminds us that there is a clear danger from the aesthetic purification of life. We see this danger anew if we return to the urn-jar motif and refer to yet another aesthetic jar, this time in Wallace Stevens's "Anecdote of the Jar":

> I placed a jar in Tennessee,
> And round it was, upon a hill.
> It made the slovenly wilderness
> Surround that hill.
>
> The wilderness rose up to it,
> And sprawled around, no longer wild.
> The jar was round upon the ground
> And tall and of a port in air.
>
> It took dominion everywhere.
> The jar was gray and bare.
> It did not give of bird or bush,
> Like nothing else in Tennessee.[20]

The jar's roundedness and—in its aesthetic "dominion everywhere"—its grayness and bareness do no justice to the sprawling "slovenly wilderness" that surrounds its hilltop heights. (Indeed, it is only the jar's round presence that forces the formal impulse to attribute the function of "surrounding" to the aimless wilderness.) Only transcendent, the jar has nothing of life—"of bird or bush"—in it.[21] Here is the warning against the deadening of life, the freezing of movement, caused by too simple and Platonic a sense of aesthetic purity, of the jar or urn motif which, in my ekphrastic mood, I have described admiringly only. Time, in its unique empirical particularity, must always be celebrated in its flow even as we arrest it to make its movement a forever-now movement. Or else poetry is hardened into static, Platonic discourse that has lost touch with— indeed that disdains to touch—our existential motions. But as poetry, even

Stevens's poem, in its persistence, itself becomes the jar, though more insistently involved with flowing existence than was the hilltop jar it decries. Like Eliot's, it has absorbed a liveliness whose moving slovenliness it must cherish.

Writers on time in the vitalistic tradition of Bergson have commonly claimed that, in its inevitable universalizing, language tends to give death to the dynamism of experience by spatializing it and thus freezing its undemarcated ceaseless flow of unrepeatable and indefinable, unentitied units. Thus phenomenological literary critics in the spirit of this tradition have tended to antiformalism, to the neglect of the object and the accentuation of the subjective flow in the transcription of their authors' consciousness of time. However just their charges against the spatializing, and thus the killing, power of language generally, I must maintain—in the tradition of Keats in his "Urn" and Yeats in his Byzantium poems—that aesthetic jars usually avoid the inadequacy recorded by Stevens, that the specially endowed language of poetry frees as well as freezes temporality, frees it into an ever-repeated motion that has all the motion together with its repeatability, through the rounded sculpture-like inevitability that guarantees its endless repetition. For this aesthetically formalized language takes on plasticity as well as spatiality. Through its ekphrastic principle, literature as poetic context proclaims at once its use of the empirically progressive and its transcendent conversion of the empirical into the archetypal even as it remains empirical, into the circular even as it remains progressive.

In this sense poetry must be at once immediate *and* objective: neither the mediated objectivity of the normal discourse that through freezing kills, nor the unmediated subjectivity that our idolaters of time-philosophy would want to keep as the unstoppable, unrepeatable, unentitied all; neither life only frozen as archetypal nor life only flowing as endlessly empirical, but at once frozen and flowing (like the urn), at once objective and immediate, archetypal and empirical. I would share the interest of the Georges Poulets and the Maurice Blanchots; but I would give the special liberating license to our best poetry, insisting on its ekphrastic completeness that allows us to transfer the human conquest of time from the murky subjective caverns of phenomenology to the well-wrought, well-lighted place of aesthetics. For the poetic context can defy the apparently mutually exclusive categories of time and space to become fixed in the still movement of the Chinese jar that poets have summoned to their poetry as the emblem of its aesthetic, which that poetry's very existence, its way of being and meaning, has implicitly proclaimed. The patterned and yet passing words can, as Eliot has suggested, "reach into the silence," "reach the stillness."

NOTES

1 The subject of the first conference of the Iowa Center for Modern Letters, held at the University of Iowa, October 28–30, 1965. This essay was the opening paper of that conference.

2 The beginnings of the sort of study I am undertaking here were made by Joseph Frank in his essays on "Spatial Form in Modern Literature" in *The Sewanee Review* 53 (spring, summer, autumn, 1945), which appear in revised form as the first chapter of his book *The Widening Gyre: Crisis and Mastery in Modern Literature* (New Brunswick, N.J.: Rutgers University Press, 1963), 3–62. But Frank is interested more in the use of these spatial metaphors by recent authors than in the generic spatiality of literary form and—even more to *my* point— in the inevitability of spatial language by the critic or by the poem as its own aesthetician. French literary critics of time-consciousness and space-consciousness, like Gaston Bachelard and Georges Poulet, also touch matters relevant to my interests here—though with a crucial difference of emphasis, as should become clear toward the end of this essay.

3 This quotation and the one which follows are from T. S. Eliot, *The Complete Poems and Plays 1909–1950* (New York: Harcourt, Brace & World, Inc., 1952), 121 and 193 respectively.

4 Sigurd Burckhardt, "The Poet as Fool and Priest," *ELH*, 23 (December, 1956), 280.

5 Jean H. Hagstrum, *The Sister Arts: The Tradition of Literary Pictorialism and English Poetry from Dryden to Gray* (Chicago: University of Chicago Press, 1948), 20. Hagstrum, trying to be etymologically faithful to the word *ekphrasis,* uses this word more narrowly than I do as I follow its other users. To be true to the sense of "speaking out," he restricts it "to that special quality of giving voice and language to the otherwise mute art object." The other descriptions of spatial works of art, those that are not made to "speak out," he merely calls "iconic," even as he admits this is a narrower use of *ekphrasis* than that of his predecessors (*The Sister Arts,* 18n.). Since I confess from the start that I intend to broaden poetry's ekphrastic propensities, it would be expected that I also am using *ekphrasis* here to include what Hagstrum calls "iconic" as well as what he calls "ekphrastic."

6 There is a very different and common use of *still* in the aesthetic realm to which I must call attention since it is so single-minded in its rejection of Keats's secondary and more subtle meaning. The "still" of the genre called still-life painting unhappily means only "stilled," inanimate, even in a sense dead—as we are told in the equivalent French phrase, *nature morte.* This sense of the timeless, of the motionless, may recall, for example, Pope's use of *still* to deny change in *An Essay on Criticism:*

> First follow Nature, and your judgment frame
> By her just standard, which is *still* the same:
> Unerring Nature, *still* divinely bright,
> One clear, unchanged, and universal light. . . .
> (1, 68–71 [italics are mine])

How much less aware is this "still" than the pun which restores vitality, and an eternal vitality, to a word that means primarily to deny motion and sound. For a more profound vision of *nature morte,* one that is more just to the dynamics of the still-life genre in painting, see Rosalie L. Colie, "Still Life: Paradoxes of Being," *Paradoxia Epidemica: The Renaissance Tradition of Paradox* (Princeton: Princeton University Press, 1966), 273–99.

7   "The 'Ode on a Grecian Urn,' or Content vs. Metagrammar," in Leo Spitzer, *Essays on English and American Literature*, ed. Anna Hatcher (Princeton: Princeton University Press, 1962), 72–73.

8   Ibid., p. 73.

9   *Hydriotaphia, Urne-Buriall, or A Brief Discourse of the Sepulchrall Urnes Lately Found in Norfolk, in the Works of Sir Thomas Browne*, ed. Geoffrey Keynes (London, 1929), IV, 23.

10 *The Well Wrought Urn: Studies in the Structure of Poetry* (New York, 1947). He discusses "urn" in "The Canonization," "The Phoenix and the Turtle," "Elegy Written in a Country Churchyard," and "Ode on a Grecian Urn." See 16–20, 101, 112–13, 139–52.

11 Ibid., 17–20.

12 C. Hugh Holman, "The Unity of Faulkner's *Light in August*," PMLA 73 (March 1958): 155–66, especially 159, 161, 164. There is reference here also to Norman H. Pearson's treatment of Lena in terms of Keats's "Grecian Urn" in his "Lena Grove," *Shenandoah*, 3 (spring, 1952): 3–7. Faulkner's awareness of Keats's urn as a source for allusion is more explicitly shown us in *The Bear*.

13 William Faulkner, *Light in August*, Modern Library ed. (New York: Random House, Inc., 1950), 6; other references are to this edition.

14 In "The 'Frail China Jar' and the Rude Hand of Chaos," above.

15 *The Well Wrought Urn*, 87.

16 I clearly mean here to propose an alternative view of poetry as archetype to that of Northrop Frye.

17 None more incisively than Geoffrey H. Hartman. See his *Wordsworth's Poetry 1784–1814* (New Haven: Yale University Press, 1964), especially 153, 211–19, and his "Wordsworth, Inscriptions, and Romantic Nature Poetry," in *From Sensibility to Romanticism, Essays Presented to Frederick A. Pottle*, ed. Frederick W. Hilles and Harold Bloom (New York: Oxford University Press, 1965), 389–413.

18 Again it is the alternative to Frye's archetypal universality that I am insisting upon.

19 *Urne-Buriall*, 44.

20 *Collected Poems of Wallace Stevens* (New York: Alfred A. Knopf, Inc., 1954), 76.

21 For a very persuasive reading, together with a summary of conflicting readings of the poem and of corroborative passages in Stevens's work (especially those relating the jar to the urn), see Patricia Merivale, "Wallace Stevens's 'Jar': The Absurd Detritus of Romantic Myth," *College English* 26 (April 1965): 527–32.

5. *Examples of Wallace Stevens*
R. P. Blackmur

THE MOST STRIKING if not the most important thing about Mr. Stevens's verse is its vocabulary—the collection of words, many of them uncommon in English poetry, which on a superficial reading seems characteristic of the poems. An air of preciousness bathes the mind of the casual reader when he finds such words as fubbed, girandoles, curlicues, catarrhs, gobbet, diaphanes, clopping, minuscule, pipping, pannicles, carked, ructive, rapey, cantilene, buffo, fiscs, phylactery, princox, and funest. And such phrases as "thrum with a proud douceur," or "A pool of pink, clippered with lilies scudding the bright chromes," hastily read, merely increase the feeling of preciousness. Hence Mr. Stevens has a bad reputation among those who dislike the finicky, and a high one, unfortunately, among those who value the ornamental sounds of words but who see no purpose in developing sound from sense.

Both classes of reader are wrong. Not a word listed above is used preciously; not one was chosen as an elegant substitute for a plain term; each, in its context, was a word definitely meant. The important thing about Mr. Stevens's vocabulary is not the apparent oddity of certain words, but the uses to which he puts those words with others. It is the way that Mr. Stevens combines kinds of words, unusual in a single context, to reveal the substance he had in mind, which is of real interest to the reader.

Good poets gain their excellence by writing an existing language *as if* it were their own invention; and as a rule success in the effect of originality is best secured by fidelity, in an extreme sense, to the individual words as they appear in the dictionary. If a poet knows precisely what his words represent, what he writes is much more likely to seem new and strange—and even difficult to understand—than if he uses his words ignorantly and at random. That is because when each word has definite character the combinations cannot avoid uniqueness. Even if a text is wholly quotation, the condition of quotation itself qualifies the text and makes it so far unique. Thus a quotation made from Marvell by Eliot has a force slightly different from what it had when Marvell wrote it. Though the combination of words is unique it is read, if the reader knows his words either by usage or dictionary, with a shock like that of recognition. The recognition is not limited, however, to what was already known in the words; there is a perception of something previously unknown, something new which is a result of the combination of the words, something which is literally an access of knowledge. Upon the poet's skill in combining words as much as upon his private feelings, depends the importance or the value of the knowledge.

In some notes on the language of e. e. cummings I tried to show how that poet, by relying on his private feelings and using words as if their meanings were spontaneous with use, succeeded mainly in turning his words into empty shells. With very likely no better inspiration in the life around him, Mr. Stevens, by combining the insides of those words he found fit to his feelings, has turned his words into knowledge. Both Mr. Stevens and cummings issue in ambiguity —as any good poet does; but the ambiguity of cummings is that of the absence of known content, the ambiguity of a phantom which no words could give being; while Mr. Stevens's ambiguity is that of a substance so dense with being, that it resists paraphrase and can be truly perceived only in the form of words in which it was given. It is the difference between poetry which depends on the poet and poetry which depends on itself. Reading cummings you either guess or supply the substance yourself. Reading Mr. Stevens you have only to know the meanings of the words and to submit to the conditions of the poem. There is a precision in such ambiguity all the more precise because it clings so closely to the stuff of the poem that separated it means nothing.

Take what would seem to be the least common word in the whole of *Harmonium*—*funest* (74, 1.6).[1] The word means "sad" or "calamitous" or "mournful" and is derived from a French word meaning fatal, melancholy, baneful, and has to do with death and funerals. It comes ultimately from the Latin *funus* for funeral. Small dictionaries do not stock it. The poem in which it appears is called "Of the Manner of Addressing Clouds," which begins as follows:

> Gloomy grammarians in golden gowns,
> Meekly you keep the mortal rendezvous,
> Eliciting the still sustaining pomps
> Of speech which are like music so profound
> They seem an exaltation without sound.

> Funest philosophers and ponderers,
> Their evocations are the speech of clouds.
> So speech of your processionals returns
> In the casual evocations of your tread
> Across the stale, mysterious seasons. . . .

The sentence in which *funest* occurs is almost a parenthesis. It *seems* the statement of something thought of by the way, suggested by the clouds, which had better be said at once before it is forgotten. In such a casual, disarming way, resembling the way of understatement, Mr. Stevens often introduces the most important elements in his poems. The oddity of the word having led us to look it up we find that, once used, *funest* is better than any of its synonyms. It is the essence of the funeral in its sadness, not its sadness alone, that makes it the right word: the clouds are going to their death, as not only philosophers but less indoctrinated ponderers know; so what they say, what they evoke, in pondering, has that much in common with the clouds. Suddenly we realize that the effect of funest philosophers is due to the larger context of the lines preceding, and at the same time we become aware that the statement about their evocations is central to the poem and illuminates it. The word *pomps*, above, means ceremony and comes from a Greek word meaning "procession," often, by association, a funeral, as in the phrase *funeral pomps.* So the pomps of the clouds suggests the funeral in *funest.*

The whole thing increases in ambiguity the more it is analyzed, but if the poem is read over after analysis, it will be seen that *in the poem* the language is perfectly precise. In its own words it is clear, and becomes vague in analysis only because the analysis is not the poem. We use analysis properly in order to discard it and return that much better equipped to the poem.

The use of such a word as *funest* suggests more abstract considerations, apart from the present instance. The question is whether or not and how much the poet is stretching his words when they are made to carry as much weight as *funest* carries above. Any use of a word stretches it slightly, because any use selects from among many meanings the right one, and then modifies that in the context. Beyond this necessary stretching, words cannot perhaps be stretched without coming to nullity—as the popular stretching of *awful, grand, swell,* has more or less nullified the original senses of those words. If Mr. Stevens stretches his words slightly, as a live poet should and must, it is in such a way as to make them seem more precisely themselves than ever. The context is so delicately illuminated, or adumbrated, that the word must be looked up, or at least thought carefully about, before the precision can be seen. This is the precision of the expert pun, and every word, to a degree, carries with it in any given sense the puns of all its senses.

But it may be a rule that only the common words of a language, words with several, even groups of meanings, can be stretched the small amount that is possible. The reader must have room for his research; and the more complex words are usually plays upon common words, and limited in their play. In the instance above the word *funest* is not so much itself stretched by its association with *philosophers* as the word *philosophers*—a common word with many senses— stretches *funest*. That is, because Mr. Stevens has used the word *funest*, it cannot easily be detached and used by others. The point is subtle. The meaning so doubles upon itself that it can be understood only in context. It is the context that is stretched by the insertion of the word *funest*; and it is that stretch, by its ambiguity, that adds to our knowledge.

A use of words almost directly contrary to that just discussed may be seen in a very different sort of poem—"The Ordinary Women" (13). I quote the first stanza to give the tone:

> Then from their poverty they rose.
> From dry catarrhs, and to guitars
> They flitted
> Through the palace walls.

Then skipping a stanza, we have this, for atmosphere:

> The lacquered loges huddled there
> Mumbled zay-zay and a-zay, a-zay.
> The moonlight
> Fubbed the girandoles.

The loges huddled probably because it was dark or because they didn't like the ordinary women, and mumbled perhaps because of the moonlight, perhaps because of the catarrhs, or even to keep key to the guitars. Moonlight, for Mr. Stevens, is mental, fictive, related to the imagination and meaning of things; naturally it fubbed the girandoles (which is equivalent to cheated the chandeliers, was stronger than the artificial light, if any) . . . Perhaps and probably but no doubt something else. I am at loss, and quite happy there, to know anything literally about this poem. Internally, inside its own words, I know it quite well by simple perusal. The charm of the rhymes is enough to carry it over any stile. The strange phrase, "Fubbed the girandoles," has another charm, like that of the rhyme, and as inexplicable: the approach of language, through

the magic of elegance, to nonsense. That the phrase is not nonsense, that on inspection it retrieves itself to sense, is its inner virtue. Somewhere between the
realms of ornamental sound and representative statement, the words pause and
balance, dissolve and resolve. This is the mood of Euphues, and presents a poem
with fine parts controlled internally by little surds of feeling that save both the
poem and its parts from preciousness. The ambiguity of this sort of writing consists in the double importance of both sound and sense where neither has direct connection with the other but where neither can stand alone. It is as if
Mr. Stevens wrote two poems at once with the real poem somewhere between,
unwritten but vivid.

A poem which exemplifies not the approach merely but actual entrance
into nonsense is "Disillusionment of Ten O'Clock" (88). This poem begins by
saying that houses are haunted by white nightgowns, not nightgowns of various
other colors, and ends with these lines:

> People are not going
> To dream of baboons and periwinkles.
> Only, here and there, an old sailor,
> Drunk and asleep in his boots,
> Catches tigers
> In rcd weather.

The language is simple and declarative. There is no doubt about the words or
the separate statements. Every part of the poem makes literal sense. Yet the
combination makes a nonsense, and a nonsense much more convincing than
the separate sensible statements. The statement about catching tigers in red
weather coming after the white nightgowns and baboons and periwinkles, has
a persuasive force out of all relation to the sense of the words. Literally, there is
nothing alarming in the statement, and nothing ambiguous, but by so putting
the statement that it appears as nonsense, infinite possibilities are made terrifying and plain. The shock and virtue of nonsense is this: it compels us to
scrutinize the words in such a way that we see the enormous ambiguity in the
substance of every phrase, every image, every word. The simpler the words are
the more impressive and certain is the ambiguity. Half our sleeping knowledge
is in nonsense; and when put in a poem it wakes.

The edge between sense and nonsense is shadow thin, and in all our deepest convictions we hover in the shadow, uncertain whether we know what our
words mean, nevertheless bound by the conviction to say them. I quote the
second half of "The Death of a Soldier" (129):

Death is absolute and without memorial,
As in a season of autumn,
When the wind stops,
When the wind stops and, over the heavens,
The clouds go, nevertheless,
In their direction.

To gloss such a poem is almost impertinent, but I wish to observe that in the passage just quoted, which is the important half of the poem, there is an abstract statement, "Death is absolute and without memorial," followed by the notation of a natural phenomenon. The connection between the two is not a matter of course; it is syntactical, poetic, human. The point is, by combining the two, Mr. Stevens has given his abstract statement a concrete, sensual force; he has turned a conviction, an idea, into a feeling which did not exist, even in his own mind, until he had put it down in words. The feeling is not exactly in the words, it is because of them. As in the body sensations are definite but momentary, while feelings are ambiguous (with reference to sensations) but lasting; so in this poem the words are definite but instant, while the feelings they raise are ambiguous (with reference to the words) and have importance. Used in this way, words, like sensations, are blind facts which put together produce a feeling no part of which was in the data. We cannot say, abstractly, in words, any better what we know, yet the knowledge has become positive and the conviction behind it indestructible, because it has been put into words. That is one business of poetry, to use words to give quality and feeling to the precious abstract notions, and so doing to put them beyond words and beyond the sense of words.

A similar result from a different mode of the use of words may be noticed in such a poem as "The Emperor of Ice-Cream" (85):

Call the roller of big cigars,
The muscular one, and bid him whip
In kitchen cups concupiscent curds.
Let the wenches dawdle in such dress
As they are used to wear, and let the boys
Bring flowers in last month's newspapers.
Let be be finale of seem.
The only emperor is the emperor of ice-cream.

Take from the dresser of deal,
Lacking the three glass knobs, that sheet
On which she embroidered fantails once

And spread it so as to cover her face.
If her horny feet protrude, they come
To show how cold she is, and dumb.
Let the lamp affix its beam.
The only emperor is the emperor of ice-cream.

The poem might be called Directions for a Funeral, with Two Epitaphs. We have a corpse laid out in the bedroom and we have people in the kitchen. The corpse is dead; then let the boys bring flowers in last month's (who would use today's?) newspapers. The corpse is dead; but let the wenches wear their everyday clothes—or is it the clothes they are used to wear at funerals? The conjunction of a muscular man whipping desirable desserts in the kitchen and the corpse protruding horny feet, gains its effect because of its oddity—not of fact, but of expression: the light frivolous words and rapid meters. Once made the conjunction is irretrievable and in its own measure exact. Two ideas or images about death—the living and the dead—have been associated, and are now permanently fused. If the mind is a rag-bag, pull out two rags and sew them together. If the materials were contradictory, the very contradiction, made permanent, becomes a kind of unison. By associating ambiguities found in nature in a poem we reach a clarity, a kind of transfiguration even, whereby we learn *what* the ambiguity was.

The point is, that the oddity of association would not have its effect without the couplets which conclude each stanza with the pungency of good epitaphs. Without the couplets the association would sink from wit to low humor or simple description. What, then, do the couplets mean? Either, or both, of two things. In the more obvious sense, "Let be be finale of seem," in the first stanza, means, take whatever seems to be, as really being; and in the second stanza, "Let the lamp affix its beam," means let it be plain that this woman is dead, that these things, impossibly ambiguous as they may be, are as they are. In this case, "The only emperor is the emperor of ice-cream," implies in both stanzas that the only power worth heeding is the power of the moment, of what is passing, of the flux.[2]

The less obvious sense of the couplets is more difficult to set down because, in all its difference, it rises out of the first sense, and while contradicting and supplanting, yet guarantees it. The connotation is, perhaps, that ice-cream and what it represents is the only power *heeded,* not the only power there is to heed. The irony recoils on itself: what seems *shall* finally be; the lamp *shall* affix its beam. The only emperor is the emperor of ice-cream. The king is dead; long live the king.

The virtue of the poem is that it discusses and settles these matters without mentioning them. The wit of the couplets does the work.

Allied to the method of this poem is the method of much of "Le Monocle de Mon Oncle." The light word is used with a more serious effect than the familiar, heavy words commonly chosen in poems about the nature of love. I take these lines from the first stanza (16):

> The sea of spuming thought foists up again
> The radiant bubble that she was. And then
> A deep up-pouring from some saltier well
> Within me, bursts its watery syllable.

The words *foist* and *bubble* are in origin and have remained in usage both light. One comes from a word meaning to palm false dice, and the other is derived by imitation from a gesture of the mouth. Whether the history of the words was present in Mr. Stevens's mind when he chose them is immaterial; the pristine flavor is still active by tradition and is what gives the rare taste to the lines quoted. By employing them in connection with a sea of spuming thought and the notion of radiance whatever vulgarity was in the two words is purged. They gain force while they lend their own lightness to the context; and I think it is the lightness of these words that permits and conditions the second sentence in the quotation, by making the contrast between the foisted bubble and the bursting syllable possible.

Stanza IV of the same poem (17–18) has a serious trope in which apples and skulls, love and death, are closely associated in subtle and vivid language. An apple, Mr. Stevens says, is as good as any skull to read because, like the skull, it finally rots away in the ground. The stanza ends with these lines:

> But it excels in this, that as the fruit
> Of love, it is a book too mad to read
> Before one merely reads to pass the time.

The light elegance and conversational tone give the stanza the cumulative force of understatement, and make it seem to carry a susurrus of irony between the lines. The word *excels* has a good deal to do with the success of the passage; superficially a syntactical word as much as anything else, actually, by its literal sense it saves the lines from possible triviality.

We have been considering poems where the light tone increases the gravity of the substance, and where an atmosphere of wit and elegance assures poignancy of meaning. It is only a step or so further to that use of language where tone and atmosphere are very nearly equivalent to substance and meaning themselves. "Sea Surface Full of Clouds" (132) has many lines and several images in its five sections which contribute by their own force to the sense of the poem, but it would be very difficult to attach special importance to any one of them. The burden of the poem is the color and tone of the whole. It is as near a tone-poem, in the musical sense, as language can come. The sense of single lines cannot profitably be abstracted from the context, and literal analysis does nothing but hinder understanding. We may say, if we like, that Mr. Stevens found himself in ecstasy—that he stood aside from himself emotionally—before the spectacle of endlessly varied appearances of California seas off Tehuantepec; and that he has tried to equal the complexity of what he saw in the technical intricacy of his poem. But that is all we can say. Neither the material of the poem nor what we get out of it is by nature susceptible of direct treatment in words. It might at first seem more a painter's subject than a poet's, because its interest is more obviously visual and formal than mental. Such an assumption would lead to apt criticism if Mr. Stevens had tried, in his words, to present a series of seascapes with a visual atmosphere to each picture. His intention was quite different and germane to poetry; he wanted to present the tone, in the mind, of five different aspects of the sea. The strictly visual form is in the background, merely indicated by the words; it is what the visual form gave off after it had been felt in the mind that concerned him. Only by the precise interweaving of association and suggestion, by the development of a delicate verbal pattern, could he secure the overtones that possessed him. A looser form would have captured nothing.

The choice of certain elements in the poem may seem arbitrary, but it is an arbitrariness without reference to their rightness and wrongness. That is, any choice would have been equally arbitrary, and, esthetically, equally right. In the second stanza of each section, for example, one is reminded of different kinds of chocolate and different shades of green, thus: rosy chocolate and paradisal green; chop-house chocolate and sham-like green; porcelain chocolate and uncertain green; musky chocolate and too-fluent green; Chinese chocolate and motley green. And each section gives us umbrellas variously gilt, sham, pied, frail, and large. The ocean is successively a machine which is perplexed, tense, tranced, dry, and obese. The ocean produces sea-blooms from the clouds, mortal massives of the blooms of water, silver petals of white blooms, figures of the clouds like blooms, and, finally, a wind of green blooms. These items, and many more, repeated and modified, at once impervious to and merging each in the other, make up the words of the poem. Directly they do nothing but rouse the small sensations and smaller feelings of atmosphere and tone. The poem itself, what it means, is somewhere in the background; we know it through the tone. The motley hue we see is crisped to "clearing opalescence."

> Then the sea
> And heaven rolled as one and from the two
> Came fresh transfigurings of freshest blue.

Here we have words used as a tone of feeling to secure the discursive evanescence of appearances; words bringing the senses into the mind which they created; the establishment of interior experience by the construction of its tone in words. In "Tattoo" (108), we have the opposite effect, where the mind is intensified in a simple visual image. The tone existed beforehand, so to speak, in the nature of the subject.

> The light is like a spider.
> It crawls over the water.
> It crawls over the edges of the snow.
> It crawls under your eyelids
> And spreads its webs there—
> Its two webs.
>
> The webs of your eyes
> Are fastened
> To the flesh and bones of you
> As to rafters or grass.
>
> There are filaments of your eyes
> On the surface of the water
> And in the edges of the snow.

The problem of language here hardly existed: the words make the simplest of statements, and the poet had only to avoid dramatizing what was already drama in itself, the sensation of the eyes in contact with what they looked at. By attempting *not* to set up a tone the tone of truth is secured for statements literally false. Fairy tales and Mother Goose use the same language. Because there is no point where the statements stop being true, they leap the gap unnoticed between literal truth and imaginative truth. It is worth observing that the strong sensual quality of the poem is defined without the use of a single sensual word; and it is that ambiguity between the words and their subject which makes the poem valuable.

There is nothing which has been said so far about Mr. Stevens's uses of language which might not have been said, with different examples, of any good poet equally varied and equally erudite[3]—by which I mean intensely careful of effects. We have been dealing with words primarily, and words are not limited either to an author or a subject. Hence they form unique data and are to be understood and commented on by themselves. You can hardly more compare two poets' use of a word than you can compare, profitably, trees to cyclones. Synonyms are accidental, superficial, and never genuine. Comparison begins to be possible at the level of more complicated tropes than may occur in single words.

Let us compare then, for the sake of distinguishing the kinds of import, certain tropes taken from Ezra Pound, T. S. Eliot, and Mr. Stevens.

From Mr. Pound—the first and third from the *Cantos* and the second from *Hugh Selwyn Mauberley:*

> In the gloom, the gold gathers the light against it.

> Tawn foreshores
> Washed in the cobalt of oblivion.

> A catalogue, his jewels of conversation.

From T. S. Eliot—one from "Prufrock," one from *The Waste Land,* and one from *Ash Wednesday:*

> I should have been a pair of ragged claws
> Scuttling across the floors of silent seas.

> The awful daring of a moment's surrender
> Which an age of prudence can never retract.

> Struggling with the devil of the stairs who wears
> The deceitful face of hope and of despair.

The unequaled versatility of Ezra Pound (Eliot in a dedication addresses him as *Il miglior fabbro*) prevents assurance that the three lines quoted from him are typical of all his work. At least they are characteristic of his later verse, and the kind of feeling they exhibit may be taken as Pound's own. Something like their effect may be expected in reading a good deal of his work.

The first thing to be noticed is that the first two tropes are visual images— not physical observation, but something to be seen in the mind's eye; and that as the images are so seen their meaning is exhausted. The third trope while not directly visual acts as if it were. What differentiates all three from physical observation is in each case the nonvisual associations of a single word—*gathers,* which in the active voice has an air of intention; *oblivion,* which has the purely mental sense of forgetfulness; and, less obviously, *conversation,* in the third trope, which while it helps *jewels* to give the line a visual quality it does not literally possess, also acts to condense in the line a great many nonvisual associations.

The lines quoted from T. S. Eliot are none of them in intention visual; they deal with a totally different realm of experience—the realm in which the mind dramatizes, at a given moment, its feelings toward a whole aspect of life. The emotion with which these lines charge the reader's mind is a quality of emotion which has so surmounted the senses as to require no longer the support of direct contact with them. Abstract words have reached the intensity of thought and feeling where the senses have been condensed into abstraction. The first distich is an impossible statement which in its context is terrifying. The language has sensual elements but as such they mean nothing: it is the act of abstract dramatization which counts. In the second and third distichs words such as *surrender* and *prudence, hope,* and *despair,* assume, by their dramatization, a definite sensual force.

Both Eliot and Pound condense; their best verse is weighted—Pound's with sensual experience primarily, and Eliot's with beliefs. Where the mind's life is concerned the senses produce images, and beliefs produce dramatic cries. The condensation is important.

Mr. Stevens's tropes, in his best work and where he is most characteristic, are neither visual like Pound nor dramatic like Eliot. The scope and reach of his verse are no less but are different. His visual images never condense the matter of his poems; they either accent or elaborate it. His dramatic statements, likewise, tend rather to give another, perhaps more final, form to what has already been put in different language.

The best evidence of these differences is the fact that it is almost impossible to quote anything short of a stanza from Mr. Stevens without essential injustice to the meaning. His kind of condensation, too, is very different in character and degree from Eliot and Pound. Little details are left in the verse to show what it is he has condensed. And occasionally, in order to make the details fit into the poem, what has once been condensed is again elaborated. It is this habit of slight reelaboration which gives the firm textural quality to the verse.

Another way of contrasting Mr. Stevens's kind of condensation with those of Eliot and Pound will emerge if we remember Mr. Stevens's *intentional* ambiguity. Any observation, as between the observer and what is observed, is the notation of an ambiguity. To Mr. Stevens the sky, "the basal slate," "the universal hue," which surrounds us and is always upon us is the great ambiguity.

Mr. Stevens associates two or more such observations so as to accent their ambiguities. But what is ambiguous in the association is not the same as in the things associated; it is something new, and it has the air of something condensed. This is the quality that makes his poems grow, rise in the mind like a tide. The poems cannot be exhausted, because the words that make them, intentionally ambiguous at their crucial points, are themselves inexhaustible. Eliot obtains many of his effects by the sharpness of surprise, Pound his by visual definition; they tend to exhaust their words in the individual use, and they are successful because they know when to stop, they know when sharpness and definition lay most hold on their subjects, they know the maximal limit of their kinds of condensation. Mr. Stevens is just as precise in his kind; he brings ambiguity to the point of sharpness, of reality, without destroying, but rather preserving, clarified, the ambiguity. It is a difference in subject matter, and a difference in accent. Mr. Stevens makes you aware of how much is *already* condensed in any word.

The first stanza of "Sunday Morning" may be quoted (89). It should be remembered that the title is an integral part of the poem, directly affecting the meaning of many lines and generally controlling the atmosphere of the whole.

> Complacencies of the peignoir, and late
> Coffee and oranges in a sunny chair,
> And the green freedom of a cockatoo
> Upon a rug mingle to dissipate
> The holy hush of ancient sacrifice.
> She dreams a little, and she feels the dark
> Encroachment of that old catastrophe,
> As a calm darkens among water-lights.
> The pungent oranges and bright, green wings
> Seem things in some procession of the dead,
> Winding across wide water, without sound.
> The day is like wide water, without sound,
> Stilled for the passing of her dreaming feet
> Over the seas, to silent Palestine,
> Dominion of the blood and sepulchre.

A great deal of ground is covered in these fifteen lines, and the more the slow ease and conversational elegance of the verse are observed, the more wonder it seems that so much could have been indicated without strain. Visually, we have a woman enjoying her Sunday morning breakfast in a sunny room with a green rug. The image is secured, however, not as in Pound's image about the gold gathering the light against it, in directly visual terms, but by the almost casual combination of visual images with such phrases as *"complacencies* of the peignoir," and "the green *freedom* of the cockatoo," where the italicized words are abstract in essence but rendered concrete in combination. More important, the purpose of the images is to show how they dissipate the "holy hush of ancient sacrifice," how the natural comfort of the body is aware but mostly unheeding that Sunday is the Lord's day and that it commemorates the crucifixion.

From her half-awareness she feels the more keenly the "old catastrophe" merging in the surroundings, subtly, but deeply, changing them as a "calm darkens among water-lights." The feeling is dark in her mind, darkens, changing the whole day. The oranges and the rug and the day all have the quality of "wide water, without sound," and all her thoughts, so loaded, turn on the crucifixion.

The transit of the body's feeling from attitude to attitude is managed in the medium of three water images. These images do not replace the "complacencies of the peignoir," nor change them; they act as a kind of junction between them and the Christian feeling traditionally proper to the day. By the time the stanza is over the water images have embodied both feelings. In their own way they make a condensation by appearing in company with and showing what was already condensed.

If this stanza is compared with the tropes quoted from Pound, the principal difference will perhaps seem that while Pound's lines define their own meaning and may stand alone, Mr. Stevens's various images are separately incomplete and, on the other hand, taken together, have a kind of completeness to which Pound's lines may not pretend: everything to which they refer is present. Pound's images exist without syntax, Mr. Stevens's depend on it. Pound's images are formally simple, Mr. Stevens's complex. The one contains a mystery, and the other, comparatively, expounds a mystery.

While it would be possible to find analogues to Eliot's tropes in the stanzas of "Sunday Morning," it will be more profitable to examine something more germane in spirit. Search is difficult and choice uncertain, for Mr. Stevens is not a dramatic poet. Instead of dramatizing his feelings, he takes as fatal the drama that he sees and puts it down either in its least dramatic, most meditative form, or makes of it a simple statement. Let us then frankly take as pure a mediation as may be found, "The Snow Man" (12), where, again, the title is integrally part of the poem:

> One must have a mind of winter
> To regard the frost and the boughs
> Of the pine-trees crusted with snow;

And have been cold a long time
To behold the junipers shagged with ice,
The spruces rough in the distant glitter

Of the January sun; and not to think
Of any misery in the sound of the wind,
In the sound of a few leaves,

Which is the sound of the land
Full of the same wind
That is blowing in the same bare place

For the listener, who listens in the snow,
And, nothing himself, beholds
Nothing that is not there and the nothing that is.

The last three lines are as near as Mr. Stevens comes to the peculiar dramatic
emotion which characterizes the three tropes quoted from Eliot. Again, as in
the passage compared to Pound's images, the effect of the last three lines depends entirely on what preceded them. The emotion is built up from chosen
fragments and is then stated in its simplest form. The statement has the force
of emotional language but it remains a statement—a modest declaration of circumstance. The abstract word *nothing*, three times repeated, is not in effect abstract at all; it is synonymous with the data about the winter landscape which
went before. The part which is not synonymous is the emotion: the overtone
of the word, and the burden of the poem. Eliot's lines,

The awful daring of a moment's surrender
Which an age of prudence can never retract,

like Pound's lines, for different reasons, stand apart and on their own feet. The
two poets work in contrary modes. Eliot places a number of things side by side.
The relation is seldom syntactical or logical, but is usually internal and sometimes, so far as the reader is concerned, fatal and accidental. He works in violent contrasts and produces as much by prestidigitation as possible. There was
no reason in the rest of "Prufrock" why the lines about the pair of ragged claws
should have appeared where they did and no reason, perhaps, why they should
have appeared at all; but once they appeared they became for the reader irretrievable, complete in themselves, and completing the structure of the poem.

That is the method of a dramatic poet, who molds wholes out of parts themselves autonomous. Mr. Stevens, not a dramatic poet, seizes his wholes only in

imagination; in his poems the parts are already connected. Eliot usually moves from point to point or between two termini. Mr. Stevens as a rule ends where he began; only when he is through, his beginning has become a chosen end. The differences may be exaggerated but in their essence is a true contrast.

If a digression may be permitted, I think it may be shown that the different types of obscurity found in the three poets are only different aspects of their modes of writing. In Pound's verse, aside from words in languages the reader does not know, most of the hard knots are tied round combinations of classical and historical references. A passage in one of the Cantos, for example, works up at the same time the adventures of a Provençal poet and the events in one of Ovid's *Metamorphoses.* If the reader is acquainted with the details of both stories, he can appreciate the criticism in Pound's combination. Otherwise he will remain confused: he will be impervious to the plain facts of the verse.

Eliot's poems furnish examples of a different kind of reference to and use of history and past literature. The reader must be familiar with the ideas and the beliefs and systems of feeling to which Eliot alludes or from which he borrows, rather than to the facts alone. Eliot does not restrict himself to criticism; he digests what he takes; but the reader must know what it is that has been digested before he can appreciate the result. The Holy Grail material in *The Waste Land* is an instance: like Tiresias, this material is a dramatic element in the poem.

Mr. Stevens's difficulties to the normal reader present themselves in the shape of seemingly impenetrable words or phrases which no wedge of knowledge brought from outside the body of Mr. Stevens's own poetry can help much to split. The wedge, if any, is in the words themselves, either in the instance alone or in relation to analogous instances in the same or other poems in the book. Two examples should suffice.

In "Sunday Morning," there is in the seventh stanza (93) a reference to the sun, to which men shall chant their devotion—

> Not as a god, but as a god might be,
> Naked among them, like a savage source.
> Their chant shall be a chant of paradise,
> Out of their blood, returning to the sky; . . .

Depending upon the reader this will or will not be obscure. But in any case, the full weight of the lines is not felt until the conviction of the poet that the sun is origin and ending for all life is shared by the reader. That is why the god might be naked among them. It takes only reading of the stanza, the poem, and other poems where the fertility of the sun is celebrated, to make the notion sure. The only bit of outside information that might help is the fact that in an earlier version this stanza concluded the poem.—In short, generally, you need only the dictionary and familiarity with the poem in question to clear up a good part of Mr. Stevens's obscurities.

The second example is taken from "The Man whose Pharynx was Bad" (128):

> Perhaps, if winter once could penetrate
> Through all its purples to the final slate.

Here, to obtain the full meaning, we have only to consult the sixth stanza of "Le Monocle de Mon Oncle" (18):

> If men at forty will be painting lakes
> The ephemeral blues must merge for them in one,
> The basic slate, the universal hue.
> There is a substance in us that prevails.

Mr. Stevens has a notion often intimated that the sky is the only permanent background for thought and knowledge; he would see things against the sky as a Christian would see them against the cross. The blue of the sky is the prevailing substance of the sky, and to Mr. Stevens it seems only necessary to look at the sky to share and be shared in its blueness.

If I have selected fairly types of obscurity from these poets, it should be clear that whereas the obscurities of Eliot and Pound are intrinsic difficulties of the poems, to which the reader must come well armed with specific sorts of external knowledge and belief, the obscurities of Mr. Stevens clarify themselves to the intelligence alone. Mode and value are different—not more or less valuable, but different. And all result from the concentrated language which is the medium of poetry. The three poets load their words with the maximum content; naturally, the poems remain obscure until the reader takes out what the poet puts in. What still remains will be the essential impenetrability of words, the bottomlessness of knowledge. To these the reader, like the poet, must submit.

Returning, this time without reference to Pound and Eliot, among the varieties of Mr. Stevens's tropes we find some worth notice which comparison will not help. In "Le Monocle de Mon Oncle," the ninth stanza (20), has nothing logically to do with the poem; it neither develops the subject nor limits it, but is rather a rhetorical interlude set in the poem's midst. Yet it is necessary to the poem, because its rhetoric, boldly announced as such, expresses the feeling of the poet toward his poem, and that feeling, once expressed, becomes incorporated in the poem.

In verses wild with motion, full of din,
Loudened by cries, by clashes, quick and sure
As the deadly thought of men accomplishing
Their curious fates in war, come, celebrate
The faith of forty, ward of Cupido.
Most venerable heart, the lustiest conceit
Is not too lusty for your broadening.
I quiz all sounds, all thoughts, all everything
For the music and manner of the paladins
To make oblation fit. Where shall I find
Bravura adequate to this great hymn?

It is one of the advantages of a nondramatic, meditative style, that pure rhetoric may be introduced into a poem without injuring its substance. The structure of the poem is, so to speak, a structure of loose ends, spliced only verbally, joined only by the sequence in which they appear. What might be fustian ornament in a dramatic poem, in a meditative poem casts a feeling far from fustian over the whole, and the slighter the relation of the rhetorical interlude to the substance of the whole, the more genuine is the feeling cast. The rhetoric does the same thing that the action does in a dramatic poem, or the events in a narrative poem; it produces an apparent medium in which the real substance may be borne.

Such rhetoric is not reserved to set interludes; it often occurs in lines not essentially rhetorical at all. Sometimes it gives life to a serious passage and cannot be separated without fatal injury to the poem. Then it is the trick without which the poem would fall flat entirely. Two poems occur where the rhetoric is the vital trope—"A High-Toned Old Christian Woman" (79), and "Bantams in Pine-Woods" (101), which I quote entire:

Chieftain Iffucan of Azcan in caftan
Of tan with henna hackles, halt!

Damned universal cock, as if the sun
Was blackamoor to bear your blazing tail.

Fat! Fat! Fat! I am the personal.
Your world is you. I am my world.

You ten-foot poet among inchlings. Fat!
Begone! An inchling bristles in these pines,

Bristles, and points their Appalachian tangs,
And fears not portly Azcan nor his hoos.

The first and last distichs are gauds of rhetoric; nevertheless they give not only the tone but the substance to the poem. If the reader is deceived by the rhetoric and believes the poem is no more than a verbal plaything, he ought not to read poetry except as a plaything. With a different object, Mr. Stevens's rhetoric is as ferociously comic as the rhetoric in Marlowe's *Jew of Malta*, and as serious. The ability to handle rhetoric so as to reach the same sort of intense condensation that is secured in bare, nonrhetorical language is very rare, and since what rhetoric can condense is very valuable it ought to receive the same degree of attention as any other use of language. Mr. Stevens's successful attempts in this direction are what are make him technically most interesting. Simple language, dealing obviously with surds, draws emotion out of feelings; rhetorical language, dealing rather, or apparently, with inflections, employed with the same seriousness, creates a surface *equivalent* to an emotion by its approximately complete escape from the purely communicative function of language.[4]

We have seen in a number of examples that Mr. Stevens uses language in several different ways, either separately or in combination; and I have tried to imply that his success is due largely to his double adherence to words and experience as existing apart from his private sensibility. His great labor has been to allow the reality of what he felt personally to pass into the superior impersonal reality of words. Such a transformation amounts to an access of knowledge, as it raises to a condition where it may be rehearsed and understood in permanent form that body of emotional and sensational experience which in its natural condition makes life a torment and confusion.

With the technical data partly in hand, it ought now to be possible to fill out the picture, touch upon the knowledge itself, in Mr. Stevens's longest and most important poem, "The Comedian as the Letter C." Everywhere characteristic of Mr. Stevens's style and interests, it has the merit of difficulty—difficulty which when solved rewards the reader beyond his hopes of clarity.

Generally speaking the poem deals with the sensations and images, notions and emotions, ideas and meditations, sensual adventures and introspective journeyings of a protagonist called Crispin. More precisely, the poem expounds the shifting of a man's mind between sensual experience and its imaginative interpretation, the struggle, in that mind, of the imagination for sole supremacy and the final slump or ascent where the mind contents itself with interpreting plain and common things. In short, we have a meditation, with instances, of man's struggle with nature. The first line makes the theme explicit: "Nota: man is the intelligence of his soil, the sovereign ghost." Later, the theme is continued in reverse form: "His soil is man's intelligence." Later still, the soil is qualified as suzerain, which means sovereign over a semi-independent or internally autonomous state; and finally, at the end of the poem, the sovereignty is still further reduced when it turns out that the imagination can make nothing better of the world (here called a turnip), than the same insoluble lump it was in the beginning.

The poem is in six parts of about four pages each. A summary may replace pertinent discussion and at the same time preclude extraneous discussion. In part I, called "The World without Imagination," Crispin, who previously had cultivated a small garden with his intelligence, finds himself at sea, "a skinny sailor peering in the sea-glass." At first at loss and "washed away by magnitude," Crispin, "merest minuscule in the gales," at last finds the sea a vocable thing,

> But with a speech belched out of hoary darks
> Noway resembling his, a visible thing,
> And excepting negligible Triton, free
> From the unavoidable shadow of himself
> That elsewhere lay around him.

The sea "was no help before reality," only "one vast subjugating final tone," before which Crispin was made new. Concomitantly, with and because of his vision of the sea, "The drenching of stale lives no more fell down."

Part II is called "Concerning the Thunder-Storms of Yucatan," and there, in Yucatan, Crispin, a man made vivid by the sea, found his apprehensions enlarged and felt the need to fill his senses. He sees and hears all there is before him, and writes fables for himself

> Of an aesthetic tough, diverse, untamed,
> Incredible to prudes, the mint of dirt,
> Green barbarism turning paradigm.

The sea had liberated his senses, and he discovers an earth like "A jostling festival of seeds grown fat, too juicily opulent," and a "new reality in parrot-squawks." His education is interrupted when a wind "more terrible than the revenge of music on bassoons," brings on a tropical thunder-storm. Crispin, "this connoisseur of elemental fate," identifies himself with the storm, finding himself free, which he was before, and "more than free, elate, intent, profound and studious" of a new self:

> the thunder, lapsing in its clap,
> Let down gigantic quavers of its voice,
> For Crispin to vociferate again.

With such freedom taken from the sea and such power found in the storm, Crispin is ready for the world of the imagination. Naturally, then, the third part of the poem, called "Approaching Carolina," is a chapter in the book of moonlight, and Crispin "a faggot in the lunar fire." Moonlight is imagination, a reflection or interpretation of the sun, which is the source of life. It is also, curiously, this moonlight, North America, and specifically one of the Carolinas. And the Carolinas, to Crispin, seemed north; even the spring seemed arctic. He meditates on the poems he has denied himself because they gave less than "the relentless contact he desired." Perhaps the moon would establish the necessary liaison between himself and his environment. But perhaps not. It seemed

> Illusive, faint, more mist than moon, perverse,
> Wrong as a divagation to Peking. . . .
> Moonlight was an evasion, or, if not,
> A minor meeting, facile, delicate.

So he considers, and teeters back and forth, between the sun and moon. For the moment he decides against the moon and imagination in favor of the sun and his senses. The senses, instanced by the smell of things at the river wharf where his vessel docks, "round his rude aesthetic out" and teach him "how much of what he saw he never saw at all."

> He gripped more closely the essential prose
> As being, in a world so falsified,
> The one integrity for him, the one
> Discovery still possible to make,
> To which all poems were incident, unless
> That prose should wear a poem's guise at last.

In short, Crispin conceives that if the experience of the senses is but well enough known, the knowledge takes the form of imagination after all. So we find as the first line of the fourth part, called "The Idea of a Colony," "Nota: his soil is man's intelligence," which reverses the original statement that man is the intelligence of his soil. With the new distinction illuminating his mind,

Crispin plans a colony, and asks himself whether the purpose of his pilgrimage is not

> to drive away
> The shadow of his fellows from the skies,
> And, from their stale intelligence released,
> To make a new intelligence prevail?

The rest of the fourth part is a long series of synonymous tropes stating instances of the new intelligence. In a torment of fastidious thought, Crispin writes a prolegomena for his colony. Everything should be understood for what it is and should follow the urge of its given character. The spirit of things should remain spirit and play as it will.

> The man in Georgia waking among pines
> Should be pine-spokesman. The responsive man,
> Planting his pristine cores in Florida,
> Should prick thereof, not on the psaltery,
> But on the banjo's categorical gut.

And as for Crispin's attitude toward nature, "the melon should have apposite ritual" and the peach its incantation. These "commingled souvenirs and prophecies"—all images of freedom and the satisfaction of instinct—compose Crispin's idea of a colony. He banishes the masquerade of thought and expunges dreams; the ideal takes no form from these. Crispin will be content to "let the rabbit run, the cock declaim."

In part V, which is "A Nice Shady Home," Crispin dwells in the land, contented and a hermit, continuing his observations with diminished curiosity. His discovery that his colony has fallen short of his plan and that he is content to have it fall short, content to build a cabin,

> who once planned
> Loquacious columns by the ructive sea,

leads him to ask whether he should not become a philosopher instead of a colonizer.

> Should he lay by the personal and make
> Of his own fate an instance of all fate?

The question is rhetorical, but before it can answer itself, Crispin, sapped by the quotidian, sapped by the sun, has no energy for questions, and is content to realize, that for all the sun takes

> it gives a humped return
> Exchequering from piebald fiscs unkeyed.

Part VI, called "And Daughters with Curls," explains the implications of the last quoted lines. The sun, and all the new intelligence which it enriched, mulcted the man Crispin, and in return gave him four daughters, four questioners and four sure answerers. He has been brought back to social nature, has gone to seed. The connoisseur of elemental fate has become himself an instance of all fate. He does not know whether the return was "Anabasis or slump, ascent or chute." His cabin—that is the existing symbol of his colony—seems now a phylactery, a sacred relic or amulet he might wear in memorial to his idea, in which his daughters shall grow up, bidders and biders for the ecstasies of the world, to repeat his pilgrimage, and come, no doubt, in their own cabins, to the same end.

Then Crispin invents his doctrine and clothes it in the fable about the turnip:

> The world, a turnip once so readily plucked,
> Sacked up and carried overseas, daubed out
> Of its ancient purple, pruned to the fertile main,
> And sown again by the stiffest realist,
> Came reproduced in purple, family font,
> The same insoluble lump. The fatalist
> Stepped in and dropped the chuckling down his craw,
> Without grace or grumble.

But suppose the anecdote was false, and Crispin a profitless philosopher,

> Glozing his life with after-shining flicks,
> Illuminating, from a fancy gorged
> By apparition, plain and common things,
> Sequestering the fluster from the year,
> Making gulped potions from obstreperous drops,
> And so distorting, proving what he proves
> Is nothing, what can all this matter since
> The relation comes, benignly, to its end.

> So may the relation of each man be clipped.

The legend or subject of the poem and the mythology it develops are hardly new nor are the instances, intellectually considered, very striking. But both the clear depth of conception and the extraordinary luxuriance of rhetoric and image in which it is expressed, should be at least suggested in the summary here furnished. Mr. Stevens had a poem with an abstract subject—man as an instance of fate, and a concrete experience—the sensual confusion in which the man is waylaid; and to combine them he had to devise a form suitable to his own peculiar talent. The simple statement—of which he is a master—could not be prolonged to meet the dimensions of his subject. To the dramatic style his talents were unsuitable, and if by chance he used it, it would prevent both the meditative mood and the accent of intellectual wit which he needed to make the subject his own. The form he used is as much his own and as adequate, as the form of *Paradise Lost* is Milton's or the form of *The Waste Land* is Eliot's. And as Milton's form filled the sensibility of one aspect of his age, Mr. Stevens's form fits part of the sensibility—a part which Eliot or Pound or Yeats do little to touch—of our own age.

I do not know a name for the form. It is largely the form of rhetoric, language used for its own sake, persuasively to the extreme. But it has, for rhetoric, an extraordinary content of concrete experience. Mr. Stevens is a genuine poet in that he attempts constantly to transform what is felt with the senses and what is thought in the mind—if we can still distinguish the two—into that realm of being, which we call poetry, where what is thought is felt and what is felt has the strict point of thought. And I call his mode of achieving that transformation rhetorical because it is not lyric or dramatic or epic, because it does not transcend its substance, but is a reflection upon a hard surface, a shining mirror of rhetoric.

In its nature depending so much on tone and atmosphere, accenting precise management of ambiguities, and dealing with the subtler inflections of simple feelings, the elements of the form cannot be tracked down and put in order. Perhaps the title of the whole poem, "The Comedian as the Letter C," is as good an example as any where several of the elements can be found together. The letter C is, of course, Crispin, and he is called a letter because he is small (he is referred to as "merest minuscule," which means small letter, in the first part of the poem) and because, though small, like a letter he stands for something— his colony, cabin, and children—as a comedian. He is a comedian because he deals finally with the quotidian (the old distinction of comedy and tragedy was between everyday and heroic subject matter), gorged with apparition, illuminating plain and common things. But what he deals with is not comic; the comedy, in that sense, is restricted to his perception and does not touch the things perceived or himself. The comedy is the accent, the play of the words. He is at various times a realist, a clown, a philosopher, a colonizer, a father, a faggot in the lunar fire, and so on. In sum, and any sum is hypothetical, he may be a comedian in both senses, but separately never. He is the hypothesis of comedy. He is a piece of rhetoric—a persona in words—exemplifying all these characters, and summing, or masking, in his persuasive style, the essential prose he read. He is the poem's guise that the prose wears at last.

Such is the title of the poem, and such is the poem itself. Mr. Stevens has created a surface, a texture, a rhetoric in which his feelings and thoughts are preserved in what amounts to a new sensibility. The contrast between his subjects—the apprehension of all the sensual aspects of nature as instances of fate,—and the form in which the subjects are expressed is what makes his poetry valuable. Nature becomes nothing but words and to a poet words are everything.

NOTES

1 Wallace Stevens, *Harmonium* (New York: Alfred A. Knopf, 1931), 74; all subsequent references are to the new edition of *Harmonium.* This differs from the first edition in that three poems have been cut out and fourteen added.

2 Mr. Stevens wrote me that his daughter put a superlative value on ice-cream. Up daughters!

3 See Logan Pearsall Smith, *Words and Idioms* (Boston: Houghton Mifflin, 1926), 121. "One of the great defects of our critical vocabulary is the lack of a neutral, nonderogatory name for these great artificers, these artists who derive their inspiration more from the formal than the emotional aspects of their art, and who are more interested in the masterly control of their material, than in the expression of their own feelings, or the prophetic aspects of their calling." Mr. Smith then suggests the use of the words *erudite* and *erudition* and gives as reason their derivation "from *erudire* (*E* 'out of,' and *rudis*, 'rude,' 'rough' or 'raw'), a verb meaning in classical Latin to bring out of the rough, to form by means of art, to polish, to instruct." Mr. Stevens is such an *erudite;* though he is often more, when he deals with emotional matters as if they were matters for *erudition.*

4 There is a point at which rhetorical language resumes its communicative function. In the second of "Six Significant Landscapes" (98), we have this image:

> A pool shines
> Like a bracelet
> Shaken at a dance,

which is a result of the startling associations induced by an ornamental, social, rhetorical style in dealing with nature. The image perhaps needs its context to assure its quality.

6. How to Do Things with Wallace Stevens
FRANK LENTRICCHIA

T HERE'S A LITTLE story told by Wallace Stevens that I need to retell—
actually it's an anecdote (*anekdota*, in the Greek, meaning unpublished
items; more familiarly, in English, a small gossipy narrative generally
of an amusing and biographical incident in the life of an important person). The
anecdote I have in mind (like all anecdotes) is also a representation; in Kenneth
Burke's searching phrase, a "representative anecdote."[1] So a hitherto unpublished little story, funny and biographical, apparently stands in for a bigger story,
a socially pivotal and culturally pervasive biography which it illuminates—in
an anecdotal flash it reveals the essence of the larger unspoken story, and in
that very moment becomes exegesis of a public text; the unpublished items become published. The teller of anecdotes must presume the cultural currency of
a containing biographical narrative which he draws upon for the sharp point he
would give his anecdote, whose true function is political: to trigger a narrative
sense of community that the evoked master biography helps to sustain by shaping. Biography so become cultural myth underwrites collective cohesion—we
feel ourselves to be part of a social narrative—even as the myth gives cohesion
to, as it contains, its various constituent anecdotes.

One day, when he was a little boy, George Washington chopped down a
cherry tree in his father's orchard. Americans usually get the point in a hurry;
the punch line need not be said. One day, my grandfather, my mother's father,
at age seventy-nine, while rocking and smoking (but not inhaling) on his front
porch in Utica, New York, in mid-August heat (which he refused to recognize by
wearing his long johns), directed his grandson's attention (who was then about
thirteen) to the man sitting on *his* front porch across the street: not rocking
or smoking but huddled into himself, as if it were cold, aged eighty. Gesturing

with cigarette in hand toward "this American," as he called him (in Italian he inserted between "this" and "American" an adjective best left untranslated), all the while nodding, and in a tone that I recognized only later as much crafted, he said: "La vecchiáia è carógna." A story of biographical incident, funny if you can translate the Italian, but representative? Probably only in the mind of yours truly. You don't because through no fault of your own you probably can't get the point, though some in my family would—as would many first-generation Italian Americans, some fewer of the second generation, and fewer yet of my generation. My mother's father is dead, and those who remember him (and immigrants like him) in the right way, with necessary specificity, where do I find them? Soon this will be an anecdote for me alone because soon it will have no claim whatsoever to being what all we anecdotalists want our stories to be—a social form which instigates cultural memory: the act of narrative renewal, the reinstatement of social cohesion. Stevens's story is no more accessible than the one I just told about my grandfather. There is no Italian to trouble us in Stevens's story but its language is equally foreign and its representational power equally in peril.

So when the relation of the teller of anecdotes to a potential audience ceases altogether to be unified by a single myth, anecdotes will lose their rhetorical power. The anecdote will become (alas!) autonomous, a story for itself alone, not a literary form whose genealogy, in parable and fable, underwrites an equation of literary and social forms as forms of instruction. If anecdotes had minds of their own they'd probably say, we don't like modernist literary theories of aesthetic self-sufficiency; restore us, good reader, to the way we were. The anecdotes about George Washington are of course ceaselessly renewed—their subject (in both senses) is redeemed by the political process of American history. But who will renew my grandfather's cultural story? For whom can my grandfather's biography be important? What might it mediate? Who, anyway, makes an anecdote work—its first author or its cultural authorizer (who is rarely the first author), who by providing us with its mediations thereby both binds and activates us collectively with its cultural power?

Anecdotes would appear by their very nature to depend on a stable outside narrative, given and known, but in fact—and most dramatically in their written, high literary style—they work at critical turning points of cultural crisis when the outside narrative seems to be slipping away and its ideological energy is at lowest ebb. The anecdotalist's role (or desire) is to represent but by way of retrieval and recreation. To tell us what we think we already know is an effect of the genial style (trick) of his rhetoric—a literary bonding proleptic, he hopes, for the social and historical bonding that he wants to resuscitate and whose absence is the trigger of his little storytelling. The anecdotalist's act of memory is generative, critical, and cautionary: his implication is always let us remember together, take it to heart, see the bigger picture. The anecdotalist is therefore necessarily a deliberately cryptic teacher; he knows that what he wants he can't achieve alone; his largest hope is to engender an engaged readership whose cohesion will lie in a common commitment to a social project and the sustaining of life therein.

So here's the little story that I promised at the beginning as it was originally told by Wallace Stevens:

> Anecdote of the Jar
>
> I placed a jar in Tennessee,
> And round it was, upon a hill.
> It made the slovenly wilderness
> Surround that hill.
>
> The wilderness rose up to it,
> And sprawled around, no longer wild.
> The jar was round upon the ground
> And tall and of a port in air.
>
> It took dominion everywhere.
> The jar was gray and bare.
> It did not give of bird or bush,
> Like nothing else in Tennessee.

The advantage of beginning with this odd little genre of anecdotal lyric in the practice of Wallace Stevens is that we are forced at the outset into confronting the inadequacy of the modernist literary theory of aesthetic autonomy (inadequate but possessed of many more than nine lives) and its corollary critical stance of trying to situate and constrain all commentary within the text's formal boundaries. In its own most deeply felt metaphor, the classic formalist reading featured in Anglo-American New Criticism is "close" reading—a desire for textual intimacy whose logic implies the end of reading in self-effacement, all the while, against its logic, elaborating itself in complex performances more complex, say its detractors, than the text being read. The American New Criticism, whose death has been periodically announced ever since the late 1950s, remains in force as the basis (what goes without saying) of undergraduate literary pedagogy, so that, having passed into the realm of common sense, it has the ideological effect in the United States of sustaining, under conditions of mass higher education, the romantic cult of genius by dispossessing middle-class readers of their active participation in the shaping of a culture and a society "of and for the people." The New Criticism strips those readers of their right to think of themselves as culturally central storytellers: an extraordinary irony for a critical method whose initial effect was entirely democratic—to make the reading of classics available to all, even to those of us whose early cultural formation did not equip us to read Shakespeare and Milton—but a predictable irony, in retrospect, when we remember that new critical reading at the same time defined and valued itself as secondary reading of explication. So while the New Criticism taught us to read, it simultaneously taught us how to subordinate our reading powers and humble ourselves before the "creative" authority of an ontologically superior primary writing. (The bibliographical convention of distinguishing between primary and secondary texts is here politically symptomatic.)

As a metaliterary phenomenon, anecdotal form is a representation of radical aesthetic unself-sufficiency: at the very moment of formal engagement, which cryptically crafted, riddle-like anecdotes (like this one of Wallace Stevens) force us into with all possible zeal for close reading, we are led beyond the assumptions of formalism. The anecdotal lyric is (at best) a marginal and eccentric literary form, but its eccentricity may bring all the way forward what is most typical about literary form—its resistance to formalist desire for closure: there is always something outside the text. The title of Stevens's poem and the first line make the point: "I placed a jar in Tennessee," but this is not an anecdote about a jar: it is an anecdote of *the* jar. However stylized for the purposes of anecdotal point making, however absurd if thought about through the norms of realism, the act described in the first line must nevertheless be imagined *as if* it were existentially typical. The little action of this little story begins when someone places a single object some place, but the poem asks us in its title to conceive of the particular act and the particular object placed by this particular "I" as an expressive instance of what can't be perceived and what isn't and can't be directly written about: a generic act, a generic object, a generic "I." Moreover, this is an anecdote that does not, apparently, centrally involve the human actor who places the jar and without whom presumably the jar could not be placed (since jars cannot place themselves). This is an anecdote about the jar itself, not jar placing: a fragment from the jar's biography. The larger narrative of which this poem is an unpublished item has to do with the jar's ideal form, its *jarness* not its *thisness*. Apparently the ideal character of the jar is the larger narrative text of which this specific jar that was placed in Tennessee is an example. In this light, the preposition in the title ("of") means not "about" but something like "belonging to," as if the jar could speak, as if the poem were really about a story that a jar might tell about itself.

But if we learn anything from Plato about ideal things we learn that there is no time in them or for them: ideal entities are part of no story. In anecdote, however, we must have narrative and the temporal dimension, and this specific anecdote of Stevens does not disappoint us: it unfolds initially as the description of an action and the effects or consequences of that action—not as the description of a jar (and not as *the consequences of a jar*: absurd phrasing for an absurd but importantly mystifying idea). The connection of jar and human subject is unavoidable in Stevens's poem (for a while); this is a poem (or so it appears in the first line) about the consequences of jar placing. The devout formalist critic can notice but not respond (as a formalist) to questions of an economic sort that begin to press upon him at this point; nothing would seem to be further from the literary texture of this poem's mode and content. Can the consequences of jars be conceived apart from the intentional human process which produces and manipulates them? Puts them, for example, on hills in Tennessee? How can any inert product of human labor ever be spoken of as having in itself consequences, as if the thing had intentions of its own? These questions are precisely questions that the poem forces us to ask because the "I" who does the initial act of placing gets lost after the first line. The human actor becomes a panoramic onlooker, a distant voice, an innocent bystander: the jar takes on, somehow, an intentional life of its own: "I placed" but "It made" and "It took" and "It did not give." The jar did it. This jar, and the character of being possessed by any jar, are necessarily implicated with human activity, yet that fact is what is shunted aside after this poem's first line. The formalist critic, forced to talk about content, and Stevens's form gives him no choice, will quickly move to the humanist's favorite sort of generalization. Human action will be essentialized: with all specific determinants of history drained off, the activity of jar placing becomes an archetypal human act, and the anecdote/parable/fable called "Anecdote of the Jar" concerns the consequences of the type of human activity (what shall it be called?) best particularized and named by the qualities possessed by a jar, and not just any jar but the sort signaled by the modifications of grayness and bareness. This story is getting curiouser and curiouser: a human act that is like a gray, bare jar?

The act of jar placing is contextualized, almost literally—it is surrounded by wilderness—and its consequences are illuminated by the natural setting within which the act is said to take place. At the point in our formalist moment at which we notice *that,* we are tempted to step outside the aesthetic monad of the single, isolated text and step into Northrop Frye's decisively postulated closed literary universe of modes and mythoi, a synchronic totality of ever-present literary forms. We quickly translate "jar" and "wilderness" into the generative structural binary of art and nature always present to the pastoral mode, though this move from the closed, atemporal world of the isolated text to the closed, atemporal world of the autonomous literary universe will be made with a clean conscience only if the critic making that jump can ignore the word "Tennessee": a political designation, out of the lexicon of sovereignty, social order placed in the wild. Jar placing, then, is a second placing and a second ordering whose action is an echo and repetition of a politically original act of state placing? Our formalism, which couldn't help but also be a humanism, now seems poised to serve the historicist interests of American studies.

It's hard to get through our formalist moment to whatever it is that is always outside the text: the textual woods is so lovely, dark and deep. Wanting to get on with it, see the thing whole, we find it hard to get out of the first stanza. The transpositions come easily, maybe too easily: jar vs. wilderness, as art vs. nature, as culture vs. nature. But a *slovenly* nature? This eye-catching and provocative little breakdown in decorum, firmly foregrounded by the only significant metrical substitution in the poem, sends us off into etymological research (Stevens was mad for etymologies) where we find not only what we expect ("untidy especially in dress or person, largely slipshod") but, also, in close company, *sloven,* a noun in Flemish signifying a woman of low character; in adjectival form, "uncultivated, undeveloped" (in a social as well as agricultural sense). So: culture vs. nature as masculine vs. feminine? Mother Nature as a low-class slut? Is *that* somehow being said in this poem? We'd better look harder at point of view: mainly panoramic, yes, but at two crucial spots limited. In the first stanza, we see the world for a moment according to a jar, refusing to keep its proud sense of its own well-formed self to itself, smugly taking itself as the distributing point of order and sole topographical coordinate; we see wilderness forced out of itself into order: "It made the slovenly wilderness / Surround that hill"; and in the third and last stanza we experience the point of view of the wilderness in the sense that the panoramic speaker takes the side of the wilderness. An old point of controversy about this poem—is Stevens *for* art or *for* nature?—disappears when we note that he lets nature get the last word in by characterizing the autonomous jar of art, at the end of the poem, as an absence of nature. Nature: maternal, creative, pliant; the jar: a receptacle that doesn't receive and from which nothing emerges—inflexible, hard, and possessed by a classic case of womb envy. "It did not give of bird or bush, / Like nothing else in Tennessee."

Formalists must all sooner or later come to the grievous conclusion about

"Anecdote of the Jar" that the aged Ezra Pound came to about his *Cantos:* it will not cohere. And things only get worse: the imposing jar is also a "port" (haven? gate? but for whom?). The original structural opposition of "jar" and "wilderness," an opposition of nouns as substances, modulates into an opposition of verbs or actions: jars "take," the wilderness "gives." Jars take power—"dominion" (supreme authority, sovereignty, absolute ownership). Who is responsible for this power? Certainly not "I"; the jar did it. No longer can we avoid the question of tone; the postulate of the literary universe will not help us now, no amount of knowledge—not even Frye's—about literary structure will help us here to hear. Structuralists, by definition, cannot attend to nonrepeatable textures of voice; structuralists, by definition, are tone-deaf. So what are we to make of the reiterated sounds of jar music, in the major key of "round"? A whole lot of "round" for such a short poem: surround, around, round (twice), ground. "Round": an insidiously invasive sound which evokes at this poem's aural level all of the big thematic points condensed in the key word of the poem: "dominion." Dominion "everywhere"—"everywhere"/"air"/"bare"—this triplet, in a poem otherwise devoid of rhyme, is unavoidable to the ear: a saturating totality, a faceless totality of authority. The jar is into every damn thing. In the world according to the jar, this aural imperialist, there is barely, just barely, one letter's worth of ground: mainly, in this world, there is "g-round." This madly incisive and potentially scary jabberwockian sense is the decisive entry to the poet's panoramic point of view, his presiding tonality: detached, above it all, neither for jars nor for nature, he writes in playful self-possession (whatever else you can say about him he's certainly not frightened of anything) this line, best read in the manner of W. C. Fields: "The jar was round upon the ground."

Northrop Frye's structuralist postulate of a literary universe of forms, always and simultaneously present to literary choice, encourages us to see Stevens's poem as a variant of traditional pastoral, and Stevens himself as on the side of nature and spontaneity (against art, culture, and systematic literariness). But the key to interpretation is not really *in* the genre that he's working with. It's in the peculiar, particular, and surprising tonal textures—in the mockery of the jar on its own aural terms ("round" being the sound which echoes the jar's essential formal property), in the individual talent over whom no tradition takes dominion. Having come to that conclusion, however, we are not much closer to answering the most pressing question of form that this poem poses: what, really, is this an anecdote of, what cautionary tale is embedded in the last line ("Like nothing else in Tennessee"), which is beginning to sound more and more like a finger-wagging warning to all us actual and would-be jar placers. If the tonal posture of this poem could not possibly be predicted, no matter how much we know about the binary oppositions of pastoral poetry, if this vocal feature seems original with this poet's handling of the genre, then maybe we need to look more deeply into this poet. And suddenly the next interpretive move virtually presents itself to us as our most enticing option yet. It seems so necessary: what is the place of "Anecdote of the Jar" within Stevens's corpus, the literary universe that inheres peculiarly in his writings taken as a totality? Not as texts written over a period of years but as texts present to one another as if they had been written all at once, in a single expressive act, bearing the poet's vision as if that vision were somehow wholly and always present to its constitutive texts, as their shaping presence.

"Anecdote of the Jar" has two contexts in Stevens's corpus. In the first, its occasion of publication, in Harriet Monroe's *Poetry*, in 1919, the poem appeared as part of an ensemble, under a title expressive of Stevens's early self-conscious decadence: "Pecksniffiana." After the original ensemble of fourteen poems was accepted, but not yet published, Stevens made several substitutions: one of them was "Anecdote of the Jar," and another he calls a "trifle" whose title, "The Indigo Glass in the Grass," will make us hear once again the aural joke "The jar was round upon the ground." In "Anecdote of the Jar" Stevens's self-deprecating decadent theory of the poem as "trifle," as his inconsequential toy (Peck's bad boy as self-ironic aesthete?) reaches through itself, in trifling play, to something more than play. The odd harmony of the Pecksniffiana ensemble consists of a blending of the tones of playfulness and dead seriousness—a blend that "Anecdote of the Jar," better than any poem in the ensemble, perfectly concentrates. In the poetic corpus as a whole, the other context or occasion, Stevens's jar poem joins several other early poems with the formal term "anecdote" as part of their title, and, then, in his middle and later years, joins a continuing and troubled meditative strain present to virtually everything that he wrote. In this context "Anecdote of the Jar" is something like a microcosm in which jars find essential kinship with various artifacts like glasses, bowls, poetic images, thought itself, even poems, and with large conceptions, in his middle and later career, of the "hero" and "major man": all various forms and effects of systematic endeavor; all the creation of structure, systems, reasons; all effects—in a word ambivalently dear to him—of "abstraction." But:

> It was when I said,
> "There is no such thing as the truth,"
> That the grapes seemed fatter.
> The fox ran out of his hole.

It is posed and it is posed
But in nature it merely grows.

. . .

You must become an ignorant man again
And see the sun again with an ignorant eye. . . .

. . .

How clean the sun when seen in its idea,
Washed in the remotest cleanliness of a heaven
That has expelled us and our images. . . .[2]

That last ellipsis is not mine; it belongs most originally to Wallace Stevens: a subtle signifier of awe, what motivates the words preceding it but what can't be said in words, imaged, or conceived. The ellipsis: not words left out, but words impossible. In 1913, in the midst of modernist revolution in poetry and philosophy, Josiah Royce replayed George Santayana's attack on Whitman as a poet of barbarism by characterizing this yearning for pure perception as a sign of the modernist times: perception as a moment of consciousness utterly final, with perceiver and perceived unified in an isolated fulfillment before all community and all conversation.[3] This unspeakable moment represented by the ellipsis, this radical desire for the first perception, prior to reason, would wipe out our history and our tradition ("us and our images"): perception, the image, the attack on reason, and the interest in the primitive are all code terms for the literary and artistic modernisms whose solidarity consists in the hatred of what sociologists call modernization. Santayana's word, "barbarism," is fair as far as it goes. What it does not do justice to is the modernist's nostalgia for the barbarous, his feeling of being out of place ("You must become an ignorant man again"): his willingness to suspend social relations, not because he's antisocial but because the society he finds himself in seems to have designs upon his health.

Jars are metonyms of modernization: they get in the way, they mediate. Jars are like bowls: cold, a cold porcelain, low and round . . . a bowl brilliant in its clarity. The day becomes a bowl of white, the world becomes a world of white.[4] Jars and bowls have centers because they are the products of rationalists, those fanciers of square hats. We want so much more than that; the imperfect is our paradise:

It was when the trees were leafless first in November
And their blackness became apparent, that one first
Knew the eccentric to be the base of design.[5]

The "eccentric," or uncentered, as subversive foundation of "design" understood as intention without prior conception, purpose, plan, project, scheme, plot: intention somehow unintended. The eccentric, or uncentered, as also the subversive foundation of "design" understood as structure (shape, pattern) without classic structurality—structure somehow unstructured yet still structured. The eccentric is the base of *design*. Design, from the Latin *designare,* and *signare* from *signum* (a mark or sign): eccentric signs would be signs unplotted, surprising. Eccentric design would resolve the greatest of antinomies because it would be both necessary and spontaneous; a form of determination, yet free. Jars—they're not that kind of design, and what's more they seem to have designs upon power. They take dominion, they can even make something as unmanageable as a wilderness shape up, imitate their structural roundedness. A jar can make a wilderness surround itself; a jar can make the very ground into its mirror. Jars are humorless narcissists who think they are ungrounded. And they are involved in a secret, undercover narrative (a "plot"): What is it?

To move, as I just have, from the single poem as closed, isolate, verbal system, a world unto itself, to the poem as microcosmic fragment of a poetic corpus, is to move, in a sense, not at all: for the corpus so conceived, as a synchronic whole, is likewise closed and isolate. And to invoke an agent called "the poet" as creator of a corpus is to invoke a subject who always contained and expressed it all, so that those temporal distinctions of career ("early," "middle," and "late") are truly gratuitous—they make no difference. Not even "career," in this interpretive context, makes much sense since the term suggests a determinate act of will to shape a life, to set an ordered narrative in motion and thereby bring your life into control (into art) by making it a story. To so read either the single poem or the corpus, as I have, is to read *for* (look for, read on behalf of, from the perspective of) self-sufficient system. To invoke "the poet" in this context is not to invoke a human being who needs to be differentiated by categories of, say, class, or gender, or race (or all three) and who would need to be historically located; it is to invoke an agent whose function is to trigger a verbal agency which, once triggered, mysteriously operates itself as a rule-bound machine. In either instance, single poem or corpus, the verbal system must be treated as if it were its own magnificent cause of being. "The poet" so invoked as an originator is a necessary fiction (we have to invoke an individual at some point), yet at some other level he must be real. ("Wallace Stevens" after all is the name of a person who was born, went to Harvard, liked his mother better than his father, married, worked for an insurance company and loved it, often took vacations to Florida alone, listened to the Saturday afternoon broadcasts from the Metropolitan Opera House, did not get divorced, made a lot of money, died of cancer, and maybe converted on his deathbed if you want to believe the nuns who attended him at the end, which I do.) Wallace Stevens, "the poet," is not subject to those modifications. For devout critics of system—all structuralists by deed if not by name—he is a verbal operator who functions in an ideal space.

But to pose the question about narratives, secret or otherwise, as I have throughout, is to move to history, or at least to be poised (or seem to be poised) at the brink of concerted historical reading. Even the devoutest formalist critic cheats; history makes them do it. I'm not devout; I've cheated two or three times to this point, I'm not quite sure how many, contaminating formal purity by mentioning Tennessee and American studies, and it could have been worse. I held back mentioning that Tennessee is an englishing of a Cherokee place name—a Cherokee village named Tanasi. And no use getting too sentimental about Indians and the wilderness. It was here first, apparently, I mean the wilderness, then the Indians, who "our forefathers" (whose forefathers?) slaughtered. Tennessee eventually took dominion over Tanasi, but the Indians did a little political placing of their own; they engaged frequently in their own territorial wars with considerable intensity. They set their cultures in the wilderness first; then we placed ours over theirs: we supplanted them, plowed them under. Jar placing, then, is a third-order placing? A metonymic representation of a repetitive action of domination, hard to separate from the course of American history?

I also brought in Josiah Royce and what he thought of modernism—he didn't like it but he knew what it was—and I wrote down dates, 1913, when Royce published the statements I alluded to, and 1919, when Stevens published "Anecdote of the Jar." Nineteen-nineteen becomes a readable fact for interpretation within the historical horizon of avant-garde modernist upheaval; that is the poem's immediate cultural context; its date of publication makes that context surround the poem. "Tennessee" is more difficult. It is surely a term for interpretation but one that resists formalist reading, though not altogether if we can count, as "reading," formalist forgetting ("jarring") of its ground, a covering of the ground not unlike the way Tennessee covers up Tanasi. "Tennessee" looks like a determinate historical and political term in Stevens's poem, looks like an unambiguous invitation to do the work of historicizing this poem, but probably "gap" is better than "term." What are the limits of the historical horizon within which we would situate "Tennessee"? How far back does it go? To the Cherokee Indians? How far forward? Maybe all the way to Vietnam.

In its immediate literary culture Stevens's critique of artifice joins the general critique, at the center of the imagist movement and polemically (and entrepreneurially) urged in the criticism of Ezra Pound, of what was passing for "literature." It was a critique not of literature *tout court* but of official poetic practice in the 1890s and early years of this century, when those who would become the chief modernists were growing up and beginning to read what was being honored as "contemporary" poetry—an exercise, or so it seemed to Pound, Frost, and others, in ever-increasing poetic vagueness inversely proportioned to the ever-increasing particularity (often of a harsh sort) in the language of realist fiction; frightened literariness, withdrawal into genteel hermitage. As Frost tirelessly pointed out, it was a language that never was, except in books: real people, at any rate—Frost meant those not born to high cultural privilege—don't talk *that* way. In this light, poetic modernism is round two of English romanticism, especially in its Wordsworthian phase. Pound's revisions of Yeats's early poems are in the mode of Wordsworth's legendary attack on Thomas Gray in the preface to *Lyrical Ballads,* as is Stevens's late meditation in *Notes toward a Supreme Fiction,* when he evokes and then one-ups Wordsworth's attack on Gray's use of archaic language. Stevens writes, "the sun must bear no name," not even the name "sun," which is just as artificial as "Phoebus"—the mythological object of Wordsworth's literary and social-revolutionary scorn. The sun must simply be, let be, "in the difficulty of what it is to be." Words are like jars: Shelley thought the truth to be imageless;[6] Stevens, immoralist of modernist lyric, appeared to think it altogether silent.

Wordsworth's critique of Gray is part of the larger romantic injunction: to "strip the evil of familiarity" from the world.[7] Not to make it strange but to see the strangeness there: a radically realist epistemological project replayed in the theoretical premises of imagism by Pound and T. E. Hulme. ("Could reality come into direct contact with sense and consciousness, art would be useless," Hulme wrote, "or rather we should all be artists."[8] Or as Pound urged the project of the image: "Direct treatment of the 'thing,' whether subjective or objective."[9]) A radically realist project, epistemologically, and an ethical and political project as well. Wordsworth's attack, like Frost's later on mannered language, is also an attack on the manners (social and poetic) of a class. Wordsworth argues, on behalf of a newly emergent class (of which Frost may be the great American modernist representative), that the poetry of privilege speaks nothing like the language spoken by real men in a state of nature, who work farms, or the language of the new urban worker sunk into "savage torpor" by the self-alienating nature of his labor. The poetry of privilege—Frost is especially strong on this point— does not *speak;* it has no aural referent in the various worlds of communication (not even in the world of the privileged). Stevens, who had none of Frost's vocal sentiments, makes critical allusion to the issue by surrounding the pompous and empty "port" (comportment, carriage, syntax) of jar-speak ("of a port in air") with plain-speaking syntax ("I placed a jar in Tennessee"). A new poetry would presumably clear our consciousness—"wash" it "clean" of artifice and a contaminating social discourse and bring us into contact with (help us to see again, re-cognize) a social outside, a "ground" ruled and exploited by the class represented by Gray, the social outside now seen in an act of sympathy which a new poetry would encourage. The social and socialist implications of Wordsworth's theory of the poet (an instigator of radical community, he "binds together by passion and knowledge the vast empire of human society, as it is spread over the whole earth"; he does "not write for poets alone, but for men"),[10] these implications were drawn out by Shelley: "The great secret of morals is love; or a going out of our own nature, and an identification of ourselves with [a] person not our own. A man, to be greatly good, must imagine intensely and comprehensively; he must put himself in the place of another and of many others."[11] As a figure for the poetry opposed (not for the same reasons and on behalf of different goals) by Wordsworth, Frost, and Pound, the jar shows kinship with the letter that kills (jars do not "give of bird or bush"). Jars are representations not of the spirit of love but of the spirit of abstraction. In the romantic lexicon, from Wordsworth to Stevens, "artifice" and "abstraction" are synonyms and key coded words in a political anecdote of struggle.

Stevens's is an American jar, plain, bare, and gray, not Thomas Gray-like and not richly worked and elaborated, like Keats's Grecian urn, but something of a commentary on Keats's most famous ode and on Keats himself: commentary not in anxiety and competitiveness but in self-definition and political critique very close to home. This is a jar that provokes in Stevens no Keatsian desire for the death of identification and therefore no Keatsian pulling back from self-extinguishment, no Keatsian shock of awareness that the urn's life is dead life, no need to say "cold pastoral." And Stevens's jar is not tempting for another reason. It represents nothing like Keats's double-edged Western cultural heritage maybe worth being embarrassed by because maybe (for Keats) worth recuperating, sustaining, being engaged with. Nor is Stevens replaying Henry James's criticism of American culture as too thin to support really "fine" writing. Stevens's biographical formation is close to that of Keats, but its American ground kept him from wishing to die out of his unprivileged class into the class of a precapitalist landed aristocracy (there is no American memory for this) which bears the burden of tradition. Keats's desire to die, reread from Stevens's perspective, is a desire for social death and rebirth: to become not a sod or a nightingale but a gentleman.

Stevens's poem, in this double focus of literary and social history, is an American poem which at once works as a metapoem, an anecdote of the wider cultural story of romantic and early-modernist poetics, an antipoetics urging a literature against official literature, and a critical evaluation of the wider story. The literary criticism which Stevens called "Anecdote of the Jar" is a criticism not of Grecian urns and Thomas Gray's poetry but of plain old democratic American jars which he insists we see as figuring a work of oppression that cannot be explained in classic European terms of class relations (in classic Marxist terms). Wordsworth and Keats had the griefs and consolations of English society at a moment of decisive social change—they might have said: "The jar is them." Stevens, who has some of Wordsworth's and Frost's feeling for ordinary people, who celebrated ignorance in his poems as the pure access to the real, who once said of himself, in self-congratulation, that he had been working like an immigrant Italian,[12] who never wanted to write in the language of real men and, like Shelley, never did, has no sentimentality for democratic myths. He forces us to say: "The jar is us."

Had Wallace Stevens lived through our Vietnam period he might have had the right answer to the question posed by Norman Mailer in 1967: *Why Are We in Vietnam?* Had he forgotten what he knew, long before our military intervention in Southeast Asia, he would have been (had he lived so long) reminded by Michael Herr who at the end of his book *Dispatches* (1970) wrote: "Vietnam Vietnam Vietnam, we've all been there." Herr maybe in part knew what he knew because he had read Stevens, who taught him about where we've all been, all along: "Once it was all locked in place, Khe Sanh became like the planted jar in Wallace Stevens's poem. It took dominion everywhere."[13] Herr's perversely perfect mixed metaphor of the "planted jar," if it might have struck Stevens as an incisive reading of his poem, might also have awakened in him an obscure memory of one of the powerful philosophical presences of his Harvard days, William James, writing out of the bitterness of his political awakening, writing on 1 March 1899 in the *Boston Transcript* against our first imperial incursion in the Orient: "We are destroying down to the root every germ of a healthy national life in these unfortunate people. . . . We must sow our ideals, plant our order, impose our God."[14] James might have ended his letter: "The Philippines the Philippines the Philippines, we've all been there."

The hypothetical "ifs" and subjunctive "mights" which fairly pepper my preceding paragraph may represent something like the lure of bad-faith political criticism: the desire for objective laws of historical force to offer themselves to the reader who then need only record them as the true causes of texts like "Anecdote of the Jar" and *Dispatches.* James and Stevens, of course, did not read Herr; Herr did read Stevens, but I see no reason to think that he read James.

Herr, Stevens, and James can be constellated as a single discursive body only because I've read them in a certain way; I name the constellation, I give it a shape: "can be constellated," a deluded construction; its passivity obscures what goes on in the act of interpretation. So my hypotheticals and subjunctives may be taken in another way, as an indication of where we always stand in the interpretive act: not on the realist's terra firma but in active ideological contest to shape our culture's sense of history. I offer Herr, Stevens, and James (in that order, reading backward, which is always the way reading takes place: through our cultural formation) as three voices from a tradition of American anti-imperialist writing (a unified cultural practice) that cuts through the boundaries of philosophy, poetry, and journalism, a discourse of political criticism.

Stevens's poem is an anecdote of that political story, but to reach for American anti-imperialism and isolationism in the first two decades of this century, when he was coming of age as a writer, as the political cause of his poem is absurd, yet no more absurd perhaps than to reach for objective laws of historical influence. In either instance what is longed for is direct reflection of political reality in a literary text, a vulgar form of historicism, periodically practiced in Marxist circles (though hardly limited to those), in which the "time" of the literary text is treated as one and the same with political "time," as if the episode in the Philippines gave rise to the poem. The varieties of vulgar formalism are more useful; they at least put the stress where it belongs, on the strange differences; it is easier to believe in literary causalities of literary texts, as if literature were self-originating. For the text in question, these causalities might be: Stevens's verbal play, the generic history of pastoral, the inner imperatives of Stevens's unfolding corpus, the literary-historical forces of romanticism, the first surge of modernist literary polemic, manifesto, and experiment (the ethical imperative of imagism). As an "effect" of such "causes," "Anecdote of the Jar" partakes of the time of literature whose integrity seems impervious to "outside" pressures. But it isn't: cultural practices are neither autonomous nor homogeneous. With all differences respected, they sometimes are made to stand in unity by acts of reading, acts of retelling or cultural constellating like Herr's remembering of Stevens in Vietnam, like my remembering of Herr's and James's anti-imperialist efforts; like my placing of Stevens as a writer "between" James and Herr and "between" our first intervention in Cuba, 21 April 1898, and our second intervention in Cuba, 21 April 1961. The storyteller's most powerful effect comes when he convinces us that what is particular, integrated, and different in a cultural practice (like the writing of rarefied high-modernist poetry) is part of a cultural plot that makes coherent sense of all cultural practices as a totality: not a totality that is there, waiting for us to acknowledge its presence, but a totality fashioned when the storyteller convinces us to see it his way.

It would have been possible to speak, as I have not yet spoken, of the intersection of literary causes and Stevens's personal social history: his literary self-consciousness as a middle-class American male who faced economic imperatives that his aristocratic European and English predecessors did not have to face. It would have been possible to link his sexual pun on "slovenly nature" and his phallic parody of the jar—it may look like a port but nothing enters, it receives nothing—with his sexual self-consciousness, the suspicion which his father encouraged that real men don't write poems. Those are in fact the sorts of possibilities that I pursue in the third section of *Ariel and the Police*,[15] "Writing after Hours," in an effort to redeem the personal subject of Wallace Stevens for history by thinking about his poems as literary actions. In the course of pursuing that effort I write small critiques of new historicism, neopragmatism, and essentialist feminism, but I've written critically at no one isolable place on literary Marxism because I intend the book as a whole to be a dialogue with Marxism precisely on the issue of the personal subject which it dismisses by calling a bourgeois illusion.[16] Like other contemporary styles of criticism, Marxism has a way of jarring the subject out of its historical orbit: either by ignoring it or by merging it much too soon with a social text—obliterating the subject by making it immediately typical. Contemporary literary Marxism is a representation of the broad range of contemporary critical theory whose origins in France and the United States constitute the triumph of structuralism over Sartre's desire to turn Marxist thought to actual individuals acting in history. Sartre's *Search for a Method*, the road not taken in contemporary theory, was simply routed by the voracious Abstractionism put into vogue by Lévi-Strauss and Frye—and still with us. Literary Marxists, like other contemporary theorists, will have virtually nothing to do with biography—impatient for the secret plot, they get there too quickly. I think we most believe in plots when they are hard to see; and a conspiracy that includes James, Foucault, and Stevens had better be hard to see.

Contemporary styles of literary theory and practice resemble nothing so much as Don DeLillo's funny anecdotal personification (in *Ratner's Star*) of a terrible fear not really separable from the modernist dream. Consider DeLillo's "Supreme Abstract Commander": one Chester Greylag Dent, "unaffiliated and stateless," who lives in a nuclear-powered submarine, thirty-five thousand feet under the sea ("just idling there in the dark and cold . . . the quietest place on earth") attended by a eunuch who talks of an international cartel interested in "abstract economic power" and named ACRONYM (a "combination of letters formed to represent the idea of a combination of letters"); who is so old as to verge on transparency; who has been awarded a Nobel Prize in literature for his books on mathematics and logic, "handblocked in a style best described as undiscourageably diffuse"; who says in response to the question, What do you do? "I think of myself as the Supreme Abstract Commander. That's what I do"; who considers us mortals "not as a collection of races and nationalities but as a group that shows the same taxonomic classification, that of Earth-planet extant"; who never laughs but instead, when moved to such spontaneous expression, says, "Hilarious," or "Extremely mirth-provoking"—Chester Greylag Dent, who believes that the reason that he has been referred to "more than a few times as the greatest man in the world" has to do with "the life choice I've made. To suspend myself in the ocean zone of perpetual darkness. To inhabit an environment composed almost solely of tiny sightless feeble-minded creatures palpitating in the ooze"; who when asked about his shawls says he buys them from "this man in Sausalito."[17]

When he wants to, DeLillo can evoke the horrors of abstraction, not impotently removed, but actively engaged in a deadly work of the sort which Herr describes in the work of MACV (an acronym representing Military Assistance Command, Vietnam), or in the cartographic work of reinscribing Vietnam as a military arena "which made for clear communication, at least among members of the Mission and the many components of . . . the fabulous MACV." And "fabulous" is just right: of a fable, not Vietnamese, generating and imposing a fable not Vietnamese: "Since most of the journalism from the war was framed in that language [MACV, I Corps, II Corps, DMZ] it would be as impossible to know what Vietnam looked like from reading most newspaper stories as it would be to know how it smelled." Like Stevens's and like DeLillo's, Herr's writing is a counterdiscourse, working to undermine discourses of abstraction and domination—Supreme Abstract Commanders, whether they are called jars, the ruling class, Khe Sanh, or MACV, or imperialism. These counterdiscourses imply (rarely state) their deepest alternative values in desires for particularity; in the way it looked and smelled; in little scraps of dialogue about "this man in Sausalito." For life in the small things, "birds and bushes," which ought to be but are not invulnerable to imperial imposition.[18]

The object of DeLillo's unmasking humor is captured in other stories which are not funny, told with great penetration by William James and Michel Foucault in reaction to their nightmare of system and discipline: the horrific accompaniments of what sociologists call modernization. Foucault's disciplinary society and James's systematic life are the outcomes of a historical process and are twin accounts insofar as they take the price of modernity to be the loss of self-determination in the normalizing actions of institutional life that James, long before Foucault, excoriated for "branding, licensing and degree-giving, authorizing and appointing, and in general regulating and administering by system the lives of human beings."[19] James, writing before the paranoid age of surveillance and computer information banks, had his hopes: "I am against all bigness and greatness in all their forms, and with the invisible molecular forces that work from individual to individual, stealing in through the crannies of the world like so many soft rootlets, or like the capillary oozing of water, and yet rending the hardest monuments of man's pride, if you give them time."[20] James believed that somehow the Supreme Abstract Commanders would lose and that history would finally come around to putting the individual on top. In this light, contemporary styles of literary theory, including Marxism, are part of the problem, not—as in their self-description—part of the solution; cultural effects of the technology of modernization, literary normalizations of individuality via the impositions of structure, myth, textuality, essentialized gender and class relations, the mode of production. They are expressions of system and discipline, not their critique: destructions of the subject.

Foucault is not sanguine about the survival of the individual. Discipline insidiously invades the ground of individuality in order to master it. Discipline takes us all through the gate of modernization, into safe port, where our individuality is studied so much the better to be controlled. Foucault's antidote is writing: not as a space for the preservation of identity and the assertion of voice, but as a labyrinth into which he can escape, to "lose myself," and, there, in the labyrinth, never have to be a self (a self is a dangerous thing to be)—write yourself off, as it were, "write in order to have no face." Give no target to discipline: "Do not ask who I am and do not ask me to remain the same: leave it to our bureaucrats and our police to see that our papers are in order. At least spare us their morality when we write."[21] If for James "individuality" translates into a philosophical positive—a given of liberalism—a holdout in freedom and the site of the personal and of "full ideality,"[22] then for Foucault undisciplined individuality may be precisely the unintended effect of a system which would produce individuality as an object of its knowledge and power (the disciplinary appropriation of biography), but which instead, and ironically, inside its safe, normalized subject, instigates the move to the underground where a deviant selfhood may nurture sullen counterschemes of resistance and revolution.

Stevens inhabits the world of James and Foucault; he is wary of system and surveillance and of the police in all their contemporary and protean guises. But Prospero-like he called upon his Ariel and Ariel rarely failed to respond, sometimes bearing unexpected gifts. After the jars, glasses, bowls, designs of various sorts, and images, after the (male) hero and (male) major man—all of them "must be abstract"—comes the fat girl. Who is she? No "central man" who, "cold and numbered," "sums us up," no canonical men ("men but artificial men"), "admired by all men"—those major men, they may be seated in cafés, but we will never see them. Instead we will see the "dish of country cheese / And a pineapple on the table." If we're lucky, we'll hear someone—could it possibly be the major man?—talk about "this man in Sausalito" who makes beautiful shawls. Coming late, after all his anecdotal portraits, so allegorical in intent,[23] the fat girl seems real: not a literary device, not what anyone wants her to be—she's a fulfillment that can be wished for, as Stevens wishes for her in some of the most moving of his lyric lines, but what his writing itself cannot grant.

In the key verbs of "Anecdote of the Jar," the fat girl gives but she cannot be taken. Refusing to show herself in anecdotal lyric, she awaits, instead, the purer romantic lyricist in his mood of praise. In "Anecdote of the Jar" Stevens tells a story whose most cryptically encoded lesson is the necessity of forsaking action, and the genre of action—storytelling—in favor of aesthesis, praise's ultimate awestruck medium. (Conjure if you can your grandparents' cultural difference.) Stevens's story against story represents a longing for lyric itself and its imperative: a politics of lyricism which in James, Stevens, Herr, and Foucault amounts to a directive not to set molecular individuals into social system, not even into literary systems of narrative; not to reencode Vietnam in the coordinates of American imperial cartography. To find the fat girl is not to impose—it is to find a "moving contour," unfixed and incomplete because alive, and moving because we are moved. She appears:

> Fat girl, terrestrial, my summer, my night,
> How is it I find you in difference, see you there
> In a moving contour, a change not quite completed? . . .
> Bent over work, anxious, content, alone,
> You remain the more than natural figure. You
> Become the soft-footed phantom. . . .[24]

NOTES

1   Kenneth Burke, *A Grammar of Motives* (1945; reprint, Berkeley: University of California Press, 1969), 59–61, 323–325.
2   *The Collected Poems of Wallace Stevens* (New York: Alfred A. Knopf, 1954), 203, 198, 380–381. All citations of Stevens's poems are to this volume.

3   Josiah Royce, *The Problem of Christianity*, with a new introduction by John E. Smith (Chicago: University of Chicago Press, 1968), 244–245, 253, 273–295. George Santayana, *Interpretation of Poetry and Religion* (New York: Harper and Row, 1957), 166–216.

4   Stevens, *Collected Poems*, 193–194.

5   Ibid., 151.

6   *The Complete Poetical Works of Percy Bysshe Shelley*, ed. Thomas Hutchinson (London: Oxford University Press, 1965), 238 (*Prometheus Unbound*, 2. 4. 116).

7   Shelley, "A Defense of Poetry," in *Critical Theory since Plato*, ed. Hazard Adams (New York: Harcourt, Brace, Jovanovich, 1971), 512.

8   T. E. Hulme, "Bergson's Theory of Art," in *Critical Theory since Plato*, 779.

9   T. S. Eliot, ed., *Literary Essays of Ezra Pound* (New York: New Directions, 1968), 3.

10 Wordsworth, Preface to Second Edition of "Lyrical Ballads," in *Critical Theory since Plato*, 439, 440.

11 Shelley, "Defense of Poetry," 503.

12 Holly Stevens, ed., *Letters of Wallace Stevens* (New York: Alfred A. Knopf, 1966), 198.

13 Michael Herr, *Dispatches* (New York: Avon Books, 1978), 260, 107.

14 F. O. Matthiessen, *The James Family: A Group Biography* (New York: Alfred A. Knopf, 1961), 626.

15 Frank Lentricchia, *Ariel and the Police* (Madison: University of Wisconsin Press, 1988).

16 See Fredric Jameson's suggestive essay "Wallace Stevens," in *New Orleans Review* 11 (spring 1984), 10–19, and his methodological meditation in *The Political Unconscious: Narrative as a Socially Symbolic Act* (Ithaca: Cornell University Press, 1981), 74–102, for a powerful historicist approach both different from and sometimes opposed to mine. On Sartre's defeat in contemporary theory, see Perry Anderson, *In the Tracks of Historical Materialism* (Chicago: University of Chicago Press, 1984), chap. 2.

17 Don DeLillo, *Ratner's Star* (New York: Alfred A. Knopf, 1976), 306–307, 340–351.

18 Herr, *Dispatches*, 92–93.

19 Matthiessen, *James Family*, 633–634.

20 Ibid., 633.

21 Michel Foucault, *The Archaeology of Knowledge*, trans. from the French by A. M. Sheridan Smith (New York: Harper and Row, 1976), 17.

22 Matthiessen, *James Family*, 633.

23 Stevens, *Collected Poems*, 250–251, 334–335.

24 Ibid., 406.

7. Stevens and Keats's "To Autumn"

HELEN VENDLER

THROUGHOUT HIS LONG life as a poet, Stevens returned again and again to Keats's ode "To Autumn." The history of those returns provides a classic example of how literary materials can be reworked by a modern artist. We are accustomed to this process in modern art, especially in painting and sculpture. Gombrich has pointed out how artists reproduce, not what they see, but some amalgam of that and an antecedent pictorial schema already in their minds. For Stevens, Keats's ode offered an irresistible antecedent model; Stevens hovered over the ode repeatedly in his musings. He became, to my way of thinking, the best reader of the ode, the most subtle interpreter of its rich meanings. Our understanding of latent significance in the older poem broadens when the ode is seen refracted through Stevens's lines. At the same time we may perceive, in Stevens's departures from the ode, implicit critiques of its stance.

A modern work of art may comment on an older one in several different ways. Stevens defined poetry as an art embracing two different "poetries"—the poetry of the idea and the poetry of the words. My own work on Stevens has hitherto been chiefly a commentary on the poetry of the words, but here I turn to the poetry of the idea. Stevens helpfully remarked that the idea of God was a poetic idea; it seems from his poetry that he considered the idea of a seasonal cycle a poetic idea as well, since it embodied the natural counterpart to the poetic "exhilarations of changes," the motive for metaphor:

> You like it under the trees in autumn,
> Because everything is half dead . . .

In the same way, you were happy in spring,
With half colors of quarter-things.

The seasonal idea, though immemorially present in lyric, seems to have been mediated to Stevens through Keats, no doubt through the sonnet on the human seasons as well as through the odes. In commenting on a received aesthetic form, an artist can take various paths. He may make certain implicit "meanings" explicit; he may extrapolate certain possibilities to greater lengths; he may choose a detail, center on it, and turn it into an entire composition; he may alter the perspective from which the form is viewed; or he may view the phenomenon at a different moment in time. We are familiar with these strategies in painting, in the expansion and critique of classical forms practiced by all subsequent schools, but most noticeably for us, perhaps, in the dramatic and radical experimentation with classic forms in our own century. Stevens is modern as Cézanne is modern; he keeps the inherited shapes, is classic in his own disposition of materials, is rarely bizarre, and stays within the central tradition of Western art. Stevens's "copies" never forget their great originals; but we may see, in following Stevens's experiments with the materials of the autumn ode, how a modern originality gradually declares itself, while deliberately recalling, even into old age, the earlier master's prototype.

The presence of Keats's ode within a great many of Stevens's poems is self-evident. The single most derivative moment in Stevens is the end of "Sunday Morning;" in "Credences of Summer" and "The Auroras of Autumn" Stevens composed two "panels" to the autumn ode; and there are lesser appearances of fragments of the ode throughout Stevens's work. Anyone familiar with the poem will recognize in Stevens's verse the replication of Keats's fruits, autumnal female presence, cottage (transmuted to an American cabin), cornfields (changed to American hayfields), wind, muted or unmelodious birds, stubble plains (reduced to bare stalks or thin grass), clouds, and bees. Our recognition of such echoes is usually intermittent; but to read through Stevens's poetry with the ode "To Autumn" in mind is to be suffused by the lights that Stevens saw presiding over the trash can at the end of the world, that resting place of tradition:

. . . Above that urn two lights
Commingle, not like the commingling of sun and moon
At dawn, nor of summer-light and winter-light
In an autumn afternoon, but two immense
Reflections, whirling apart and wide away.

The end of "Sunday Morning" is a rewritten version of the close of Keats's "To Autumn"; such risk-taking in a young poet argues a deep engagement with the earlier poem. The resemblances are obvious and have been often remarked. Both poets use successive clauses of animal presence (gnats, lambs, crickets, redbreast, and swallows in Keats; deer, quail, and pigeons in Stevens); both poems close with birds in the sky (gathering swallows in Keats, flocks of pigeons in Stevens) and with the sense of sound (including a whistling bird in each); Keats's soft-dying day becomes Stevens's evening. Stevens's stance, unlike that of Keats, is the homiletic and doctrinal one inherited from religious poetry and so dear to American poets. However, Stevens, as a modern poet, offers no single doctrine but rather a choice among truths: we live either (1) in chaos, or (2) in a system of mutual dependency, or (3) in a condition of solitude, which may itself be seen as (3a) lonely ("unsponsored") or (3b) liberated ("free"), but which is in any case inescapable. The passage allowing doctrinal choices is followed by the passage on deer, quail, berries, and pigeons (those wilderness forms replacing Keats's domestic ones), in which the doctrinal options are alluded to but, in the end, left undecided. The quail utter "spontaneous" cries, and their adjective hearkens back phonemically to our "unsponsored" state; the pigeons fly in an "isolation" etymologically resembling our "island" solitude; the "chaos" of the sun recalls orthographically the "casual" flocks of pigeons. In the end, as the pigeons inscribe their transient motions in the air, their calligraphy is read (by the poet seeking significance) as elusively ambiguous, and doctrinal choice dissolves in mystery. But although metaphysical certainty remains unattainable, the truth of existence is clear. The final motion, whether or not definable as one of chaos, dependency, solitude, freedom, or unsponsoredness, is "downward to darkness." In such an ending, *be* is finale of *seem,* and death is the only certainty uninvaded by metaphysical doubt. While Keats rests in the polyphony of the creatures in their autumnal choir, Stevens (though his adoption of Keats's principal trope, enumeration, shows him as not insensible to the plenitude around him in the scene) makes his landscape depend for its significance on what it can explicitly suggest about metaphysical truth.

   With the example of Keats's beautiful implicit meanings before us, we may tend to recoil from what seems crudity in Stevens, as he speckles the visible scene with invisible queries: chaos? dependency? solitude? unsponsoredness? freedom? isolation? casualness? ambiguity? The coercion of cadence forces the innocent landscape to enact a Stevensian entropy:

                 And,
                      in the isolation of the sky,

<pre>
                    at evening,
           casual flocks of pigeons make
     Ambiguous undulations as they sink,
           downward to darkness,
                on extended wings.
</pre>

Stevens's final clause is, of course, imitated from Keats's passage on the gnats among the river sallows,

<pre>
              aloft   lives
     borne   or   as the light wind   or
              sinking   dies.
</pre>

Keats's imitation of randomness is changed by Stevens into an imitation of decline. But Keats, after writing about the gnats, went on to forbid himself such naïve stylistic equivalences:

> And full-grown lambs loud bleat from hilly bourn;
>   Hedge-crickets sing; and now with treble soft
> The red-breast whistles from a garden-croft;
>   And gathering swallows twitter in the skies.

These clauses are the source for Stevens's earlier ones (such as "Deer walk upon our mountains"), but Stevens has reversed Keats's rhetorical order. Keats writes a long clause about the gnats, then follows it with shorter ones dwindling to "hedge-crickets sing," then broadens out to end his poem. Stevens writes short clauses followed by a final long one. The result is a gain in climactic force and explicit pathos, but a loss in stoicism and discretion of statement. Keats's pathos (at its most plangent in the small gnats who mourn in a wailful choir, helpless in the light wind; less insistent but still audible in the bleating lambs; but largely absent in the whistle and twitter of the closing lines) reaches us with steadily diminishing force, in inverse relation to Keats's recognition of the independent worth of autumnal music, without reference to any dying fall. Stevens's pathos, on the other hand, is at its most evident in the closing lines. In short, Stevens has adopted Keats's manner—the population of animals, the types of clause, the diction, even the sunset landscape—without embracing Keats's essential stylistic argument against nostalgia. Nor has he imitated Keats's reticent diction and chaste rhetoric; instead, he writes with an increasing opulence of rhetorical music, and imposes explicit metaphysical dimensions on the landscape.

The imitation, however inferior to its source, argues that Keats's ode had penetrated Stevens's consciousness and imagination and was already provoking him to see the world in its light, even if he found the world insufficient without attendant metaphysics. Keats's ode continued to provide Stevens with material to the very end of his life. In the "Adagia," Stevens asks the question which the ode, among other works, must have prompted: "How has the human spirit ever survived the terrific literature with which it has had to contend?"

If, on the total evidence of Stevens's poetry, we ask how he read "To Autumn," we can isolate, for the moment neglecting the chronology of the *Collected Poems*, elements of his understanding of the ode. He thought, at first, that Keats was being evasive in the stasis of the first stanza, that he was avoiding the most repellent detail of natural process—death. (Stevens was, in taking this severe view, misinterpreting Keats, whose subject was not natural processes, but human intervention in natural process—harvest, rather than death.) In "Le Monocle de Mon Oncle" and "Sunday Morning" Stevens, insisting that everything "comes rotting back to ground" and that "this luscious and impeccable fruit of life / Falls, it appears, of its own weight to earth," writes what seem taunts directed at the changeless ripeness of Keats's first stanza:

> Is there no change of death in paradise?
> Does ripe fruit never fall? Or do the boughs
> Hang always heavy in that perfect sky?

Allowing the fruit to follow its natural trajectory, Stevens lets Autumn not only "swell the gourd" but strain it beyond its own capacity to swell until it becomes distorted in shape and its skin becomes streaked and rayed:

> It comes, it blooms, it bears its fruit and dies . . .
> Two golden gourds distended on our vines,
> Into the autumn weather, splashed with frost,
> Distorted by hale fatness, turned grotesque.
> We hang like warty squashes, streaked and rayed,
> The laughing sky will see the two of us
> Washed into rinds by rotting winter rains.

In spite of this "realist" critique of Keats's benign autumn, Stevens's poetry here is still Keatsian: no new style of language has been invented to support the new harshness of position. And the unfairness of the critique is of a piece with the "realist" position. Stevens comes much closer to the true Keatsian stance in a later poem, "On the Road Home," where plenitude is seen to stem not so much from any group of items in the landscape as from the refusal of doctrine in favor of perception, of measuring the world not by thought but by eye:

It was when I said,
"There is no such thing as the truth,"
That the grapes seemed fatter . . .

It was at that time, that the silence was largest
And longest, the night was roundest,
The fragrance of the autumn warmest,
Closest and strongest.

Whatever the objections that could be urged against the final formulation here, it is, in its near-tautology and solemn playfulness, recognizably Stevensian and not Keatsian in language. Even when metaphysically in agreement with Keats, the later Stevens speaks in his own voice.

When Stevens writes, in "The Rock," his final retraction of the "realist" view expressed in "Le Monocle," he alludes to his own dictum from the early poem ("It comes, it blooms, it bears its fruit and dies") but he quietly corrects himself by omitting the death. The leaves which cover the rock, standing for the poem as icon, "bud and bloom and bear their fruit without change." This is not written in agreement with Keats, who allowed his fruit to change, if not through death at least through harvest, winnowing, and cider-making. But neither is it written to correct him. It is written to give credence to the plenty of the world as it is preserved not on the earth but in the mind, always Stevens's chosen territory. The leaves

. . . bloom as a man loves, as he lives in love.
They bear their fruit so that the year is known,

As if its understanding was brown skin,
And honey in its pulp, the final found,
The plenty of the year and of the world.

Here, precisely because he is speaking of internal, not external fruition, Stevens is able to leave the fruit on the tree, the honey in the hive, without irritably reaching out to force them to fall and rot, or to be harvested.

No other source in poetry was so rich for Stevens as Keats's second stanza. Keats's goddess of autumn, nearer to us than pagan goddesses because, unlike them, she labors in the fields and is herself threshed by the winnowing wind, varies in her manifestations from careless girl to burdened gleaner to patient watcher—erotic in her abandon to the fume of poppies, intimate of light in her bosom friendship with the maturing sun, worn by her vigil over the last oozings. She reappears in innumerable guises in Stevens's work, but is more often than not maternal: "The mother's face, / The purpose of the poem, fills the room" ("The Auroras of Autumn"). It is probable that her maternal nature was suggested by Keats's ode (which itself borrows from Shakespeare's image of "the teeming autumn, big with rich increase, / Bearing the wanton burden of the prime, / Like widow'd wombs after their lord's decease"). Keats's season is an earth-goddess whose union with the sun makes her bear fruit; the sun, his part in procreation done, departs from the poem as the harvest begins, and the season gradually ages from the careless figure on the granary floor to the watcher over the last drops of the crushed apples. Finally, when she becomes herself the "soft-dying day," she is mourned by creatures deliberately infantine, as even full-grown sheep are represented as bleating lambs: these creatures are filial forms, children grieving for the death of the mother. Stevens, I believe, recognized these implications and brought them into explicitness.

The most beautiful modern commentary on Keats's invention of a humanized goddess of the ripe fields is Stevens's poem "The Woman in Sunshine":

> It is only that this warmth and movement are like
> The warmth and movement of a woman.
>
> It is not that there is any image in the air
> Nor the beginning nor end of a form:
>
> It is empty. But a woman in threadless gold
> Burns us with brushings of her dress
>
> And a dissociated abundance of being,
> More definite for what she is—
>
> Because she is disembodied,
> Bearing the odors of the summer fields,
>
> Confessing the taciturn and yet indifferent,
> Invisibly clear, the only love.

The "poetry of the idea" here comes from Keats, the "poetry of the words" from Stevens. The iconic "image," surrounded by words like "empty," "dissociated," "disembodied," "taciturn," "indifferent," and "invisibly clear," is wholly Stevensian, as is the rhetoric of "it is only," "it is not," and "it is empty." Stevens has taken a detail from his source—Keats's form of an autumn goddess—and has enlarged it to fill a new and more modern space. This goddess assumes various forms in Stevens, most of them beneficent. When Stevens is depressed, "mother nature" (as she is named along with a matching invention, "father nature," in

"Lulu Morose") turns either actively malevolent (curdling the kind cow's milk with lightning in "Lulu Morose") or, worse, devouring but indifferent (as in "Madame La Fleurie," where mother and father nature are conflated into one androgynous mother who feeds on her son, "a bearded queen, wicked in her dead light"). But such "corrections" of Keats's goddess are infrequent in Stevens. Rather, Stevens tends to expand Keats's figure until she becomes one of "the pure perfections of parental space, / . . . the beings of the mind / In the light-bound space of the mind." Though he acknowledges fully the fictive nature of the goddess, Stevens can move insensibly into speaking of her as if she were real, as if she were in fact all there is of reality. In this, he learned from Keats's fully formed and fully imagined relation to the autumn goddess, whom Keats begins by celebrating in tones of worship and ends by consoling in the accents of intimacy: "Think not of them, thou hast thy music too."

Keats's third stanza gave Stevens his crickets, his bare spaces, and all his autumn refrains of thinning music. But, more centrally, it invited him to participate in its debate on the value of a diminished music, and in its speculation on the relation of that music to the ampler choirs of spring. Stevens recognized, I think, that Keats's ode is spoken by one whose poetic impetus arises from a recoil at the stubble plains; the method of the ode is to adopt a reparatory fantasy whereby the barren plains are "repopulated" with fruit, flowers, wheat, and a providential goddess. But Keats subsides, at the end, into the barrenness which had first stimulated his compensatory imagination, and he leaves in the fields nothing but his poem—that autumnal thin music—where there had briefly been an imagined feast for sight and touch.

Nostalgia, so gently put aside by Keats when his goddess sighs for the songs of spring, is more vindictively suppressed by Stevens in one of the more astonishing poetic descendants of the ode. "Think not of them," says Keats to that part of himself which has looked longingly backward to the nightingales' spring songs. Stevens begins his corresponding late passage in "Puella Parvula" by telling us that "every thread of summer is at last unwoven." It is the "season of memory, / When the leaves fall like things mournful of the past." But over the dissolving wind, "the mighty imagination triumphs," saying to inner nostalgia not Keats's kind words but rather,

> Keep quiet in the heart, O wild bitch. O mind
> Gone wild, be what he tells you to be: *Puella.*
> Write *pax* across the window pane. And then
>
> Be still. The *summarium in excelsis* begins.

The taming of mind to the season is common to Keats and Stevens, but Stevens's regret, the regret of the man who rarely had the satisfactions of summer, is more bitter. What is left from romance is "the rotted rose," and the later poet must squeeze "the reddest fragrance from the stump / Of summer." The violence of the modern supervenes on the Romantic sunset.

These, as Stevens would say, are only instances. For Stevens's grandest meditation on "To Autumn" we must look to two of his long poems. "Credences of Summer" centers on the moment when "the hay, / Baked through long days, is piled in mows," the moment before the stubble plains. "The Auroras of Autumn" centers on the approach of "boreal night" after "the season changes." The light wind of Keats's soft-dying day modulates into a fiercer form: "A cold wind chills the beach." The stubble plains, at the end of "The Auroras," are metaphorically ignited to form the flares of the aurora borealis, "the lights / Like a blaze of summer straw, in winter's nick." In between "Credences" and "Auroras," radiating back to the one and forward to the other, stands Keats's ode.

The boldness of "Credences of Summer" lies in its suggestion that the perception of Keats's bees—that "warm days will never cease"—is no self-deception to be patronized, however wistfully, by the poet, but rather one of the authentic human states of being:

> . . . Fill the foliage with arrested peace,
> Joy of such permanence, right ignorance
> Of change still possible . . .
>   The utmost must be good and is
> And is our fortune and honey hived in the trees.

And yet Stevens knows that the song of "summer in the common fields" is sung by singers not themselves partaking of that summer, just as Keats's ode of summer fruition and repose is sung by one gazing at the shorn stubble fields. Stevens's singers are "far in the woods":

> Far in the woods they sang their unreal songs,
> Secure. It was difficult to sing in face
> Of the object. The singers had to avert themselves
> Or else avert the object. Deep in the woods
> They sang of summer in the common fields.
>
> They sang desiring an object that was near,
> In face of which desire no longer moved,
> Nor made of itself that which it could not find.

In spite of this admission that singers sing out of desire rather than out of satisfaction, Stevens's poem begins, as Keats's does, with the benevolent fiction that the singers are in the midst of the landscape they celebrate:

> Young broods
> Are in the grass, the roses are heavy with a weight
> Of fragrance and the mind lays by its trouble.

This is the moment of the marriage of earth and sky, the time of conspiracy between the sky-god, the sun, and the earth-goddess, the queen, to produce the young broods: this is "green's apogee / And happiest folk-land, mostly marriage hymns."

Keats had begun his ode with the symbolic marriage of earth and air, but had sketched it with the lightest of suggestions: in Stevens the family constellation appears and reappears, as he draws Keats out to iconic completion:

> These fathers standing round,
> These mothers touching, speaking, being near,
> These lovers waiting in the soft dry grass.

The queen is "the charitable majesty of her whole kin," and "the bristling soldier" is "a filial form and one / Of the land's children, easily born." Like the earthly paradise where flowers and fruit coexist, this paradise contains harmoniously all stages of human existence—the young broods, lovers, fathers and mothers, and an old man—but its chief emblem is "the youth, the vital son, the heroic power," the filial form whom age cannot touch. Yet, after the admission that "a mind exists, aware of division," the heroic attempt to maintain the privileged moment falters, and Stevens's more grotesque version of stubble fields makes its appearance, with a presiding form resembling Keats's redbreast. There is even a recollection of Keats's river sallows:

> Fly low, cock bright, and stop on a bean pole. Let
> Your brown breast redden, while you wait for warmth.
> With one eye watch the willow, motionless.
> The gardener's cat is dead, the gardener gone
> And last year's garden grows salacious weeds.

Keats's twice-repeated "soft" appears in this canto: "Soft, civil bird," and "not / So soft." For the agricultural laborer-goddess and her creatures Stevens substitutes the gardener and his cat, deriving the gardener perhaps from Keats's "gardener Fancy" in the "Ode to Psyche." Stevens's way of solving the encroachments of decay on his scene of happiness is to attribute to his singers, although they are only the creations of "an inhuman author," a will of their own, as though the author is himself mastered by the rise of desire in the hearts of his characters:

> . . . The characters speak because they want
> To speak, the fat, the roseate characters,
> Free, for a moment, from malice and sudden cry,
> Complete in a completed scene, speaking
> Their parts as in a youthful happiness.

These characters who speak of their own free will resemble Keats's creatures, who, in spite of the season's sadness, sing their own music. It is clear from Stevens's ending that "malice and sudden cry" are likely to be the ordinary states of the characters of the inhuman author, and that the miraculous lifting for a moment of their usual oppressive state enables, not youthful happiness, but a state resembling it. Seen in this way, "Credences of Summer" becomes, like "To Autumn," a backward-glancing poem, as its author, for a moment liberated from misery, looks for the perfect metaphor for the feeling he experiences in that moment and decides that youthful happiness (after spring's infuriations are over, after one's mortifying adolescent foolish selves are slaughtered) is the vehicle he needs. It is only in retrospect that we see the hovering of a divided mental state at the end of the second stanza:

> This is the last day of a certain year
> Beyond which there is nothing left of time.
> It comes to this and the imagination's life.

"This"—the perfect day—staves off for a while the full realization of the other— the imagination's life. But by the end of the poem, in the meditation on the observant mind, imagination is in the ascendant and the rich day has decayed into the salacious garden. The war in the poem between the warmth of Keatsian language and the chill of metaphysical analysis means that Stevens has not achieved a style which would embrace both the physical pine and the metaphysical pine. The presentation of summer cannot coexist, in tone or diction, with the anatomy of summer; and the anatomy, skirted and then suppressed in Keats in favor of self-forgetfulness, is allowed full play by Stevens. If the bees are given credence, so is the undeceiving questioning of the aloof, divided mind, and Stevens's poem, unable to maintain a Keatsian harmony, divides sharply in consequence of its "mind, aware of division."

If "Credences of Summer" goes both backward from Keats and further with his questioning (thereby losing the miraculous, if precarious Keatsian balance),

"The Auroras of Autumn" fastens on the question "Where are the songs of spring?" and makes a poetics of it. Keats stops in autumn to imagine spring and rebukes himself for his nostalgia, which implies a criticism of the season in which he finds himself. "Think not of them," he says of the spring songs. Stevens, in contrast, decides to think deliberately about them. What does it mean—for life, for poetry—that we cannot rest in the present, in any present? It means that the desire for change is more deep-rooted than the pleasure of any permanence, no matter how luxurious:

> Is there an imagination that sits enthroned
> As grim as it is benevolent, the just
> And the unjust, which in the midst of summer stops
>
> To imagine winter?

Every making of the mind moves to find "what must unmake it and, at last, what can." After being "fattened as on a decorous honeycomb," "we lay sticky with sleep," like Keats's bees. Stevens is Keatsian in accepting the fact of change; he is also Keatsian in his elegiac strain, substituting a Keatsian "farewell" for the even more Keatsian "adieu":

> Farewell to an idea . . . A cabin stands,
> Deserted, on a beach.

Stevens is Keatsian, too, in making the goddess who presides over the dissolution of the season a maternal figure who says not farewell or adieu but (as to children) goodnight, goodnight:

> Farewell to an idea . . . The mother's face,
> The purpose of the poem, fills the room.
>
> She gives transparence. But she has grown old.
> The necklace is a carving not a kiss.

Stevens offers a critique of Keats by leaping over Keats's set piece of sunset and twilight bird song and taking his poem beyond the death of the mother, after sunset, into boreal night. The birds, instead of going downward to darkness or gathering into a Keatsian flock, are set wildly flying:

> The theatre is filled with flying birds,
> Wild wedges, as of a volcano's smoke.

Across his sky Stevens displays his auroras, his earthly equivalent to the heavenly serpent-god sloughing skins at the opening of the poem, both symbols of change. The auroras are beautiful and intimidating at once; they leave us in the state of Keats's gnats and bleating lambs, "a shivering residue, chilled and foregone." The auroras change "idly, the way / A season changes color to no end, / Except the lavishing of itself in change." All natural changes are equal; there is no entropy in nature; all events are simply songs of "the innocent mother." The spectre of the spheres, like the inhuman author of "Credences of Summer," contrives a balance to contrive a whole. This new poetic wishes not only to relish everything equally (in itself a Keatsian ideal), but to relish everything at once, to imagine winter in summer and summer in winter, to meditate

> The full of fortune and the full of fate,
> As if he lived all lives, that he might know,
>
> In hall harridan, not hushful paradise,
> To a haggling of wind and weather, by these lights
> Like a blaze of summer straw, in winter's nick.

This finale of "The Auroras" is an implicit boast. Everything, however, is intrinsically less expressible than something. The close of the poem is less beautiful than the vision of the aurora itself. In this respect Stevens is Keatsian, substituting one form of landscape, the later auroras, for another, the Romantic sunset.

An earlier poem of Stevens arises from the Keatsian injunction that prompted "The Auroras"—"Think not of them"—and is in fact an extended thinking-and-not-thinking; "The Snow Man" might well be called "The Man Standing in the Stubble Plains." Snow, like harvest, eliminates vegetation; and Stevens, like Keats, faces the question of how to praise a world from which the summer growth has disappeared. Keats's "light wind" blowing over the bare fields is intensified, always, in Stevens into a "wind" of "winter" (and Stevens relishes the phonemic echo). Oddly enough, beheld with a mind of winter, the world does not appear bare: the boughs of the pine trees are crusted with snow, the junipers are shagged with ice, the spruces are rough in the distant glitter of the January sun. It is only with the introduction of the wind, and misery and the few remaining leaves on the deciduous trees that the world becomes "the same bare place" and the regarder and beholder—who saw such a rich world—becomes a listener who, nothing himself, "beholds / Nothing that is not there and the nothing that is." The turn from beholding to listening, borrowed from Keats's ode, coincides, as it does in Keats, with a pained turning from plenitude to absence. But Keats finds a new plenitude—of the ear—to substitute for the visual absence. Stevens, finding it impossible to sustain the plenitude perceivable by a mind of winter—that plenitude of encrustation, shagginess and rough snow-glitter—reverses Keats and finds bareness in listening. He turns, therefore, from the Keatsian trope of plenitude—enumeration—which he had employed in his listing of pines, junipers, and spruce trees, and uses instead a trope of reductiveness, becoming a modernist of minimal art: he hears, in a deadly repetition of the same few words (italics mine),

> *the sound of the wind*
> *the sound of a few* leaves
> *the sound of the* land
>   full *of the same wind*
>   that is blowing *in the same* bare place
>   for the *listener* who *listens in the* snow
>   and, *nothing* himself, beholds
>   *nothing that is* not there
>   and the *nothing that is.*

Another fairly early attempt at "thinking with the season" occurs in "Anatomy of Monotony," where Stevens, conceding the pathetic fallacy, urges us to have it on nature's terms, not our own. Since the earth "bore us as a part of all the things / It breeds," it follows that "our nature is her nature":

>   Hence it comes,
>   Since by our nature we grow old, earth grows
>   The same. We parallel the mother's death.

But the earth has a wider vision than our narrow personal pathos:

>   She walks an autumn ampler than the wind
>   Cries up for us and colder than the frost
>   Pricks in our spirits at the summer's end,
>   And over the bare spaces of our skies
>   She sees a barer sky that does not bend.

This widening of perspective is borrowed from Keats too, though it applies Keats's technique (broadening from the cottage and its kitchen garden and orchard to the cornfields and outbuildings and finally extending to the horizon, the boundary hill and hedges, the river, and the sky) only to the bare spaces of Keats's final stanza. It seems, as we read Stevens, that each aspect of the autumn ode called out to him to be reinterpreted, reused, recreated into a poem.

Much later, in "World without Peculiarity," Stevens "rewrites" "Anatomy of Monotony," achieving at last, however briefly, the power to think with the season. What is most human is now no longer (in Stevens's hard saying) sadness, pathos, nostalgia—that projection of ourselves into and onto other things which fail, die, or wane—but rather solitary existence as a natural object. Stevens may be remembering, in his extraordinary central stanza, Whitman's line about "the justified mother of men":

> What good is it that the earth is justified,
> That it is complete, that it is an end,
> That in itself it is enough?
>
> It is the earth itself that is humanity . . .
> He is the inhuman son and she,
> She is the fateful mother, whom he does not know.
>
> She is the day.

Though there are here no verbal echoes of Keats, this seems to me a poem that could not have been thought of except by someone who had incorporated into his imagination that sense of the independent life of nature voiced in the autumn ode.

Just as Stevens's "Woman in Sunshine" removes the mythological solidity from Keats's goddess in the fields and reminds us of what she is, a fictive construct, so "Less and Less Human, O Savage Spirit" wishes for a god both silent and quiet, "saying things," if he must, as light and color and shape "say things," a god who "will not hear us when we speak." This god, unable to say "Where are the songs of spring," is at once more earthly and more disembodied than Keats's goddess, pressing further toward the fictive and the inanimate at once.

Always in Stevens there is a new precipitate from the Keatsian solution, because mind and sense cannot coexist in equilibrium. No writer, in Stevens's view, could avoid the asking of the fatal question about the songs of spring. Stevens writes, in "The Ultimate Poem is Abstract," a second-order reflection on the inevitability of questions: Keats (or a poet like him) is treated ironically and called "the lecturer / On This Beautiful World of Ours," who "hems the planet rose and haws it rope, / And red, and right." But his hemming and hawing into roses and rosehips and red haws cannot last:

> One goes on asking questions. That, then, is one
> Of the categories. So said, this placid space
>
> Is changed. It is not so blue as we thought. To be blue,
> There must be no questions.

> . . . It would be enough
> If we were ever, just once, at the middle, fixed
> In This Beautiful World of Ours and not as now,
>
> Helplessly at the edge, enough to be
> Complete, because at the middle, if only in sense,
> And in that enormous sense, merely enjoy.

Such a poem is a rewriting, at a second-order level, of the Keats ode; it recounts in an abstract way Keats's attempt to remain "at the middle" of the beautiful world, praising its generosity to all the senses, its plenitude of being. The invasion of Keats's enjoyment by questioning, an *event* in the ode, becomes a *topic* for Stevens. And in other poems Stevens comments on each stage of the Keatsian process—how one sees first the earth "as inamorata," but then sees her "without distance . . . and naked or in rags, / Shrunk in the poverty of being close." She has been a celestial presence among laborers, an angel surrounded by paysans, an "archaic form / . . . evoking an archaic space." But then her appurtenances fade (the moon is "a tricorn / waved in pale adieu") and "she is exhausted and a little old" ("Things of August").

Stevens's late poetry of receptivity and inception, coming after the poetry of age and exhaustion, is nothing short of astonishing. Here Stevens follows Keats's "Human Seasons" beyond the winter of gross misfeature, finding "the cricket of summer forming itself out of ice," "not autumn's prodigal returned, / But an antipodal, far-fetched creature" ("A Discovery of Thought"). As he listens to winter sounds in "A Quiet Normal Life," he hears "the crickets' chords, / Babbling each one, the uniqueness of its sound," and decides to do without the archaic forms:

> There was no fury in transcendent forms.
> But his actual candle blazed with artifice.

Stevens forgoes (in "Looking across the Fields and Watching the Birds Fly") "the masculine myths we used to make" in favor of "a transparency through which the swallow weaves, / Without any form or any sense of form," and he decides that our thinking is nothing but our preestablished harmony with the grand motions of nature:

> We think, then, as the sun shines or does not.
> We think as wind skitters on a pond in a field . . .
>
> The spirit comes from the body of the world . . .

> The mannerism of nature caught in a glass
> And there become a spirit's mannerism,
> A glass aswarm with things going as far as they can.

This sublime self-transformation into a modern version of an Aeolian harp immolates the mind. If we pose questions, it is because the earth poses them. There is no longer any need to say "Think not of them": everything is permitted, because everything is a natural motion.

Stevens's last tribute to the stubble plains is his transmutation of Keats's bareness into "The Plain Sense of Things." This poem presses Keats's *donnée* to its ultimate point. There is no goddess, even a dying one; there is no memorial gleam cast through rosy clouds; there is no music; there are no touching filial forms; the surrogate animal for the human is not the laden honeybee, but the inquisitive pond rat:

> After the leaves have fallen, we return
> To a plain sense of things. It is as if
> We had come to an end of the imagination,
> Inanimate in an inert savoir . . .
>
> Yet the absence of the imagination had
> Itself to be imagined. The great pond,
> The plain sense of it, without reflections, leaves,
> Mud, water like dirty glass, expressing silence
>
> Of a sort, silence of a rat come out to see,
> The great pond and its waste of the lilies, all this
> Had to be imagined as an inevitable knowledge,
> Required, as a necessity requires.

"To Autumn" represented, for Keats, a retraction of the "Ode to Psyche." In the earlier ode Keats had hoped that the imagination could be fully reparatory for an external absence; piece by piece, in "Psyche" he constructs his interior fane to compensate, warmly and luxuriously, for the earthly temple that the goddess lacks. By the time he writes "To Autumn," he has lost, not the impulse (his impulse on seeing uninhabited stubble plains is to go home and write a stanza loaded and blessed with fruit and to invent an indwelling harvest goddess), but the ability to close with "a bright torch, and a casement ope at night, / To let the warm Love in!" "The absence of fantasia" in the bare fields might have tempted Stevens earlier to a compensatory opulence of reconstruction (like his populating his cabin with four daughters with curls in "The Comedian"), but now he finds a discipline in poverty. The comedian Crispin had boasted that he would find "a new reality" at last in another detail borrowed from Keats and expanded into its own poem: an unmusical bird cry. The "wailful choir" of the autumn ode gives way, in Stevens's poetry of old age, to an imagined choir of aubade, as Stevens draws the ode forward from its sunset into the new sunrise of "Not Ideas about the Thing but the Thing Itself":

> At the earliest ending of winter,
> In March, a scrawny cry from outside
> Seemed like a sound in his mind . . .
>
> That scrawny cry—it was
> A chorister whose c preceded the choir.
> It was part of the colossal sun,
>
> Surrounded by its choral rings,
> Still far away. It was like
> A new knowledge of reality.

There is no "new reality": there is only a "new knowledge of reality." The "marvellous sophomore" had boasted "Here was the veritable ding an sich, at last." But his boast was premature. Stevens did not find "the thing itself" until very late, and then in a scale Keatsian in its humility. "Not Ideas about the Thing but the Thing Itself" is Stevens's most beautiful late reflection on his own beginnings (as the comedian as the letter "C" becomes the chorister whose "c" preceded the choir) and on Keats's ode and its minimal music. Nonetheless I close not with this last successful meditation but instead with a poem that in its own relative failure shows Stevens's stubborn ambition, even at the expense of violent dislocation of form, to have plenitude and poverty at once, to possess Keats's central divine figure opulently whole and surrounded by her filial forms, while at the same time asserting the necessary obsolescence of her form and of the literature about her. She remains, he asserts, for all her inevitable vanishing, "The Hermitage at the Centre":

> The leaves on the macadam make a noise—
>   How soft the grass on which the desired
>   Reclines in the temperature of heaven—
>
> Like tales that were told the day before yesterday—
>   Sleek in a natural nakedness,
>   She attends the tintinnabula—

And the wind sways like a great thing tottering—
   Of birds called up by more than the sun,
   Birds of more wit, that substitute—

Which suddenly is all dissolved and gone—
   Their intelligible twittering
   For unintelligible thought.

And yet this end and this beginning are one,
   And one last look at the ducks is a look
   At lucent children round her in a ring.

Stevens's response to Keats's ode was so long-lived that the central problems of the ode—process, termination, interruption of ripeness, the human seasons, the beauty of the minimal, the function of nostalgia, the relation between sense and thought, and so on—became central to Stevens's poetry as well. His attempts to go "beyond" Keats in various ways—to take the human seasons further, into winter, into boreal apocalypse, into inception; to find new imagery of his own, while retaining Keats's crickets and bees and birds and sun and fields; to create his own archaic forms in the landscape—define in their evolution Stevens's own emerging originality. Though he retains a classical structure to his verse, his diction and rhetoric become ever less visibly Romantic, as a plain sense of things and an absence of fantasia supervene. Everywhere we hear Stevens meditating on Keats, whose fashion of beholding without comment must have seemed to Stevens prophetically modern. Stevens sensed that the poem of presentation was the poem of earth: Just to behold, just to be beheld, what is there here but weather—these are the assumptions Stevens found and grasped for himself in the most untranscendental of the great Romantic odes.

8. "Lycidas": A Poem Finally Anonymous
STANLEY FISH

THE SWAIN SPEAKS

THE TENSION between the desire to lose oneself in a union with deity
—and the desire either to defer the moment of union or to master it by
intellectualizing it—is a feature of the poetry as early as the *Nativity
Ode*. In *Lycidas*, it is a master theme; and once it is steadily seen as such, it
provides a vantage point from which we can make a kind of narrative sense of
the poem's many and surprising twists and turns.

Much of *Lycidas* criticism is an extended answer to those who, in the tradition of Dr. Johnson, see the poem as an "irreverent combination" of "trifling fictions" and "sacred truths," or as a lament marred by intrusive and unassimilated
digressions, or, more sympathetically, as "an accumulation of magnificent fragments,"[1] or simply (and rather notoriously) as a production more "willful and
illegal in form" than any other of its time.[2] This last judgment—it is John Crowe
Ransom's in his famous essay "A Poem Nearly Anonymous"—indicates the extent to which the poem has been brought before the bar. The indictment has
included, among others, the following charges: the tenses are inconsistent and
frustrate any attempt to trace a psychological progression; there are frequent
and unsettling changes in style and diction; the structure is uncertain, hesitat-
ing between monologue, dialogue, and something that is not quite either; the
speaker assumes a bewildering succession of poses; the lines on Fame are poorly
integrated; the procession of mourners is perfunctory; the Pilot's speech is over-
long and overharsh; the flower passage is merely decorative; the Christian consolation (beginning "Weep no more, woeful Shepherds")[3] is unconvincing and
insufficiently prepared for; the shift to the third person in the final lines is dis-

concerting and without any persuasive justification. Together and individually, these characterizations constitute a challenge to the poem's unity, and it is as an assertion of unity that the case for the defense is always presented.

Typically, that defense proceeds by first acknowledging and then domesticating the discontinuities that provoke it. Thus, William Madsen observes that the voice that says "Weep no more, woeful Shepherds" at line 165 does not sound at all like the voice we have been listening to; but no sooner does he note this breach in the poem's logic than he mends it by assigning the line and what follows to the angel Michael,[4] although he fails to explain, as Donald Friedman points out, why among all the speakers in *Lycidas*, Michael is the only one who "is introduced without comment or identification."[5] Friedman himself is concerned with another moment of disruption, occasioned by the voice of Phoebus, whose unexpected appearance as a speaker in the past tense blurs the narrative line and creates "confusion about the nature of the utterance we are listening to" (13). That confusion, however, is only "momentary," at least in Friedman's argument, where it is soon brought into a relationship with "the coda in which Milton subsumes the entire experience of the swain" (13). That coda, of course, brings its own problem; for, as Stewart Baker observes, the appearance of a third-person narrator after 185 lines constitutes a "surprise." But after acknowledging the surprise in the opening sentence of his essay, Baker proceeds to accommodate it, and by the time he finishes, it has been removed, along with Saint Peter's dread voice, as a possible threat "to the unity of the poem."[6] Defending the poem's unity is also the concern of H. V. Ogden, who writes in part to refute G. W. Knight's early characterization of *Lycidas* "as an effort to bind and clamp together a universe trying to fly off into separate bits."[7] Ogden cannot but acknowledge that the poem abounds in "abrupt turns in new directions," but these turns are explained or explained away by invoking the seventeenth-century principle of "aesthetic variety," and one can almost hear Ogden's sigh of relief as he declares triumphantly that "*Lycidas* is a disciplined interweaving of contrasting passages into a unified whole."[8]

Examples could be multiplied, but the pattern is clear: whatever *Lycidas* is, *Lycidas* criticism is "an effort to bind and clamp together a universe trying to fly off into separate bits." It is, in short, an effort to put the poem together, and the form that effort almost always takes is the putting together of an integrated and consistent first-person voice. Indeed, it is the assumption that the poem is a dramatic lyric and hence the expression of a unified consciousness that generates the pressure to discover a continuity in the narrative. The unity in relation to which the felt discontinuities must be brought into line is therefore a *psychological* unity; the drama whose coherence everyone is in the business of demonstrating is mental. In the history of the criticism, that coherence has been achieved by conceiving of the speaker as an actor in one of several possible biographical dramas: he may be remembering a past experience from a position of relative tranquillity (the position of the last eight lines); or he may be performing a literary exercise in the course of which he creates a naive persona (the uncouth swain); or he may be in the process of breaking out of the conventional limitations imposed on him by a tradition; or he may be passing from a pagan to a Christian understanding of the world and the possibilities it offers him. These readings are written in opposition to one another, but in fact they all share an assumption that is made explicit by John Henry Raleigh when he declares that *Lycidas* is "an existential poem. . . . It is about 'becoming,' the emergence of the ego to its full power."[9] Given this assumption, the poem can only be read as one in which the first-person speaker is a seventeenth-century anticipation of a Romantic hero.

The notorious exception to this way of dealing with *Lycidas* is John Crowe Ransom, who explains the discontinuities in the poem as evidence of a failure to *suppress* the ego, a failure to realize the proper poetic intention of remaining "always anonymous" (66). In Ransom's account, the "logical difficulties of the work" (80), the shifts in tense, the changes in tone, the interpolations of different speakers, the roughness of the verse, are the intrusive self-advertisements of a poet who cannot keep himself out of his poem, who is "willful and illegal" so that "nobody will make the mistake of not remarking his personality" (80). In general the Milton establishment has not been impressed by Ransom's argument, which is now viewed as something of a curiosity. In what follows, I will attempt to revive it, but with a difference. Ransom is right, I believe, to see that the shifts and disruptions in the poem reflect a tension between anonymity and personality; but I do not think, as he seems to, that the personality in the poem is triumphant because it is irrepressible. Indeed, it will be my contention that the suppressing of the personal voice is the poem's achievement, and that the energy of the poem derives not from the presence of a controlling and self-contained individual, but from forces that undermine his individuality and challenge the fiction of his control. If the poem records a struggle of personality against anonymity, it is a struggle the first-person speaker loses, and indeed the triumph of the poem occurs when his voice can no longer be heard.

That voice, when we first encounter it, is heard complaining about the task to which it has been called by "sad occasion" (6). The complaint is all the more bitter because it takes the form of an apology. "I am sorry to have to do this to you," the speaker says to the apostrophized berries, but what he is really sorry about is something that has been done to him. The double sense of the lines is nicely captured in the ambiguity of "forc'd" in line 4 ("And with forc'd fingers rude"), which can be read either as a characterization of his own action, or as an indictment of that which has made the action necessary (he is forced to do the forcing). In the same way, "rude" is at once a deprecation of his poetic skills and an expression of anger at having to exercise them prematurely: his fingers are rude because they have been forced to an unready performance. The pretense of an apology is continued through line 5, where it is once again undermined by the phrase "the mellowing year." Thomas Warton objected to an "inaccuracy" here, because "the 'mellowing year' could not affect the leaves of the laurel, the myrtle, and the ivy . . . characterized before as 'never sere.'"[10] Just so. The "inaccuracy" is there to call ironic and mocking attention to the inappropriateness of the apology: the laurel, the myrtle, and the ivy have no "mellowing year" to shatter; what has been shattered, in different ways, are the mellowing years of Lycidas and the speaker; and it is in response to the violence (interruption) done to them that these lines are spoken. By the time we reach line 7, it is impossible to read "disturb your season due" as anything but a bitter joke. It is the speaker's season that has been disturbed and by a disturbance (the death of Lycidas) even more final; and it is with the greatest reluctance that he is compelled to give voice to this "melodious tear" (14).

This posture of reluctance is one often assumed by Milton's characters, most notably by the Attendant Spirit in *Comus,* who is more than a little loath to leave the "Regions mild of calm and serene Air"[11] for the "smoke and stir of this dim spot, / Which men call Earth" (5–6). It is also the posture in which Milton likes to present himself in the prose tracts, so that typically he will declare with what small willingness he leaves the "still time" of his studies to engage in "tedious antiquities and disputes,"[12] or announce that only in response to the "earnest entreaties and serious conjurements" of a friend has he been "induc't" to break off pursuits "which cannot but be a great furtherance . . . to the enlargement of truth."[13] The labor to which he is called in these tracts is always an *interruption,* something that comes between him and a preferred activity, a discontinuity that threatens the completion of his real work.

This is especially true of *The Reason of Church Government* where his situation, as he characterizes it, exactly parallels that of the speaker in *Lycidas.* He writes, he tells us, "out of mine own season, when I have neither yet completed to my minde the full circle of my private studies."[14] "I should not," he says, "chuse this manner of writing wherin knowing my self inferior to my self . . . I have the use . . . but of my left hand" (808). He would rather be "soaring in the high region of his fancies with his garland and singing robes about him," where, in response to the "inward prompting" of thoughts that have long "possest" him, he "might perhaps leave something so written to aftertimes, as they should not willingly let it die" (810). It is from those exalted "intentions" that hc has been "pluckt" by the "abortive and foredated discovery" (820) of the present occasion ("sad occasion dear"), and he knows that the reader will understand how reluctant he is "to interrupt the pursuit of no lesse hopes than these . . . to imbark in a troubl'd sea of noises and hoars disputes, put from beholding the bright countenance of truth in the quiet and still air of delightful studies" (821–822). In *Lycidas*, the still and quiet air of studies is punctuated by the "Oaten Flute" and by the song beloved of "old *Damaetas*" (33, 36); but as in *The Reason of Church Government*, this is a lost tranquillity now recollected from the vantage point of a present turmoil, of a "heavy change" (37). In both contexts the change is the occasion for premature activity, for the hazarding of skills that are not yet ready in the performance of a task that is unwelcome.

There is one great difference however. The Milton of *The Reason of Church Government*, like the Attendant Spirit in *Comus*, is soon reconciled to that task because he is able to see it not as an interruption but as an extension of the activity from which he has been called away. He may be "put from beholding the bright countenance of truth," but it is as a witness to the same truth that he takes up the labor forced upon him by the moment. All acts performed in response to the will of God are equally virtuous, and "when God commands to take the trumpet and blow a dolorous or a jarring blast, it lies not in mans will what he shall say" (803). Indeed, "were it the meanest under-service, if God by his Secretary conscience injoyn it" (822), then it is impossible for a man to draw back. It is the same reasoning that leads him in *Of Education* to accede to the entreaties of Hartlib, for although the reforming of education is not the pursuit to which the love of God was taking him, he is able to see the present assignment as one "sent hither by some good providence" (363) and therefore as an opportunity to manifest that same love. In *An Apology*, he has decided, even before he descends to the disagreeable business of replying to slanders and calumnies, that it is his duty to do so, lest the truth and "the religious cause" which he had "in hand" be rendered "odious." "I conceav'd my self," he declares, "to be not now as mine own person, but as a member incorporate into that truth whereof I was perswaded."[15]

This conception of himself as "not . . . mine own person" is essential to his ability to see the disrupting activity as an instance or manifestation of the activity from which he has been *unwillingly* torn. That is, the disruption looms large only from the perspective of his personal desires—he would rather be writing poetry, or reading the classics, or furthering some long-term project—but from the vantage point of the truth whereof he is but a member incorporate, there is no disruption at all, simply a continuity of duty and service. It is here that the point of contrast with the speaker in *Lycidas* is most obvious: he takes everything *personally*, and as a consequence whatever happens is seen only as it relates to the hopes he has for his own career. This, of course, is the great discovery of twentieth-century criticism—that in *Lycidas* Milton is "primarily taking account of the meaning of the experience to himself";[16] but for Milton to be *primarily* doing this is for him to be doing something very different from what he does in the prose tracts, where egocentric meanings are rejected as soon as they are identified. That is, the stance of the speaker in *Lycidas* is anomalous in the Milton canon; for rather than relinquishing the conception of himself as "his own person," he insists on it, and by insisting on it he resists incorporation into a body of which he is but an extending member.

Indeed, insofar as the poem can be said to have a plot, it consists of the speaker's efforts to resist assimilation. He does this in part by maintaining an ironic distance from the conventions he proceeds to invoke. As we have seen, that irony is compounded largely of bitterness, and it takes the form both of questioning the adequacy of the conventions to the occasion, and of claiming a knowledge superior to any the conventions are able to offer. Irony is itself a mode of superiority: the ironic voice always issues from a perspective of privilege and presents itself as having penetrated to meanings that have been missed by the naive and the innocent. The ironic voice, in short, always knows *more*.

In this case it knows more than the traditions of consolation; it knows that they are fictions, false surmises. The method in the opening sections is to let these fictions have their say, only so that the speaker can enter to expose their shallowness. "He must not float upon his wat'ry bier" (*Lycidas*, 12) seems, as we read it, to be the sentiment of someone who believes that there is something to be done, but this belief is dismissed and mocked by the first word of line 13, "Unwept." He will, in fact, continue to float on his watery bier, and the only thing that will be done is what the speaker is doing now—producing laments in the form of "some melodious tear" (14). This characterization of his own activity is slighting, but it does not mean that he is assuming a stance of modesty or self-deprecation; the criticism extends only to the means or tools, and not to the workman who finds them inadequate. It is their failure and not his that is culpable; and indeed, his recognition, even before he employs them, that they will not do the job validates the superiority of his perception.

Even when the pastoral conventions are invoked, they are invoked in such a way as to call into question their capacities. The elegy proper begins with an echo of Virgil's messianic eclogue: "Begin . . . and somewhat loudly sweep the string" (15, 17). That eclogue, however, specifically promises to transcend the genre, and therefore to invoke it is already to assume the insufficiency of the tradition in the very act of rehearsing its tropes. One of those tropes is the recollection of past delights, and it is given an extended, even lingering evocation in lines 25–36 (the lines to which Dr. Johnson so objected); but even as we listen, in the place of "old *Damaetas*," to this song, we are aware, with Douglas Bush, that it is "a picture of pastoral innocence, of carefree youth unconscious of the fact of death."[17] We therefore hear it with *condescension* and with an expectation that it will be succeeded by a perspective less naive. As a result, when the speaker breaks in with "But O the heavy change" (*Lycidas*, 37), the tone may be elegiac but the gesture is a triumphant one, made by someone who is able to present himself as "sadder, but wiser." What he is wiser than is the pastoral mode and all of the ways by which it attempts to render comfortable what is so obviously distressing. One of those ways is the doctrine of natural sympathy, which would tell us that in response to the death of Lycidas, "The Willows and the Hazel Copses green / Shall now no more be seen" (42–43); but that assertion is allowed to survive only for the moment, before the succeeding line at once completes the syntax and, in an ironic reversal, changes the meaning: "Shall now no more be seen, / Fanning their joyous Leaves to thy soft lays." The willows and the hazel copses green will in fact be seen, but they will be seen fanning their joyous leaves to someone else's soft lays, for it is Lycidas who will be "no more." This new meaning does not simply displace but mocks the old: "How foolish of any one to believe that nature takes notice of the misfortunes of man." Obviously, the speaker is not such a one, and, as always, the superimposition of his perspective on the perspective of the convention has the effect of establishing him in a removed and superior position. He maintains this position even when he appears to be turning on himself. "Ay me, I fondly dream" (56) has the form of a self-rebuke, but the fondness is displaced onto the tradition and its representative figures—the nymphs, the bards, the druids, the Muses, Orpheus, and even Universal Nature. It is their ineffectiveness that has led the speaker to break off his performance and to exclaim, "For what could that have done? / What could the Muse herself that *Orpheus* bore . . . ?" (57–58). What *he* can do, and very effectively, is to see and say just that and so disassociate himself from the failures he continues to expose.

I am aware that in other accounts of the poem this questioning of pastoral efficacy has received another reading, and is seen not as evidence of egocentricity but as a kind of heroism. B. A. Rajan, for example, reads the poem as the anguished discovery by the first-person voice that ritual and tradition are inadequate when confronted by the "assault of reality."[18] The poem is thus an attack on "its own assumptions" (56), an attack that is "mounted by the higher mood against the pastoral form" (54). In the struggle that ensues, "convention and elementality are the basic forces of contention" (54), and for "elementality" we may read the personal voice, characterized by Rajan, as the "cry out of the heart of experience" (62). His argument is more finely tuned than Raleigh's, but its point is the same: *Lycidas* is about becoming, the emergence of the ego to its full power; or in Rajan's more guarded vocabulary, "it is a voyage toward recognition" (63), a recognition that is won to some extent at the expense of the claims to adequacy of pastoral and other ritual or public forms.

For Rajan, then, the contest between the conventional and the real or personal is the story the poem tells; what I am suggesting is that it is a story the *speaker* tells, and that he tells it in an effort to situate himself in a place not already occupied by public and conventional meanings. It is less "a cry out of the heart of experience" than a *strategy*, a strategy designed to privilege experience, and especially *individual* experience, in relation to the impersonality of public and institutional structures. That is why the efficacy of the pastoral is called into question: so that the efficacy of the speaker, as someone who stands apart from conventions and is in a position to evaluate them, can be that much more firmly established. In other words, the characterization of the pastoral is deliberately low and feeble in order to display to advantage the authority and prescience of the speaker when he pronounces in his own voice, as he does at line 64: "Alas! What boots it with uncessant care . . ." Here, and in the lines that follow, the speaker is at the height of his powers, in the sense that he seems to have earned the questions he hurls at the world, questions whose force is in direct proportion to the claim (silently but effectively made) to sincerity. Here is no mediated pastoral voice, heard through a screen of tradition and ritual; here is the thing itself, the expression of a distinctive perspective on a problem that many have considered ("Yet once more" [1]), but never with such poignancy and perceptiveness. It is precisely what Rajan says it is, a cry out of the heart of experience, a cry which emerges from the wreckage of failed conventions to pose the ultimate question: In a world like this, what does one do?

THE SWAIN IS SILENCED

It is all the more startling, then, when that cry is interrupted by the voice of Apollo, a moment characterized by Ransom as "an incredible interpolation" and "a breach in the logic of composition." These are strong words, but they are in response to a very strong effect given the extent to which the speaker has, to this point, asserted his control over the poem and its progression. Here the control is taken from him in so complete a way that we as readers do not even know when it happens. The identification of Apollo's voice occurs at the beginning of line 77 ("*Phoebus* repli'd"), but the identification is after the fact, with the result that there is no way of determining who has been speaking. Many editors add punctuation so as to make it "clear" that Phoebus enters with "But not the praise" (76); yet as we read Milton's unpunctuated text, "But not the praise" seems to be part of a dialogue the first-person voice is having with himself on the nature of Fame and its relationship to effort ("uncessant care" [64]). The correction supplied by "*Phoebus* repli'd" does not result in a simple reassignment of the half-line, but blurs, retroactively, the assignment of the lines preceding. When does Phoebus begin to speak? Is this his first reply or has he begun to respond to the first-person complaint at line 70: "*Fame* is the spur"? The first person would then return in line 73—"But the fair Guerdon when we hope to find"—and *then* Phoebus would be heard to reply "But not the praise." My point is not to argue for this particular redistribution of the lines, but to demonstrate that it is possible; and because it is just one among other possibilities, and because the matter cannot be settled once and for all, the question of just who is in charge of the poem becomes a real one.

This is not the only question raised by Apollo's intervention. Because "repli'd" is in the past tense, what had presented itself as speech erupting in the present is suddenly revealed to be recollected or reported speech. As Ransom observes, "dramatic monologue has turned . . . into narrative" (79); and the result, in Friedman's words, is "a momentary confusion about the nature of the utterance we are listening to."[19] The confusion not only is generic (monologue or narrative), but extends to the kind of hearing we are to give to that utterance, for "if the memory of Phoebus's words is reported by the swain as part of the elegy, then what has happened to the pretense of spontaneity and present creation?" Friedman's question contains its own answer (although it is not the one he eventually gives): it is here that the spontaneity begins to be exposed precisely as a pretense, as a claim elaborately made by the speaker from his very first words: "Yet once more." Although these words acknowledge convention (by acknowledging that this has been done before), they are themselves unconventional, because they are not produced within the frame or stage setting that traditionally encloses the pastoral lament. From Theocritus to Spenser, elegiac song is introduced into a situation that proclaims its status as artifice, as a piece of currency in a social exchange (song for bowl), or as a performance offered in competition. In *Lycidas,* however, the frame is omitted, and what we hear, or are encouraged to hear, is an unpremeditated outpouring of grief and anger. When Apollo's reply is reported in the past tense, the pastoral frame is introduced retroactively, and the suggestion is that it has been there all the while.

Immediately the spontaneity of the preceding lines is compromised, and compromised too are the claims of the speaker to independence. At the very moment he dismisses the pastoral, he is revealed to be a narrated pastoral figure, no longer the teller of his tale but told by it—identified and made intelligible, as it were, by the very tradition he scorns. Moreover, he is identified in such a way as to call into question his identity. When Apollo plucks his trembling ear, he repeats an action already performed in response to another poet who also has dreams of transcending the pastoral conventions: "When I tried a song of kings and battles, Phoebus / Plucked my ear and warned, 'A shepherd, Tityrus, / Should feed fat sheep, recite a fine-spun song.' "[20] Apollo, in short, puts Virgil in his place, and by doing so establishes a place (or commonplace) that is now occupied by the present speaker. That is, the desire of the poet to rise above the pastoral is itself a pastoral convention, and when the speaker of *Lycidas* gives voice to that desire, he succeeds only in demonstrating the extent to which his thoughts and actions are already inscribed in the tradition from which he would be separate. Not only are his ambitions checked by Apollo,[21] but they are not *his* ambitions, insofar as he is only playing out the role assigned him in a drama not of his making.

It is not too much to say, then, that the intervention of Apollo changes everything: the speaker loses control of his poem when another voice simply dislodges him from center stage (where he had been performing in splendid isolation), and, at the same time, the integrity of his own voice is compromised when this voice becomes indistinguishable from its Virgilian predecessor. Apollo poses a threat to the speaker not only as a maker, as someone who is in the act of building the lofty rhyme, but as a selfcontained consciousness, as a mind that is fully present to itself and responsible for its own perceptions. The speaker meets this twin threat by rewriting, or misreading, what has happened to him in such a way as to reinstate, at least for the moment, the fiction of his independence:

> O Fountain *Arethuse*, and thou honor'd flood,
> Smooth-sliding *Mincius*; crown'd with vocal reeds,
> That strain I heard was of a higher mood:
> But now my Oat proceeds . . .
> (*Lycidas*, 85–88)

The picture in these lines is of someone who has paused to listen, no doubt politely, to the opinion of another before proceeding resolutely on *his* way (the strong claim is in the *my* of "my Oat"). There is no acknowledgment at all of the violence of Apollo's entrance, of his brusque and dismissive challenge to the speaker's sentiments, of the peremptory and unceremonious manner in which he seizes the floor. Moreover, the action Apollo performs is misrepresented when it is reported as an action *against* the pastoral ("That strain . . . was of a higher mood"). In fact, it is an action against the speaker—a rebuke, as Mary Christopher Pecheux observes, to his "rebellious questioning."[22] If Apollo's words are higher, they are higher than the speaker's own; rather than supporting his denigration of the pastoral, they are precisely pastoral words, and mark the moment when the tradition interrupts the "bold discourse"[23] of one who scorns it and exposes the illusion of his control.

It is in order to maintain the illusion that the speaker sets Apollo against the pastoral, for he can then present himself as the judge of their respective assertions. But no sooner has he reclaimed the central and directing role ("But now my Oat proceeds") than it is once again taken from him: "But now my Oat proceeds, / And listens to the Herald of the Sea / That came in *Neptune's* plea" (88–90). Suddenly the voices competing for attention, and for the position of authority, multiply and become difficult to distinguish. Triton comes, but he comes in Neptune's plea, and therefore when we read of someone who "ask'd" the waves and felon winds (91) it is not clear whether that someone is Triton or Neptune, nor when it is that whoever it is speaks (it could be that Triton reports the investigative queries of Neptune—he "ask'd"—or that Triton *now* asks in the present of the narrative, but is reported as having done so in the present of the narrator, i.e., the voice that tells us Phoebus "repli'd"). The one thing that *is* clear is that the questioner is not the speaker, who is now reduced to the role of a listener while someone else conducts the investigation. Again, this someone else could be Triton or Neptune or the yet unknown third-person voice of whose existence we have had only hints; or, after line 96, it could be the "sage *Hippotades*" who brings someone's (it seems to be everyone's) unsatisfactory answers. By the time we reach the most unsatisfactory answer of all—"It was that fatal and perfidious Bark" (100)—there is absolutely no way of determining who delivers it. A poem that began as the focused utterance of a distinctive personal voice is by this point so diffused that it is spoken, quite literally, by everybody.

Not only is the original speaker now indistinguishable from a chorus, but he is not even the object of direct address, as he was when he listened to Apollo. Whoever it is that indicts the fatal and perfidious bark, he directs his remarks to Lycidas: "That sunk so low that sacred head of *thine*" (102; italics mine). Moreover, the indictment and the entire investigation are once again proceeding in a narrated past. The fading of the speaker from the scene of his own poem coincides with the almost imperceptible slide into the past tense, and both movements are complete when we hear (we have displaced the speaker, who is no longer even a prominent listener) that "Last came, and last did go / The Pilot of the *Galilean* lake" (108–109).

It would seem that with this figure the poem is once again dominated by a single controlling presence, but his identity (in two senses) is perhaps not so firm as we have been taught to think. Taking up a suggestion first made by R. E. Hone, Mary Pecheux has argued persuasively that the Pilot of the Galilean lake (who significantly is not named) is not Peter but a composite of Peter, Moses, and Christ. The speech thus dramatizes Milton's assertion in the *Christian Doctrine* that revelation was disclosed in various ages by Christ even though he was not always known under that name: "Under the name of Christ are also comprehended Moses and the Prophets, who were his forerunners, and the Apostles whom he sent."[24] This splitting of the "dread voice" has the advantage, as Pecheux points out, of being "consonant with the extraordinary richness and ambivalence" of the poem, with the sense one has "of having heard a multitude of overtones difficult to disentangle one from the other" (239). Again, the details of her argument are less important than the fact that it can be made, for this means that the question is an open one and that the Pilot's speech too proceeds from a source that is not *uniquely* identified.

That speech is also addressed to Lycidas ("How well could I have spar'd for thee, young swain" [113]), and its "stern" (112) message further shifts attention away from the first-person voice by replacing his very personal concerns with the concerns of the church as a whole. That is, the complaint one hears in these lines is quite different from the complaint that precedes Apollo's interruption: it is not an answer to the speaker's questions ("What boots it . . ." [64]) but a "higher" questioning in which the ambitions of any one shepherd or singer are absorbed into a more universal urgency, as rot and "foul contagion" spread (127). The focus of the Pilot's words is continually expanding, until it opens in the end on a perspective so wide that all of our attempts to name it are at once accurate and hopelessly inadequate. Whatever the two-handed engine is—and we shall never know—the action for which it stands ready will not be in response to any cry out of the heart of experience, and in this moment of apocalyptic prophecy the private lament that was, for a time, the poem's occasion is so much transcended that one can scarcely recall it.

This movement away from the personal is a structural component of Milton's work from the very beginning. It is seen as early as the *Nativity Ode,* where the poet begins by desiring to be first, to stand out ("Have thou the honor first, thy Lord to greet" [26]) and ends by being indistinguishable from the others (animals, angels, shepherds) who "all about the Courtly Stable, / . . . sit in order serviceable."[25] The glory he had hoped to win by being first is won when, in a sense, he no longer is, and is able to pronounce the glorious death of his own poetic ambitions ("Time is our tedious Song should here have ending" [239]). While the career of the speaker in *Lycidas* is parallel, it is also different because he does not relinquish his position voluntarily. He holds tenaciously to his own song and must be forcibly removed from the poem by voices that preempt him or displace him or simply ignore him, until at the end of the Pilot's speech he seems to have disappeared.

Indeed, so long has it been since he was last on stage (line 90) that when he suddenly pops up again he seems an interpolation more incredible than Apollo. He seems, in fact, a digression, a departure from what we have come to recognize as the poem's true concerns; and as a digression his gesture of reassertion is, in every sense, reactionary:

> Return *Alpheus*, the dread voice is past
> That shrunk thy streams; Return *Sicilian* Muse,
> And call the Vales, and bid them hither cast
> Their Bells and Flowrets of a thousand hues.
> (*Lycidas*, 132–135)

Once again the return of the speaker is marked by a rewriting that is a misrepresentation. He acts as if all had been proceeding under his direction, as if the voices in the poem require his permission to come and go—a permission he now extends to the pastoral, which is characterized as if it were a child that had been frightened by the sound of an adult voice. His strategy is two-pronged and it is familiar. He opposes the pastoral to the speech of the Galilean Pilot (as he had earlier opposed it to Apollo) and thus denies it the responsibility for documenting ecclesiastical abuses, a responsibility it was given in the Scriptures. In effect, it is he, not the Pilot, who shrinks, or attempts to shrink, the pastoral stream, and he does it, characteristically, in a denial of the extent to which his own stream has been shrunk in the course of the poem. It is a classic form of displacement in which he attempts, for the last time, to project a story in which he is a compelling and powerful figure.

It is as part of that story that he calls the role of flowers, a gesture intended not so much "to interpose a little ease" (152) but to set the stage for still another assertion of pastoral inadequacy: "Let our frail thoughts dally with false surmise" (153). As before, what is presented as self-deprecation is an act of self-promotion. The "frail thoughts" are detached from the speaker—he merely dallies with them—and identified with the failure of the convention; if, in some sense, he can do no better, at least he is able to recognize a false surmise when he sees one, and that ability in itself is evidence of a vision that is superior even if it is (realistically) dark: "Ay me! Whilst thee the shores and sounding Seas / Wash far away, where'er thy bones are hurl'd" (154–155). This is, of course, exactly what he has said before, when he breaks off his address to the nymphs to exclaim, "Ay me, I fondly dream" (56), and again, when his rehearsal of Orpheus's death (he also was hurled by shores and sounding seas) is followed by a bitter question: "Alas! What boots it with uncessant care?" (64). What is remarkable about the speaker is how little he is affected by those sections of the poem that unfold between his intermittent appearances. Higher moods and dread voices may come and go, but when he manages to regain the stage, it is to sing the same old song: Ay me, alas, what am I to do? What's the use? It's all so unfair. As the poem widens its perspective to include ever larger considerations (eternal fame, the fate of the church, the condition of the Christian community, the Last Judgment), the speaker remains within the perspective of his personal disappointment, remains very much "his own person," and therefore he becomes, as I have said, a digression in (what began as) his own poem. While he has been busily exposing the false surmises of pastoral consolation, the poem has been even more insistently exposing the surmise that enables him (or so he thinks) to do so—the surmise that his vision is both inclusive and conclusive, that he sees what there is to see and knows what there is to know.

What he sees is that there is no laureate hearse (only the "wat'ry bier" he saw at line 12), and what he knows is that there is neither justice nor meaning in the world. He seems to have heard in the Pilot's speech none of the resonances that have been reported by so many readers. His words remain determinedly bleak, and therefore they are all the more discontinuous with the call that is sounded at line 165: "Weep no more, woeful Shepherds, weep no more, / For *Lycidas* your sorrow is not dead." These are entirely new accents spoken by an entirely new voice. It is a voice that counsels rather than complains, that turns outward rather than inward, a voice whose confident affirmation of a universal benevolence could not be further from the dark and self-pitying questioning of the swain. Everything, in short, has been changed, and it has changed not even in a line but in the space between lines. It is at this point that the orthodox reading of the poem, in which "the troubled thought of the elegist" traces out a sequence of "rise, evolution, and resolution," founders.[26] There is no evolution here, simply a disjunction, a gap, and the seekers of unity are left with the problem of explaining it. In general, their explanations have taken one of two forms. Either the change is explained theologically as a "leap from nature to revelation"[27] and a "dramatization of the infusion of grace,"[28] or it is explained away by assigning the lines to another speaker. This is the solution of William Madsen, who notes the abrupt transition from the "plaintive" and "ineffectual" to the authoritative, and concludes that the consolation is spoken not by the swain but by Michael, who responds in a fuller measure than might have been expected to the speaker's appeal ("Look homeward Angel now, and melt with ruth" [Lycidas, 163]). Madsen offers his emendation as an alternative to the theological reading; but in fact there is very little difference between them, since in either reading this point marks the appearance in the poem of "a new voice." For Madsen that voice is Michael's; for Abrams and Friedman (among others) it is the voice of a regenerated (made new) swain. In either case, there is agreement that the voice we had been hearing is heard no more and that what takes its place is something wholly different. This is of course not the first time this has happened, and it is only because in Madsen's reading the event is unusual that he feels moved to assign the new voice a specific name (it is this assignment that has been objected to). In the reading that has been developed here, however, the appearance of new voices and the merging of old is occurring all the time; the speaker is repeatedly dislodged or overwhelmed or absorbed, and his disappearance at line 164 is just one in a series.

There is, however, a difference. This disappearance is the last; the speaker is never heard from again. Or if he is heard from again, it is not as his "own person" but as a "member incorporate" of a truth from which he is now indistinguishable. That is to say, Madsen is right to hear the voice as different, but he is wrong to hear it as anyone's in particular. The accents here, as Marjorie Nicolson long ago observed, are "choral" as "all voices combine in virtuous crescendo."[29] If the speaker is among them, he is literally unrecognizable, since what allowed him to stand out was the "dogged insistence"[30] with which he held on to the local perspective of his own ambitions. In the end he is not even distinguishable as an addressee: the choral voice responds not to one but to a mass of complaints; the consolation is for "woeful Shepherds," and the plural noun silently denies the speaker even the claim to have been uniquely grieving; the grief is as general as the consolation, and it simply doesn't leave room for anything personal. The distance that has been traveled is the distance from the melodious tear of line 14 to the "unexpressive nuptial Song" of line 176. The tear falls from a single eye; it is the poem as the product of one voice that demands to be heard, if only as an expression of inconsolability; but the nuptial song is produced by everyone and therefore *heard* by no one, in the sense that there is no one who is at a sufficient distance from it for there to be a question of hearing. That is why it is called "unexpressive," which means both inexpressible (can't be said) and inaudible (it can't be apprehended): both speaking and receiving assume a separation between communicating agents; but this song is not a communication at all—it is a testimony to a joy which, since it binds all, need not be transmitted to any. The mistake of the first-person voice has been his desire to speak, to proclaim from an analytic and judgmental distance a truth he only sees; but in the great vision of these soaring lines, the truth proclaims, because it fills, its speakers, who are therefore not speakers at all but witnesses. They are in the happy condition for which Milton prays at the end of "At a Solemn Music":

> O may we soon again renew that Song,
> And keep in tune with Heav'n, till God ere long
> To his celestial consort us unite,
> To live with him, and sing in endless morn of light.
> (25–28)

The wish that we may join that choir is the wish that we *not* be heard as a distinctive and therefore alienated voice, the wish that we might utter sounds in such a way as to remain silent (unexpressive). It is a wish that is here granted the would-be elegist, whether he wants it or not, as finally he is no longer his own person but a member incorporate into that truth whereof he has been persuaded.

I am aware that this might seem a backdoor way into the usual reading of *Lycidas;* for just like any other critic, I have gotten the swain into heaven or at least into a position where a heavenly vision is available to him. But if he is now one of those who sing and singing in their glory move, he could not be picked out from among the other members of troops and societies, and therefore his "triumph," if one can call it that, is not achieved in terms that he would understand or welcome. As Friedman remarks, the speaker "fights *against* the knowledge" offered by the poem's higher moods; his experience is "one of active struggle" (5). My point is that it is a struggle he loses, and that the poem achieves its victory first by preempting him and finally by silencing him. Rather than the three-part structure traditionally proposed for *Lycidas,* I am proposing a structure of two parts: a first part (lines 1 through 75.5) where the first-person voice proceeds under the illusion of independence and control, and a second, longer part where that illusion is repeatedly exposed and finally dispelled altogether. In place of an interior lyric punctuated by digressive interpolations, we have a poem that begins in digression—the first-person voice is the digression—and regains the main path only when the lyric note is no longer sounded. We have, in short, a poem that relentlessly denies the privilege of the speaking subject, of the unitary and separate consciousness, and is finally, and triumphantly, anonymous.

It is anonymous twice. The last eight lines of *Lycidas* have always been perceived as problematic, because they insist on a narrative frame that was not apparent in the beginning, because the frame or coda is spoken by an unidentified third-person voice, and because that voice is so firmly impersonal. One advantage of the reading offered here is that these are not problems at all: if the introduction of a narrative perspective suggests that everything presented as spontaneous was in fact already spoken, this is no more than a confirmation of what has long since become obvious; if the new voice is unidentified, it is only the last in a series of unidentified voices or of voices whose single identities have long since been lost or blurred; and if the unidentified voice is impersonal it is merely a continuation of the mode the poem has finally achieved. In fact, the crucial thing about these lines is that there is no one to whom they can be plausibly assigned. They are certainly not the swain's, for he is what they describe, and they describe him significantly as someone who is "uncouth"—that is, unknown, someone who departs the poem with less of an identity than he displayed at its beginning; nor is there any compelling reason to assign them to any of the previous speakers, to the Pilot, or Hippotades, or Triton, or Neptune, or Cambridge, or Apollo. The only recourse, and it is one that has appealed to many, is to assign the lines to Milton; but of all the possibilities, this is the least persuasive. No voice in English poetry is more distinctive than Milton's, so much so that the characters he creates almost always sound just like him. But these lines do not sound like anyone; they are perfectly—that is, unrelievedly—conventional, and as such they are the perfect conclusion to a poem from which the personal has been systematically eliminated. Indeed, if these lines were written in accents characteristically Miltonic, they would constitute a claim exactly like that which is denied to the poem's first speaker: the claim to be able to pronounce, to sum up, to say it conclusively and once and for all. Instead Milton gives over the conclusion of the poem to a collection of pastoral commonplaces which are not even structured into a summary statement, but simply follow one another in a series that is unconstrained by any strong syntactic pressures. (The lines are markedly paratactic and conform to what Thomas Rosenmeyer has called the "disconnective decorum" of the pure pastoral.)[31] In short, Milton silences himself, just as the first-person voice is silenced, and performs (if that is the word) an act of humility comparable to that which allows him to call his *Nativity Ode* "tedious" at the very moment its intended recipient falls asleep. Rosemond Tuve once observed that in Herbert's career we can see a life-long effort to achieve the "immolation of the individual will." This has not usually been thought to be Milton's project, but the determined anonymity of *Lycidas* should remind us that the poet's fierce egoism is but one-half of his story.

NOTES

1   G. W. Knight, *The Burning Oracle* (London: Oxford University Press, 1939), 70.

2   J. C. Ransom, "A Poem Nearly Anonymous," in *Milton's Lycidas: The Tradition and the Poem*, ed. C. A. Patrides (New York: Holt, Rinehart, Winston, 1961), 71. This essay was first published in *American Review* 4 (1953).

3   *Lycidas*, line 165, in *John Milton: Complete Poems and Major Prose*, ed. M. Y. Hughes (New York, 1957).

4   William Madsen, *From Shadowy Types to Truth* (New Haven: Yale University Press, 1968), 13.

5   Donald Friedman, "*Lycidas:* The Swain's Paideia," *Milton Studies* 3 (1971): 33.

6   Stewart Baker, "Milton's Uncouth Swain," *Milton Studies* 3 (1971): 35, 50.

7   Knight, *The Burning Oracle*, 70.

8   H. V. Ogden, "The Principles of Variety and Contrast in Seventeenth-Century Aesthetics, and Milton's Poetry," *Journal of the History of Ideas* 10 (1949): 181.

9   J. H. Raleigh, "*Lycidas:* 'Yet Once More,'" *Prairie Schooner* (winter 1968–1969): 317.

10 S. Elledge, ed., *Milton's Lycidas* (New York: Harper and Row, 1966), 254.

11 *Comus*, line 4, in *John Milton: Complete Poems and Major Prose.*

12 *An Apology against a Pamphlet*, in *Complete Prose Works of John Milton*, vol. 1, ed. D. M. Wolfe (New Haven: Yale University Press, 1953), 953.

13 *Of Education*, in *Complete Prose Works of John Milton*, vol. 2, ed. E. Sirluck (New Haven: Yale University Press, 1959), 363.

14 *The Reason of Church Government*, in *Complete Prose Works of John Milton*, vol. 1, 807.

15 *An Apology against a Pamphlet*, 871.

16 J. H. Hanford, *The Milton Handbook* (New York: F. S. Croft, 1954), 168.

17 A. S. P. Woodhouse and D. Bush, eds., *A Variorum Commentary on the Poems of John Milton* (New York: Columbia University Press, 1972), vol. 2, part 2, 647.

18 B. A. Rajan, "*Lycidas:* The Shattering of the Leaves," *Studies in Philology* 64 (1967): 59.

19 Friedman, "*Lycidas:* The Swain's Paideia," 13.

20 Virgil, *Eclogue VI*, trans. Paul Alpers, in Alpers, *The Singer of the Eclogues* (Berkeley: University of California Press, 1979), 37.

21 Friedman, "*Lycidas:* The Swain's Paideia," 13.

22 M. C. Pecheux, "The Dread Voice in *Lycidas*," *Milton Studies*, 9 (1976): 238.

23 See *Paradise Lost*, book V, lines 803–807: "Thus far his bold discourse without control / Had audience, when among the Seraphim, / *Abdiel* . . . / Stood up." In *John Milton: Complete Poems and Major Prose.*

24 Quoted in Pecheux, "The Dread Voice in *Lycidas*," 235.

25 *Nativity Ode,* lines 26, 243–244, in *John Milton: Complete Poems and Major Prose.*

26 M. H. Abrams, "Five Types of *Lycidas,*" in Patrides, ed., *Lycidas: The Tradition and the Poem,* 224.

27 Ibid., 229.

28 Friedman, "*Lycidas:* The Swain's Paideia," 19.

29 Marjorie Nicolson, *John Milton: A Reader's Guide to His Poetry* (New York: Farrar, Straus, 1963), 110.

30 The phrase is Madsen's (*From Shadowy Types to Truth,* 13).

31 Thomas Rosenmeyer, *The Green Cabinet* (Berkeley: University of California Press, 1969), 53.

AFTER FORMALISM?

9. *Literary History and Literary Modernity*
Paul de Man

To WRITE REFLECTIVELY about modernity leads to problems that put the usefulness of the term into question, especially as it applies, or fails to apply, to literature. There may well be an inherent contradiction between modernity, which is a way of acting and behaving, and such terms as "reflection" or "ideas" that play an important part in literature and history. The spontaneity of being modern conflicts with the claim to think and write about modernity; it is not at all certain that literature and modernity are in any way compatible concepts. Yet we all speak readily about modern literature and even use this term as a device for historical periodization, with the same apparent unawareness that history and modernity may well be even more incompatible than literature and modernity. The innocuous-sounding title of this essay may therefore contain no less than two logical absurdities—a most inauspicious beginning.

The term "modernity" reappears with increasing frequency and seems again to have become an issue not only as an ideological weapon, but as a theoretical problem as well. It may even be one of the ways by means of which the link between literary theory and literary praxis is being partly restored. At other moments in history, the topic "modernity" might be used just as an attempt at self-definition, as a way of diagnosing one's own present. This can happen during periods of considerable inventiveness, periods that seem, looking back, to have been unusually productive. At such actual or imaginary times, modernity would not be a value in itself, but would designate a set of values that exist independently of their modernity: Renaissance art is not admired because it may have been, at a certain moment, a distinctively "modern" form of art. We do not feel this way about the present, perhaps because such self-assurance can exist only retrospectively. It would be a hopeless task to try to define descriptively the elusive pattern of our own literary modernity; we draw nearer to the problem, however, by asking how modernity can, in itself, become an issue and why this issue seems to be raised with particular urgency with regard to literature or, even more specifically, with regard to theoretical speculations about literature.

That this is indeed the case can be easily verified in Europe as well as in the United States. It is particularly conspicuous, for example, in Germany where, after being banned for political reasons, the term "modernity" now receives a strong positive value-emphasis and has of late been much in evidence as a battlecry as well as a serious topic of investigation. The same is true in France and in the United States, perhaps most clearly in the renewed interest shown in the transfer of methods derived from the social sciences to literary studies.

Not so long ago, a concern with modernity would in all likelihood have coincided with a commitment to avant-garde movements such as dada, surrealism, or expressionism. The term would have appeared in manifestoes and proclamations, not in learned articles or international colloquia. But this does not mean that we can divide the twentieth century into two parts: a "creative" part that was actually modern, and a "reflective" or "critical" part that feeds on this modernity in the manner of a parasite, with active modernity replaced by theorizing about the modern. Certain forces that could legitimately be called modern and that were at work in lyric poetry, in the novel, and the theater have also now become operative in the field of literary theory and criticism. The gap between the manifestoes and the learned articles has narrowed to the point where some manifestoes are quite learned and some articles—though by no means all—are quite provocative. This development has by itself complicated and changed the texture of our literary modernity a great deal and brought to the fore difficulties inherent in the term itself as soon as it is used historically or reflectively. It is perhaps somewhat disconcerting to learn that our usage of the word goes back to the late fifth century of our era and that there is nothing modern about the concept of modernity. It is even more disturbing to discover the host of complications that beset one as soon as a conceptual definition of the term is attempted, especially with regard to literature. One is soon forced to resort to paradoxical formulations, such as defining the modernity of a literary period as the manner in which it discovers the impossibility of being modern.

It is this complication I would like to explore with the help of some examples that are not necessarily taken from our immediate present. They should illuminate the problematic structure of a concept that, like all concepts that are in essence temporal, acquires a particularly rich complexity when it is made to refer to events that are in essence linguistic. I will be less concerned with a description of our own modernity than with the challenge to the methods or the possibility of literary history that the concept implies.

Among the various antonyms that come to mind as possible opposites for "modernity"—a variety which is itself symptomatic of the complexity of the term—none is more fruitful than "history." "Modern" can be used in opposition to "traditional" or even to "classical." For some French and American contemporaries, "modern" could even mean the opposite of "romantic," a usage that would be harder to conceive for some specialists of German literature. Antimodernists such as Emil Staiger do not hesitate to see the sources of a modernism they deplore in the Frühromantik of Friedrich Schlegel and Novalis, and the lively quarrel now taking place in Germany is still focused on the early nineteenth-century tensions between Weimar and Jena. But each of these antonyms—ancient, traditional, classical, and romantic—would embroil us in qualifications and discriminations that are, in fact, superficial matters of geographical and historical contingency. We will reach further if we try to think through the latent opposition between "modern" and "historical," and this will also bring us closest to the contemporary version of the problem.

The vested interest that academics have in the value of history makes it difficult to put the term seriously into question. Only an exceptionally talented and perhaps eccentric member of the profession could undertake this task with sufficient energy to make it effective, and even then it is likely to be accompanied by the violence that surrounds passion and rebellion. One of the most striking instances of such a rebellion occurred when Nietzsche, then a young philologist who had been treated quite generously by the academic establishment, turned violently against the traditional foundations of his own discipline in a polemical essay entitled "Of the Use and Misuse of History for Life" ("Vom Nutzen und Nachteil der Historie für das Leben"). The text is a good example of the complications that ensue when a genuine impulse toward modernity collides with the demands of a historical consciousness or a culture based on the disciplines of history. It can serve as an introduction to the more delicate problems that arise when modernity is applied more specifically to literature.

It is not at once clear that Nietzsche is concerned with a conflict between modernity and history in his Second Unzeitgemässe Betrachtung. That history is being challenged in a fundamental way is obvious from the start, but it is not obvious that this happens in the name of modernity. The term "modern" most frequently appears in the text with negative connotations as descriptive of the way in which Nietzsche considers his contemporaries to be corrupted and enfeebled by an excessive interest in the past. As opposed to the Greeks, Nietzsche's "moderns" escape from the issues of the present, which they are too weak and sterile to confront, into the sheltering inwardness that history can provide, but that bears no relation to actual existence.[1] History and modernity seem to go hand in hand and jointly fall prey to Nietzsche's cultural criticism. Used in this sense, modernity is merely a descriptive term that designates a certain state of mind Nietzsche considers prevalent among the Germans of his time. A much more dynamic concept of modernity, far-reaching enough to serve as a first definition, appears in what is here directly being opposed to history, namely what Nietzsche calls "life."

"Life" is conceived not just in biological but in temporal terms as the ability to *forget* whatever precedes a present situation. Like most opponents of Rousseau in the nineteenth century, Nietzsche's thought follows purely Rousseauistic patterns; the text starts with a contrasting parallel between nature and culture that stems directly from the *Second Discourse on the Origins of Inequality*. The restlessness of human society, in contrast to the placid state of nature of the animal herd, is diagnosed as man's inability to forget the past.

> [Man] wonders about himself, about his inability [to learn] to forget, and about his tendency to remain tied to the past: No matter how far and how swiftly he runs, the chain runs with him . . . Man says "I remember," and envies the animal that forgets at once, and watches each moment die, disappear in night and mist, and disappear forever. Thus the animal lives unhistorically: It hides nothing and coincides at all moments exactly with that which it is; it is bound to be truthful at all times, unable to be anything else. (211)

This ability to forget and to live without historical awareness exists not only on an animal level. Since "life" has an ontological as well as a biological meaning, the condition of animality persists as a constitutive part of man. Not only are there moments when it governs his actions, but these are also the moments when he reestablishes contact with his spontaneity and allows his truly human nature to assert itself.

> We saw that the animal, which is truly unhistorical and lives confined within a horizon almost without extension, exists in a relative state of happiness: We will therefore have to consider the ability to experience life in a nonhistorical way as the most important and most original of experiences, as the foundation on which right, health, greatness, and anything truly human can be erected. (215)

Moments of genuine humanity thus are moments at which all anteriority vanishes, annihilated by the power of an absolute forgetting. Although such a radical rejection of history may be illusory or unfair to the achievements of the past, it nevertheless remains justified as necessary to the fulfillment of our human destiny and as the condition for action. "As the man who acts must, according to Goethe, be without a conscience, he must also be without knowledge; he forgets everything in order to be able to *do* something; he is unfair toward what lies behind and knows only one right, the right of what is now coming into being as the result of his own action" (216).

We are touching here upon the radical impulse that stands behind all genuine modernity when it is not merely a descriptive synonym for the contemporaneous or for a passing fashion. Fashion (mode) can sometimes be only what remains of modernity after the impulse has subsided, as soon—and this can be almost at once—as it has changed from being an incandescent point in time into a reproducible cliché, all that remains of an invention that has lost the desire that produced it. Fashion is like the ashes left behind by the uniquely shaped flames of the fire, the trace alone revealing that a fire actually took place. But Nietzsche's ruthless forgetting, the blindness with which he throws himself into an action lightened of all previous experience, captures the authentic spirit of modernity. It is the tone of Rimbaud when he declares that he has no antecedents whatever in the history of France, that all one has to expect from poets is "du nouveau" and that one must be "absolutely modern"; it is the tone of Antonin Artaud when he asserts that "written poetry has value for one single moment and should then be destroyed. Let the dead poets make room for the living . . . the time for masterpieces is past."[2] Modernity exists in the form of a desire to wipe out whatever came earlier, in the hope of reaching at last a point that could be called a true present, a point of origin that marks a new departure. This combined interplay of deliberate forgetting with an action that is also a new origin reaches the full power of the idea of modernity. Thus defined, modernity and history are diametrically opposed to each other in Nietzsche's text. Nor is there any doubt as to his commitment to modernity, the only way to reach the metahistorical realm in which the rhythm of one's existence coincides with that of the eternal return. Yet the shrill grandiloquence of the tone may make one suspect that the issue is not as simple as it may at first appear.

Of course, within the polemical circumstances in which it was written, the essay has to overstate the case against history and to aim beyond its target in the hope of reaching it. This tactic is less interesting, however, than the question of whether Nietzsche can free his own thought from historical prerogatives, whether his own text can approach the condition of modernity it advocates. From the start, the intoxication with the history-transcending life-process is counterbalanced by a deeply pessimistic wisdom that remains rooted in a sense of historical causality, although it reverses the movement of history from one of development to one of regression. Human "existence," we are told near the beginning of the essay, "is an uninterrupted pastness that lives from its own denial and destruction, from its own contradictions." ("Das Dasein ist nur ein ununterbrochenes Gewesensein, ein Ding, das davon lebt, sich selbst zu verneinen and zu verzehren, sich selbst zu widersprechen.")[3] This description of life as a constant regression has nothing to do with cultural errors, such as the excess of historical disciplines in contemporary education against which the essay polemicizes, but lies much deeper in the nature of things, beyond the reach of culture. It is a temporal experience of human mutability, historical in the deepest sense of the term in that it implies the necessary experience of any present as a *passing* experience that makes the past irrevocable and unforgettable, because it is inseparable from any present or future. Keats gained access to the same awareness when, in *The Fall of Hyperion*, he contemplated in the fallen Saturn the past as a foreknowledge of his own mortal future:

> Without stay or prop
> But my own weak mortality, I bore
> The load of this eternal quietude,
> The unchanging gloom . . .

Modernity invests its trust in the power of the present moment as an origin, but discovers that, in severing itself from the past, it has at the same time severed itself from the present. Nietzsche's text leads him irrevocably to this discovery, perhaps most strikingly (because most implicitly) when he comes close to describing his own function as a *critical* historian and discovers that the rejection of the past is not so much an act of forgetting as an act of critical judgment directed against himself.

> [The critical student of the past] must possess the strength, and must at times apply this strength, to the destruction and dissolution of the past in order to be able to live. He achieves this by calling the past into court, putting it under indictment, and finally condemning it; any past, however, deserves to be condemned, for such is the condition of human affairs that they are ruled by violence and weakness. . . . "It takes a great deal of strength to be able to live and forget to what extent life and injustice go together." . . . But this very life that has to forget must also at times be able

to stop forgetting; then it will become clear how illegitimate the existence of something, of a privilege, a caste or a dynasty actually is, and how much it deserves to be destroyed. Then the past is judged critically, attacked at its very roots with a sharp knife, and brutally cut down, regardless of established pieties. This is always a dangerous process, dangerous for life itself. Men and eras that serve life in this manner, by judging and destroying the past, are always dangerous and endangered. For we are inevitably the result of earlier generations and thus the result of their mistakes, their passions and aberrations, even of their crimes; it is not possible to loosen oneself entirely from this chain. . . . Afterwards, we try to give ourselves a new past from which we should have liked to descend instead of the past from which we actually descended. But this is also dangerous, because it is so difficult to trace the limit of one's denial of the past, and because the newly invented nature is likely to be weaker than the previous one. . . . (230)

The parricidal imagery of the passage, the weaker son condemning and killing the stronger father, reaches the inherent paradox of the denial of history implied in modernity.

As soon as modernism becomes conscious of its own strategies—and it cannot fail to do so if it is justified, as in this text, in the name of a concern for the future—it discovers itself to be a generative power that not only engenders history, but is part of a generative scheme that extends far back into the past. The image of the chain, to which Nietzsche instinctively resorts when he speaks of history, reveals this very clearly. Considered as a principle of life, modernity becomes a principle of origination and turns at once into a generative power that is itself historical. It becomes impossible to overcome history in the name of life or to forget the past in the name of modernity, because both are linked by a temporal chain that gives them a common destiny. Nietzsche finds it impossible to escape from history, and he finally has to bring the two incompatibles, history and modernity (now using the term in the full sense of a radical renewal), together in a paradox that cannot be resolved, an aporia that comes very close to describing the predicament of our own present modernity:

For the impulse that stands behind our history-oriented education—in radical inner contradiction to the spirit of a "new time" or a "modern spirit"—must in turn be understood historically; history itself must resolve the problem of history, historical knowledge must turn its weapon against itself—this threefold "must" is the imperative of the "new times," if they are to achieve something truly new, powerful, life-giving, and original. (261)

Only through history is history conquered; modernity now appears as the horizon of a historical process that has to remain a gamble. Nietzsche sees no assurance that his own reflective and historical attempt achieves any genuine change; he realizes that his text itself can be nothing but another historical document (277), and finally he has to delegate the power of renewal and modernity to a mythical entity called "youth" to which he can only recommend the effort of self-knowledge that has brought him to his own abdication.

The bad faith implied in advocating self-knowledge to a younger generation, while demanding from this generation that it act blindly, out of a self-forgetting that one is unwilling or unable to achieve oneself, forms a pattern all too familiar in our own experience to need comment. In this way Nietzsche, at this early point in his career, copes with a paradox that his thought has revealed with impressive clarity: Modernity and history relate to each other in a curiously contradictory way that goes beyond antithesis or opposition. If history is not to become sheer regression or paralysis, it depends on modernity for its duration and renewal; but modernity cannot assert itself without being at once swallowed up and reintegrated into a regressive historical process. Nietzsche offers no real escape out of a predicament in which we readily recognize the mood of our own modernity. Modernity and history seem condemned to being linked together in a self-destroying union that threatens the survival of both.

If we see in this paradoxical condition a diagnosis of our own modernity, then literature has always been essentially modern. Nietzsche was speaking of life and of culture in general, of modernity and history as they appear in all human enterprises in the most general sense possible. The problem becomes more intricate when it is restricted to literature. Here we are dealing with an activity that necessarily contains, within its own specificity, the very contradiction that Nietzsche discovered at the endpoint of his rebellion against a historically minded culture. Regardless of historical or cultural conditions, beyond the reach of educational or moral imperatives, the modernity of literature confronts us at all times with an unsolvable paradox. On the one hand, literature has a constitutive affinity with action, with the unmediated, free act that knows no past; some of the impatience of Rimbaud or Artaud echoes in all literary texts, no matter how serene and detached they may seem. The historian, in his function as historian, can remain quite remote from the collective acts he records; his language and the events that the language denotes are clearly distinct entities. But the writer's language is to some degree the product of his own action; he is both the historian and the agent of his own language. The ambivalence of writing is such that it can be considered both an act and an interpretative process that follows after an act with which it cannot coincide. As such, it both affirms and denies its own nature or specificity. Unlike the historian, the writer remains so closely involved with action that he can never free himself of the temptation to destroy whatever stands between him and his deed, especially the temporal distance that makes him dependent on an earlier past. The appeal of modernity haunts all literature. It is revealed in numberless images and emblems that appear at all periods—in the obsession with a *tabula rasa*, with new beginnings—that finds recurrent expression in all forms of writing. No true account of literary language can bypass this persistent temptation of literature to fulfill itself in a single moment. The temptation of immediacy is constitutive of a literary consciousness and has to be included in a definition of the specificity of literature.

The manner in which this specificity asserts itself, however, the form of its actual manifestation, is curiously oblique and confusing. Often in the course of literary history writers openly assert their commitment to modernity thus conceived. Yet whenever this happens, a curious logic that seems almost uncontrolled, a necessity inherent in the nature of the problem rather than in the will of the writer, directs their utterance away from their avowed purpose. Assertions of literary modernity often end up by putting the possibility of being modern seriously into question. But precisely because this discovery goes against an original commitment that cannot simply be dismissed as erroneous, it never gets stated outright, but hides instead behind rhetorical devices of language that disguise and distort what the writer is actually saying, perhaps in contrast to what he meant to say. Hence the need for the interpreter of such texts to respond to levels of meaning not immediately obvious. The very presence of such complexities indicates the existence of a special problem: How is it that a specific and important feature of a literary consciousness, its desire for modernity, seems to lead outside literature into something that no longer shares this specificity, thus forcing the writer to undermine his own assertions in order to remain faithful to his vocation?

It is time to clarify what we are trying to convey with some examples taken from texts that openly plead the cause of modernity. Many, but by no means all, of these texts are written by people who stand outside literature from the start, either because they instinctively tend toward the interpretative distance of the historian, or because they incline toward a form of action no longer linked to language. During the quarrel between the Ancients and the Moderns, the debate between a traditional conception of literature and modernity that took place in France near the end of the seventeenth century and that is still considered by some as the starting point of a "modern" sense of history,[4] it is striking that the modern camp not only contained men of slighter literary talent, but that their arguments against classical literature were often simply against literature as such. The nature of the debate forced the participants to make comparative critical evaluations of ancient versus contemporary writing; it obliged them to offer something resembling readings of passages in Homer, Pindar, or Theocritus. Although no one covered himself with critical glory in the performance of this task—mainly because the powerful imperative of decorum (*bienséance*) tends to become a particularly opaque screen that stands between the antique text and the classical reading[5]—the partisans of the Ancients still performed a great deal better than the promoderns. If one compares the remarks of a "moderne" such as Charles Perrault on Homer or his application in 1688 of seventeenth-century bienséance to Hellenic texts in *Parallèle des anciens et des modernes* with Boileau's reply in *Réflexions critiques sur quelques passages du rhéteur Longin* of 1694,[6] it then becomes clear that the "anciens" had a notion of decorum that remained in much closer contact with literature, including its constitutive impulse toward literary modernity, than the "modernes." This fact undoubtedly strengthens, in the long run, the cause of the moderns, despite their own critical shortcomings, but the point is precisely that a partisan and deliberately promodern stance is much more easily taken by someone devoid of literary sensitivity than by a genuine writer. Literature, which is inconceivable without a passion for modernity, also seems to oppose from the inside a subtle resistance to this passion.

Thus we find in the same period a detached and ironical mind like that of the early Fontenelle openly take the side of the moderns in asserting that "nothing stands so firmly in the way of progress, nothing restricts the mind so effectively as an excessive admiration for the Ancients."[7] Having to demystify the merit of invention and origin on which the superiority of the Ancients is founded—and which, in fact, roots their merit in their genuine modernity—Fontenelle becomes himself entertainingly inventive in his assertion that the prestige of so-called origins is merely an illusion created by the distance separating us from a remote past. At the same time he expresses the mock-anxious fear that our own progressing rationality will prevent us from benefiting, in the eyes of future generations, from the favorable prejudice we were silly enough to bestow on the Greeks and the Romans.

> By virtue of these compensations, we can hope to be excessively admired in future centuries, to make up for the little consideration we are given in our own. Critics will vie to discover in our works hidden beauties that we never thought of putting there; obvious weaknesses, that the author would be the first to acknowledge if they were pointed out to him today, will find staunch

defenders. God knows with what contempt the fashionable writers of these future days—which may well turn out to be Americans—will be treated in comparison with us. The same prejudice that degrades us at one time enhances our value at another; we are first the victims, then the gods of the same error in judgment—an amusing play to observe with detached eyes.

The same playful indifference prompts Fontenelle to add the remark: "But, in all likelihood, reason will grow more perfect in time and the crude prejudice in favor of the Ancients is bound to vanish. It may well not be with us much longer. We may well be wasting our time admiring the Ancients in vain, without expectations of ever being admired in the same capacity. What a pity! (195–96, 199).

Fontenelle's historical irony is far from being unliterary, but if taken at face value it stands at the very opposite pole of the impulse toward action without which literature would not be what it is. Nietzsche admired Fontenelle, but it must have been as an Apollinian antiself, for nothing is more remote from the spirit of modernity than Fontenelle's *perfectibilité*, a kind of statistical, quantitative balance between right and wrong, a process of trial-by-chance that may perhaps lead to certain rules by means of which aberrations could be prevented in the future. In the name of perfectibilité, he can reduce critical norms to a set of mechanical rules and assert, with only a trace of irony, that literature progressed faster than science because the imagination obeys a smaller number of easier rules than does reason. He can easily dismiss poetry and the arts as "unimportant," since he pretends to have moved so far away from their concerns. His stance is that of the objective, scientific historian. Even if taken seriously, this stance would engage him in a task of interpretation closer to literature than that of Charles Perrault, for example, who has to resort to the military and imperial achievements of his age to find instances of the superiority of the moderns. That such a type of modernism leads outside literature is clear enough. The topos of the antiliterary, technological man as an incarnation of modernity is recurrent among the *idées reçues* of the nineteenth century and symptomatic of the alacrity with which modernity welcomes the opportunity to abandon literature altogether. The opposite temptation toward a purely detached interpretation, of which we find an ironic version in Fontenelle, also reveals the inherent trend to draw away from the literary. Perrault's committed, as well as Fontenelle's detached, modernism both lead away from literary understanding.

Our examples may have been one-sided, however, since we were dealing with nonliterary figures. More revealing is the case of writers whose proximity to literature is beyond dispute and who find themselves, in true accordance with their literary vocation, defenders of modernity—not just in the choice of their themes and settings, but as representative of a fundamental attitude of mind. The poetry of Baudelaire, as well as his plea for modernity in several critical texts, would be a good case in point.

As seen in the famous essay on Constantin Guys, "Le peintre de la vie moderne," Baudelaire's conception of modernity is very close to that of Nietzsche in his second *Unzeitgemässe Betrachtung*. It stems from an acute sense of the present as a constitutive element of all aesthetic experience: "The pleasure we derive from the *representation of the present* (la représenstation du présent) is not merely due to the beauty it may display, but also to the essential 'presentness' of the present."[8] The paradox of the problem is potentially contained in the formula "représentation du présent," which combines a repetitive with an instantaneous pattern without apparent awareness of the incompatibility. Yet this latent tension governs the development of the entire essay. Baudelaire remains faithful throughout to the seduction of the present; any temporal awareness is so closely tied for him to the present moment that memory comes to apply more naturally to the present than it does to the past: "Woe be to him who, in Antiquity, studies anything besides pure art, logic and general method! By plunging into the past he may well lose the *memory of the present* (la mémoire du présent). He abdicates the values and privileges provided by actual circumstance, for almost all our originality stems from the stamp that time prints on our sensations" (224–25, italics mine). The same temporal ambivalence prompts Baudelaire to couple any evocation of the present with terms such as "représentation," "mémoire," or even "temps," all opening perspectives of distance and difference within the apparent uniqueness of the instant. Yet his modernity too, like Nietzsche's, is a forgetting or a suppression of anteriority. The human figures that epitomize modernity are defined by experiences such as childhood or convalescence, a freshness of perception that results from a slate wiped clear, from the absence of a past that has not yet had time to tarnish the immediacy of perception (although what is thus freshly discovered prefigures the end of this very freshness), of a past that, in the case of convalescence, is so threatening that it has to be forgotten.

All these experiences of immediacy coupled with their implicit negation, strive to combine the openness and freedom of a present severed from all other temporal dimensions, the weight of the past as well as the concern with a future, with a sense of totality and completeness that could not be achieved if a more extended awareness of time were not also involved. Thus we find Constantin Guys, who is made to serve as a kind of emblem for the poetic mind, to be a curious synthesis of a man of action (that is, a man of the moment, severed from past and future) with an observer and recorder of moments that are necessarily combined within a larger totality. Like the photographer or reporter of today, he has to be present at the battles and the murders of the world not to inform, but to freeze what is most transient and ephemeral into a recorded image. Constantin Guys, before being an artist, has to be "homme du monde," driven by curiosity and "always, spiritually, in the state of mind of the convalescent." The description of his technique offers perhaps the best formulation of this ideal combination of the instantaneous with a completed whole, of pure fluid movement with form—a combination that would achieve a reconciliation between the impulse toward modernity and the demand of the work of art to achieve duration. The painting remains steadily in motion and exists in the open, improvised manner of a sketch that is like a constant new beginning. The final closing of the form, constantly postponed, occurs so swiftly and suddenly that it hides its dependence on previous moments in its own precipitous instantaneity. The entire process tries to outrun time, to achieve a swiftness that would transcend the latent opposition between action and form.

In Monsieur Guy's manner, two features can be observed; in the first place, the contention of a highly suggestive, resurrecting power of memory, a memory that addresses all things with: "Lazarus, arise!"; on the other hand, a fiery, intoxicating vigor of pencil and brushstroke that almost resembles fury. He seems to be in anguish of not going fast enough, of letting the phantom escape before the synthesis has been extracted from it and recorded. . . . M. G. begins by slight pencil-marks that merely designate the place assigned to various objects in space. Then he indicates the main surfaces. . . . At the last moment, the definitive contour of the objects is sealed with ink. . . . This simple, almost elementary method . . . has the incomparable advantage that, at each point in the process of its elaboration, each drawing seems sufficiently completed; you may call this a sketch, if you like, but it is a perfect sketch. (228)

That Baudelaire has to refer to this synthesis as a "fantôme" is another instance of the rigor that forces him to double any assertion by a qualifying use of language that puts it at once into question. The Constantin Guys of the essay is himself a phantom, bearing some resemblance to the actual painter, but differing from him in being the fictional achievement of what existed only potentially in the "real" man. Even if we consider the character in the essay to be a mediator used to formulate the prospective vision of Baudelaire's own work, we can still witness in this vision a similar disincarnation and reduction of meaning. At first, in the enumeration of the themes that the painter (or writer) will select, we again find the temptation of modernity to move outside art, its nostalgia for the immediacy, the facticity of entities that are in contact with the present and illustrate the heroic ability to ignore or to forget that this present contains the prospective self-knowledge of its end. The figure chosen can be more or less close to being aware of this: it can be the mere surface, the outer garment of the present, the unwitting defiance of death in the soldier's colorful coat, or it can be the philosophically conscious sense of time of the dandy. In each case, however, the "subject" Baudelaire chose for a theme is preferred because it exists in the facticity, in the modernity, of a present that is ruled by experiences that lie outside language and escape from the successive temporality, the duration involved in writing. Baudelaire states clearly that the attraction of a writer toward his theme—which is also the attraction toward an action, a modernity, and an autonomous *meaning* that would exist outside the realm of language—is primarily an attraction to what is not art. The statement occurs with reference to the most anonymous and shapeless "theme" of all, that of the crowd: "C'est un moi insatiable de non-moi." (It is a self insatiable for non-selfhood) . . . (219). If one remembers that this "moi" designates, in the metaphor of a subject, the specificity of literature, then this specificity is defined by its inability to remain constant to its own specificity.

This, at least, corresponds to the first moment of a certain mode of being, called literature. It soon appears that literature is an entity that exists not as a single moment of self-denial, but as a plurality of moments that can, if one wishes, be represented—but this is a mere representation—as a succession of moments or a duration. In other words, literature can be represented as a movement and is, in essence, the fictional narration of this movement. After the initial moment of flight away from its own specificity, a moment of return follows that leads literature back to what it is—but we must bear in mind that terms such as "after" and "follows" do not designate actual moments in a diachrony, but are used purely as *metaphors* of duration. Baudelaire's text illustrates this return, this *reprise*, with striking clarity. The "moi insatiable de non-moi . . ." has been moving toward a series of "themes" that reveal the impatience with which it tries to move away from its own center. These themes become less and less concrete and substantial, however, although they are being evoked with increasing realism and mimetic rigor in the description of their surfaces. The more realistic and pictorial they become, the more abstract they are, the slighter the residue of meaning that would exist outside their specificity as mere language and mere *significant*. The last theme that Baudelaire evokes, that of the carriages, has nothing whatever to do with the facticity of the carriage— although Baudelaire insists that in the paintings by Constantin Guys "the entire structure of the carriage-body is perfectly orthodox: every part is in its place and nothing needs to be corrected" (259). The substantial, thematic *meaning* of the carriage as such, however, has disappeared:

> Regardless of attitude and position, regardless of the speed at which it is launched, a carriage, like a ship, receives from its motion a mysteriously complex graceful air, very hard to capture in shorthand (très difficile à sténographier). The pleasure that the artist's eye derives from it is drawn, or so it seems, from the sequence of geometrical figures that this already so complicated object engenders successively and swiftly in space. (259)

What is here being stenographed is the movement by which, in apparent and metaphorical succession, literature first moves away from itself and then returns. All that remains of the theme is a mere outline, less than a sketch, a time-arabesque rather than a figure. The carriage has been allegorized into nothingness and exists as the purely temporal vibration of a successive movement that has only linguistic existence—for nothing is more radically metaphorical than the expression "figures géométriques" that Baudelaire is compelled to use to make himself understood. But that he wants to be understood, and not misunderstood in the belief that this geometry would have recourse to anything that is not language, is clear from its implied identification with a mode of writing. The *stenos* in the word stenography, meaning narrow, could be used to designate the confinement of literature within its own boundaries, its dependence on duration and repetition that Baudelaire experienced as a curse. But the fact that the word designates a form of writing indicates the compulsion to return to a literary mode of being, as a form of language that knows itself to be mere repetition, mere fiction and allegory, forever unable to participate in the spontaneity of action or modernity.

The movement of this text—that could be shown to parallel the development of Baudelaire's poetry as it moves from the sensory richness of the earlier poems to their gradual allegorization in the prose versions of the *Spleen de Paris*—recurs with various degrees of explicitness in all writers and measures the legitimacy of their claim to be called writers. Modernity turns out to be indeed one of the concepts by means of which the distinctive nature of literature can be revealed in all its intricacy. No wonder it had to become a central issue in critical discussions and a source of torment to writers who have to confront it as a challenge to their vocation. They can neither accept nor reject it with good conscience. When they assert their own modernity, they are bound to discover their dependence on similar assertions made by their literary predecessors; their claim to being a new beginning turns out to be the repetition of a claim that has always already been made. As soon as Baudelaire has to replace the single instant of invention, conceived as an act, by a successive movement that involves at least two distinct moments, he enters into a world that assumes the depths and complications of an articulated time, an interdependence between past and future that prevents any present from ever coming into being.

The more radical the rejection of anything that came before, the greater the dependence on the past. Antonin Artaud can go to the extreme of rejecting all forms of theatrical art prior to his own; in his own work, he can demand the destruction of any form of written text—he nevertheless finally has to ground his own vision in examples such as the Balinese theater, the least modern, the most text-frozen type of theater conceivable. And he has to do so with full knowledge that he thus destroys his own project, with the hatred of the traitor for the camp that he has chosen to join. Quoting the lines in which Artaud attacks the very concept of the theater on which he has waged his entire undertaking ("Rien de plus impie que le système des Balinais . . ."), Jacques Derrida can rightly comment: "[Artaud] was unable to resign himself to a theater based on repetition, unable to renounce a theater that would do away with all forms of repetition."[9] The same fatal interplay governs the writer's attitude toward modernity: he cannot renounce the claim to being modern but also cannot resign himself to his dependence on predecessors—who, for that matter, were caught in the same situation. Never is Baudelaire as close to his predecessor Rousseau as in the extreme modernity of his latest prose poems, and never is Rousseau as tied to his literary ancestors as when he pretends to have nothing more to do with literature.

The distinctive character of literature thus becomes manifest as an inability to escape from a condition that is felt to be unbearable. It seems that there can be no end, no respite in the ceaseless pressure of this contradiction, at least as long as we consider it from the point of view of the writer as subject. The discovery of his inability to be modern leads him back to the fold, within the autonomous domain of literature, but never with genuine appeasement. As soon as he can feel appeased in this situation he ceases to be a writer. His language may be capable of a certain degree of tranquillity; it is, after all, the product of a renunciation that has allowed for the metaphorical thematization of the predicament. But this renunciation does not involve the subject. The continuous appeal of modernity, the desire to break out of literature toward the reality of the moment, prevails and, in its turn, folding back upon itself, engenders the repetition and the continuation of literature. Thus modernity, which is fundamentally a falling away from literature and a rejection of history, also acts as the principle that gives literature duration and historical existence.

The manner in which this inherent conflict determines the structure of literary language cannot be treated within the limits of this essay. We are more concerned, at this point, with the question of whether a history of an entity as self-contradictory as literature is conceivable. In the present state of literary studies this possibility is far from being clearly established. It is generally admitted that a positivistic history of literature, treating it as if it were a collection of empirical data, can only be a history of what literature is not. At best, it would be a preliminary classification opening the way for actual literary study, and at worst, an obstacle in the way of literary understanding. On the other hand, the intrinsic interpretation of literature claims to be anti- or ahistorical, but often presupposes a notion of history of which the critic is not himself aware.

In describing literature, from the standpoint of the concept of modernity, as the steady fluctuation of an entity away from and toward its own mode of being, we have constantly stressed that this movement does not take place as an actual sequence in time; to represent it as such is merely a metaphor making a sequence out of what occurs in fact as a synchronic juxtaposition. The sequential, diachronic structure of the process stems from the nature of literary language as an entity, not as an event. Things do not happen as if a literary text (or a literary vocation) moved for a certain period of time away from its center, then turned around, folding back upon itself at one specific moment to travel back to its genuine point of origin. These imaginary motions between fictional points cannot be located, dated, and represented as if they were places in a geography or events in a genetic history. Even in the discursive texts we have used—in Baudelaire, in Nietzsche, or even in Fontenelle—the three moments of flight, return, and the turning point at which flight changes into return or vice versa, exist simultaneously on levels of meaning that are so intimately intertwined that they cannot be separated. When Baudelaire, for example, speaks of "représentation du présent," of "mémoire du présent," of "synthèse du fantôme," or of "ébauche finie," his language names, at the same time, the flight, the turning point, and the return. Our entire argument lies compressed in such formulations. This would even be more obvious if we had used poetic instead of discursive texts. It follows that it would be a mistake to think of literary history as the diachronic narrative of the fluctuating motion we have tried to describe. Such a narrative can be only metaphorical, and history is not fiction.

With respect to its own specificity (that is, as an existing entity susceptible to historical description), literature exists at the same time in the modes of error and truth; it both betrays and obeys its own mode of being. A positivistic history that sees literature only as what it is not (as an objective fact, an empirical psyche, or a communication that transcends the literary text as text) is, therefore, necessarily inadequate. The same is true of approaches to literature that take for granted the specificity of literature (what the French structuralists, echoing the Russian formalists, call literarity [littérarité] of literature). If literature rested at ease within its own self-definition, it could be studied according to methods that are scientific rather than historical. We are obliged to confine ourselves to history when this is no longer the case, when the entity steadily puts its own ontological status into question. The structuralist goal of a science of literary forms assumes this stability and treats literature as if the fluctuating movement of aborted self-definition were not a constitutive part of its language. Structuralist formalism, therefore, systematically bypasses the necessary component of literature for which the term "modernity" is not such a bad name after all, despite its ideological and polemical overtones. It is a very revealing paradox, confirming again that anything touching upon literature becomes at once a Pandora's box, that the critical method which denies literary modernity would appear—and even, in certain respects, would be—the most modern of critical movements.

Could we conceive of a literary history that would not truncate literature by putting us misleadingly *into* or *outside* it, that would be able to maintain the literary aporia throughout, account at the same time for the truth and the falsehood of the knowledge literature conveys about itself, distinguish rigorously between metaphorical and historical language, and account for literary modernity as well as for its historicity? Clearly, such a conception would imply a revision of the notion of history and, beyond that, of the notion of time on which our idea of history is based. It would imply, for instance, abandoning the pre-assumed concept of history as a generative process that we found operative in Nietzsche's text—although this text also began to rebel against it—of history as a temporal hierarchy that resembles a parental structure in which the past is like an ancestor begetting, in a moment of unmediated presence, a future capable of repeating in its turn the same generative process. The relationship between truth and error that prevails in literature cannot be represented genetically, since truth and error exist simultaneously, thus preventing the favoring of the one over the other. The need to revise the foundations of literary history may seem like a desperately vast undertaking; the task appears even more disquieting if we contend that literary history could in fact be paradigmatic for history in general, since man himself, like literature, can be defined as an entity capable of putting his own mode of being into question. The task may well be less sizable, however, than it seems at first. All the directives we have formulated as guidelines for a literary history are more or less taken for granted when we are engaged in the much more humble task of reading and understanding a literary text. To become good literary historians, we must remember that what we usually call literary history has little or nothing to do with literature and that what we call literary interpretation—provided only it is good interpretation—is in fact literary history. If we extend this notion beyond literature, it merely confirms that the bases for historical knowledge are not empirical facts but written texts, even if these texts masquerade in the guise of wars or revolutions.

NOTES

1 Friedrich Nietzsche, "Vom Nutzen und Nachteil der Historie für das Leben," *Unzeitgemässe Betrachtung II* in Karl Schlechta, ed., *Werke I* (Munich: 1954), 232–33, 243.

2 Antonin Artaud, *Le Théâtre et son double*, vol. 4, *Oeuvres complètes* (Paris, 1956).

3 Nietzsche, "Vom Nutzen," 212.

4 See, for example, Werner Krauss, "Cartaud de la Villate und die Entstehung des geschichtlichen Weltbildes in der Frühaufklärung," *Studien zur Deutschen und Französischen Aufklärung* (Berlin: 1963), and H. R. Jauss's substantial introduction to his facsimile edition of Charles Perrault, *Parallèle des anciens et des modernes* (Munich: 1964), 12–13.

5 Critical utterances concerning the Homeric question are particularly revealing in this respect, in a partisan of the Moderns like Charles Perrault as well as in a partisan of the Ancients like Boileau.

6 H. R. Jauss, *Parallèle des anciens*, mentions as other convincing instances of critical insight among the defenders of the Ancients La Bruyère's *Discours sur Théophraste* (1699) and Saint-Evremont's *Sur les poèmes des anciens* (1685).

7 Fontenelle, "Digression sur les anciens et les modernes," *Oeuvres*, 4 (Paris: 1767), 170–200.

8 Charles Baudelaire, "Le peintre de la vie moderne," in *l'Art romantique, Oeuvres complètes*, vol. 4, ed. F. F. Gautier (Paris, 1923), 208. Italics are mine.

9 Jacques Derrida, "Le théâtre de la cruauté et la clôture de la représentation," *L'Écriture et la différence* (Paris: Édition du Seuil, 1967), 367.

10. Acts of Cultural Criticism
ROLAND BARTHES

THE ROMANS IN FILMS

I N MANKIEWICZ'S *Julius Caesar*, all the characters are wearing fringes. Some have them curly, some straggly, some tufted, some oily, all have them well combed, and the bald are not admitted, although there are plenty to be found in Roman history. Those who have little hair have not been let off for all that, and the hairdresser—the king-pin of the film—has still managed to produce one last lock which duly reaches the top of the forehead, one of those Roman foreheads, whose smallness has at all times indicated a specific mixture of self-righteousness, virtue and conquest.

What then is associated with these insistent fringes? Quite simply the label of Roman-ness. We therefore see here the mainspring of the Spectacle—the *sign*—operating in the open. The frontal lock overwhelms one with evidence, no one can doubt that he is in Ancient Rome. And this certainty is permanent: the actors speak, act, torment themselves, debate "questions of universal import," without losing, thanks to this little flag displayed on their foreheads, any of their historical plausibility. Their general representativeness can even expand in complete safety, cross the ocean and the centuries, and merge into the Yankee mugs of Hollywood extras; no matter, everyone is reassured, installed in the quiet certainty of a universe without duplicity, where Romans are Romans thanks to the most legible of signs: hair on the forehead.

A Frenchman, to whose eyes American faces still have something exotic, finds comical the combination of the morphologies of these gangster-sheriffs with the little Roman fringe: it rather looks like an excellent music hall gag. This is because for the French the sign in this case overshoots the target and discredits itself by letting its aim appear clearly. But this very fringe, when combed on the only naturally Latin forehead in the film, that of Marlon Brando, impresses us and does not make us laugh; and it is not impossible that part of the success of this actor in Europe is due to the perfect integration of Roman capillary habits with the general morphology of the characters he usually portrays. Conversely, one cannot believe in Julius Caesar, whose physiognomy is that of an Anglo-Saxon lawyer—a face with which one is already acquainted through a thousand bit parts in thrillers or comedies, and a compliant skull on which the hairdresser has raked, with great effort, a lock of hair.

In the category of capillary meanings, here is a subsign, that of nocturnal surprises: Portia and Calpurnia, woken up at dead of night, have conspicuously uncombed hair. The former, who is young, expresses disorder by flowing locks: her unreadiness is, so to speak, of the first degree. The latter, who is middle-aged, exhibits a more painstaking vulnerability: a plait winds round her neck and comes to rest on her right shoulder so as to impose the traditional sign of disorder, asymmetry. But these signs are at the same time excessive and ineffectual: they postulate a "nature" which they have not even the courage to acknowledge fully: they are not "fair and square."

Yet another sign in this *Julius Caesar:* all the faces sweat constantly. Labourers, soldiers, conspirators, all have their austere and tense features streaming (with Vaseline). And close-ups are so frequent that evidently sweat here is an attribute with a purpose. Like the Roman fringe or the nocturnal plait, sweat is a sign. Of what? Of moral feeling. Everyone is sweating because everyone is debating something within himself; we are here supposed to be in the locus of a horribly tormented virtue, that is, in the very locus of tragedy, and it is sweat which has the function of conveying this. The populace, upset by the death of Caesar, then by the arguments of Mark Antony, is sweating, and combining economically, in this single sign, the intensity of its emotion and the simplicity of its condition. And the virtuous men, Brutus, Cassius, Casca, are ceaselessly perspiring too, testifying thereby to the enormous physiological labour produced in them by a virtue just about to give birth to a crime. To sweat is to think—which evidently rests on the postulate, appropriate to a nation of businessmen, that thought is a violent, cataclysmic operation, of which sweat is only the most benign symptom. In the whole film, there is but one man who does not sweat and who remains smooth-faced, unperturbed and water-tight: Caesar. Of course Caesar, the *object* of the crime, remains dry since *he* does not know, *he does not think,* and so must keep the firm and polished texture of an exhibit standing isolated in the courtroom.

Here again, the sign is ambiguous: it remains on the surface, yet does not for all that give up the attempt to pass itself off as depth. It aims at making people understand (which is laudable) but at the same time suggests that it is spontaneous (which is cheating); it presents itself at once as intentional and ir-repressible, artificial and natural, manufactured and discovered. This can lead us to an ethic of signs. Signs ought to present themselves only in two extreme forms: either openly intellectual and so remote that they are reduced to an algebra, as in the Chinese theatre, where a flag on its own signifies a regiment; or deeply rooted, invented, so to speak, on each occasion, revealing an internal, a hidden facet, and indicative of a moment in time, no longer of a concept (as in the art of Stanislavsky, for instance). But the intermediate sign, the fringe of Roman-ness or the sweating of thought, reveals a degraded spectacle, which is equally afraid of simple reality and of total artifice. For although it is a good thing if a spectacle is created to make the world more explicit, it is both rep-rehensible and deceitful to confuse the sign with what is signified. And it is a duplicity which is peculiar to bourgeois art: between the intellectual and the visceral sign is hypocritically inserted a hybrid, at once elliptical and preten-tious, which is pompously christened *"nature."*

NOVELS AND CHILDREN

If we are to believe the weekly *Elle*, which some time ago mustered seventy women novelists on one photograph, the woman of letters is a remarkable zoo-logical species: She brings forth, pell-mell, novels and children. We are intro-duced, for example, to Jacqueline Lenoir (two daughters, one novel); Marina Grey (one son, one novel); Nicole Dutreil (two sons, four novels), and so on.

What does it mean? This: to write is a glorious but bold activity; the writer is an "artist," one recognizes that he is entitled to a little bohemianism. As he is in general entrusted—at least in the France of *Elle*—with giving society reasons for its clear conscience, he must, after all, be paid for his services: one tacitly grants him the right to some individuality. But make no mistake: let no women believe that they can take advantage of this pact without having first submitted to the eternal statute of womanhood. Women are on the earth to give children to men; let them write as much as they like, let them decorate their condition, but above all, let them not depart from it: let their Biblical fate not be disturbed by the promotion which is conceded to them, and let them pay immediately, by the tribute of their motherhood, for this bohemianism which has a natural link with a writer's life.

Women, be therefore courageous, free; play at being men, write like them; but never get far from them; live under their gaze, compensate for your books by your children; enjoy a free rein for a while, but quickly come back to your condition. One novel, one child, a little feminism, a little connubiality. Let us tie the adventure of art to the strong pillars of the home: both will profit a great deal from this combination: where myths are concerned, mutual help is always fruitful.

For instance, the Muse will give its sublimity to the humble tasks of the home; and in exchange, to thank her for this favour, the myth of childbearing will lend to the Muse, who sometimes has the reputation of being a little wanton, the guarantee of its respectability, the touching decor of the nursery. So that all is well in the best of all worlds—that of *Elle*. Let women acquire self-confidence: they can very well have access, like men, to the superior status of creation. But let men be quickly reassured: women will not be taken from them for all that, they will remain no less available for motherhood by nature. *Elle* nimbly plays a Molièresque scene, says yes on one side and no on the other, and busies herself in displeasing no one; like Don Juan between his two peasant girls, *Elle* says to women: you are worth just as much as men; and to men: your women will never be anything but women.

Man at first seems absent from this double parturition; children and novels alike seem to come by themselves, and to belong to the mother alone. At a pinch, and by dint of seeing seventy times books and kids bracketed together, one would think that they are equally the fruits of imagination and dream, the miraculous products of an ideal parthenogenesis able to give at once to woman, apparently, the Balzacian joys of creation and the tender joys of motherhood. Where then is man in this family picture? Nowhere and everywhere, like the sky, the horizon, an authority which at once determines and limits a condition. Such is the world of *Elle:* women there are always a homogeneous species, an established body jealous of its privileges, still more enamoured of the burdens that go with them. Man is never inside, femininity is pure, free, powerful; but man is everywhere around, he presses on all sides, he makes everything exist; he is in all eternity the creative absence, that of the Racinian deity: the feminine world of *Elle*, a world without men, but entirely constituted by the gaze of man, is very exactly that of the gynaeceum.

In every feature of *Elle* we find this twofold action: lock the gynaeceum, then and only then release woman inside. Love, work, write, be businesswomen or women of letters, but always remember that man exists, and that you are not made like him; your order is free on condition that it depends on his; your freedom is a luxury, it is possible only if you first acknowledge the obligations of your nature. Write, if you want to, we women shall all be very proud of it; but don't forget on the other hand to produce children, for that is your destiny. A

Jesuitic morality: adapt the moral rule of your condition, but never compromise about the dogma on which it rests.

TOYS

French toys: one could not find a better illustration of the fact that the adult Frenchman sees the child as another self. All the toys one commonly sees are essentially a microcosm of the adult world; they are all reduced copies of human objects, as if in the eyes of the public the child was, all told, nothing but a smaller man, a homunculus to whom must be supplied objects of his own size.

Invented forms are very rare: a few sets of blocks, which appeal to the spirit of do-it-yourself, are the only ones which offer dynamic forms. As for the others, French toys *always mean something*, and this something is always entirely socialized, constituted by the myths or the techniques of modern adult life: the Army, Broadcasting, the Post Office, Medicine (miniature instrument cases, operating theaters for dolls), School, Hairstyling (driers for permanent waving), the Air Force (Parachutists), Transport (trains, Citroëns, Vedettes, Vespas, petrol stations), Science (Martian toys).

The fact that French toys *literally* prefigure the world of adult functions obviously cannot but prepare the child to accept them all, by constituting for him, even before he can think about it, the alibi of a Nature which has at all times created soldiers, postmen and Vespas. Toys here reveal the list of all the things the adult does not find unusual: war, bureaucracy, ugliness, Martians, etc. It is not so much, in fact, the imitation which is the sign of an abdication, as its literalness: French toys are like a Jivaro head, in which one recognizes, shrunken to the size of an apple, the wrinkles and hair of an adult. There exist, for instance, dolls which urinate; they have an oesophagus, one gives them a bottle, they wet their nappies; soon, no doubt, milk will turn to water in their stomachs. This is meant to prepare the little girl for the causality of housekeeping, to "condition" her to her future role as mother. However, faced with this world of faithful and complicated objects, the child can only identify himself as owner, as user, never as creator; he does not invent the world, he uses it: there are, prepared for him, actions without adventure, without wonder, without joy. He is turned into a little stay-at-home householder who does not even have to invent the mainsprings of adult causality; they are supplied to him ready-made: he has only to help himself, he is never allowed to discover anything from start to finish. The merest set of blocks, provided it is not too refined, implies a very different learning of the world: then, the child does not in any way create meaningful objects, it matters little to him whether they have an adult name; the actions he performs are not those of a user but those of a demiurge. He creates forms which walk, which roll, he creates life, not property: objects now act by themselves, they are no longer an inert and complicated material in the palm of his hand. But such toys are rather rare: French toys are usually based on imitation, they are meant to produce children who are users, not creators.

The bourgeois status of toys can be recognized not only in their forms, which are all functional, but also in their substances. Current toys are made of a graceless material, the product of chemistry, not of nature. Many are now moulded from complicated mixtures; the plastic material of which they are made has an appearance at once gross and hygienic, it destroys all the pleasure, the sweetness, the humanity of touch. A sign which fills one with consternation is the gradual disappearance of wood, in spite of its being an ideal material because of its firmness and its softness, and the natural warmth of its touch. Wood removes, from all the forms which it supports, the wounding quality of angles which are too sharp, the chemical coldness of metal. When the child handles it and knocks it, it neither vibrates nor grates, it has a sound at once muffled and sharp. It is a familiar and poetic substance, which does not sever the child from close contact with the tree, the table, the floor. Wood does not wound or break down; it does not shatter, it wears out, it can last a long time, live with the child, alter little by little the relations between the object and the hand. If it dies, it is in dwindling, not in swelling out like those mechanical toys which disappear behind the hernia of a broken spring. Wood makes essential objects, objects for all time. Yet there hardly remain any of these wooden toys from the Vosges, these fretwork farms with their animals, which were only possible, it is true, in the days of the craftsman. Henceforth, toys are chemical in substance and colour; their very material introduces one to a coenaesthesis of use, not pleasure. These toys die in fact very quickly, and once dead, they have no posthumous life for the child.

STEAK AND CHIPS

Steak is a part of the same sanguine mythology as wine. It is the heart of meat, it is meat in its pure state; and whoever partakes of it assimilates a bull-like strength. The prestige of steak evidently derives from its quasi-rawness. In it, blood is visible, natural, dense, at once compact and sectile. One can well imagine the ambrosia of the Ancients as this kind of heavy substance which dwindles under one's teeth in such a way as to make one keenly aware at the same time of its original strength and of its aptitude to flow into the very blood of man. Fullbloodedness is the raison d'être of steak; the degrees to which it is cooked are expressed not in calorific units but in images of blood; rare steak is said to be *saignant* (when it recalls the arterial flow from the cut in the animal's throat), or *bleu* (and it is now the heavy, plethoric, blood of the veins which is suggested by the purplish colour—the superlative of redness). Its cooking, even moderate, cannot openly find expression; for this unnatural state, a euphemism is needed: one says that steak is *à point*, "medium," and this in truth is understood more as a limit than as a perfection.

To eat steak rare therefore represents both a nature and a morality. It is supposed to benefit all the temperaments, the sanguine because it is identical, the nervous and lymphatic because it is complementary to them. And just as wine becomes for a good number of intellectuals a mediumistic substance which leads them towards the original strength of nature, steak is for them a redeeming food, thanks to which they bring their intellectualism to the level of prose and exorcize, through blood and soft pulp, the sterile dryness of which they are constantly accused. The craze for steak tartare, for instance, is a magic spell against the romantic association between sensitiveness and sickliness; there are to be found, in this preparation, all the germinating states of matter: the blood mash and the glair of eggs, a whole harmony of soft and life-giving substances, a sort of meaningful compendium of the images of preparturition.

Like wine, steak is in France a basic element, nationalized even more than socialized. It figures in all the surroundings of alimentary life: flat, edged with yellow, like the sole of a shoe, in cheap restaurants; thick and juicy in the bistros which specialize in it; cubic, with the core all moist throughout beneath a light charred crust, in haute cuisine. It is a part of all the rhythms, that of the comfortable bourgeois meal and that of the bachelor's bohemian snack. It is a food at once expeditious and dense, it effects the best possible ratio between economy and efficacy, between mythology and its multifarious ways of being consumed.

Moreover, it is a French possession (circumscribed today, it is true, by the invasion of American steaks). As in the case of wine there is no alimentary constraint which does not make the Frenchman dream of steak. Hardly abroad, he feels nostalgia for it. Steak is here adorned with a supplementary virtue of elegance, for among the apparent complexity of exotic cooking, it is a food which unites, one feels, succulence and simplicity. Being part of the nation, it follows the index of patriotic values: it helps them to rise in wartime, it is the very flesh of the French soldier, the inalienable property which cannot go over to the enemy except by treason. In an old film (*Deuxième Bureau contre Kommandantur*), the maid of the patriotic *curé* gives food to the Boche spy disguised as a French underground fighter: "Ah, it's you, Laurent! I'll give you some steak."

And then, when the spy is unmasked: "And when I think I gave him some of my steak!"—the supreme breach of trust.

Commonly associated with chips, steak communicates its national glamour to them: chips are nostalgic and patriotic like steak. *Match* told us that after the armistice in Indo-China "General de Castries, for his first meal, asked for chips." And the President of the Indo-China Veterans, later commenting on this information added: "The gesture of General de Castries asking for chips for his first meal has not always been understood." What we were meant to understand is that the General's request was certainly not a vulgar materialistic reflex, but an episode in the ritual of appropriating the regained French community. The General understood well our national symbolism; he knew that *la frite*, chips, are the alimentary sign of Frenchness.

THE GREAT FAMILY OF MAN

A big exhibition of photographs has been held in Paris, the aim of which was to show the universality of human actions in the daily life of all the countries of the world: birth, death, work, knowledge, play, always impose the same types of behaviour; there is a family of Man.

The Family of Man, such at any rate was the original title of the exhibition which came here from the United States. The French have translated it as *The Great Family of Man.* So what could originally pass for a phrase belonging to zoology, keeping only the similarity in behaviour, the unity of a species, is here amply moralized and sentimentalized. We are at the outset directed to this ambiguous myth of the human "community," which serves as an alibi to a large part of our humanism.

This myth functions in two stages: first the difference between human morphologies is asserted, exoticism is insistently stressed, the infinite variations of the species, the diversity in skins, skulls and customs are made manifest, the image of Babel is complacently projected over that of the world. Then, from this pluralism, a type of unity is magically produced: man is born, works, laughs and dies everywhere in the same way; and if there still remains in these actions some ethnic peculiarity, at least one hints that there is underlying each one an identical "nature," that their diversity is only formal and does not belie the existence of a common mould. Of course this means postulating a human essence, and here is God reintroduced into our Exhibition: the diversity of men proclaims his power, his richness; the unity of their gestures demonstrates his will. This is what the introductory leaflet confides to us when it states, by the pen of M. André Chamson, that "this look over the human condition must somewhat resemble the benevolent gaze of God on our absurd and sublime ant-hill." The pietistic intention is underlined by the quotations which accompany each chapter of the Exhibition: these quotations often are "primitive" proverbs or verses from the Old Testament. They all define an eternal wisdom, a class of assertions which escape History: "The Earth is a Mother who never dies, Eat bread and salt and speak the truth, etc." This is the reign of gnomic truths, the meeting of all the ages of humanity at the most neutral point of their nature, the point where the obviousness of the truism has no longer any value except in the realm of a purely "poetic" language. Everything here, the content and appeal of the pictures, the discourse which justifies them, aims to suppress the determining weight of History: we are held back at the surface of an identity, prevented precisely by sentimentality from penetrating into this ulterior zone of human behaviour where historical alienation introduces some "differences" which we shall here quite simply call "injustices."

This myth of the human "condition" rests on a very old mystification, which always consists in placing Nature at the bottom of History. Any classic humanism postulates that in scratching the history of men a little, the relativity of their institutions or the superficial diversity of their skins (but why not ask the parents of Emmet Till, the young Negro assassinated by the Whites what *they* think of *The Great Family of Man?*), one very quickly reaches the solid rock of a universal human nature. Progressive humanism, on the contrary, must always remember to reverse the terms of this very old imposture, constantly to scour nature, its "laws" and its "limits" in order to discover History there, and at last to establish Nature itself as historical.

Examples? Here they are: those of our Exhibition. Birth, death? Yes, these are facts of nature, universal facts. But if one removes History from them, there is nothing more to be said about them; any comment about them becomes purely tautological. The failure of photography seems to me to be flagrant in this connection: to reproduce death or birth tells us, literally, nothing. For these natural facts to gain access to a true language, they must be inserted into a category of knowledge which means postulating that one can transform them, and precisely subject their naturalness to our human criticism. For however universal, they are the signs of an historical writing. True, children are *always* born: but in the whole mass of the human problem, what does the "essence" of this process matter to us, compared to its modes which, as for them, are perfectly historical? Whether or not the child is born with ease or difficulty, whether or not his birth causes suffering to his mother, whether or not he is threatened by a high mortality rate, whether or not such and such a type of future is open to him: this is what your Exhibitions should be telling people, instead of an eternal lyricism of birth. The same goes for death: must we really celebrate its essence once more, and thus risk forgetting that there is still so much we can do to fight it? It is this very young, far too young power that we must exalt, and not the sterile identity of "natural" death.

And what can be said about work, which the Exhibition places among great universal facts, putting it on the same plane as birth and death, as if it was quite evident that it belongs to the same order of fate? That work is an age-old fact does not in the least prevent it from remaining a perfectly historical fact. Firstly, and evidently, because of its modes, its motivations, its ends and its benefits, which matter to such an extent that it will never be fair to confuse in a purely gestural identity the colonial and the Western worker (let us also ask the North African workers of the Goutte d'Or district in Paris what they think of *The Great Family of Man*). Secondly, because of the very differences in its inevitability: we know very well that work is "natural" just as long as it is "profitable," and that in modifying the inevitability of the profit, we shall perhaps one day modify the inevitability of labour. It is this entirely historified work which we should be told about, instead of an eternal aesthetics of laborious gestures.

So that I rather fear that the final justification of all this Adamism is to give to the immobility of the world the alibi of a "wisdom" and a "lyricism" which only make the gestures of man look eternal the better to defuse them.

11. *Nostalgia for the Present*

FREDRIC JAMESON

THERE IS A NOVEL by Philip K. Dick, which, published in 1959, evokes the fifties: President Eisenhower's stroke; Main Street, U.S.A.; Marilyn Monroe; a world of neighbors and PTAs; small retail chain stores (the produce trucked in from the outside); favorite television programs; mild flirtations with the housewife next door; game shows and contests; sputniks distantly revolving overhead, mere blinking lights in the firmament, hard to distinguish from airliners or flying saucers. If you were interested in constructing a time capsule or an "only yesterday" compendium or documentary-nostalgia video film of the 1950s, this might serve as a beginning: to which you could add short haircuts, early rock and roll, longer skirts, and so on. The list is not a list of facts or historical realities (although its items are not invented and are in some sense "authentic"), but rather a list of stereotypes, of ideas of facts and historical realities. It suggests several fundamental questions.

First of all, did the "period" see itself this way? Did the literature of the period deal with this kind of small-town American life as its central preoccupation; and if not, why not? What other kinds of preoccupations seemed more important? To be sure, in retrospect, the fifties have been summed up culturally as so many forms of protest against the fifties "themselves"; against the Eisenhower era and its complacency, against the sealed self-content of the American small (white, middle-class) town, against the conformist and the family-centered ethnocentrism of a prosperous United States learning to consume in the first big boom after the shortages and privations of the war, whose immediacy has by now largely lost its edge. The first Beat poets; an occasional "anti-hero" with "existentionalist" overtones; a few daring Hollywood impulses; nascent rock and roll itself; the compensatory importation of European books, movements, and art films; a lonely and premature political rebel or theorist like C. Wright Mills: such, in retrospect, seems to be the balance sheet of fifties culture. All the rest is Peyton Place, bestsellers, and TV series. And it is indeed just those series—living room comedies, single-family homes menaced by *Twilight Zone*, on the one hand, and gangsters and escaped convicts from the outside world, on the other—that give us the content of our positive image of the fifties in the first place. If there is "realism" in the 1950s, in other words, it is presumably to be found there, in mass cultural representation, the only kind of art willing (and able) to deal with the stifling Eisenhower realities of the happy family in the small town, of normalcy and nondeviant everyday life. High art apparently cannot deal with this kind of subject matter except by way of the oppositional: the satire of Lewis, the pathos and solitude of Hopper or Sherwood Anderson. Of naturalism, long after the fact, the Germans used to say that it "stank of cabbage"; that is, it exuded the misery and boredom of its subject matter, poverty itself. Here too the content seems somehow to contaminate the form, only the misery here is the misery of happiness, or at least contentment (which is in reality complacency), of Marcuse's "false" happiness, the gratifications of the new car, the TV dinner and your favorite program on the sofa— which are now themselves secretly a misery, an unhappiness that doesn't know its name, that has no way of telling itself apart from genuine satisfaction and fulfillment since it has presumably never encountered this last.

When the notion of the oppositional is contested, however, in the mid eighties, we will know a fifties revival in which much of this "degraded mass culture" returns for possible reevaluation. In the fifties, however, it is high culture that is still authorized to pass judgment on reality, to say what real life is and what is, on the other hand, mere appearance; and it is by leaving out, by ignoring, by passing over in silence and with the repugnance one may feel for the dreary stereotypes of television series, that high art palpably issues its judgments. Faulkner and Hemingway, the southerners and the New Yorkers, pass this small-town U.S. raw material by in a detour considerably greater than the proverbial ten-foot pole; indeed, of the great writers of the period, only Dick himself comes to mind as the virtual poet laureate of this material: of squabbling couples and marital dramas, of petit bourgeois shopkeepers, neighborhoods, and afternoons in front of television, and all the rest. But, of course, he does something to it, and it was already California anyway.

This small-town content was not, in the postwar period, really "provincial" any longer (as in Lewis or John O'Hara, let alone Dreiser): you might want to leave, you might still long for the big city, but something had happened—perhaps something as simple as television and the other media—to remove the pain and sting of absence from the center, from the metropolis. On the other hand, today, none of it exists any longer, even though we still have small towns (whose downtowns are now in decay—but so are the big cities). What has happened is that the autonomy of the small town (in the provincial period a source of claustrophobia and anxiety; in the fifties the ground for a certain comfort and even a certain reassurance) has vanished. What was once a separate point on the map has become an imperceptible thickening in a continuum of identical products and standardized spaces from coast to coast. One has the feeling, however, that the autonomy of the small town, its complacent independence, also functioned as an allegorical expression for the situation of Eisenhower America in the outside world as a whole—contented with itself, secure in the sense of its radical difference from other populations and cultures, insulated from their vicissitudes and from the flaws in human nature so palpably acted out in their violent and alien histories.

This is clearly, however, to shift from the realities of the 1950s to the representation of that rather different thing, the "fifties," a shift which obligates us in addition to underscore the cultural sources of all the attributes with which we have endowed the period, many of which seem very precisely to derive from its own television programs; in other words, its own representation of itself. However, although one does not confuse a person with what he or she thinks of himself/herself, such self-images are surely very relevant indeed and constitute an essential part of the more objective description or definition. Nonetheless, it seems possible that the deeper realities of the period—read, for example, against the very different scale of, say, diachronic and secular economic rhythms, or of synchronic and systemic global interrelationships, have little to do with either our cultural stereotypes of years thus labeled and defined in terms of generational decades. The concept of "classicism," for example, has a precise and functional meaning in German cultural and literary history which disappears when we move to a European perspective in which those few key years vanish without a trace into some vaster opposition between Enlightenment and Romanticism. But this is a speculation which presupposes the possibility that at an outer limit, the sense people have of themselves and their own moment of history may ultimately have *nothing* whatsoever to do with its reality: that the existential may be absolutely distinct, as some ultimate "false consciousness," from the structural and social significance of a collective phenomenon, surely a possibility rendered more plausible by the fact of global imperialism, in terms of which the meaning of a given nation-state—for everyone else on the globe—may be wildly at odds from their own inner experiences and their own interior daily life. Eisenhower wore a well-known smile for us but an equally well-known scowl for foreigners beyond our borders, as the state portraits in any U.S. consulate during those years dramatically attested.

There is, however, an even more radical possibility; namely, that period concepts finally correspond to no realities whatsoever, and that whether they are formulated in terms of generational logic, or by the names of reigning monarchs, or according to some other category or typological and classificatory system, the collective reality of the multitudinous lives encompassed by such terms is nonthinkable (or nontotalizable, to use a current expression) and can never be described, characterized, labeled, or conceptualized. This is, I suppose, what one could call the Nietzschean position, for which there are no such things as "periods," nor have there ever been. In that case, of course, there is no such thing as "history" either, which was probably the basic philosophical point such arguments sought to make in the first place.

This is the moment, however, to return to Dick's novel and record the twist that turns it into science fiction: for it transpires, from an increasing accumulation of tiny but aberrant details, that the environment of the novel, in which we watch the characters act and move, is not really the fifties after all (I do not know that Dick ever uses this particular word). It is a Potemkin village of a historical kind: a reproduction of the 1950s—including induced and introjected memories and character structures in its human population—constructed (for reasons that need not detain us here) in 1997, in the midst of an interstellar atomic civil war. I will only note that a twofold determination plays across the main character, who must thus be read according to a negative and a positive hermeneutic simultaneously. The village has been constructed in order to trick him, against his will, into performing an essential wartime task for the government. In that sense, he is the victim of this manipulation, which awakens all our fantasies of mind control and unconscious exploitation, of anti-Cartesian predestination and determinism. On this reading, then, Dick's novel is a nightmare and the expression of deep, unconscious, collective fears about our social life and its tendencies.

Yet Dick also takes pains to make clear that the 1950s village is also very specifically the result of infantile regression on the part of the protagonist, who has also, in a sense, unconsciously chosen his own delusion and has fled the anxieties of the civil war for the domestic and reassuring comforts of his own childhood during the period in question. From this perspective, then, the novel is a collective wish-fulfillment, and the expression of a deep, unconscious yearning for a simpler and more human social system and a small-town Utopia very much in the North American frontier tradition.

We should also note that the very structure of the novel articulates the position of Eisenhower America in the world itself and is thereby to be read as a kind of distorted form of cognitive mapping, an unconscious and figurative projection of some more "realistic" account of our situation, as it has been described earlier: the hometown reality of the United States surrounded by the implacable menace of world communism (and, in this period to a much lesser degree, of Third World poverty). This is also, of course, the period of the classic science fiction films, with their more overtly ideological representations of external threats and impending alien invasions (also generally set in small towns). Dick's novel can be read in that way—the grimmer "reality" disclosed behind the benign and deceptive appearance—or it can be taken as a certain approach to self-consciousness about the representations themselves.

What is more significant from the present perspective, however, is the paradigmatic value of Dick's novel for questions of history and historicity in general. One of the ways of thinking about the subgenre to which this novel belongs—that "category" called science fiction, which can be either expanded and dignified by the addition of all the classical satiric and Utopian literature from Lucian on or restricted and degraded to the pulp-and-adventure tradition—is as a historically new and original form which offers analogies with the emergence of the historical novel in the early nineteenth-century. Lukács has interpreted this last as a formal innovation (by Sir Walter Scott) which provided figuration for the new and equally emergent sense of history of the triumphant middle classes (or bourgeoisie), as that class sought to project its own vision of its past and its future and to articulate its social and collective project in a temporal narrative distinct in form from those of earlier "subjects of history" such as the feudal nobility. In that form, the historical novel—and its related emanations, such as the costume film—has fallen into disrepute and infrequency, not merely because, in the postmodern age, we no longer tell ourselves our history in that fashion, but also because we no longer experience it that way, and, indeed, perhaps no longer experience it at all.

One would want, in short, to stress the conditions of possibility of such a form—and of its emergence and eclipse—less in the existential experience of history of people at this or that historical moment than rather in the very structure of their socioeconomic system, in its relative opacity or transparency, and the access its mechanisms provide to some greater cognitive as well as existential contact with the thing itself. This is the context in which it seems interesting to explore the hypothesis that science fiction as a genre entertains a dialectical and structural relationship with the historical novel—a relationship of kinship and inversion all at once, of opposition and homology (just as comedy and tragedy have often been supposed to do, or lyric and epic, or satire and Utopia, as Robert C. Elliott analyzed them). But time itself plays a crucial role in this generic opposition, which is also something of an evolutionary compensation. For if the historical novel "corresponded" to the emergence of historicity, of a sense of history in its strong modern post-eighteenth-century sense, science fiction equally corresponds to the waning or the blockage of that historicity, and, particularly in our own time (in the postmodern era), to its crisis and paralysis, its enfeeblement and repression. Only by means of a violent formal and narrative dislocation could a narrative apparatus come into being capable of restoring life and feeling to this only intermittently functioning organ that is our capacity to organize and live time historically. Nor should it be thought overhastily that the two forms are symmetrical on the grounds that the historical novel stages the past and science fiction the future.

Historicity is, in fact, neither a representation of the past nor a representation of the future (although its various forms *use* such representations): it can first and foremost be defined as a perception of the present as history; that is, as a relationship to the present which somehow defamiliarizes it and allows us that distance from immediacy which is at length characterized as a historical perspective. It is appropriate, in other words, also to insist on the historicality of the operation itself, which is our way of conceiving of historicity in this particular society and mode of production; appropriate also to observe that what is at stake is essentially a process of reification whereby we draw back from our immersion in the here and now (not yet identified as a "present") and grasp it as a kind of thing—not merely a "present" but a present that can be dated and called the eighties or the fifties. Our presupposition has been that today this is more difficult to achieve than at the time of Sir Walter Scott, when a contemplation of the past seemed able to renew our sense of our own reading present as the sequel, if not particularly the culmination, of that genetic series.

Time Out of Joint, however, offers a very different machine for producing historicity than Sir Walter Scott's apparatus: what one might in the strong sense call a trope of the future anterior—the estrangement and renewal as history of our own reading present, the fifties, by way of the apprehension of that present as the past of a specific future. The future itself—Dick's 1997—is not, however, centrally significant as a representation or an anticipation; it is the narrative means to a very different end, namely the brutal transformation of a realistic representation of the present, of Eisenhower America and the 1950s small town, into a memory and a reconstruction. Reification is here indeed built into the novel itself and, as it were, defused and recuperated as a form of praxis: the fifties is a thing, but a thing that we can build, just as the science fiction writer builds his own small-scale model. At that point, then, reification ceases to be a baleful and alienating process, a noxious side-effect of our mode of production, if not, indeed, its fundamental dynamic, and is rather transferred to the side of human energies and human possibilities. (The reappropriation has, of course, a good deal to do with the specificity of Dick's own themes and ideology—in particular, the nostalgia about the past and the "petit bourgeois" valorization of small craftsmanship, as well as small business and collecting.)

This novel has necessarily become for us a historical one: for its present—the 1950s—has become our past in a rather different sense than that proposed by the text itself. The latter still "works": we can still feel and appreciate the transformation and reification of its readers' present into a historical period; we can even, by analogy, extrapolate something similar for our own moment in time. Whether such a process today can be realized concretely, in a cultural artifact, is, however, a rather different question. The accumulation of books like *Future Shock*, the incorporation of habits of "futurology" into our everyday life, the modification of our perception of things to include their "tendency" and of our reading of time to approximate a scanning of complex probabilities—this new relationship to our own present both includes elements formerly incorporated in the experience of the "future" and blocks or forestalls any global vision of the latter as a radically transformed and different system. If catastrophic "near-future" visions of, say, overpopulation, famine, and anarchic violence are no longer as effective as they were a few years ago, the weakening of those effects and of the narrative forms that were designed to produce them is not necessarily due only to overfamiliarity and overexposure; or rather, this last is perhaps also to be seen as a modification in our relationship to those imaginary near futures, which no longer strike us with the horror of otherness and radical difference. Here a certain Nietzscheanism operates to defuse anxiety and even fear: the conviction, however gradually learned and acquired, that there is only the present and that it is always "ours," is a kind of wisdom that cuts both ways. For it was always clear that the terror of such near futures—like the analogous terror of an older naturalism—was class based and deeply rooted in class comfort and privilege. The older naturalism let us briefly experience the life and the life world of the various underclasses, only to return with relief to our own living rooms and armchairs: the good resolutions it may also have encouraged were always, then, a form of philanthropy. In the same way, yesterday's terror of the overcrowded conurbations of the immediate future could just as easily be read as a pretext for complacency with our own historical present, in which we do not yet have to live like that. In both cases, at any rate, the fear is that of proletarianization, of slipping down the ladder, of losing a comfort and a set of privileges which we tend increasingly to think of in spatial terms: privacy, empty rooms, silence, walling other people out, protection against crowds and other bodies. Nietzschean wisdom, then, tells us to let go of that kind of fear and reminds us that whatever social and spatial form our future misery may take, it will not be alien because it will by definition be ours. *Dasein ist je mein eigenes*—defamiliarization, the shock of otherness, is a mere aesthetic effect and a lie.

Perhaps, however, what is implied is simply an ultimate historicist breakdown in which we can no longer imagine the future at all, under any form—Utopian or catastrophic. Under those circumstances, where a formerly futurological science fiction (such as so-called cyberpunk today) turns into mere "realism" and an outright representation of the present, the possibility Dick offered us—an experience of our present as past and as history—is slowly excluded. Yet everything in our culture suggests that we have not, for all that, ceased to be preoccupied by history; indeed, at the very moment in which we complain, as here, of the eclipse of historicity, we also universally diagnose contemporary culture as irredeemably historicist, in the bad sense of an omnipresent and indiscriminate appetite for dead styles and fashions; indeed, for all the styles and fashions of a dead past. Meanwhile, a certain caricature of historical thinking—which we may not even call *generational* any longer, so rapid has its momentum become—has also become universal and includes at least the will and intent to return upon our present circumstances in order to think of them—as the nineties, say—and to draw the appropriate marketing and forecasting conclusions. Why is this not historicity with a vengeance? and what is the difference between this now generalized approach to the present and Dick's rather cumbersome and primitive laboratory approach to a "concept" of his own fifties?

In my opinion, it is the structure of the two operations which is instructively different: the one mobilizing a vision of the future in order to determine its return to a now historical present; the other mobilizing, but in some new allegorical way, a vision of the past, or of a certain moment of the past. Several recent films (I will here mention *Something Wild* and *Blue Velvet*) encourage us to see the newer process in terms of an allegorical encounter; yet even this formal possibility will not be properly grasped unless we set in place its preconditions in the development of nostalgia film generally. For it is by way of so-called nostalgia films that some properly allegorical processing of the past becomes possible: it is because the formal apparatus of nostalgia films has trained us to consume the past in the form of glossy images that new and more complex "postnostalgia" statements and forms become possible. I have elsewhere tried to identify the privileged raw material or historical content of this particular operation of reification and of the transformation into the image in the crucial antithesis between the twenties and the thirties, and in the historicist revival of the very stylistic expression of that antithesis in art deco. The symbolic working out of that tension—as it were, between Aristocracy and Worker—evidently involves something like the symbolic reinvention or production of a new Bourgeoisie, a new form of identity. Yet like photorealism, the products themselves are bland in their very visual elegance, while the plot structures of such films suffer from a schematization (or typification) which seems to be inherent in the project. While we may anticipate more of these, therefore, and while the taste for them corresponds to more durable features and needs in our present economicopsychic constitution (image fixation *cum* historicist cravings), it was perhaps only to be expected that some new and more complicated and interesting formal sequel would rapidly develop.

What was more unexpected—but very "dialectical" indeed, in a virtually textbook way—was the emergence of this new form from a kind of cross, if not synthesis, between the two filmic modes we had until now been imagining as antithetical: namely, the high elegance of nostalgia films, on the one hand, and the grade-B simulations of iconoclastic punk film, on the other. We failed to see that both were significantly mortgaged to music, because the musical signifiers were rather different in the two cases—the sequences of high-class dance music, on the one hand, the contemporary proliferation of rock groups, on the other. Meanwhile, any "dialectical" textbook of the type already referred to might have alerted us to the probability that an ideologeme of "elegance" depends in some measure on an opposite of some kind, an opposite and a negation which seems in our time to have shed its class content (still feebly alive when the "beats" were felt to entertain a twin opposition to bourgeois respectability and high modernist aestheticism), and to have gradually migrated into that new complex of meanings that bears the name *punk*.

The new films, therefore, will first and foremost be allegories of that, of their own coming into being as a synthesis of nostalgia-deco and punk: they will in one way or another tell their own stories as the need and search for this "marriage" (the wonderful thing about aesthetics—unlike politics, alas—being that the "search" automatically becomes the thing itself: to set it up is by definition to realize it). Yet this resolution of an aesthetic contradiction is not gratuitous, because the formal contradiction itself has a socially and historically symbolic significance of its own.

But now the stories of these two films need to be briefly outlined. In *Something Wild* a young "organization man" is abducted by a crazy girl, who initiates him into cutting corners and cheating on credit cards, until her husband, an exconvict, shows up and, bent on vengeance, pursues the couple. In *Blue Velvet*, on the other hand, a young high school graduate discovers a severed ear, which puts him on the trail of a torch singer mysteriously victimized by a local drug dealer, from whom he is able to save her.

Such films indeed invite us to return somehow to history: the central scene of *Something Wild*—or at least the one on which the plot structure pivots decisively—is a class reunion, the kind of event which specifically demands historical judgments of its participants: narratives of historical trajectories, as well as evaluations of moments of the past nostalgically reevoked but necessarily rejected or reaffirmed. This is the wedge, or opening, through which a hitherto aimless but lively filmic narrative suddenly falls into the deeper past (or that deeper past into it); for the ten year reunion in reality takes us back twenty more, to a time when the "villain" unexpectedly emerges, over your shoulder, marked as "familiar" in all his unfamiliarity to the spectator (he is the heroine's husband, Ray, and worse). "Ray" is, of course, in one way yet another reworking of that boring and exhausted paradigm, the gothic, where—on the individualized level—a sheltered woman of some kind is terrorized and victimized by an "evil" male. I think it would be a great mistake to read such literature as a kind of protofeminist denunciation of patriarchy and, in particular, a protopolitical protest against rape. Certainly the gothic mobilizes anxieties about rape, but its structure gives us the clue to a more central feature of its content which I have tried to underscore by means of the word *sheltered*.

Gothics are indeed ultimately a class fantasy (or nightmare) in which the dialectic of privilege and shelter is exercised: your privileges seal you off from other people, but by the same token they constitute a protective wall through which you cannot see, and behind which therefore all kinds of envious forces may be imagined in the process of assembling, plotting, preparing to give assault; it is, if you like, the shower-curtain syndrome (alluding to Hitchcock's *Psycho*). That its classical form turns on the privileged content of the situation of middle-class women—the isolation, but also the domestic idleness, imposed on them by newer forms of middle-class marriage—adds such texts, as symptoms, to the history of women's situations but does not lend them any particular political significance (unless that significance consists merely in a coming to self-consciousness of the disadvantages of privilege in the first place). But the form can also, under certain circumstances, be reorganized around young men, to whom some similarly protective distance is imputed: intellectuals, for example, or "sheltered" young briefcase-carrying bureaucrats, as in *Something Wild* itself. (That this gender substitution risks awakening all kinds of supplementary sexual overtones is here self-consciously dramatized in the extraordinary tableau moment in which the stabbing, seen from behind—and from the woman's visual perspective—looks like a passionate embrace between the two men.) The more formal leap, however, will come when for the individual "victim"—male or female—is substituted the collectivity itself, the U.S. public, which now lives out the anxieties of its economic privileges and its sheltered "exceptionalism" in a pseudopolitical version of the gothic—under the threats of stereotypical madmen and "terrorists" (mostly Arabs or Iranians for some reason). These collective fantasies are less to be explained by some increasing "feminization" of the American public self than by its guilt and the dynamics of comfort already referred to. And like the private version of the traditional gothic romance, they depend for their effects on the revitalization of ethics as a set of mental categories, and on the reinflation and artificial reinvigoration of that tired and antiquated binary opposition between virtue and vice, which the eighteenth century cleansed of its theological remnants and thoroughly sexualized before passing it on down to us.

The modern gothic, in other words—whether in its rape-victim or its political-paranoid forms—depends absolutely in its central operation on the construction of *evil* (forms of the good are notoriously more difficult to construct, and generally draw their light from the darker concept, as though the sun drew its reflected radiance from the moon). Evil is here, however, the emptiest form of sheer Otherness (into which any type of social content can be poured at will). I have so often been taken to task for my arguments against ethics (in politics as well as in aesthetics) that it seems worth observing in passing that Otherness is a very dangerous category, one we are well off without; but fortunately, in literature and culture, it has also become a very tedious one. Ridley Scott's *Alien* may still get away with it (but then, for science fiction, all of Lem's work—in particular the recent *Fiasco*—can be read as an argument against the use of such a category even there); but surely Ray of *Something Wild* and Frank Booth of *Blue Velvet* don't scare anybody any longer; nor ought we really to require our flesh to creep before reaching a sober and political decision as to the people and forces who are collectively "evil" in our contemporary world.

On the other hand, it is only fair to say that Ray is not staged demonically, as a representation of evil as such, but rather as the representation of someone *playing at being evil*, which is a rather different matter. Nothing about Ray, indeed, is particularly authentic; his malevolence is as false as his smile; but his clothes and hairstyle give a further clue and point us in a different direction from the ethical one. For not only does Ray offer a simulation of evil, he also offers a simulation of the *fifties*, and that seems to me a far more significant matter. I speak of the oppositional fifties, to be sure: the fifties of Elvis rather than the fifties of Ike, but I'm not sure we can really tell the difference any more, as we peer across our historical gap and try to focus the landscape of the past through nostalgia-tinted spectacles.

At this point, however, the gothic trappings of *Something Wild* fall away and it becomes clear that we have to do here with an essentially allegorical narrative in which the 1980s meet the 1950s. What kind of accounts actuality has to settle with this particular historicist ghost (and whether it manages to do so) is for the moment less crucial than how the encounter was arranged in the first place: by the intermediary and the good offices of the 1960s, of course—inadvertent good offices to be sure, since Audrey/Lulu has very little reason to desire the connection, or even to be reminded of her own past, or Ray's (he has just come out of prison).

Everything turns, therefore, or so one would think, on this distinction between the sixties and the fifties: the first desirable (like a fascinating woman), the second fearful and ominous, untrustworthy (like the leader of a motorcycle gang). As the title suggests, it is the nature of "something wild" which is at stake, the inquiry into it focused by Audrey's first glimpse of Charley's nonconformist character (he skips out on his lunch bill). Indeed, the nonpaying of bills seems to function as the principal index for Charley's "hipness" or "squareness"—it being understood that neither of these categories (nor those of conformity/nonconformity used above) corresponds to the logic of this film, which can be seen as an attempt very precisely to construct new categories with which to replace those older, historically dated and period-bound (uncontemporary, unpostmodern) ones. We may describe this particular "test" as involving white-collar crime, as opposed to the "real," or lower-class, crime—grand theft and mayhem—practiced by Ray himself. Only it is a petit-bourgeois white-collar crime (even Charley's illicit use of company credit cards is scarcely commensurable with the genuine criminality his corporation can be expected, virtually by definition, to imply). Nor are such class markers present in the film itself, which can in another sense be seen very precisely as an effort to repress the language and categories of class and class differentiation and to substitute for them other kinds of semic oppositions still to be invented.

Those necessarily emerge in the framework of the Lulu character, within the sixties allegory (which is something like the "black box" of this particular semic transformation). The fifties stands for genuine rebellion, with genuine violence and genuine consequences, but also for the *romantic representations* of such rebellion, in the films of Brando and James Dean. Ray thus functions both as a kind of gothic villain, within this particular narrative, and also, on the allegorical level, as the sheer idea of the romantic hero—the tragic protagonist of another kind of film, that can no longer be made. Lulu is not herself an alternate possibility, unlike the heroine of *Desperately Seeking Susan*. The framework here remains exclusively male, as the lamentable ending—her chastening, or taming—testifies, along with the significance of clothing, which we will look at in a moment. Everything depends, therefore, on the new kind of *hero* Lulu somehow allows or enables Charley to become, by virtue of her own semic composition (since she is a good deal more than a mere woman's body or fetish).

What is interesting about that composition is that it first of all gives us the sixties seen, as it were, through the fifties (or the eighties?): alcohol rather than drugs. The schizophrenic, drug-cultural side of the sixties is here systematically excluded along with its politics. What is dangerous, in other words, is not Lulu at her most frenzied but rather Ray; not the sixties and its countercultures and "life-styles" but the fifties and its revolts. Yet the continuity between the fifties and the sixties lay in what was being revolted *against*, in what life-style the "new" life-styles were alternatives *to*. It is, however, difficult to find any content in Lulu's stimulating behavior, which seems organized around sheer caprice; that is to say, around the supreme value of remaining unpredictable and immune to reification and categorization. Shades of André Gide, in *Lafcadio's Adventures*, or of all those Sartrean characters desperately attempting to evade that ultimate objectification by another's Look (it is impossible, and they end up simply being labeled "capricious"). The costume changes lend this otherwise purely formal unpredictability a certain visual content; they translate it into the language of image culture and afford a purely specular pleasure in Lulu's metamorphoses (which are not really psychic).

Yet viewers and protagonist still have to feel that they are on their way somewhere (at least until the appearance of Ray gives the film a different kind of direction): as thrilling and improvised as it seems, therefore, Lulu's abduction of Charley from New York has at least an empty form that will be instructive, for it is the archetypal descent into Middle America, into the "real" United States, either of lynching and bigotry or of true, wholesome family life and American ideals; one doesn't quite know which. Nonetheless, like those Russian populist intellectuals in the nineteenth century setting forth on foot to discover "the people," something like this journey is or was the *scène à faire* for any American allegory worthy of its vocation: what this one reveals, however, is that there is no longer anything to discover at the end of the line. For Lulu/Audrey's family—reduced in this case to a mother—is no longer the bourgeoisie of sinister memory: neither the sexual repression and respectability of the fifties nor the Johnsonian authoritarianism of the sixties. This mother plays the harpsichord, "understands" her daughter, and is fully as much an oddball as everybody else. No Oedipal revolts are possible any longer in this American small town, and with them all the tension goes out of the social and cultural dynamics of the period. Yet if there are no longer any "middle classes" to be found in the heartland, there is something else that may serve as something for a substitute for them, at least in the dynamic of narrative structure itself: for what we find at Lulu's class reunion (besides Ray and her own past) is Charley's business colleague, that is to say, a yuppie bureaucrat, along with his pregnant wife. These are unquestionably the baleful parents we sought, but of some distant and not quite imaginable future, not of the older, traditional American past: they occupy the semic slot of the "squares," but without any social basis or content any longer (they can scarcely be read as embodiments of the Protestant ethic, for example, or of puritanism or white racism or patriarchy). But they at least help us to identify the deeper ideological purpose of this film, which is to differentiate Charley from his fellow yuppies by making him over into a hero or protagonist of a different generic type than Ray. Unpredictability, as we have shown, is a matter of *fashion* (clothing, hairstyle, and general body language): Charley himself must therefore pass through this particular matrix, and his metamorphosis is concretely realized, appropriately enough, when he sheds his suit for a more relaxed and tourist-type disguise (T-shirt, shorts, dark glasses, etc.). At the end of the film, of course, he also sheds his corporate job; but it would probably be asking too much to wonder what he does or can become in its stead, except in the "relationship" itself, where he becomes the master and the senior partner. The semic organization of all this might be laid out as follows (and symmetry preserved by seeing the pregnant and disapproving yuppie wife as the concrete manifestation of the neutral term):

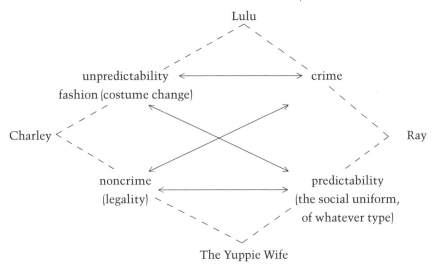

We have not yet mentioned the handcuffs, which can serve as the transition to a similar type of narrative allegory, one whose combinations and atmosphere are very different from this one. *Blue Velvet*, indeed, tries to place sadomasochism squarely on the mass-cultural map with an earnestness altogether lacking in the Demme movie (whose handcuff love scene is as sexy as it is "frivolous"). S&M thus becomes the latest and the last in the long line of those taboo forms of content which, beginning with Nabokov's nymphets in the 1950s, rise one after the other to the surface of public art in that successive and even progressive widening of transgressions which we once called the counterculture, or the sixties. In *Blue Velvet*, however, it is explicitly related to drugs, and therefore to crime—although not exactly organized crime, rather to a collectivity of misfits and oddballs—the transgressive nature of this complex of things being tediously reinforced by repetitive obscenity (on the part of the Dennis Hopper character).

Yet if history is discreetly evoked and invoked in *Something Wild*, it is rather its opposite—Nature—which is given us as the overall frame and inhuman, transhuman perspective in which to contemplate the events of *Blue Velvet*. The father's stroke, which opens the film like an incomprehensible catastrophe—an act of God which is peculiarly an act of scandalous violence within this peaceful American small town—is itself positioned by David Lynch (director of *Eraserhead* and *Dune*) within the more science fictional horizon of the Darwinian violence of all nature. From the shot of the father lying paralyzed, the camera withdraws into the bushes surrounding the house, enlarging its microscopic focus as it does so, until we confront a horrible churning which we take first and generically, in good horror-film format, to be the hidden presence of the maniac, until it proves to be the mandibles of an insatiable insect. The later insistence on robins with worms twisting desperately in their beaks also reinforces this cosmic sense of the dizzying and nauseating violence of all nature—as though within this ferocity without boundaries, this ceaseless bloodshed of the universe as far as the eye can see or thought can reach, a single peaceful oasis had been conquered by the progress of humanity and whatever divine providence guided it; namely—unique in the animal kingdom as well as in the horrors of human history as well—the North American small town. Into this precious and fragile conquest of civilized decorum wrenched from a menacing outside world, then, comes violence—in the form of a severed ear; in the form of an underground drug culture and of a sadomasochism about which it is finally not yet really clear whether it is a pleasure or a duty, a matter of sexual gratification or just another way of expressing yourself.

History therefore enters *Blue Velvet* in the form of ideology, if not of myth: the Garden and the Fall, American exceptionalism, a small town far more lovingly preserved in its details like a simulacrum or Disneyland under glass some-where than anything the protagonists of *Something Wild* were able to locate on their travels, complete with high school leads on the order of the most au-thentic fifties movies. Even a fifties-style pop psychoanalysis can be invoked around this fairy tale, since besides a mythic and sociobiological perspective of the violence of nature, the film's events are also framed by the crisis in the paternal function—the stroke that suspends paternal power and authority in the opening sequence, the recovery of the father and his return from the hospi-tal in the idyllic final scene. That the other father is a police detective lends a certain plausibility to this kind of interpretation, which is also strengthened by the abduction and torture of the third, absent, father, of whom we only see the ear. Nonetheless the message is not particularly patriarchal-authoritarian, par-ticularly since the young hero manages to assume the paternal function very handily: rather, this particular call for a return to the fifties coats the pill by insistence on the unobtrusive benevolence of all these fathers—and, contrari-wise, on the unalloyed nastiness of their opposite number.

For this gothic subverts itself fully as much as *Something Wild*, but in a rather different way. There, it was the simulated nature of Ray's evil that was underscored for us even while he remained a real threat: revolt, statutory ille-gality, physical violence, and ex-convicts are all genuine and serious matters. What *Blue Velvet* gives us to understand about the sixties, in contrast, is that despite the grotesque and horrendous tableaux of maimed bodies, this kind of evil is more distasteful than it is fearful, more disgusting than threatening: here evil has finally become an image, and the simulated replay of the fifties has gen-eralized itself into a whole simulacrum in its own right. Now the boy without fear of the fairy tale can set out to undo this world of baleful enchantment, free its princess (while marrying another), and kill the magician. The lesson implied by all this—which is rather different from the lesson it transmits—is that it is better to fight drugs by portraying them as vicious and silly, than by awakening the full tonal range of ethical judgments and indignations and thereby endow-ing them with the otherwise glamorous prestige of genuine Evil, of the Trans-gressive in its most august religious majesty. Indeed, this particular parable of the end of the sixties is also, on another metacritical level, a parable of the end of theories of transgression as well, which so fascinated that whole period and its intellectuals. The s&m materials, then—even though contemporary with a whole new postmodern punk scene—are finally called on to undo themselves and to abolish the very logic on which their attraction/repulsion was based in the first place.

Thus these films can be read as dual symptoms: they show a collective unconscious in the process of trying to identify its own present at the same time that they illuminate the failure of this attempt, which seems to reduce itself to the recombination of various stereotypes of the past. Perhaps, indeed, what follows upon a strongly generational self-consciousness, such as what the "people of the sixties" felt, is often a peculiar aimlessness. What if the crucial identifying feature of the next "decade" is, for example, a lack of just such strong self-consciousness, which is to say a constitutive lack of identity in the first place? This is what many of us felt about the seventies, whose specificity seemed most of the time to consist in having no specificity, particularly after the uniqueness of the preceding period. Things began to pick up again in the eighties, and in a variety of ways. But the identity process is not a cyclical one, and this is essentially the dilemma. Of the eighties, as against the seventies, one could say that there were new political straws in the wind, that things were moving again, that some impossible "return of the sixties" seemed to be in the air and in the ground. But the eighties, politically and otherwise, have not really resembled the sixties, especially, particularly if one tried to define them as a return or a reversion. Even that enabling costume-party self-deception of which Marx spoke—the wearing of the costumes of the great moments of the past—is no longer on the cards in an ahistorical period of history. The generational *combinatoire* thus seems to have broken down at the moment it confronted serious historicity, and the rather different self-concept of "postmodernism" has taken its place.

Dick used science fiction to see his present as (past) history; the classical nostalgia film, while evading its present altogether, registered its historicist deficiency by losing itself in mesmerized fascination in lavish images of specific generational pasts. The two 1986 movies, while scarcely pioneering a wholly new form (or mode of historicity), nonetheless seem, in their allegorical complexity, to mark the end of that and the now open space for something else.

12. The Mousetrap

CATHERINE GALLAGHER AND
STEPHEN GREENBLATT

OR AT LEAST a thousand years the Passover Seder has included a
midrash about four sons—the wise son, the wicked son, the simple son,
and the son who does not know how to ask—representing four distinct attitudes toward the evening's ritual and toward the religious community it helps
to define.[1] To the son who does not know how to ask, who is too young or too
ignorant to seek enlightenment, the father must take the initiative and begin
the story, as he is enjoined to do in the book of Exodus: "This is because of that
which the Lord did for me when I came forth from Egypt." To the simple son
who can at least notice that something unusual is happening but can only ask,
"*Ma zot?*"—"What is this?"—the father moves from the personal to the collective and adds a crucial bit of information: "With a strong hand did God bring us
out from Egypt, from the House of Bondage." But the crucial distinction is between the questions asked by the first two sons and the responses to their questions. The wise son recites a question taken from Deuteronomy (6:20): "What
mean the testimonies, and the statutes / and the ordinances, which the Lord
our God hath commanded you?" The wicked son recites a question taken from
Exodus (12:26): "What mean you by this service?"

On the face of it, the two questions are quite similar—nothing in
their original context suggests any moral difference between them—but the
Haggadah treats them as diametrically opposed. To the wise son, the father
patiently expounds the laws of the Passover; to the wicked son, he delivers a
stinging rebuke. This is because the midrash chooses to hear in the wicked son's
question a failure of identification:[2]

> The Wicked Son—what does he say? "What mean you by this service?"
> "You," he says, not himself. Since he has excluded himself, he has repudi-

ated God; and you should set his teeth too on edge, replying: "This is because of that which the Lord did for me when I came forth from Egypt"; for
me, not for him—if he had been there he would not have been saved.

You may have noticed that the reply to the wicked child is identical to that
given to the child who does not know how to ask—"This is because of that
which the Lord did for me when I came forth from Egypt" (Exodus 13:8); but
where the words in one instance are spoken as the gentle prelude to an initiation, in the other they are recited as a denunciation, an act of exclusion that
corresponds to an unacceptable self-exclusion, a refusal of communal participation. The issue here and throughout the Seder is a Jew's relation to historical
memory. The Haggadah enjoins a continual renewal of the ancient experience:
"In each and every generation, it is a man's duty to regard himself as though
[ke-*ee*-loo] he went forth out of Egypt, as it is said, 'And thou shalt tell thy son
in that day, saying, This is done because of that which the Lord did unto me
when I came forth out of Egypt.'" The wicked child refuses to incorporate the
memory of enslavement and the Exodus from Egypt; he refuses to swallow the
story as his own.

Our words are something more than metaphorical, of course, for the Passover Seder is a meal, derived from the ancient slaughtering and eating of the
paschal lamb. In the Bible certain features of the feast are carefully prescribed—
for example, "They shall eat the flesh that same night; they shall eat it roasted
over the fire, with unleavened bread and with bitter herbs"—as is its formal
and decisive closure: "You shall not leave any of it over until morning; whatever is left of it until morning you shall burn" (Exodus 12:1–20). After the destruction of the Temple, the sacrifice of the lamb ceased to be the central ritual
event of the festival, though some of its elements survived, as in the Mishnah's
scrupulous attempt to reinforce the prohibition of leftovers: "After midnight the
Passover offering imparts uncleanness to the hands; *piggul* and *notar* impart
uncleanness to the hands." *Notar*—food that is kept after its proper time—becomes *piqqul*, carrion, and hence a source of pollution. Symbolically, then, the
paschal lamb begins to rot at midnight. More familiarly, of course, the Passover
meal came to focus on the injunction to eat matzoth—unleavened bread—and
to drink the obligatory four cups of wine. As they eat the matzoth and drink the
wine, all males are required to recline on the left side—for this was the position
of free men at Roman banquets—but the festive celebration of freedom is qualified by the eating of bitter herbs and, traditionally, by the injunction to show
some sign of hurry or anxiety in order to reenact the flight from the pursuing
Egyptians. For the entire meal is an acting out of the Exodus story, as well as a

commentary upon it, in order to fulfill the commandment that the events be experienced as though they were your own, or rather that you speak of them to your child as your own personal history. And your child in turn must make your history his own—the one who declines the memory, who does not eat the bread of affliction, who refuses to regard himself as though he personally has been brought out of the house of bondage is wicked. He has repudiated God, and his teeth must be set on edge.

Even a very small Jewish child knows perfectly well, of course, that his father has been born, say, in Boston and not in Cairo, that his uncle Abraham has played semipro baseball in Cheyenne and not slaved for the Pharaohs, and that his uncle Moses, despite his name, has not parted the Red Sea. The wicked son would seem, from this perspective, the only sane or, alternatively, the only honest person at the table. This integrity is purchased by a refusal of an ambiguous injunction: to regard yourself *as though* means in part to pretend to be something you are not—the term acknowledges some distance between your actual and your imagined identity—but it also means to accept something that you are, something that you may not have understood about yourself and your origin and your destiny, something that you have inherited from your father and he from his. To escape this inheritance the wicked son would have to refuse the supper—or so it would appear—for the ritual meal seems an irresistible realization of the Haggadah's "as though."[3] Eating the matzoth and drinking the wine performatively make good on the claim to living memory by making that memory part of your own body even as your own body is part of the community engaged in the ritual of eating. This performance is closely related to the symbolic logic of the Eucharist, which was probably instituted, after all, at or in proximity to a Passover supper:[4]

> And as they were eating, Jesus took bread, and blessed it, and brake it, and gave it to the disciples, and said, "Take, eat; this is my body." And he took the cup, and gave thanks, and gave it to them, saying, "Drink ye all of it; For this is my blood of the new testament, which is shed for many for the remission of sins." (Matthew 26:26–28; with variations in Mark 14:22–24 and Luke 22:19–20)

In what is thought to be the oldest part of the Passover ritual, the matzoth are uncovered and held aloft, while the following words are recited in Aramaic: "This is the bread of affliction that our fathers ate in the land of Egypt."[5] How does this differ from Jesus' "This is my body," words associated with a comparable elevation of the bread in the Catholic Mass? At the moment of elevation in the Seder, historical time is drastically foreshortened; the distant past is made so intensely present that it lays claim to the material world here and now. But Jesus' words and the cultic practice that grew up around them go beyond anything intended by the rabbis who compiled the Haggadah; they pass from memory to miracle.

In the Jewish ritual, historical distance is continually reinvoked even as it is abrogated by the act of eating what is imagined as a piece of history. And the piece of history remains crucially what it always was—a piece of bread baked in a certain way. There is no transformation of its substance; on the contrary, history suffuses the object and passes into the body of the celebrant precisely to the extent that it is what it appears to be, in a plain and literal sense. Hence the claim to a direct personal experience of bondage and liberation is at once confirmed and qualified in the sentence "This is the bread of affliction that our fathers ate in the land of Egypt." The words oscillate between identification and recollection, proximity and distance, and the whole Seder similarly oscillates between a commemoration of the Exodus from Egypt and a commemoration of the rabbinical exegesis of these events. If the participants at the Seder reenact the liberation of the ancient Hebrews, they also explicitly reenact the narrative reenactment of the event by the most celebrated rabbis of late antiquity: "It once happened that Rabbi Eliezer, Rabbi Joshua, Rabbi Eleazar, the son of Azariah, Rabbi Akiba, and Rabbi Tarphon were reclining on Passover at Bene Berak, and were telling the story of the departure from Egypt all that night, until their pupils came and said to them: 'Masters! The time has come for reciting the morning Shema.' "[6] In the sentence "This is my body," by contrast, all traces of the rabbinical "as though" are erased, and according to Catholic doctrine, the actual substance of the bread is transmuted. Communal memory gives way to outright corporeal transformation and eating as an acknowledgment of communal membership by descent gives way to eating as the actual incorporation of the body of God.

The extreme radicalism of Jesus' speech act is underscored, of course, by the centuries of speculation, disputation, and competing institutional practice that it engendered.[7] The apparently simple sentence put enormous pressure on communal understanding of words and of matter, pressure that reached the breaking point in the sixteenth and seventeenth centuries. Are the bread and the wine the body and blood of Christ really or figuratively? Ontologically and substantially, or symbolically and in signification? How and under what conditions does something become a sign? How and at what moment does it cease to be one thing and become another? What are the entailments of the different and often incompatible terms applied to the Eucharist, terms that open an almost infinite linguistic space between God's body and a piece of common baked bread: flesh, sign, word, promise, mystery, representation, presentation, shadow, memorial, commemoration, figure, pledge, token, metaphor, metonymy, covenant, even real estate lease?[8] Should every member of the community receive the sacramental bread or only those who are worthy to receive it? If an unbeliever eats the Eucharist, has he or she actually received the body of God? Can it be efficaciously consecrated by an evil priest? Is the Lord's Supper a public, common feast or what one sixteenth-century polemicist contemptuously called "a private churlish breakfast"?[9] Can it be administered to the sick or dying in their own homes? Should observers be allowed to watch the administration of the Sacrament, as if it were a performance, or should only those who are themselves participating be present? What preparation is required before receiving Communion, and how often can or should it be received? Should it be consecrated at an altar or is a table to be preferred? Should those administering it wear special vestments? Should those receiving it kneel? Should the bread be lifted up and shown to the congregants? Should it be dipped in the wine? Should it be received in the hand or taken directly in the mouth? What happens if the sacramental bread corrupts? What is the status of the fragments that are left over and what is to be done with them?

These questions and many others like them troubled men and women in the late Middle Ages and the early modern period; they occasioned vast amounts of polemical writing, bitter denunciations, intellectual heroics, spectacular feats of the imagination, and murderous violence. As Miri Rubin's wonderfully capacious study *Corpus Christi: The Eucharist in Late Medieval Culture* argues, eucharistic interpretations are too complex, various, and unpredictable to submit to any overarching theory: "No single Eucharist is to be sought," she writes, "and no single category such as class or gender can adequately capture the variety of eucharistic meaning."[10] We have no intention of trying to do anything of the kind. But we want to make three observations: first, most of the significant and sustained thinking in the early modern period about the nature of linguistic signs centered on or was deeply influenced by eucharistic controversies; second, most of the literature that we care about from this period was written in the shadow of these controversies; and third, their significance for English literature in particular lies less in the problem of the sign than in what we will call "the problem of the leftover," that is, the status of the material remainder. This problem is never entirely absent from eucharistic theology, for, as Louis Marin observes in *La Critique du discours*, transubstantiation raises a question at the intersection of physics and linguistics. But when the Port-Royal logicians thought about the Eucharist, they focused not on matter but on words. The formula of the consecration begins with *hoc*, a neuter demonstrative pronoun whose function, according to the *Logic*, is to point as with a finger at the thing about which one is speaking. In the case of the matzoth, this pointing is not a problem, but how does it work in the formula of the Eucharist?[11] And what exactly is the thing at which it points? The solution for the Port-Royal logicians lies in the word *est*, which not only links the terms *hoc* and *corpus meum*, but also transforms the thing that *hoc* designates from bread into body, the body which is that of the subject who originally pronounces the words. A stable ideology of representation is challenged by a complex intuition of language as force.[12]

There is some comparable speculation in early modern England, but Reformation theology pulled in a different direction, away from the transforming power of sacramental words—words that were satirized as "hocus-pocus." English reformers focused instead upon the spiritual power of signification—*est*, Zwingli and others argued, here means only *significat*—and they focused too on the persistence and what we might call the embarrassments of matter.[13] Those embarrassments were not unfamiliar to medieval defenders of eucharistic orthodoxy, who rehearsed them as the imagined arguments of the enemies of the faith. "The beleve of thes[e] Cristen men is false, as I wene," says the rich Jewish merchant Jonathas in the late-fifteenth-century Croxton *Play of the Sacrament*. "For the[y] beleve on a cake."[14] Jonathas and his fellow Jews—who have the disquieting habit of swearing by Mohammed—purchase a consecrated Host from a corrupt Christian and put it to the test in order to mock its crudely material nature. But when they stab the Host, the Jews find to their horror that it bleeds, and their panicky reactions, which include nailing the bread to a post and casting it into an oven, only succeed in reenacting the Crucifixion and entombment for which their race was held responsible. Finally, the oven bursts asunder, and the figure of the bleeding Christ emerges. In the face of incontrovertible proof of the eucharistic miracle, the terrified Jews convert, whereupon the figure of Christ returns once again to the form of bread and is carried in solemn triumph into the church.

But the triumph was evidently less decisive than the pious authors of the miracle play hoped. For the skepticism attributed to carnal Israel continually resurfaced within the Christian community and by the early sixteenth century had flared into open and irrepressible revolt. "Is that bread," Thomas Becon asks the "mass-mongers," "which a little afore was corn in the ploughman's barn, meal in the miller's trough, flour in the baker's boulting-tub, and afterward tempered with a little water and baken of the wafer-man between a pair of hot printing-irons, come now suddenly through your charming into such dignity that it is 'the Lamb of God, that taketh away the sins of the world?' "[15] For Becon the Catholic Mass is a shameless theatrical imposture. "Like another Roscius, with his foolish, player-like, and mad gestures," the priest, decked out in "scenical and game-player's garments," puts on a performance designed to make the crowd forget that *Hoc est corpus meum*, 'This is my body,' is a figurative speech."[16] To recite these words in an alien tongue, to pretend that they have the power to call Christ's body down from heaven, is a horrible pollution of the Sacrament, a kind of magic.[17] The gullible are induced to believe that they are actually glimpsing God: "If the priest be weak in the arms, and heave not up high enough," Becon writes, with the eye of the ethnographer and the detachment of the wicked son, "the rude people of the country in divers parts of England will cry out to the priest, 'Hold up, sir John, hold up; heave it a little higher.' And one will say to another, 'Stoop down, thou fellow afore, that I may see my Maker: for I cannot be merry except I see my Lord God once in a day.' "[18]

Becon tells a story of a Christian who took a Jew of his acquaintance, an honest and upright man whom he wished to convert, to church. The Jew enjoyed the festiveness of the service—"jolly ringing, pleasant singing, and merry organs playing"—but he declared that he was shocked to see the congregants "fall down and worship a piece of bread and a silver cup" (281–82). For Becon then, as for Luther, the Jews have refused to convert to Christianity because Christianity, in the corrupt form of Catholicism, has sunk to idolatry. Gorgeously robed magicians mumble a Latin formula and hold up a thin round cake that they claim is God: "What is idolatry, if this be not idolatry?" (274). To shock his readers into a recognition of its grotesque absurdity, Becon indulges in strange Gogol-like fantasies: Mary the Virgin gives birth to a lump of bread that sucks at her breasts; the bread walks upon the earth; the bread is stretched out and, as in the *Play of the Sacrament*, nailed to the cross. The insistent materiality pulls at the fabric of the sacred story and threatens to unravel it; such is the risk Becon must take in order to free the spiritual truth from its corrupt and idolatrous imprisonment in a piece of ordinary bread.

The threat that recalcitrant, ineradicable matter posed for eucharistic theology was not, as we have already seen, only a Reformation concern, nor was it the exclusive province of the male intellectual elite. In the heresy trials in Norwich in 1428, for example, testimony was taken against Margery Baxter, who was accused of Lollardy by her friend Johanna Clyfland in the wake of an argument in which Margery allegedly warned her (*in lingua materna*): "Dame, bewar of the bee, for every bee wil styngge, and therfor loke that ye swer nother be Godd ne by Our Ladi ne be non other seynt, and if ye don the contrarie the be will styngge your tunge and veneme your sowle."[19] Johanna was an orthodox believer—she told the inquisitors that she said to Margery that after the consecration the sacrament was *verum corpus Christi in specie panis*—but Margery had other ideas: "You believe wrongly, since if every such sacrament were god and Christ's real body, then gods would be infinite in number, because a thousand priests and more confect a thousand such gods every day and then eat them, and once eaten emit them from their back side in filthy and stinking pieces; and you can find plenty of these gods there if you are willing to look."[20]

The scatological joke here is a vivid way of insisting on the problem of the leftover, a way of making the point that—as the Lollard John Reve put it during the same inquisition—"aftir the sacramentall wordis said of a prest at messe ther remaneth nothyng but only a cake of material bred" (III). If it is a cake of material bread, it must be chewed with teeth, swallowed, and digested. The nastiness of the natural process—that fact that the remains of the wafer must eventually pass out of the body in filthy and stinking pieces—is emphasized in order to identify matter with shameful pollution.

The only way to save Christ's Glorified Body, or rather Christian faith in that body, from material contamination is to pry it loose from the visible Church, to separate it off from the grossly physical bread and wine, by insisting that Christ—single, whole, and beyond corruption—dwells in heaven at the right hand of his Father. The Church has no power, Reformers argued, to draw Christ's body back to earth, nor could that body, if it were so drawn, violate the laws of physics. Becon told his Catholic opponents:

> It is directly against the verity and truth of Christ's natural body to be in more places at once than in one, as he must be in an hundred thousand places at once, if your doctrine be true. A stinking sodomite or a wicked whoremonger, being dressed in his fool's coat, and standing at an altar with a little thin round cake in his hand, shall with these five words, *Hoc est enim corpus meum*, and with blowing and breathing upon the bread, make Christ, the King of glory, to come from the right hand of his Father, and to touch himself in the accidents of the little cake, till ye have eaten him. . . .[21]

In the Middle Ages the Pope had extracted from the heretic Berengar a strikingly literal doctrinal confession: "The bread and wine are the true body of our Lord Jesus Christ . . . handled and broken by the hands of the priests and ground by the teeth of the faithful."[22] Even Luther, who insisted on the Real Presence, found this phraseology disturbingly crude;[23] Calvin found it monstrous.

The Reformers return again and again to the celebrated words of Augustine: "Why are you preparing your teeth and your stomach? Believe, and you have already eaten [*crede et manducasti*]."[24] It followed, according to Calvin, not that the Sacrament was pointless, but that "believers have, outside the Lord's Supper, what they receive in the Supper itself."[25] There was, as Bullinger put it, a "spiritual, divine, and life-giving presence of Christ the Lord in the Supper and outside the Lord's Supper, by which he . . . proceeds to enter our hearts, not through empty symbols, but through his Spirit."[26] Luther's theory that the body of Christ was present "in, with, and under" the bread of the Supper seemed to many Reformers to confuse the crucial distinction between spirit and matter and hence to reiterate Roman Catholic carnality. "We freely confess," Calvin wrote to the Lutheran Joachim Westphal, "that our sacred unity with Jesus Christ is beyond our corporeal understanding. . . . But must we therefore dream that his substance is transfused into us in order to be soiled with our filth?"[27] The solution is to grasp that the eucharistic formula for the bread and wine— "This is my body, this is my blood"—is a figure of speech, specifically, a metonymy in which "the sign borrows the name of the truth that it figures."[28] There are, Beza said flatly, only two possibilities: "either transubstantiation or a trope."[29]

According to the Reformers, a conspiracy of self-serving priests had contrived for centuries to transform trope into flesh, to confound what Augustine called the "visible word" with a basely "materialistic theology." The Catholic Church withholds the Host from husbands and wives who have not observed a period of sexual abstinence—as if God condemned marital love—but it is the lascivious priests themselves, the heretics argue, who have dragged the Sacrament down into the realm of the senses: you come forth to the altar with your gaudy vestments and "your shamelesse, smooth, smirking faces," Becon writes, to signify that you are ready at all times "to play *Priapus* part."[30] It is from the likes of these—from the hands and mouths and bellies of such theatrical sensualists—that the body of God must be rescued.

For the Lollards, as later for Calvinists and others, the Supper of the Lord continues to include the ritual eating of the consecrated bread—the sign must pass into and through the body—but the ritual now eschews the miraculous transformation of matter. The emphasis is on remembrance through representation: the symbol enters into the body as an exalted mnemonic device. "For Christ is not visibly present, and is not beheld with our eyes," writes Calvin, "as the symbols are which excite our remembrance by representing him. In short, in order that he may be present to us, he does not change his place, but communicates to us from heaven the virtue of his flesh as though it were present."[31] "As though it were present"—we are brought close once again to the Passover Seder and its injunction to eat and remember under the sign of "as though." But for Calvin, and for Protestants more generally, the Supper of the Lord does not finally center on the carnal rite of remembrance. The crucial agent is not historical memory, written on the flesh, but feeling faith, a faith that soars away altogether from the limitations of matter. "The sacrament is corruptible," writes the Anglican John Jewel in his controversy with the Catholic John Harding; "Christ's body is glorious, and void of all corruption. The sacrament is in the earth: Christ's body is in heaven. The sacrament is received by our bodily mouth: Christ's body is received only by faith, which is the mouth of our soul."[32]

Committed as they were to the Aristotelian distinction between substance and accidents, Catholic theologians had always recognized that there was in the Sacrament of the Mass a material residue, and committed as they were to a principle of exhaustiveness, they had vigorously debated its status. The issue of digestion was officially resolved by the argument that after the consecration, the bread was miraculously changed in substance into Christ's body, but the appearance of bread, the accidents or species, was unchanged.[33] The substance, Albertus Magnus declared, remained only as long as the form of the Eucharist continued intact; once the wafer was dissolved in the mouth (or, in Gratian's formulation, once it was touched by the teeth) it was no longer Christ's body.[34] But this sophisticated doctrine did not entirely resolve the problem of the left-over, even for church intellectuals, and heresy trials throughout the late Middle Ages, along with conflicting practices within the Church itself, suggest that it continued to be a vexing problem for a wide spectrum of people. The consecrated bread had been transformed by the touch of the transcendent, but its material accidents stubbornly persisted and were unnervingly subject to the disgraces to which all matter is vulnerable.

In the poisoned atmosphere of the sixteenth century, this vulnerability became a particularly charged point of contention between Catholics and Protestants. This accounts for several strange moments in the first examination of the Protestant Anne Askew in 1545: In the notes that she is said to have smuggled out of the Tower of London to John Bale, she relates that a priest, sent to question her on her beliefs, asked her,

> If the host shuld fall, and a beast ded eate it, whether the beast ded receyve God or no: I answered, Seynge ye have taken the paynes to aske thys questyon, I desyre yow also to take so moche payne more, as to assoyle it your selfe. For I wyll not do it, bycause I perceyve ye come to tempte me. And he sayd, it was agaynst the ordre of scoles, that he whych asked the questyon, shuld answere it. I tolde hym, I was but a woman, & knewe not the course of scoles.[35]

The question was not random: it was also asked by the chief secular interrogator: "My Lord Mayor laid one thing unto my charge which was never spoken of me, but of them: and that was, whether a mouse eating the Host received God, or no? This question did I never ask; but, indeed, they asked it of me, whereunto I made them no answer, but smiled."[36] By the middle of the sixteenth century, Catholics expected Protestants to try to mock them with the Host-eating mouse; thus, for example, Becon taunts the mass-mongers for believing that "not only the godly and faithful eat the body of Christ in the supper, but also the ungodly and misbelieving; yea, the cats, rats, mice, dogs, owls, flittermouses."[37] The taunts must have stung, for the lord mayor tries to turn the tables and lure the heretic into the mousetrap. Anne Askew's smile is a wonderfully poised response, for it gives away nothing and implies that the problem is after all the Catholic Church's and not hers.

"We suffer anxiety if anything of the cup, or even of our bread fall to the ground," Tertullian wrote, and the anxiety was reiterated through the ensuing centuries.[38] Elaborate measures were taken during the Middle Ages to protect the Host from contamination or pollution. The Mass table was situated in an elevated and enclosed place and covered by a ciborium to prevent dust from falling upon the cloth or the wafers. Though they had the right to make ornaments for the priest's apparel and napkins for the holy table, women were forbidden to approach the altar or touch the chalice, the paten, and the corporale. Before celebrating Mass, the officiating priest was combed by church servers with ivory combs so that nothing unclean might fall from his hair onto the holy things. During Mass a servant raised and lowered a *flabellum* (fan) at the side of the priest to keep flies from alighting on the bread or cup.[39] Priests wore maniples or *sudaria*, small pieces of cloth embroidered with gold, over their wrists at Mass, so that they could wipe away any drops of perspiration that might otherwise fall upon the bread and wine. After breaking the Host, the priest was supposed to keep his thumb and forefinger closed, so that no crumbs could fall from his hand; later he was supposed to rub these fingers together over the chalice, so that the small particles might drop into the holy vessel.[40] According to Durandus, "After the celebrant has taken in the sacrifice, he must not allow himself to cough or spit. Neither must he eat the Host as men do other food, but he should hold it in his mouth with discretion, modesty, and caution, using his front teeth and moistening it with his tongue, so that no crumb can fix itself in the cavities of his teeth."[41] After Mass, priests would use a separate basin to wash their hands, along with the paten and chalice, in order to collect any particles of the Host. In the later Middle Ages, pipes were laid from the washstand, carrying the water either directly to the earth or by means of a spout into the churchyard outside—in either case, only onto consecrated ground. Alternatively, ordained as early as 1212, priests were supposed to drink up the rinse water.

But as churchmen recognized, these extraordinary measures would never be perfect, and there would inevitably be accidents, thefts, and disasters, including the mouse about which Anne Askew was interrogated. Aquinas reports that "some have said that, as soon as the sacrament is touched of a mouse or a dog, the body and blood of Christ straightway departeth from it," but he regards this reassuring view as a derogation of the truth of the Sacrament. John of Burgos declares flatly that a mouse, eating the Host, receives the body of Christ—"*Mus . . . comedens hostiam suscipit corpus Christi*"—and, though there is considerable disagreement and uncertainty, other theologians concur.[42] If the bread has been miraculously transformed, then all of it—not only the leftover wafers but the crumbs on the altar cloth—must be protected from defilement. Protestant polemicists seized on these opinions and maliciously rehearsed the more extreme moments of Catholic eucharistic fervor. Hence Jewel quotes Peter of Palus: "The mouse's entrails must be drawn, and the portion of the sacrament that there remaineth, if the priest be squeamish to receive it, must reverently be laid up in the tabernacle, until it may naturally be consumed." "If the priest be squeamish to receive it"—ideally, that is, the priest should eat the bits of wafer recovered from the mouse's entrails, just as "St Hugh of Clunice much commendeth Goderanus, a priest, for receiving the like portions" vomited up by a leper. "St Laurence's gridiron was nothing so bad," Goderanus is said to have reported afterward.[43] "I protest," writes Jewel after dwelling for pages on this subject, that its "blasphemy and loathsomeness" is intolerable; "neither would I have used this unpleasant rehearsal, were it not that it behoveth each man to know how deeply the people hath been deceived, and to what villany they have been brought" (784).

These are the vicious little amusements of sixteenth-century intellectuals. But, as Anne Askew and her inquisitor both understood, the stakes for all the faithful were high. Along with questions about the materiality of the supreme signifier, they involved the nature and limits of the religious community: Who has legitimate access to the holy? What do you need to believe in order to become part of Christ's body and to make Christ's body part of yours? Where do you locate and how do you ward off threats of pollution? What is the proper relation between the Eucharist—"a most Maiesticall & diuine obiect," in the words of a late-sixteenth-century English Catholic priest—and the "exorbitant desyres" of the human body, "this sacke of durte? this meate for wormes, this gate of sinne? this bodye of myne?"[44] The skirmishing about the mouse is for

Protestants a way of exposing the Catholic Church's alleged idolatry, materialism, and indifference to the faith of its members, while for the Church it is a necessary if awkward corollary to its central dogma and to its assertions of institutional power. A priest—any priest, regardless of his personal failings or the failings of his parishioners—had the power, through his performance of the ritual of consecration, to initiate and preside over the miraculous transformation of matter. And if matter was actually transformed, how could the faithful be indifferent to the disposition of even the tiniest fragments? The concern was not merely decorum, though decorum was important enough, but rather the fate of the precious body of God.

We claimed earlier that the literature of the period was written in the shadow of these controversies, and we want at least to gesture toward making good on this claim. The point is not only that explicitly religious works are affected—as they manifestly are—but also that apparently secular works are charged with the language of eucharistic anxiety. "Now, Hamlet, where's Polonius?" Claudius asks. "At supper." "At supper? Where?" "Not where he eats," Hamlet replies, "but where a is eaten."[45] The significance of these words extends beyond the cruel and callous joke about Polonius; *the* supper where the host does not eat but is eaten is the Supper of the Lord. A theological resonance here may seem implausible, and not only because Polonius is an extremely unlikely candidate for the role of sacrificial offering: after all, though Protestants actively promoted substituting the phrase "the Supper of the Lord" for the Catholic "Mass," the word "supper" retained its principal meaning of the last meal in the day: "About the sixth hour," as one character puts it in *Love's Labour's Lost*, "when beasts most graze, birds best peck, and men sit down to that nourishment which is called supper" (1.1.227–29). Hamlet, to be sure, makes the grim point that Polonius will himself be the nourishment served up at this supper, but there scarcely seems to be any sacrificial meaning attached to his body. When at the scene's end Hamlet declares, with appalling coldness, that he'll "lug the guts into the neighbour room," we are far from an allegory of the most sacred mystery of the faith.

Yet just as we dismiss the strange resonance in the phrase "Not where he eats but where a is eaten," the next lines make it sound again: "A certain convocation of politic worms are e'en at him. Your worm is your only emperor for diet" (4.3.20–22). Scholars duly note the allusion to the Diet of Worms, where Luther's doctrines were officially condemned by the Holy Roman Emperor, but the question is what work the allusion is doing. Two answers have been proposed—showing that Hamlet was a student at Wittenberg and marking the earliest date for the play's events—but its principal function, we think, is to echo and reinforce the theological and, specifically, the eucharistic subtext, not only in the bitter jest that was just spoken but in the reverse riddle that follows: "A man may fish with the worm that hath eat of a king, and eat of the fish that hath fed of that worm." "What dost thou mean by this?" Claudius asks, and Hamlet replies, "Nothing but to show you how a king may go a progress through the guts of a beggar."

Somewhere half buried here is a death threat against the usurper-king—and Claudius understands perfectly well that the rapier thrust at the rat behind the arras had been aimed at him rather than Polonius—but Hamlet's words, with their strange blend of rage, disgust, and curiosity, reach beyond his immediate enemy, as they have already reached beyond Polonius, to touch another king, the royal father whose body is rotting in the sepulcher. And as if Hamlet's imagination knew no bounds, as if it were compelled to thrust further and still further, until it reached the ultimate point, it seems to touch another king as well, the king of kings whose transubstantiated flesh could go a progress through the guts of a beggar.

But why should the prince's imagination be seized by images of royal or even divine decomposition? After all, Hamlet has just seen the ghost of his father in Gertrude's closet—"My father, in his habit as he lived" (4.4.126), he tells his mother—and he had earlier seen him looking exactly as he had looked on the battlefield, in "that fair and warlike form," as Horatio puts it, "In which the majesty of buried Denmark / Did sometimes march" (1.1.45–47). The two apparitions are strikingly different, the one in full armor ("so majestical," says Marcellus [1.2.124]) and the other in a nightgown, but in each case the father's body is intact and his face is evidently visible.[46] Hamlet is confronted in effect with animated versions of the effigies sculpted on sixteenth-century tombs: *representacions au vif*, in the language of contracts from the period, "lifelike" figures arrayed in costumes befitting their worldly dignity and comfort.[47] But tombs in this period often had another effigy carved just below the *representacion au vif*: a *representacion de la mort*. This horrible image in the shadows of the lower register—a depiction of the decaying corpse eaten by mice and worms—is what Hamlet's imagination seems continually to force into his consciousness, compelling him, as his mother complains, to "seek for thy noble father in the dust" (1.2.71). From this perspective, the apparition of his father in the intact, uncorrupted forms found on the upper register of the period's tomb sculpture only pulls Hamlet's attention down to the still more dreadful image that lurks below, the image of the decaying corpse.

"Thou know'st 'tis common—all that lives must die," Gertrude tells her son, "Passing through nature to eternity" (1.2.72–73). It was this "passing through nature" that the representacion de la mort was presumably meant to underscore, by insisting upon the transience of the flesh: "Let the soul depart but one half hour from the body," the Catholic Robert Persons wrote in his *Christian Directory* (1582), "and this loving face is ugly to look on: let it ly but two days in the grave, or above ground dead, and those who were so earnestly in love with it before, will scarce abide to behold or to come near it."[48] Consolation lies elsewhere; to dwell obsessively upon the flesh, to persevere in mourning the fate of the body, is to pursue what Claudius calls "a course / of impious stubbornness" (1.2.93–94). Hamlet, in the usurper's devious but deeply perceptive view, is anything but a model of filial piety; rather his "obstinate condolement" is a form of aggression not only against the natural and supernatural order of things, but also against the very father he professes to mourn: "Fie, 'tis a fault to heaven, / A fault against the dead, a fault to nature" (1.2.101–2). Claudius is in effect accusing Hamlet of being the wicked son, behaving not as if his father's spirit had passed through nature to eternity, but as if instead it had been transformed into the most degraded form of matter.

This transformation played, as we have seen, a crucial role in the polemic that raged around the Mass, a polemic that lies just below the surface of Hamlet's caustic, riddling words about the Diet of Worms, the fat king and the lean beggar, the royal progress through the intestines. If these words allude to a grotesquely materialist reimagining of the Eucharist, if they conjoin "a fault to heaven" and "a fault against the dead," if they complete a circuit that links Hamlet's prospective father-in-law Polonius and his "uncle-father" Claudius to his earthly and heavenly fathers, they would seem to bear out the charge that Hamlet is the wicked son. By insisting upon the vulnerability of matter and its grotesque metamorphoses, by dwelling upon the transformation of the dead into endlessly recycled food, by dragging a king through the guts of a beggar, Hamlet bitterly protests against the ghostly transmission of patriarchal memory and against the whole sacrificial plot in which the son is fatally appointed to do his father's bidding. But how is it possible to reconcile this apparently skeptical, secular protest with Hamlet's obsessive quest to fulfill precisely the task that the ghost has set him?

The answer is that a skeptical, secular insistence on irreducible corporeality paradoxically originates in an attempt to save the Eucharist from the taint of the body. It is only by ritually defiling the Host, by imagining the Sacrament passing through the belly of the beast, by dwelling on the corruptibility of matter and its humiliating susceptibility to chain-eating that the spirit can be liberated. "But now what do thei with him, hauing thus transformed him," the preacher John Bridges asked about the Host in the Catholic Mass, in a sermon he preached at Paul's Cross in 1571,

> forsoth euen as the cat doth with the mouse, play with it, dandle it vp & downe, hoise it ouer her head, tosse it hither & thyther, & then eate it cleane vp: euen so for al the world, did they order Christ. Marke a Priest at Masse, and marke a Cat with a mouse, & tel me then what difference. Nor if Christ were not eaten vp of the Priest, did he so escape the Priests handes: Nay, euen as a mouse kept in a trap till she pine to death, as a birde in a pitfal til she be starued, as a caytif in a dungeon til he be famished, so was Christ thrust vp into a copper pixe, and there hanged vp tyll euen the wormes did eate hym, and scraule [sic] all ouer hym, and the very hoarie moulde dydd rotte him, and then was he taken down and burned, bycause he could keepe himselfe no better. O cruell *Canibali*, O barbarous Priests.[49]

"Behold the masse-Priest with his baked god," writes Thomas Adams in 1615, in a similar vein, "towzing tossing, and dandling it, to and fro, vpward and downward, forward and backward, till at last, the iest turning into earnest, he choppes it into his mouth at one bitte; whiles all stand gaping with admiration."[50] Since neither Bridges nor Adams was by any means proposing to do away with the wafer, their ridicule had its obvious dangers, but the risk of mocking the most sacred thing had to be taken in order to secure the integrity of belief and the purity of the sacrifice. This is the logic of Protestant polemics against the Mass, and this too is the logic of Shakespeare's tragedy.

Even before he learned of his mother's adultery and his father's murder, Hamlet had been sickened by the "too too solid" (or "sallied" or "sullied") flesh. Later in the play, after he has encountered the ghost, he will use many images that link this materiality with corruptibility, but here the dominant associations are not with the vulnerability of nature but rather with what for Hamlet is its nauseating vigor, its uncontrollable, metastatic power to renew itself: "'Tis an unweeded garden / That grows to seed; things rank and gross in nature / Possess it merely" (1.2.135–37). Why unchecked fecundity should be the focus is explained by his obsession in the rest of the speech with his mother's remarriage: it is as if the death of his father should properly have brought about the death of desire, the end of renewal and increase, the disappearance of matter.

Hamlet's longing is for a melting or thawing of the flesh, a turning of solid into liquid and then the "resolution" of liquid into dew.[51] But the flesh does not simply vanish; instead, it is caught up in unending cycles of renewal, strikingly figured by the recycling of leftovers: "Thrift, thrift, Horatio. The funeral bak'd meats / Did coldly furnish forth the marriage tables" (1.2.180–81). In Hamlet's bitter jest, food prepared for his father's funeral has been used for his mother's marriage, a confounding of categories that has stained both social rituals in the service of thrift. At issue is not only, as G. R. Hibbard suggests,[52] an aristocratic disdain for a bourgeois prudential virtue, but a conception of the sacred as incompatible with a restricted economy, an economy of calculation and equivalence. Such calculation has led Gertrude to marry Claudius, as if he were his brother's equal: "My father's brother," Hamlet protests, "but no more like my father / Than I to Hercules" (1.2.152–53). Her remarriage, like the reuse of the funeral baked meats, is a double defilement: it has sullied Gertrude's flesh, which becomes a leftover to be gobbled up by the loathsome Claudius, and, since "Father and mother is man and wife; man and wife is one flesh" (4.3.53–4), it has retroactively stained old Hamlet by identifying his noble spirit with the grossness of the "bloat King" (3.4.171).

The source of the pollution, according to the ghost, is unbridled sexual appetite:

> lust, though to a radiant angel linked,
> Will sate itself in a celestial bed
> And prey on garbage.
> (1.5.55–57)

The disgust provoked by the leftover is here intensified by the image of the person who, though sated, continues to eat and to eat garbage—not simply refuse, but, literally, "entrails."[53] The ghost breaks off his meditation on lust in order to recount the scene of his murder, but Hamlet becomes obsessed with his mother's sexual appetite, which seems to loom larger in his consciousness than the killing of his father. His charge that Gertrude has murdered her husband— "A bloody deed—almost as bad, good-mother, / As kill a king and marry with his brother" (3.4.27–28)[54]—gives way to a desperate, nauseated indictment of her filthy desires:

> Nay, but to live
> In the rank sweat of an enseamèd bed
> Stewed in corruption, honeying and making love
> Over the nasty sty.
> (3.4.81–84)

The lines are the culmination of a powerful current of imagery in the play, not all of it in Hamlet's own speeches, related to something sticky, greasy, cancerous, or mildewed in, around, or of the body, something that leaves a horrible stain or that swells and bursts inwardly or that is detected by a rank taste or a lingering smell.

Claudius, who intuitively shares many of Hamlet's deepest perceptions, reproaches himself for not dealing sooner with his nephew's dangerous madness:

> We would not understand what was most fit,
> But, like the owner of a foul disease,
> To keep it from divulging, let it feed
> Even on the pith of life.
> (4.1.19–23)

Hamlet is, by implication, a disease within Claudius's own body, a body that is coextensive with the state. If, as Marcellus suspected, "something is rotten in the state of Denmark," this "something" is Hamlet. "Do it, England," Claudius declares, ordering his tributary state to put Hamlet to death, "For like the hectic in my blood he rages, / And thou must cure me" (4.3.66–68). And when this cure fails, Claudius, turning to Laertes, imagines himself as the physician who must break through the skin to lance the dangerous infection: "But to the quick of th'ulcer" (4.7.95.10). The metaphor had already been used by Hamlet, devising the "Mousetrap" as a means to expose what lay hidden within his uncle: "I'll tent him to the quick. If a but blench, / I know my course" (3.1.573–74). And Hamlet returns to it again when he is pleading with his mother not to dismiss his words by attributing them to madness:

> It will but skin and film the ulcerous place
> Whilst rank corruption, mining all within,
> Infects unseen.
> (3.4.138–40)[55]

The image repeatedly is of some horrible substance, itself a life-form but one inimical to any life one actually holds dear, growing in the darkness, feeding and spreading and ultimately killing.

Even before he had encountered the ghost and learned its secret, Hamlet had had intimations of this ghastly living thing hidden within an apparently healthy living body: "some vicious mole of nature" (1.4.18.8), he termed it. "Mole" is usually glossed as an external blemish, and the subsequent phrase "the stamp of one defect" would seem to support such a meaning, but there is a latent sense as well of something deep inside a person, burrowing in the darkness like a blind mole, or growing within like the tumors or the false conceptions that were also in this period called moles, or restlessly gaping and feeding like the female genitals that were by Galen compared to moles.[56] With that sublime, half-mad verbal lightning that flashes blindingly throughout the play, confounding the vicious and the innocent, the excremental and the divine, Hamlet in the next scene returns to the image, hysterically addressing his father's ghost, whom he hears moving beneath the ground: "Well said, old mole. Canst work i'th' earth so fast?" (1.5.164).

Hamlet does not speak again of the blind mole, but the image lingers perhaps in the digging of Goodman Delver the grave maker or in Hamlet's contriving against the treachery of Rosencrantz and Guildenstern to "delve one yard below their mines" (3.4.185.7). Above all, the horror, disgust, and weird humor that it evokes in Hamlet are powerfully reiterated in his response to his mother's desires. His mother's failure to see—her inability to distinguish between her first husband and the loathsome Claudius—comes to stand in Hamlet's mind for the sexual viciousness of her nature. "Have you eyes?" he asks. "Could you on this fair mountain leave to feed, / And batten of this moor? Ha, have you eyes?" (3.4.65–66). "Eyes without feeling," he continues in a second quarto passage, "feeling without sight" (3.4.70.8). Hamlet's identification of this corrupt and corrupting and blind infection, this horrible life-within-life, with his mother's sexuality leads him to forget the vengeance to which he has dedicated himself, or so the ghost charges, interrupting Hamlet's tirade about the "enseamèd bed" to remind him of his purpose: "Do not forget. This visitation / Is but to whet thy almost blunted purpose" (3.4.100–1).

The time is out of joint, and the spirit of the father has charged his son with setting it right. But the task becomes mired in the flesh that will not melt away, that cannot free itself from its deep bonds with mother and lover, that stubbornly persists and resists and blocks the realization of the father's wishes. Generativity—the capacity for bodies, and specifically for women's bodies, to engender more and more flesh—comes to obsess Hamlet, as if it were the source of contamination that he must somehow get free of before he can serve his father's spirit:

> Get thee to a nunnery. Why wouldst thou be a breeder of sinners? I am myself indifferent honest, but yet I could accuse me of such things that it were better my mother had not borne me. . . . Go thy ways to a nunnery. Where's your father? . . . Let the doors be shut upon him, that he may play the fool nowhere but in's own house. . . . I have heard of your paintings, too, well enough. God hath given you one face, and you make yourselves another.

You jig, you amble, and you lisp, and nickname God's creatures, and make your wantonness your ignorance. Go to, I'll no more on't. It hath made me mad. I say we will have no more marriages. . . . To a nunnery, go. (3.1.122–49).

The object of the loathing here appears to be breeding itself, or rather the sexual desire that women, by the way they look and move and speak ("You jig, you amble, and you lisp"), arouse in men, leading them to play the fool.

Somewhere behind Hamlet's words is Erasmus's genial perception, in the *Praise of Folly*, that without the folly of sexual desire the world would not long continue, but the humanist's vision, here as elsewhere in the play, has been turned into disgust and a longing to free the spirit, Hamlet's father's spirit and his own, from the corrupting taint of the flesh. Sexual desire has led Hamlet's father to make his mother a breeder of such worthless sinners as Hamlet himself is: "it were better my mother had not borne me." In this self-annihilating wish, Hamlet's father is uncoupled from his mother, and all future coupling will cease: "I say we will have no more marriages."

"I hoped thou shouldst have been my Hamlet's wife," Gertrude says sadly over Ophelia's corpse. "I thought thy bride-bed to have decked, sweet maid / And not t'have strewed thy grave" (5.1.227–29). But long before Ophelia's death, the bride-bed and its pleasures have been poisoned by Hamlet's anxiety about desire, his disgust at generation, and his rejection of marriage. "For if the sun breed maggots in a dead dog, being a good kissing carrion—have you a daughter?" Hamlet asks Polonius, who replies that he has. "Let her not walk in the sun" (2.2.182–85). The association of ideas here links Ophelia to the carcass of a dog, lovemaking to the kissing of rotting flesh, and conception to the breeding of maggots. Hamlet's words also contain a famous textual crux that leads back to the theological issues with which we have been concerned. Warburton in the eighteenth century proposed that the true reading was "a God, kissing carrion." If the emendation, which Samuel Johnson thought so "noble" that it "almost sets the critic on a level with the author," is correct, it would express in the most direct way possible the deep anxiety about the yoking of the divine spirit to corrupting and corruptible matter that haunted eucharistic controversies for centuries. That anxiety, the play seems to suggest, is not only eucharistic but also incarnational: it is enfleshment that corrupts. Disgust at the idea of the Incarnation is an ancient theme, associated with many Christian heresies and, not without justification, with Jews. The twelfth-century Hebrew chronicle of Rabbi Eliezer bar Nathan, recounting the persecution of Jews during the First

Crusade, tells of a Jew named Shemariah in the Rhineland who killed his wife and children, to save them from defilement, and then unsuccessfully tried to kill himself. The chronicler reports that the Christians said to him (implausibly enough), "Although you have acted in a defiant manner, your life shall be spared if you adopt our erroneous belief. Otherwise, we will inflict a violent death upon you, burying you alive with those you have slain." Shemariah answered, "Heaven forfend that I should deny the Living God for a dead, decaying carcass."[57]

At the very least, Hamlet's task, imposed upon him by the ghost, is complicated by his own and his father's entanglements in the flesh. When alive, old Hamlet was not exempt from the thousand natural shocks that flesh is heir to, and even after death he carries about him a strange quasi-carnality, for he was taken "grossly, full of bread, / With all his crimes broad blown, as flush as May" (3.3.80–81). "Full of bread"—the words distinguish between someone living in the midst of his ordinary life and someone who, anticipating death, puts his spiritual house in order through fasting.[58]

Hamlet is disgusted by the grossness whose emblem here is the bread in his father's stomach, a grossness figured as well by drinking, sleeping, sexual intercourse, and above all perhaps by woman's flesh. The play enacts and reenacts queasy rituals of defilement and revulsion, an obsession with a corporeality that reduces everything to appetite and excretion. "We fat all creatures else to fat us, and we fat ourselves for maggots. Your fat king and your lean beggar is but variable service—two dishes, but to one table. That's the end" (4.3.22–25). Here, as in the lines about the king's progress through the guts of a beggar, the revulsion is mingled with a sense of drastic leveling, the collapse of order and distinction into polymorphous, endlessly recycled materiality. Claudius with his reechy kisses and paddling fingers, is a paddock, a bat, a gib, and this unclean beast, like Becon's priapic priest, has poisoned the entire social and symbolic system. Hamlet's response is not to attempt to shore it up but to drag it altogether into the writhing of maggots. Matter corrupts: "If you find him not within this month," Hamlet says, finally telling Claudius where to look for Polonius's corpse, "you shall nose him as you go up the stairs into the lobby" (4.3.35–36).

The spirit can only be healed by refusing all compromise and by plunging the imagination unflinchingly into the rank corruption of the ulcerous place. Such a conviction led the Reformers to dwell on the progress of the Host through the guts of a mouse, and a comparable conviction, born of intertwining theological and psychological obsessions, leads Hamlet to the clay pit and the decayed leftovers that the grave diggers bring to light. "How abhorred in my imagination it is," Hamlet says, staring at the skull of Yorick. "My gorge rises at it" (5.1.178–79). This is the primary and elemental nausea provoked by the vulnerability of matter, a nausea that reduces language to a gagging sound that the Folio registers as "Pah." Revulsion is not an end in itself; it is the precondition of a liberated spirit that finds a special providence in the fall of a sparrow, sacrificially fulfills the father's design, and declares that the readiness is all.[59]

But this is not quite all. We remarked earlier that there was some risk in the strategic insistence on the problem of the leftover, and we think we can glimpse it again at the close of *Hamlet*. For if there is a detachment from the body that culminates in Hamlet's impossible words, "I am dead, Horatio," there is at least the shadow of a different kind of detachment, a detachment from the spirit. "Remember me," the spirit of Hamlet's murdered father solemnly commands, and his son swears to erase all "baser matter" from the book and volume of his brain. But the communion of ghostly father and carnal son is more complex, troubled not only by the son's madness and suicidal despair but by the persistent, ineradicable materialism figured in the progress of a king through the guts of a beggar. The mind that dwells upon that progress has not succeeded in erasing all but the father's commandment; rather it manifests something of the restless curiosity of Montaigne, who muses that "the heart and life of a triumphant emperor is the breakfast of a little worm."[60] Montaigne's reflection comes in the course of the "Apology for Raymond Sebond," that is, in the great essay whose skeptical materialism radically undermined his own father's spiritual guide. "There is nothing so horrible to imagine," Montaigne writes in a haunting passage of this essay, "as eating one's father."[61] But there are, he observes, nations that regard this act as testimony of filial piety, "trying thereby to give their progenitors the most worthy and honorable sepulture, lodging in themselves and as it were in their marrow the bodies of their fathers and their remains, bringing them to life in a way and regenerating them by transmutation into their living flesh by means of digestion and nourishment" (438). There are echoes here of eucharistic piety and a sense of the vulnerability of the flesh, but the thoughts slip away from Catholic and Protestant orthodoxy alike, toward a tolerant acceptance of the dizzying variety of customs and the natural processes of the body.

Similarly, when Hamlet follows the noble dust of Alexander until he finds it stopping a bung-hole, he does not go on to meditate on the immortality of Alexander's incorporeal name or spirit.[62] The progress he sketches is the progress of a world that is all matter. "'Twere to consider too curiously to consider so," warns Horatio; he has heard, however fleetingly, the voice of the wicked son.

NOTES

1. The midrash is now genially revised in many contemporary Haggadoth to include daughters and mothers, but since this paper is about historical memory, it would seem misleading to do so here.

2. Similarly, it hears in the wise son's words "the Lord our God" the crucial recognition of participation.

3. Of course the child who reads the part of the wicked son is not refusing the supper but participating in the Seder, and indeed the character of the wicked son is himself participating, for his imagined self-exclusion enables the father to insist upon his own personal identification with the ancient events, an identification that would otherwise not be adequately marked. In this sense, the wicked son is essential to the reenactment, not despite but because he so clearly marks the fact that the events of the enslavement and liberation are in the past. If the present had genuinely collapsed into the past, there would be no place to ask the question of participation and meaning.

4. Dom Gregory Dix, among others, argues that the Eucharist was instituted not at a Passover Seder but at the formal supper on the night before the first Seder: "Our Lord instituted the Eucharist at a supper with His disciples which was probably *not* the Passover supper of that year, but the evening meal twenty-four hours before the actual Passover. On this S. John appears to contradict the other three gospels, and it seems that S. John is right. Nevertheless, from what occurred at it and from the way in which it was regarded by the primitive Jewish Christian church it is evident that the last supper was a Jewish religious meal, of some kind. The type to which it best conforms is the formal supper of a *chabiarah*." Dom Gregory Dix, *The Shape of the Liturgy* (Westminster: Dacre Press, n.d.), 50. According to Anthony Grafton, the first modern scholar to recognize that the Eucharist originated in a Passover Seder was the Dutch Protestant philologist and historian Joseph Justus Scaliger. Scaliger analyzes the Haggadah, showing that the oldest elements are "This is the bread of affliction" and "Next year in Jerusalem," observing that the presence of the latter means that the Haggadah postdates the destruction of the Temple and hence is not identical to any ceremony that Jesus himself would have participated in.

5. In Sephardic communities it is customary for the father of the household actually to place the dish on the head of one of his children.

6. This anecdote is sometimes associated with Roman persecutions and the legendary martyrdom of Rabbi Akiba.

7. One telling measure of its radicalism is its effect on the medieval Jewish observance of the Passover: For centuries European Jews did not dare to drink red wine at the Seder for fear of the Blood Libel, the fatal accusation that they killed Christian children in order to drink their blood and bake their flesh into matzoth.

8. "He is present as a house is in a lease"; see Roger Hutchison, *Works*, ed. Jo. Bruce (London: Parker Society, 1842), 251.

9. Thomas Becon, "The Jewel of Joy," *The Catechism of Thomas Becon*, ed. John Ayre (Cambridge: Parker Society, 1844), 2:453.

10. Miri Rubin, *Corpus Christi: The Eucharist in Late Medieval Culture* (Cambridge: Cambridge University Press, 1991), 288.

11 See Montaigne: "Most of the occasions for the troubles of the world are grammatical. Our lawsuits spring only from debate over the interpretation of the laws, and most of our wars from the inability to express clearly the conventions and treaties of agreement of princes. How many quarrels, and how important, have been produced in the world by doubt of the meaning of that syllable *Hoc!*" "Apology for Raymond Sebond," in *The Complete Essays of Montaigne*, trans. Donald Frame (Stanford, Calif.: Stanford University Press, 1948), 392.

12 Louis Marin, *La Critique du discours: Sur la "Logique de Port-Royal" et les "Pensées" de Pascal* (Paris: Minuit, 1975), 54ff.

13 For Protestant antimaterialism and its consequences for English culture, see Jeffrey Knapp, *An Empire Nowhere: England, America, and Literature from "Utopia" to "The Tempest"* (Berkeley: University of California Press, 1992).

14 *The Play of the Sacrament*, in *Medieval Drama*, ed. David Bevington (Boston: Houghton Mifflin, 1975), ll. 199–200.

15 Thomas Becon, *The Displaying of the Popish Mass*, in *Prayers and Other Pieces* (Cambridge: Parker Society, 1844), 278.

16 On priests as players, see Becon, *A Comparison between the Lord's Supper and the Pope's Mass*, in *Prayers*, 362; on Jesus' words as figurative speech, see *Displaying*, 271. See likewise Edmund Grindal, "A Fruitful Dialogue between Custom and Verity," in *Remains* (Cambridge: Parker Society, 1843): "Scripture is not so to be taken always as the letter soundeth, but as the intent and purpose of the Holy Ghost was, by whom the scripture was uttered. For if you follow the bare words, you will soon shake down and overthrow the greatest part of the Christian faith" (41).

17 See the references to Bullinger, Calvin, Zwingli, and others in Jaroslav Pelikan, *Reformation of Church and Dogma (1300–1700)*, in *The Christian Tradition: A History of the Development of Doctrine*, 5 vols. (Chicago: University of Chicago Press, 1984), 4:190.

18 Becon, *Displaying*, 270.

19 *Heresy Trials in the Diocese of Norwich, 1428–31*, ed. Norman P. Tanner, Camden series, vol. 20 (London: Royal Historical Society, 1977), 44.

20 "Et tunc dicta Mergeria dixit isti iurate, 'tu male credis quia si quodlibet tale sacramentum esset Deus et verum corpus Christi, infinite sunt dii, quia mille sacerdotes et plures omni die conficiunt mille tales deos et postea tales deos comedunt et commestos emittunt per posteriora in sepibus turpiter fetentibus, ubi potestis tales deos sufficientes invenire si volueritis perscrutari; ideoque sciatis pro firmo quod illud quod vos dicitis sacramentum altaris nunquam erit Deus meus per praciam Dei, quia tale sacramentum fuit falso et deceptorie ordinatum per presbiteros in Ecclesia ad inducendum populum simplicem ad ydolatriam, quia illud sacramentum est tantum panis materialis." In *Heresy Trials*, 44–45. Translated in part and quoted in Rubin, *Corpus Christi*, 328.

21 Becon, *Displaying*, 272.

22 Quoted in Pelikan, *Reformation of Church and Dogma*, 4:199. In terms that are repeated almost verbatim by the Reformers, Berengar had ventured to argue that "the bread is present not symbolically but actually in its ordinary material or substance. It comes from the field into the granary, from the granary to the mill, from the mill on to the Lord's Table.

Its nature is preserved, and it can be broken with the hands and ground with the teeth." He had concluded from this that "if the body of Christ were actually present on the altar, there would be in existence, every day and at the same time, a million bodies of Christ." Quoted in A. J. Macdonald, *Berengar and the Reform of Sacramental Doctrine* (London: Longmans, 1930), 305, 310.

23 Luther expressed regret that he could not bring himself to reject the doctrine of Real Presence. "If you could show me," he wrote to the Reformers, "that there is nothing in the sacrament except bread and wine, you would have done me a great service, for I have suffered much, and would have gladly been convinced, because I saw well that with that opinion I would have given to the papacy the greatest slap. . . . But I am caught; I cannot get out: the text is too forcibly there, and will not allow itself to be twisted out of the sense with words." *De Wette Luthers Briefe* 11:577 (1524), quoted in John A. Faulkner, "Luther and the Real Presence," in *The American Journal of Theology* 21 (1917): 227.

24 Quoted in Pelikan, *Reformation of Church and Dogma*, 4:54.

25 Quoted in Pelikan, *Reformation of Church and Dogma*, 4:189.

26 Quoted in Pelikan, *Reformation of Church and Dogma*, 4:189.

27 "Nous confessons bien que l'unité sacrée que nous avons avec Jésus-Christ est incompréhensible à notre sens charnel. . . . Mais faut-il pour autant songer que sa substance soit transfusée en nous pour être souillée de nos ordures?" Quoted in Bernard Cottret, "Pour une Sémiotique de la Réforme: Le *Consensus Tigurinus* (1549) et la *Brève résolution . . .* (1555) de Calvin," in *Annales ESC* (1984): 280.

28 "Nous rejetons donc comme mauvais expositeurs ceux qui insistent ric à ric au sens littéral de ces mots: Ceci est mon corps, Ceci est mon sang. Car nous tenons pour tout notoire que ces mots doivent être sainement interprétés et avec discrétion, à savoir que les noms de ce que le pain et le vin signifient leur sont attribués. Et cela ne doit être trouvé nouveau ou étrange que par une figure qu'on dit métonymie, le signe emprunte le nom de la vérité qu'il figure. . . ." *Consensus Tigurinus* (1549); the French translation, cited here, was published in 1551 and entitled "L'accord passé et conclu touchant la matière des sacrements, entre les ministres de l'église de Zurich et maître Jean Calvin, minister de l'église de Genève." Quoted in Cottret, p. 268. In *Brève résolution* (1555), Calvin writes similarly: "Mais selon que l'Écriture parle partout des sacrements, que le nom de la chose signifiée s'attribue au signe, par une figure qu'on appelle métonymie, qui vaut autant comme transport de nom" (268).

29 Quoted in Pelikan, *Reformation of Church and Dogma*, 4:201.

30 Becon, *Displaying*, 259; the passage, partly omitted by the Parker Society editor, is here restored.

31 Quoted in Kilian McDonnell, *John Calvin, the Church, and the Eucharist* (Princeton: Princeton University Press, 1967), 231.

32 John Jewel, *The Reply to Harding's Answer*, in *The Works of John Jewel*, ed. John Ayre, 4 vols. (Cambridge: Parker Society, 1847), 2:786.

33 Catholics like Rastell argued that the change in substance had taken place and that we should be able to see the body "with our bodily eyes, except divers causes were to the contrary, of which this is one, lest some horror & lothsomenes might trouble us, if it were

geaven in visible forme of flesh . . . unto us." (See, similarly, Harding: the form of wine remains, covering the blood, "ut nullus horror cruoris sit, that there might be no abhorring of bloude. . . . Thus the bread and wine are changed in substance and yet kepe stil their olde outwarde formes." Quoted in John E. Booty, *John Jewel as Apologist of the Church of England* (London: SPCK, 1963), 154, 158.

34 See Rubin, *Corpus Christi*, pp. 337–38. According to Andrew Willet, Cardinal Bellarmine says that "the body of Christ goeth downe into the stomacke, but no further: but when the formes of bread and wine begin to be corrupted there, the body of Christ goeth away." *Synopsis papismi, That is, a Generall View of Papiestrie* (London, 1600), 515.

35 Anne Askew, in *The Paradise of Women: Writings by Englishwomen of the Renaissance*, ed. Betty Travitsky (New York: Columbia University Press, 1989), 175.

36 *The First Examination of Anne Askew*, in John Bale, *Select Works*, ed. Henry Christmas (Cambridge: Parker Society, 1949), 154.

37 Becon, *Comparison*, 378. See Willet, *Synopsis*: "If a Mouse chance to creepe into your pixe, and fill her hungry belly with your god-amight, what is it that the Mouse feedeth vpon? trow you they be accidents onely? for your say that the consecrated host goeth no further then the stomacke: and yet it is to much that the housell of Christians should be hosed in a mouses belly. These are but ridiculous and light questions, yet such as haue troubled your grauest and sagest heads, and remaine vnanswered." "The thirteenth generall controversie of the Sacrament of the Lord Supper," 516.

38 W. Lockton, *The Treatment of the Remains at the Eucharist after Holy Communion and the Time of the Ablutions* (Cambridge: Cambridge University Press, 1920), 2.

39 Yrjö Hirn, from whom most of these details are taken, refers to Bishop Anno's biography, which relates how "a fly, to the horror of the holy man, snapped up a portion of the Host, which, however, at Anno's earnest prayers, the creature brought back again." Yrjö Hirn, *The Sacred Shrine: A Study of the Poetry and Art of the Catholic Church* (Boston: Beacon Press, 1957; 1st ed. in Swedish, 1909), 497 n.27.

40 On shipboard, priests celebrated a *missa sicca*, a Mass without consecration and Communion, for it was feared that the sea might cause the wine to be spilled out of the chalice.

41 Quoted in Hirn, *The Sacred Shrine*, 104.

42 Once again the controversy is associated with Berengar, who had written that if Christ was literally present in the bread and wine, His body would be subject to the digestion not only of human beings but also of animals. In c. 1073, the monk Guitmund (later bishop of Aversa) replied that the body and blood of the Lord remain in the Sacrament, even when the species are eaten by some animal. Some medieval theologians, including Odo of Ourscamp, Maurice Sully, the author of the *Commentarius Porretanus*, and Peter Comestor, concur. Others proposed counterarguments, for example, that the substance of bread miraculously returned when the mouse started nibbling. See Artur Landgraf, *Die in der Frühscholastik klassische Frage "quid sumit mus,"* in *Dogmengeschichte in der Frühscholastik* (Regensburg, 1955), 3:2; Gary Macy, "Of Mice and Manna: Quid Mus Sumit as a Pastoral Question," in *Recherches de théologie ancienne et médiévale* 58 (1991): 157–66; Rubin, *Corpus Christi*, especially 65–68.

43 For the foregoing theological opinions, and others of the same kind, see Jewel, *Reply,*

2:783–84; and Rubin, *Corpus Christi*, 65–68. The Peter of Palus quoted by Jewel is the Dominican Peter de La Palu (c. 1277–1342).

44 Thomas Wright, *The disposition or garnishmente of the soule to receiue worthily the blessed sacrament* (Antwerp [in reality, an English secret press], 1596), 1, 99.

45 *Hamlet* 4.3.17–20. All citations of Shakespeare are to *The Norton Shakespeare*, ed. Stephen Greenblatt et al. (New York: W. W. Norton, 1997). *Hamlet* exists in three distinct early texts, two of which (the second quarto and the folio) have substantial authority. Passages that appear only in the second quarto text of the play and are omitted in the folio are indicated by an extra number: for example, 4.7.95.10 refers to the tenth line of a second quarto-only passage that appears immediately after act 4, scene 7, line 95.

46 The nightgown is indicated only in a Q1 stage direction. Both Q2 and F have a stage direction in the opening scene indicating that the ghost's "beaver"—that is, his visor—is raised, and the point is reiterated in the dialogue itself. When he is informed that the apparition was in armor, "from top to toe," Hamlet concludes, "Then saw you not his face." "O yes, my lord," Horatio replies, "he wore his beaver up" (1.3.227–28). In the closet scene, Hamlet addresses the "gracious figure" and notes "how pale he glares" (3.4.95, 116).

47 Erwin Panofsky, *Tomb Sculpture*, ed. H. W. Janson (New York: Harry Abrams, n.d.), 39–66.

48 Quoted in Christopher Devlin, *Hamlet's Divinity and Other Essays* (London: Rupert Hart-Davis, 1963), 40.

49 John Bridges, "A Sermon Preached at Paules Crosse" (1571), 126. We owe this reference to Jeffrey Knapp.

50 Thomas Adams, *Mystical Bedlam, or the World of Mad-Men* (London, 1615), 70. We owe this reference to Christina Malcolmson.

51 Note the effect of the ghost's apparition on Marcellus and Bernardo, according to Horatio; they were, he says, "distill'd / Almost to jelly with the act of fear" (1.2.204–5). The image may be linked to the images of Foxe's *Book of Martyrs* that show the limbs of martyrs rendering their fat and water in the flames. There is perhaps some hint of this horrible process in the ghost's words to his son:

> My hour is almost come
> When I to sulph'rous and tormenting flames
> Must render up myself.
> (1.5.2–4)

52 *Hamlet*, ed. G. R. Hibbard (Oxford: Oxford University Press, 1987), 1.2.180n.

53 There are other images of entrails in the play, beyond those we have already noted: "Ere this," Hamlet declares in self-contempt, "I should have fatted all the region kites / With this slave's offal" (2.2.367–68). See also Hamlet on the dead Polonius: "I'll lug the guts into the neighbour room" (3.4.192).

54 Hamlet's way of laying the charge here does not present Gertrude as a mere passive accomplice to the murder, as the "Mousetrap" suggests, but seems to accuse her of being the murderer herself.

55 Another version of this image of inward corruption appears in a Q2 passage. Brooding on the apparent irrationality of Fortinbras's campaign against Poland for a plot of worthless ground, Hamlet declares:

This is th'impostume of much wealth and peace,

That inward breaks, and shows no cause without

Why the man dies.

(4.4.9.17–19)

56 "You can see something like this," Galen writes of the female genitals, "in the eyes of the
mole, which have vitreous and crystalline humors and the tunics that surround these . . .
and they have these just as much as animals do that make use of their eyes. The mole's
eyes, however, do not open, nor do they project but are left there imperfect and remain
like the eyes of other animals when these are still in the uterus." *On the Usefulness of the
Parts of the Body*, 2 vols., ed. and trans. Margaret May (Ithaca, N.Y.: Cornell University
Press, 1988), 2:14.297, 628–29.

57 Shlomo Eidelberg, trans. and ed., *The Jews and the Crusaders: The Hebrew Chronicles of
the First and Second Crusades* (Madison: University of Wisconsin Press, 1977), 90. We owe
this reference to Aaron Greenblatt.

58 It is worth noting that these words are spoken when Hamlet believes that Claudius is engaged in the "purging of his soul" through prayer. We have been told by William Bouwsma
that Hooker uses the phrase "fullness of bread" to mean "prosperity."

59 Without the divinity that shapes our ends, there would be no escape from the charnel
house, no possibility of redemption, for the works of the flesh are necessarily corrupt.
There is in *Hamlet* a passing allusion to this Protestant conception of grace that interestingly conjoins the Eucharist and the playhouse. When Polonius declares that he will
use the players "according to their desert," Hamlet exclaims, "God's bodykins, man, much
better. Use every man after his desert, and who should scape whipping?" (2.2.519–20). The
lines pull away from the immediate dramatic exchange (the minor disagreement between
Polonius and Hamlet about how the players should be "used") and from the specific social
question of the status of the actors (with Hamlet arguing that they should be treated especially well because they are the bearers of reputation after death). Hamlet's words swerve
rather in the direction of larger questions that have a moral and ultimately a theological
resonance. We are all sinners and breeders of sinners, and by our own deserts we should all
be punished; only through unmerited grace can we hope to be treated well. That grace, in
theological terms, was linked to Christ's sacrifice to redeem the sins of mankind. It is the
commemoration, the anamnesis, of this sacrifice, that lies at the heart of the Mass, and it
is this anamnesis that has evidently called forth Hamlet's exclamation, "God's bodykins."
For the diminutive "bodykin" refers specifically to the consecrated Host of the Holy Communion. The diminutive is a mark not only of affection but of the reduced size of the object
as it figures in the Mass.

60 Montaigne, "Apology for Raymond Sebond," in *Essays*, trans. Donald M. Frame (Stanford,
Calif.: Stanford University Press, 1948), 339. G. F. Stedefeld argues that "Shakespeare sought
by the drama of *Hamlet* to free himself from the impressions left upon his mind by the
reading of the book of the French skeptic, Montaigne" (*Hamlet, ein Tendenzdrama Sheak-
speare's* [sic] *gegen di skeptische und kosmopolitische Weltanschauung des Michael de
Montaigne* [Berlin, 1871], cited in Horace Howard Furness, ed. Variorum *Hamlet* [New
York: Dover, 1963; reprint of 1877 original], 2:344). If this is so, it is not clear to us that

Shakespeare succeeded in freeing himself, since his play seems haunted by Montaigne's most skeptical essay. Florio's translation of the passage we are looking at may convey some further sense of this haunting presence: "There is nothing wherein the world differeth so much, as in customes and lawes. Some things are here accompted abominable, which in another place are esteemed commendable. . . . Marriages in proximity of blood are amongst us forbidden as capitall, elsewhere they are allowed and esteemed;

> "—gentes esse feruntur,
> In quibus et nato geitrix, et nata parenti
> Jungitur, et pietas geminato crescit amore.
> (Ovid, *Met*, x.331)

> There are some people, where the mother weddeth
> Her sonne, the daughter her own father beddeth,
> And so by doubling love, their kindnesse spreddeth.

"The murthering of children and of parents; the communication with women; traffick of robbing and stealing; free license to all manner of sensuality: to conclude, there is nothing so extreame and horrible, but is found to be received and allowed by the custome of some nation. It is credible that there be naturall lawes; as may be seene in other creatures, but in us they are lost: this goodly humane reason engrafting it selfe among all men, to sway and command, confounding and topsi-turving the visage of all things, according to her inconstant vanitie and vaine inconstancy. . . . Nothing can be imagined so horrible, as for one to eate and devoure his own father. Those people, which anciently kept custome, hold it neverthelesse for a testimonie of pietie and good affection: seeking by that meane to give their fathers the worthiest and most honorable sepulchre, harboring their fathers bodies and reliques in themselves and in their marrow; in some sort reviving and regenerating them by the transmutation made in their quicke flesh, by digestion and nourishment. It is easie to be considered what abomination and cruelty it had beene, in men accustomed and trained in this inhumane superstition, to cast the carcases of their parents into the corruption of the earth, as food for beasts and worms." Montaigne, "Apology of Raymond de Sebond," in Montaigne, *Essays*, trans. John Florio, 3 vols. (London: Dent, 1965), 2:298–99.

61 In "De la coustume" (I.23), Montaigne cites from Herodotus the story of Darius asking some Greeks, "What price would persuade them to eat their fathers' dead bodies. They answered that there was no price for which they would do it." In the "Apology" then, Montaigne is being effortlessly classicizing in his anthropological speculations.

62 A "bung-hole" (5.1.189) is usually glossed as the opening of a cask, but it could also, by transference, refer to the anus, as is made clear by Cotgreve's 1611 definition of a sea anemone: "A small and ouglie fish, or excrescence of the Sea, resembling a man's bung hole" (*OED*).

13. Jane Austen's Cover Story (and Its Secret Agents)

SANDRA GILBERT AND
SUSAN GUBAR

I am like the needy knife-grinder—I have no story to tell.
—Maria Edgeworth

I dwell in Possibility—
A fairer House than Prose—
More numerous of Windows—
Superior—for Doors—
—Emily Dickinson

. . . the modes of fainting should be all as different
as possible and may be made very diverting.
—*The Girls' Book of Diversions* (ca. 1840)

From Sappho to myself, consider the fate of women.
How unwomanly to discuss it!
—Carolyn Kizer

JANE AUSTEN WAS NOT alone in experiencing the tensions inherent in being a "lady" writer, a fact that she herself seemed to stress when, in *Northanger Abbey*, she gently admonished literary women like Maria Edgeworth for being embarrassed about their status as novelists. Interestingly, Austen came close to analyzing a central problem for Edgeworth, who constantly judged and depreciated her own "feminine" fiction in terms of her father's commitment to pedagogically sound moral instruction . . .

Virginia Woolf suggests that:

If a woman wrote, she would have to write in the common sitting-room. . . .
She was always interrupted. . . . Jane Austen wrote like that to the end of her
days. "How she was able to effect all this," her nephew writes in his Memoir, "is surprising, for she had no separate study to repair to, and most of the
work must have been done in the general sitting-room subject to all kinds
of casual interruptions. She was careful that her occupation should not be
suspected by servants or visitors or any persons beyond her own family
party." Jane Austen hid her manuscripts or covered them with a piece of
blotting-paper. . . . [She] was glad that a hinge creaked, so that she might
hide her manuscript before any one came in.[1]

Despite the odd contradiction we sense between Woolf's repeated assertions elsewhere in *A Room of One's Own* that Austen was unimpeded by her
sex and her clear-sighted recognition in this passage of the limits placed on
Austen because of it, the image of the lady writing in the common sitting room
is especially useful in helping us understand both Austen's confinement and the
fictional strategies she developed for coping with it. We have already seen that
even in the juvenilia (which many critics consider her most conservative work)
there are clues that Austen is hiding a distinctly unladylike outlook behind the
"cover" or "blotter" of parody. But the blotting paper poised in anticipation of
a forewarning creak can serve as an emblem of a far more organic camouflage
existing within the mature novels, even as it calls to our attention the anxiety
that authorship entailed for Austen.

We can see Austen struggling after *Northanger Abbey* to combine her implicitly rebellious vision with an explicitly decorous form as she follows Miss
Edgeworth's example and writes in order to make herself useful, justifying her
presumptuous attempts at the pen by inspiring other women with respect for
the moral and social responsibilities of their domestic duties. . . .

Austen's propriety is most apparent in the overt lesson she sets out to teach
in all of her mature novels. Aware that male superiority is far more than a fiction, she always defers to the economic, social, and political power of men as
she dramatizes how and why female survival depends on gaining male approval
and protection. All the heroines who reject inadequate fathers are engaged in a
search for better, more sensitive men who are, nevertheless, still the representatives of authority. As in *Northanger Abbey*, the happy ending of an Austen
novel occurs when the girl becomes a daughter to her husband, an older and
wiser man who has been her teacher and her advisor, whose house can pro-

vide her with shelter and sustenance and at least derived status, reflected glory. Whether it be parsonage or ancestral mansion, the man's house is where the heroine can retreat from both her parents' inadequacies and the perils of the outside world: like Henry Tilney's Woodston, Delaford, Pemberley, Donwell, and Thornton Lacy are spacious, beautiful places almost always supplied with the loveliest fruit trees and the prettiest prospects. Whereas becoming a man means proving or testing oneself or earning a vocation, becoming a woman means relinquishing achievement and accommodating oneself to men and the spaces they provide.

Dramatizing the necessity of female submission for female survival, Austen's story is especially flattering to male readers because it describes the taming not just of any woman but specifically of a rebellious, imaginative girl who is amorously mastered by a sensible man. No less than the blotter literally held over the manuscript on her writing desk, Austen's cover story of the necessity for silence and submission reinforces women's subordinate position in patriarchal culture. Interestingly, what common law called "coverture" at this time actually defined the married woman's status as suspended or "covered": "the very being or legal existence of the woman is suspended during the marriage," wrote Sir William Blackstone, "or at least is incorporated and consolidated into that of the husband: under whose wing, protection and cover, she performs everything."[2] The happiest ending envisioned by Austen, at least until her very last novel, accepts the necessity of protection and cover for heroines who wish to perform anything at all.

At the same time, however, we shall see that Austen herself "performs everything" under this cover story. As Virginia Woolf noted, for all her "infallible discretion," Austen always stimulates her readers "to supply what is not there."[3] A story as sexist as that of the taming of the shrew, for example, provides her with a "blotter" or socially acceptable cover for expressing her own self-division. Undoubtedly a useful acknowledgment of her own ladylike submission and her acquiescence to masculine values, this plot also allows Austen to consider her own anxiety about female assertion and expression, to dramatize her doubts about the possibility of being both a woman and a writer. She describes both her own dilemma and, by extension, that of all women who experience themselves as divided, caught in the contradiction between their status as human beings and their vocation as females.

The impropriety of female creativity first emerges as a problem in *Lady Susan*, where Austen seems divided between her delight in the vitality of a talented libertine lady and her simultaneous rejection of the sexuality and selfishness of her heroine's plots. In this first version of the taming of the shrew,

Austen exposes the wicked wilfulness of Lady Susan, who gets her own way because of her "artful" (Letters 4, 13, and 17), "bewitching powers" (Letter 4), powers intimately related to her "clever" and "happy command of language" (Letter 8). Using "deep arts," Lady Susan always has a "design" (Letter 4) or "artifice" that testifies to her great "talent" (Letters 16 and 36) as a "Mistress of Deceit" (Letter 23) who knows how to play a number of parts quite convincingly. She is the first of a series of heroines, of varying degrees of attractiveness, whose lively wit and energetic imagination make them both fascinating and frightening to their creator.

Several critics have explored how Lady Susan's London ways are contrasted to her daughter's love of the country, how the mother's talkative liveliness and sexuality are balanced against the daughter's silence and chastity, how art is opposed to nature.[4] But, if Lady Susan is energetic in her pursuit of pleasure, her daughter is quite vapid and weak; indeed, she seems far more socialized into passivity than a fit representative of nature would be. Actually she is only necessary to emphasize Lady Susan's unattractiveness—her cruelty to her daughter—which can best be viewed as Austen's reflex to suppress her interest in such wilful sorts of women. For the relationship between Lady Susan and Frederica is not unlike that between the crafty Queen and her angelic step daughter, Snow White: Lady Susan seems almost obsessed with hatred of her daughter, who represents an extension of her own self, a projection of her own inescapable femininity which she tries to destroy or transcend even at the risk of the social ostracism she must inevitably incur at the end of the novel. These two, mother and daughter, reappear transformed in the mature novels into sisters, sometimes because Austen wishes to consider how they embody available options that are in some ways equally attractive yet mutually exclusive, sometimes because she seeks to illustrate how these two divided aspects of the self can be integrated.

In *Sense and Sensibility* (1811), as most readers of the novel have noted, Marianne Dashwood's sensibility links her to the Romantic imagination. Repeatedly described as fanciful, imaginative, emotionally responsive, and receptive to the natural beauty of trees and the aesthetic beauties of Cowper, Marianne is extremely sensitive to language, repelled by clichés, and impatient with the polite lies of civility. Although quite different from Lady Susan, she too allows her lively affections to involve her in an improper amorous involvement, and her indiscreet behavior is contrasted with that of her sister Elinor, who is silent, reserved, and eminently proper. If the imagination is linked with Machiavellian evil in *Lady Susan*, it is closely associated with self-destruction in *Sense and Sensibility:* when Elinor and Marianne have to confront the same painful situation—betrayal by the men they deemed future husbands—Elinor's stoical self-restraint is the strength born of her good sense while Marianne's indulgence in sensibility almost causes her own death, the unfettered play of her imagination seeming to result in a terrible fever that represents how imaginative women are infected and sickened by their dreams.

Marianne's youthful enthusiasm is very attractive, and the reader, like Colonel Brandon, is tempted to find "something so amiable in the prejudices of a young mind, that one is sorry to see them give way to the reception of more general opinions" (I, chap. II). But give way they apparently must and evidently do. Eagerness of fancy is a passion like any other, perhaps more imprudent because it is not recognized as such. As delightful as it might first seem, moreover, it is always shown to be a sign of immaturity, of a refusal to submit. Finally this is unbecoming and unproductive in women, who must exert their inner resources for pliancy, elasticity of spirit, and accommodation. *Sense and Sensibility* is an especially painful novel to read because Austen herself seems caught between her attraction to Marianne's sincerity and spontaneity, while at the same time identifying with the civil falsehoods and the reserved, polite silences of Elinor, whose art is fittingly portrayed as the painting of screens.

Pride and Prejudice (1813) continues to associate the perils of the imagination with the pitfalls of selfhood, sexuality, and assertion. Elizabeth Bennet is her father's favorite daughter because she has inherited his wit. She is talkative, satirical, quick at interpreting appearances and articulating her judgments, and so she too is contrasted to a sensible silent sister, Jane, who is quiet, unwilling to express her needs or desires, supportive of all and critical of none. While moral Jane remains an invalid, captive at the Bingleys, her satirical sister Elizabeth walks two miles along muddy roads to help nurse her. While Jane visits the Gardeners only to remain inside their house waiting hopelessly for the visitors she wishes to receive, Elizabeth travels to the Collins' establishment where she visits Lady Catherine. While Jane remains at home, lovesick but uncomplaining, Elizabeth accompanies the Gardeners on a walking tour of Derbyshire. Jane's docility, gentleness, and benevolence are remarkable, for she suffers silently throughout the entire plot, until she is finally set free by her Prince Charming. In these respects, she adumbrates Jane Fairfax of Austen's *Emma* (1816), another Jane who is totally passive and quiet, despite the fact that she is repeatedly humiliated by her lover. Indeed, although Jane Fairfax is eventually driven to a gesture of revolt—the pathetic decision to endure the "slave trade" of becoming a governess rather than wait for Frank Churchill to become her husband—she is a paragon of submissive politeness and patience throughout her ordeal, so much so that, "wrapped up in a cloak of politeness," she was to Emma and even to Mr. Knightley "disgustingly . . . suspiciously, reserved" (II, chap. 2).

Just as Jane Bennet forecasts the role and character of Jane Fairfax, Elizabeth Bennet shares much with Emma who, perhaps more than all the others, demonstrates Austen's ambivalence about her imaginative powers, since she created in Emma a heroine whom she suspected no one but herself would like.[5] A player of word games, a painter of portraits and a spinner of tales, Emma is clearly an avatar of Austen the artist. And more than all the other playful, lively girls, Emma reminds us that the witty woman is responding to her own confining situation with words that become her weapon, a defense against banality, a way of at least *seeming* to control her life. Like Austen, Emma has at her disposal worn-out, hackneyed stories of romance that she is smart enough to resist in her own life. If Emma is an artist who manipulates people as if they were characters in her own stories, Austen emphasizes not only the immorality of this activity, but its cause or motivation: except for placating her father, Emma has nothing to do. Given her intelligence and imagination, her impatient attempts to transform a mundane reality are completely understandable.

Emma and her friends believe her capable of answering questions which puzzle less quick and assured girls, an ability shown to be necessary in a world of professions and falsehoods, puzzles, charades, and riddles. But word games deceive especially those players who think they have discovered the hidden meanings, and Emma misinterprets every riddle. Most of the letters in the novel contain "nothing but truth, though there might be some truths not told" (II, chap. 2). Because readiness to talk frequently masks reticence to communicate, the vast majority of conversations involve characters who not only remain unaffected by dialogue, but barely hear each other talking: Isabella, Miss Bates and Mr. Woodhouse, Mrs. Elton and Mr. Weston are participating in simultaneous soliloquies. The civil falsehoods that keep society running make each character a riddle to the others, a polite puzzle. With professions of openness Frank Churchill has been keeping a secret that threatens to embarrass and pain both Emma and Jane Fairfax. Emma discovers the ambiguous nature of discourse that mystifies, withholds, coerces, and lies as much as it reveals.

Yet Austen could not punish her more thoroughly than she does, and in this respect too Emma resembles the other imaginative girls. For all these heroines are mortified, humiliated, even bullied into sense. Austen's heavy attack on Emma, for instance, depends on the abject failure of the girl's wit. The very brilliant and assertive playfulness that initially marks her as a heroine is finally criticized on the grounds that it is self-deluding. Unable to imagine her visions into reality, she finds that she has all along been manipulated as a character in someone else's fiction. Through Emma, Austen is confronting the inadequacy of fiction and the pain of the "imaginist" who encounters the relentless recalcitrance of the world in which she lives, but she is also exposing the vulnerable delusions that Emma shares with Catherine Morland before the latter learns that she has no story to tell. Not only does the female artist fail, then, her efforts are condemned as tyrannical and coercive. Emma feels great self-loathing when she discovers how blind she has been: she is "ashamed of every sensation but the one revealed to her—her affection for Mr. Knightley—Every other part of her mind was disgusting" (III, chap. 2).

Although Emma is the center of Austen's fiction, what she has to learn is her commonality with Jane Fairfax, her vulnerability as a female. Like the antithetical sisters we have discussed, Jane Fairfax and Emma are doubles. Since they are the most accomplished girls in Highbury, exactly the same age, suitable companions, the fact that they are not friends is in itself quite significant. Emma even believes at times that her dislike for Jane is caused by her seeing in Jane "the really accomplished young woman which she wanted to be thought herself" (II, chap. 2). In fact, she has to succumb to Jane's fate, to *become* her double through the realization that she too has been manipulated as a pawn in Frank Churchill's game. The seriousness of Emma's assertive playfulness is made clear when she behaves rudely, making uncivil remarks at Box Hill, when she talks indiscreetly, unwittingly encouraging the advances of Mr. Elton, and when she allows her imagination to indulge in rather lewd suppositions about the possible sexual intrigues of Jane Fairfax and a married man. In other words, Emma's imagination has led her to the sin of being unladylike, and her complete mortification is a prelude to submission as she becomes a friend of Jane Fairfax, at one with her too in her realization of her own powerlessness. In this respect, Mr. Elton's recitation of a well-known riddle seems ominous:

> My first doth affliction denote,
>   Which my second is destin'd to feel
> And my whole is the best antidote
>   That affliction to soften and heal.—
> (I, chap. 9)

For if the answer is woe/man, then in the process of growing up female Emma must be initiated into a secondary role of service and silence.

Similarly, in *Northanger Abbey* Catherine Morland experiences "the liberty which her imagination had dared to take" as a folly which makes her feel that "She hated herself more than she could express" (II, chap. 10) so that she too is reduced to "silence and sadness" (II, chap. 15). Although Marianne Dashwood's sister had admitted that "thirty-five and seventeen had better not have anything to do with matrimony together" (I, chap. 8), Marianne allows herself at the end to be given away to Colonel Brandon as a "reward" (III, chap. 14) for his virtuous constancy. At nineteen she finds herself "submitting to new attachments, entering on new duties" (III, chap. 14). "With such a confederacy against her," the narrator asks, "what else could she do?" Even Elizabeth Bennet, who had "prided" herself on her "discernment," finds that she had never known even herself (II, chap. 13). When "her anger was turned against herself" (II, chap. 14), Elizabeth realizes that "she had been blind, partial, prejudiced, absurd" (II, chap. 13). Significantly, "she was humbled, she was grieved; she repented, though *she hardly knew of what*" (III, chap. 8; italics are ours).

All of these girls learn the necessity of curbing their tongues: Marianne is silent when she learns submission and even when "a thousand inquiries sprung up from her heart . . . she dared not urge one" (III, chap. 10). When she finds that "For herself she was humbled; but she was proud of him" (III, chap. 10), Elizabeth Bennet displays her maturity by her modest reticence: not only does she refrain from telling both her parents about her feelings for Mr. Darcy, she never tells Jane about Mrs. Gardiner's letter or about her lover's role in persuading Mr. Bingley not to propose. Whereas before she had scorned Mr. Collins's imputation that ladies never say what they mean, at the end of *Pride and Prejudice* Elizabeth refuses to answer Lady Catherine and lies to her mother about the motives for that lady's visit. Furthermore, Elizabeth checks herself with Mr. Darcy, remembering "that he had yet to learn to be laughed at, and it was rather too early to begin" (III, chap. 16).

Emma also refrains from communicating with both Mrs. Elton and Jane Fairfax when she learns to behave discreetly. She manages to keep Harriet's secret even when Mr. Knightley proposes to her. "What did she say?" the narrator coyly asks. "Just what she ought, of course. A lady always does" (III, chap. 13). And at this point the novelist indicates her own ladylike discretion as she too refrains from detailing the personal scene explicitly. The polite talk of ladies, as Robin Lakoff has shown, is devised "to prevent the expression of strong statements,"[6] but such politeness commits both author and heroine alike to their resolve "of being humble and discreet and repressing imagination" (I, chap. 17). The novelist who has been fascinated with double-talk from the very beginning of her writing career sees the silences, evasions, and lies of women as an inescapable sign of their requisite sense of doubleness.

Austen's self-division—her fascination with the imagination and her anxiety that it is unfeminine—is part of her consciousness of the unique dilemma of all women, who must acquiesce in their status as objects after an adolescence in which they experience themselves as free agents. Simone de Beauvoir expresses the question asked by all Austen's heroines: "if I can accomplish my destiny only as the *Other*, how shall I give up my Ego?"[7] Like Emma, Austen's heroines are made to view their adolescent eroticism, their imaginative and physical activity, as an outgrown vitality incompatible with womanly restraint and survival: "how improperly had she been acting. . . . How inconsiderate, how indelicate, how irrational, how unfeeling, had been her conduct! What blindness, what madness, had led her on!" (III, chap. 11). The initiation into conscious acceptance of powerlessness is always mortifying, for it involves the fall from authority into the acceptance of one's status as a mere character, as well as the humiliating acknowledgment on the part of the witty sister that she must become her self-denying, quiet double. Assertion, imagination, and wit are tempting forms of self-definition which encourage each of the lively heroines to think that she can master or has mastered the world, but this is proven a dangerous illusion for women who must accept the fate of being mastered, and so the heroine learns the benefits of modesty, reticence, and patience.

If we recall Sophia's dying advice to Laura in *Love and Friendship*—"Run mad as often as you chuse; but do not faint"—it becomes clear that Austen is haunted by both these options and that she seems to feel that fainting, even if it only means playing at being dead, is a more viable solution for women who are acceptable to men only when they inhabit the glass coffin of silence, stillness, secondariness. At the same time, however, Austen never renounces the subjectivity of what her heroines term their own "madness" until the end of each of their stories. The complementarity of the lively and the quiet sisters, moreover, suggests that these two inadequate responses to the female situation are inseparable. We have already seen that Marianne Dashwood's situation when she is betrayed by the man she considers her fiancé is quite similar to her sister's, and many critics have shown that Elinor has a great deal of sensibility, while Marianne has some sense.[8] Certainly Elizabeth and Jane Bennet, like Emma Woodhouse and Jane Fairfax, are confronted with similar dilemmas even as they eventually reach similar strategies for survival. In consistently drawing our attention to the friendship and reciprocity between sisters, Austen holds out the hope that maturity can bring women consciousness of self as subject and object.

Although all women may be, as she is, split between the conflicting desire for assertion in the world and retreat into the security of the home—speech and silence, independence and dependency—Austen implies that this psychic conflict can be resolved. Because the relationship between personal identity and social role is so problematic for women, the emerging self can only survive with a sustained double vision. As Austen's admirers have always appreciated, she does write out accommodations, even when admitting their cost: since the polarities of fainting and going mad are extremes that tempt but destroy women, Austen describes how it is possible for a kind of dialectic of self-consciousness to emerge. While this aspect of female consciousness has driven many women to schizophrenia, Austen's heroines live and flourish *because* of their contradictory projections. When the heroines are able to live Christian lives, doing unto others as they would be done, the daughters are ready to become wives. Self-consciousness liberates them from the self, enabling them to be exquisitely sensitive to the needs and responses of others. This is what distinguishes them from the comic victims of Austen's wit, who are either imprisoned in officious egoism or incapacitated by lethargic indolence: for Austen selfishness and selflessness are virtually interchangeable.

Only the mature heroines can sympathize and identify with the self-important meddlers and the somnambulant valetudinarians who abound in Austen's novels. But their maturity implies a fallen world and the continual possibility, indeed the necessity, of self-division, duplicity, and double-talk. As the narrator of *Emma* explains, "Seldom, very seldom, does complete truth belong to any human disclosure; seldom can it happen that something is not a little disguised or a little mistaken" (iii, chap. 13). Using silence as a means of manipulation, passivity as a tactic to gain power, submission as a means of attaining the only control available to them, the heroines *seem* to submit as they get what they both want and need. On the one hand, this process and its accompanying sense of doubleness is psychologically and ethically beneficial, even a boon to women who are raised by it to real heroism. On the other hand, it is a painful degradation for heroines immersed or immured in what de Beauvoir would call their own "alterity."

The mortifications of Emma, Elizabeth, and Marianne are, then, the necessary accompaniment to the surrender of self-responsibility and definition. While Marianne Brandon, Elizabeth Darcy, and Emma Knightley never exist except in the slightly malevolent futurity of all happily-ever-afters, surely they would have learned the intricate gestures of subordination. And in *Mansfield Park* (1814), where Austen examines most carefully the price of doubleness, the mature author dramatizes how the psychic split so common in women can explode into full-scale fragmentation when reintegration becomes impossible. Nowhere in her fiction is the conflict between self and other portrayed with more sensitivity to the possibility of the personality fragmenting schizophrenically than in this novel in which Austen seems the most conflicted about her own talents.

Fanny Price and Mary Crawford enact what has developed into a familiar conflict in Austen's fiction. Fanny loves the country, where she lives quietly and contentedly, conservative in her tastes, revering old buildings and trees, and acquiescent in her behavior, submitting to indignities from every member of the household with patient humility. But "what was tranquillity and comfort to Fanny was tediousness and vexation to Mary" (II, chap. 11), because differences of disposition, habit, and circumstance make the latter a talented and restless girl, a harpist, a superb card player, and a witty conversationalist capable of parody and puns. In the famous play episode the two are most obviously contrasted: exemplary Fanny refuses to play a part, deeming the theatrical improper in Sir Bertram's absence, while Mary enters into the rehearsals with vivacity and anticipation of the performance precisely because it gives her the opportunity to dramatize, under the cover of the written script, her own amorous feelings toward Edmund. This use of art links Mary to Austen in a way further corroborated by biographical accounts of Austen's delight as a girl in such home theatricals. While many critics agree that Austen sets out to celebrate Fanny's responsiveness to nature,[9] in fact it is Mary who most resembles her creator in seeing "inanimate nature, with little observation; her attention was all for men and women, her talents for the light and lively" (I, chap. 8).

In spite of their antithetical responses, Mary and Fanny, like the other "sisters" in Austen's fiction, have much in common. Both are visitors in the country and virtually parentless outsiders at Mansfield Park. Both have disreputable family histories which they seek to escape in part through their contact with the Bertram household. Both are loving sisters to brothers very much in need of their counsel and support. Both are relatively poor, dependent on male relatives for financial security. While Mary rides Fanny's horse, Fanny wears what she thinks is one of Mary's necklaces. While Fanny loves to hear Mary's music, Mary consistently seeks out Fanny's advice. They are the only two young people aware that Henry is flirting outrageously with both Bertram sisters and thereby creating terrible jealousies. Both see Rushworth as the fool that he is, both are aware of the potential impropriety of the play, and both are in love with Edmund Bertram. Indeed, each seems incomplete because she lacks precisely the qualities so fully embodied by the other: thus, Fanny seems constrained, lacking nerve and will, while Mary is insensitive to the needs and feelings of her friends; one is too silent, the other too talkative.

Perhaps Fanny does learn enough from Mary to become a true Austen heroine. Not only does she "come out" at a dance in her honor, but she does so in a state "nearly approaching high spirits" (II, chap. 10). She rejects the attempts at persuasion made by Sir Thomas and he accuses her of "wilfulness of temper, self-conceit, and . . . independence of spirit" (III, chap. 1). In defending herself against the unwelcome addresses of Henry Crawford, Fanny also speaks more, and more angrily, than she ever has before. Finally, she does liberate herself from the need for Edmund's approval, specifically when she questions his authority and becomes "vexed into displeasure, and anger, against Edmund" (III, chap. 8). Recently, two feminist critics have persuasively argued that, when Fanny refuses to marry for social advantage, she becomes the moral model for all the other characters, challenging their social system and exposing its flimsy values.[10] And certainly Fanny does become a kind of authority figure for her younger sister Susan, whom she eventually liberates from the noisy confinement of the Portsmouth household.

Yet, trapped in angelic reserve, Fanny can never assert or enliven herself except in extreme situations where she only succeeds through passive resistance. A model of domestic virtue—"dependent, helpless, friendless, neglected, forgotten" (II, chap. 7)—she resembles Snow White not only in her passivity but in her invalid deathliness, her immobility, her pale purity. And Austen is careful to show us that Fanny can only assert herself through silence, reserve, recalcitrance, and even cunning. Since, as Leo Bersani has argued, "nonbeing is the ultimate prudence in the world of *Mansfield Park*,"[11] Fanny is destined to become the next Lady Bertram, following the example of Sir Thomas's corpselike wife. With purity that seems prudish and reserve bordering on hypocrisy, Fanny is far less likeable than Austen's other heroines: as Frank Churchill comments of Jane Fairfax, "There is safety in reserve, but no attraction" (II, chap. 6). Obedience, tears, pallor, and martyrdom are effective but not especially endearing methods of survival, in part because one senses some pride in Fanny's self-abasement.

If Fanny Price seems unable fully to actualize herself as an authentic subject, Mary Crawford fails to admit her contingency. Because of this, like the Queen who insists on telling and living her own lively stories, she is exorcised from Mansfield Park, both the place and the plot, in a manner that dramatizes Austen's obsessive anxiety over Mary's particular brand of impropriety— her audacious speech. When Mary's liberty deteriorates into license and her self-actualization into selfishness, Edmund can only defend her by claiming that "She does not *think* evil, but she speaks it—speaks it in playfulness—" and he admits this means "the mind itself was tainted" (II, chap. 9). Although Mary's only crimes do, in fact, seem to be verbal, we are told repeatedly that her mind has been "led astray and bewildered, and without any suspicion of being so; darkened, yet fancying itself light" (III, chap. 6). Because she would excuse as "folly" what both Fanny and Edmund term "evil," her *language* gives away her immodesty, her "blunted delicacy" (III, chap. 16). Edmund says in horror, "No reluctance, no horror, no feminine—shall I say? no modest loathings!" (III, chap. 16). It is, significantly, "the manner in which she spoke" (III, chap. 16) that gives the greatest offense and determines Edmund's final rejection.

When, during the episode of the theatricals, Fanny silently plays the role of the angel by refusing to play, Mary Crawford metamorphoses into a siren as she coquettishly persuades Edmund to participate in the very theatricals he initially condemned as improper. Fanny knows that in part her own reticence is caused by fear of exposing herself, but this does not stop her from feeling extremely jealous of Mary, not only because Mary is a fine actress but because she has chosen to play a part that allows her to express her otherwise silent opposition to Edmund's choice of a clerical profession. Heretical, worldly, cynical in her disdain for the institutions of the Church, Mary is a damned Eve who offers to seduce prelapsarian Edmund Bertram in the garden of the green room, when the father is away on a business trip, and she almost succeeds, at least until the absent father reappears to burn all the scripts, to repress this libidinal outbreak in paradise and call for music which "helped conceal the want of real harmony" (II, chap. 2). Since the rehearsals have brought nothing but restlessness, rivalry, vexation, pettiness, and sexual license, *Lover's Vows* illustrates Austen's belief that self-expression and artistry are dangerously attractive precisely because they liberate actors from the rules, roles, social obligations, and familial bonds of every day life.[12]

Mary's seductive allure is the same as her brother Henry's. He is the best actor, both on and off the stage, because he has the ability to be "every thing to every body" (II, chap. 13). But he can "do nothing without a mixture of evil" (II, chap. 13). Attractive precisely because of his protean ability to change himself into a number of attractive personages, Henry is an impersonator who degenerates into an imposter, not unlike Frank Churchill, who is also "acting a part or making a parade of insincere professions" (E, II, chap. 6). Indeed, Henry is a good representative of the kind of young man with whom each of the heroines falls briefly in love before she is finally disillusioned: Willoughby, Wickham, Frank Churchill, Henry Crawford, and Mr. Elliot are eminently agreeable because they are self-changers, self-shapers. In many respects they are attractive to the heroines because somehow they act as doubles: younger men who must learn to please, narcissists, they experience traditionally "feminine" powerlessness and they are therefore especially interested in becoming the creators of themselves.

In *Mansfield Park*, however, Austen defines this self-creating spirit as a "bewitching" (ii, chap. 13) "infection" (ii, chap. 1), and the epidemic restlessness represented by the Crawfords is seen as far more dangerous than Fanny's invalid passivity. Fanny's rejection of Henry represents, then, her censure of his presumptuous attempt to author his own life, his past history, and his present fictional identities. Self-divided, indulging his passions, alienated from authority, full of ambition, and seeking revenge for past injuries, the false young man verges on the Satanic. While he manages to thrive in his own fashion, finding a suitable lover or wife and generally making his fortune in the process, his way cannot be the Austen heroine's. Although his crimes are real actions while hers are purely rhetorical, she is more completely censured because her liberties more seriously defy her social role.

When her Adam refuses to taste the fruit offered by Mary Crawford, Austen follows the example of Samuel Richardson in her favorite of his novels, *Sir Charles Grandison*, where Harriet draws a complimentary analogy between Sir Charles and Adam: the former would not have been so compliant as to taste the forbidden fruit; instead he would have left it to God to annihilate the first Eve and supply a second.[13] Just as Fanny sees through the play actor, Henry Crawford, to the role-player and hypocrite, Edmund finally recognizes Mary's playfulness as her refusal to submit to the categories of her culture, a revolt that is both attractive and immoral because it gains her the freedom to become whatever she likes, even to choose not to submit to one identity but to try out a variety of voices. For all these reasons, she has to be annihilated. But, unlike Richardson, Austen in destroying this unrepentant, imaginative, and assertive girl is demonstrating her own self-division.

In all six of Austen's novels women who are refused the means of self-definition are shown to be fatally drawn to the dangerous delights of impersonation and pretense. But Austen's profession depends on just these disguises. What else, if not impersonation, is characterization? What is plot, if not pretense? In all the novels, the narrator's voice is witty, assertive, spirited, independent, even (as D. W. Harding has shown) arrogant and nasty.[14] Poised between the subjectivity of lyric and the objectivity of drama, the novel furnishes Austen with a unique opportunity: she can create Mary Crawford's witty letters or Emma's brilliant retorts, even while rejecting them as improper; furthermore, she can reprove as indecent in a heroine what is necessary to an author. Authorship for Austen is an escape from the very restraints she imposes on her female characters. And in this respect she seems typical, for women may have contributed so significantly to narrative fiction precisely because it effectively objectifies, even as it sustains and hides, the subjectivity of the author. Put another way, in the novels Austen questions and criticizes her own aesthetic and ironic sensibilities, noting the limits and asserting the dangers of an imagination undisciplined by the rigors of art.

Using her characters to castigate the imaginative invention that informs her own novels, Austen is involved in a contradiction that, as we have seen, she approves as the only solution available to her heroines. Just as they manage to survive only by seeming to submit, she succeeds in maintaining her double consciousness in fiction that proclaims its docility and restraint even as it uncovers the delights of assertion and rebellion. Indeed the comedy of Austen's novels explores the tensions between the freedom of her art and the dependency of her characters: while they stutter and sputter and lapse into silence and even hasten to perfect felicity, she attains a woman's language that is magnificently duplicitous. In this respect, Austen serves as a paradigm of the literary ladies who would emerge so successfully and plentifully in the mid-nineteenth century, popular lady novelists like Rhoda Broughton, Charlotte Mary Yonge, Home Lee, and Mrs. Craik[15] who strenuously suppressed awareness of how their own professional work called into question traditional female roles. Deeply conservative as their content appears to be, however, it frequently retains traces of the original duplicity so manifest in its origin, even as it demonstrates their own exuberant evasion of the inescapable limits they prescribe for their model heroines.

Although Austen clearly escapes the House of Prose that confines her heroines by making her story out of their renunciation of storytelling, she also dwells in the freer prospects of Emily Dickinson's "Possibility" by identifying not only with her model heroines, but also with less obvious, nastier, more resilient and energetic female characters who enact her rebellious dissent from her culture, a dissent, as we have seen, only partially obscured by the "blotter" of her plot. Many critics have already noticed duplicity in the "happy endings" of Austen's novels in which she brings her couples to the brink of bliss in such haste, or with such unlikely coincidences, or with such sarcasm that the entire message seems undercut[16]: the implication remains that a girl without the aid of a benevolent narrator would never find a way out of either her mortifications or her parents' house.

Perhaps less obvious instances of Austen's duplicity occur in her representation of a series of extremely powerful women each of whom acts out the rebellious anger so successfully repressed by the heroine and the author. Because they so rarely appear and so infrequently speak in their own voices, these furious females remain secret presences in the plots. Not only do they play a less prominent role in the novels than their function in the plot would seem to require; buried or killed or banished at the end of the story, they seem to warrant this punishment by their very unattractiveness. Like Lady Susan, they are mothers or surrogate mothers who seek to destroy their docile children. Widows who are no longer defined by men simply because they have survived the male authorities in their lives, these women can exercise power even if they can never legitimize it; thus they seem both pushy and dangerous. Yet if their energy appears destructive and disagreeable, that is because this is the mechanism by which Austen disguises the most assertive aspect of herself as the Other. We shall see that these bitchy women enact impulses of revolt that make them doubles not only for the heroines but for their author as well.

We have seen Austen at her most conflicted in *Mansfield Park*, so perhaps it is here that we can begin to understand how she quietly yet forcefully undercuts her own moral. Probably the most obnoxious character in the book, Aunt Norris, is clearly meant to be a dark parody of Mary Crawford, revealing—as she does—how easily Mary's girlish liveliness and materialism could degenerate into meddlesome, officious penny-pinching. But, as nasty as she is repeatedly shown and said to be when she tries to manage and manipulate, to condescend to Fanny, to save herself some money, Aunt Norris is in some ways castigated for moral failures which are readily understandable, if not excusable. After all, she is living on a small, fixed income, and if she uses flattery to gain pecuniary help, her pleasures are dependent on receiving it. Like Fanny Price, Aunt Norris knows that she must please and placate Sir Thomas. Even when he gives "advice," both accept it as "the advice of absolute power" (II, chap. 18). Perhaps one reason for her implacable hatred of Fanny is that Aunt Norris sees in her a rival for Sir Thomas's protection, another helpless and useful dependent. Furthermore, like Fanny, Aunt Norris uses submission as a strategy to get her own way: acquiescing to the power in authority, she manages to talk her brother-in-law into all her schemes.

Unlike "good" Lady Bertram, Aunt Norris is an embittered, manipulative, pushy female who cannot allow other people to live their own lives. At least, this is how these sisters first strike us, until we remember that, for all her benign dignity, Lady Bertram does nothing but sit "nicely dressed on a sofa, doing some long piece of needlework, of little use and no beauty, thinking more of her pug than her children" (I, chap. 2). Indeed, the contrast between her total passivity and Aunt Norris's indiscriminate exertions recalls again the options described by Sophia in *Love and Friendship*—fainting or running mad. Like all the other "good" mothers in Austen's fiction who are passive because dead, dying, or dumb, Lady Bertram teaches the necessity of submission, the all-importance of a financially sound marriage, and the empty-headedness that goes with these values. For all her noisy bustling, Aunt Norris is a much more loving mother to Lady Bertram's daughters. If she indulges them, it is in part out of genuine affection and loyalty. And as she herself actively lives her own life and pursues her own ends, Aunt Norris quite naturally identifies with her headstrong nieces. Unlike the figure of the "good" mother, the figure of bad Aunt Norris implies that female strength, exertion, and passion are necessary for survival and pleasure.

Instead of abandoning Maria after the social disgrace of the elopement and divorce, Aunt Norris goes off to live with her as her surrogate mother. Although she is thereby punished and driven from Mansfield Park, Aunt Norris (we cannot help suspecting) is probably as relieved to have escaped the dampening effect of Sir Thomas's sober rule as he is to have rid himself of the one person who has managed to assert herself against his wishes, to evade his control. This shrew is still talking at the end of the book, untamed and presumably untameable. As if to authenticate her completely unacceptable admiration for this kind of woman, Austen constructs a plot which quite consistently finds its impetus in Aunt Norris. It is she, for instance, who decides to take Fanny from her home and bring her to Mansfield; she places Fanny in Sir Thomas's household and allocates her inferior status; she rules Mansfield in Sir Thomas's absence and allows the play to progress; she plans and executes the visit to Southerton that creates the marriage between Maria and Mr. Rushworth. Quite openly dedicated to the pursuit of pleasure and activity, especially the joy of controlling other people's lives, Aunt Norris is a parodic surrogate for the author, a suitable double whose manipulations match those of Aunt Jane.

As vilified as she is, Aunt Norris was the character most often praised and enjoyed by Jane Austen's contemporaries, to the author's delight.[17] Hers is one of the most memorable voices in *Mansfield Park*. She resembles not only the hectic, scheming Queen, stepmother to Snow White, but also the Queen of the Night in Mozart's *The Magic Flute*. Actually, all the angry dowagers in Austen's novels represent a threat to the enlightened reason of the male god who eventually wins the heroine only by banishing the forces of female sexuality, capriciousness, and loquacity. But, as in *The Magic Flute*, where the Queen of the Night is carried offstage still singing her exuberantly strenuous resistance, women like Aunt Norris are never really completely stifled. The despised Mrs. Ferrars of *Sense and Sensibility*, for example, exacts the punishment which Elinor Dashwood could not help but wish on a man who has been selfishly deceiving her for the entire novel. By tampering with the patriarchal line of inheritance, Mrs. Ferrars proves that the very forms valued by Elinor are arbitrary. But even though *Sense and Sensibility* ends with the overt message that young women like Marianne and Elinor must submit to the powerful conventions of society by finding a male protector, Mrs. Ferrars and her scheming protégée Lucy Steele prove that women can themselves become agents of repression, manipulators of conventions, and survivors.

Most of these powerful widows would agree with Lady Catherine De Bourgh in seeing "no occasion for entailing estates from the female lines" (*PP*, II, 6). Opposed to the very basis of patriarchy, the exclusive right of male inheritance, Lady Catherine quite predictably earns the vilification always allotted by the author to the representatives of matriarchal power. She is shown to be arrogant, officious, egotistical, and rude as she patronizes all the other characters in the novel. Resembling Lady Susan in her disdain for her own pale, weak, passive daughter, Lady Catherine delights in managing the affairs of others. Probably most unpleasant when she opposes Elizabeth's right to marry Darcy, she questions Elizabeth's birth and breeding by admitting that Elizabeth is "a gentleman's daughter," but demanding, "who was your mother?" (III, chap. 14).

As dreadful as she seems to be, however, Lady Catherine is herself in some ways an appropriate mother to Elizabeth because the two women are surprisingly similar. Her ladyship points this out herself when she says to Elizabeth, "You give your opinion very decidedly for so young a person" (II, chap. 6). Both speak authoritatively of matters on which neither is an authority. Both are sarcastic and certain in their assessment of people. Elizabeth describes herself to Darcy by asserting, "There is a stubbornness about me that never can bear to be frightened at the will of others" (II, chap. 8), and in this respect too she resembles Lady Catherine, whose courage is indomitable. Finally, these are the only two women in the novel capable of feeling and expressing genuine anger, although it is up to Lady Catherine to articulate the rage against entailment that Elizabeth must feel since it has so rigidly restricted her own and her sisters' lives. When Elizabeth and Lady Catherine meet in conflict, each retains her decided resolution of carrying her own purpose. In all her objections to Elizabeth's match with Darcy, Lady Catherine only articulates what Elizabeth has herself thought on the subject, that her mother is an unsuitable relation for him and her sister an even less appropriate connection. Highly incensed and unresponsive to advice, Elizabeth resembles her interlocutor; it is fitting not only that she takes the place meant for Lady Catherine's daughter when she marries Darcy, but that she also sees to it that her husband is persuaded to entertain his aunt at Pemberley. As Darcy and Elizabeth both realize, Lady Catherine has been the author of their marriage, bringing about the first proposal by furnishing the occasion and place for meetings, and the second by endeavoring to separate them when she actually communicates Elizabeth's renewed attraction to a suitor waiting for precisely such encouragement.

The vitriolic shrew is so discreetly hidden in *Emma* that she never appears at all, yet again she is the causal agent of the plot. Like her predecessors, Mrs. Churchill is a proud, arrogant, and capricious woman who uses all means, including reports of her poor health, to elicit attention and obedience from her family. In fact, only her death—which clears the way for the marriage of Frank Churchill to Jane Fairfax—convinces them that her nervous disorders were more than selfish, imaginary complaints. Actually Mrs. Churchill can be viewed as the cause of all the deceit practiced by the lovers inasmuch as their secret engagement is a response to her disapproval of the match. Thus this disagreeable woman with "no more heart than a stone to people in general, and the devil of a temper" (I, chap. 14) is the "invisible presence" which, as W. J. Harvey explains, "enables Jane Austen to embody that aspect of our intuition of reality summed up by Auden—'we are lived by powers we do not understand.'"[18]

But Mrs. Churchill is more than the representative of the unpredictable contingency of reality. On the one hand, she displays an uncanny and ominous resemblance to Jane Fairfax, who will also be a penniless upstart when she marries and who is also subject to nervous headaches and fevers. Mrs. Churchill, we are told by Mr. Weston, "is as thorough a fine lady as anybody ever beheld" (II, chap. 18), so it is quite fitting that polite Jane Fairfax becomes the next Mrs. Churchill and inherits that lady's jewels. On the other hand, Mrs. Churchill seems much like Emma, who is also involved in becoming a pattern lady: selfish in their very imaginings, both have the power of having too much their own way, both are convinced of their superiority in talent, elegance of mind, fortune, and consequence, and both want to be first in society where they can enjoy assigning subservient parts to those in their company.

The model lady haunts all the characters of *Emma*, evoking "delicate plants" to Mr. Woodhouse (II, chap. 16) and the showy finery of Selena for Mrs. Elton. But it is Mrs. Churchill who illustrates the bankruptcy of the ideal, for she is not only a monitory image of what Austen's heroines could be, she is also a double of what they are already fast becoming. If Mrs. Churchill represents Austen's guilt at her own authorial control, she also reminds us that feminine propriety, reserve, and politeness can give way to bitchiness since the bitch is what the young lady's role and values imply from the beginning, built—as we have seen them to be—out of complicity, manipulation, and deceit. At the same time, however, Mrs. Churchill is herself the victim of her own ladylike silences, evasions, and lies: no one takes seriously her accounts of her own ill health, no one believes that her final illness is more than a manipulative fiction, and her death—one of the few to occur in Austen's mature fiction—is an ominous illustration of feminine vulnerability that Austen would more fully explore in her last novel.

It is not only Austen's mad matriarchs who reflect her discomfort with the glass coffin of female submission. Her last completed novel, *Persuasion* (1818), focuses on an angelically quiet heroine who has given up her search for a story and has thereby effectively killed herself off. Almost as if she were reviewing the implications of her own plots, Austen explores in *Persuasion* the effects on women of submission to authority and the renunciation of one's life story. Eight years before the novel begins, Anne Elliot had been persuaded to renounce her romance with Captain Wentworth, but this decision sickened her by turning her into a nonentity. Forced into "knowing [her] own nothingness" (I, chap. 6), Anne is a "nobody with either father or sister" so her word has "no weight" (I, chap. I). An invisible observer who tends to fade into the background, she is frequently afraid to move lest she should be seen. Having lost the "bloom" of her youth, she is but a pale vestige of what she had been and realizes that her lover "should not have known [her] again" (I, chap. 7), their relationship being "now nothing!" Anne Elliot is the ghost of her own dead self; through her, Austen presents a personality haunted with a sense of menace.

At least one reason why Anne has deteriorated into a ghostly insubstantiality is that she is a dependent female in a world symbolized by her vain and selfish aristocratic father, who inhabits the mirrored dressing room of Kellynch Hall. It is significant that *Persuasion* begins with her father's book, the *Baronetage,* which is described as "the book of books" (I, chap. I) because it symbolizes male authority, patriarchal history in general, and her father's family history in particular. Existing in it as a first name and birth date in a family line that concludes with the male heir presumptive, William Walter Elliot, Esq., Anne has no reality until a husband's name can be affixed to her own. But Anne's name is a new one in the *Baronetage:* The history of this ancient, respectable line of heirs records "all the Marys and Elizabeths they had married" (I, chap. I), as if calling our attention to the hopeful fact that, unlike her sisters Mary and Elizabeth, Anne may not be forced to remain a character within this "book of books." And, in fact, Anne will reject the economic and social standards represented by the *Baronetage,* deciding, by the end of her process of personal development, that not she but the Dowager Viscountess Dalrymple and her daughter the Honourable Miss Carteret are "nothing" (II, chap. 4). She will also discover that Captain Wentworth is "no longer nobody" (II, chap. 12), and, even more significantly, she will insist on her ability to seek and find "at least the comfort of telling the whole story her own way" (II, chap. 9).

But before Anne can become somebody, she must confront what being a no-body means: "I'm Nobody!" (J. 228), Emily Dickinson could occasionally avow, and certainly, by choosing not to have a story of her own, Anne seems to have decided to dwell in Dickinson's realm of "Possibility," for what Austen demonstrates through her is that the person who has not become anybody is haunted by everybody. Living in a world of her father's mirrors, Anne confronts the several selves she might have become and discovers that they all reveal the same story of the female fall from authority and autonomy.

As a motherless girl, Anne is tempted to become her own mother, although she realizes that her mother lived invisibly, unloved, within Sir Walter's house. Since Anne could marry Mr. Elliot and become the future Lady Elliot, she has to confront her mother's unhappy marriage as a potential life story not very different from that of Catherine Morland's Mrs. Tilney. At the same time, however, since serviceable Mrs. Clay is an unattached female who aspires to her mother's place in the family as her father's companion and her sister Elizabeth's intimate, Anne realizes that she could also become patient Penelope Clay, for she too understands "the art of pleasing" (I, chap. 2), of making herself useful. When Anne goes to Uppercross, moreover, she functions something like Mrs. Clay, "being too much in the secret of the complaints" of each of the tenants of both households (I, chap. 6), and trying to flatter or placate each and all into good humor. The danger exists, then, that Anne's sensitivity and selflessness could degenerate into Mrs. Clay's ingratiating, hypocritical service.

Of course, Mary Musgrove's situation is also a potential identity for Anne, since Charles had actually asked for Anne's hand in marriage before he settled on her younger sister, and since Mary resembles Anne in being one of Sir Walter's unfavored daughters. Indeed, Mary's complaint that she is "always the last of my family to be noticed" (II, chap. 6) could easily be voiced by Anne. Bitter about being nobody, Mary responds to domestic drudgery with "feminine" invalidism that is an extension of Anne's sickening self-doubt, as well as the only means at Mary's disposal of using her imagination to add some drama and importance to her life. Mary's hypochondria reminds us that Louisa Musgrove provides a kind of paradigm for all these women when she literally falls from the Cobb and suffers from a head injury resulting in exceedingly weak nerves. Because incapacitated Louisa is first attracted to Captain Wentworth and finally marries Captain Benwick, whose first attentions had been given to Anne, she too is clearly an image of what Anne might have become.

Through both Mary and Louisa, then, Austen illustrates how growing up female constitutes a fall from freedom, autonomy, and strength into debilitating, degrading, ladylike dependency. In direct contradiction to Captain Wentworth's sermon in the hedgerow, Louisa discovers that even firmness cannot save her from such a fall. Indeed, it actually precipitates it, and she discovers that her fate is not to jump from the stiles down the steep flight of seaside stairs but to read love poetry quietly in the parlor with a suitor suitably solicitous for her sensitive nerves. While Louisa's physical fall and subsequent illness reinforce Anne's belief that female assertion and impetuosity must be fatal, they also return us to the elegiac autumnal landscape that reflects Anne's sense of her own diminishment, the loss she experiences since her story is "now nothing."

Anne lives in a world of mirrors both because she could have become most of the women in the novel and, as the title suggests, because all the characters present her with their personal preferences rationalized into principles by which they attempt to persuade her. She is surrounded by other people's versions of her story and offered coercive advice by Sir Walter, Captain Wentworth, Charles Musgrove, Mrs. Musgrove, Lady Russell, and Mrs. Smith. Eventually, indeed, the very presence of another person becomes oppressive for Anne, since everyone but she is convinced that his or her version of reality is the only valid one. Only Anne has a sense of the different, if equally valid, perspectives of the various families and individuals among which she moves. Like Catherine Morland, she struggles against other people's fictional use and image of her; and finally she penetrates to the secret of patriarchy through absolutely no skill of detection on her own part. Just as Catherine blunders on the secret of the ancestral mansion to understand the arbitrary power of General Tilney, who does not mean what he says, Anne stumbles fortuitously on the secret of the heir to Kellynch Hall, William Elliot, who had married for money and was very unkind to his first wife. Mr. Elliot's "manoevres of selfishness and duplicity must ever be revolting" (II, chap. 7) to Anne, who comes to believe that "the evil" of this suitor could easily result in "irremediable mischief" (II, chap. 10).

For all of Austen's heroines, as Mr. Darcy explains, "detection could not be in [their] power, and suspicion certainly not in [their] inclination" (II, chap. 3). Yet Anne does quietly and attentively watch and listen and judge the members of her world and, as Stuart Tave has shown, she increasingly exerts herself to speak out, only gradually to discover that she is being heard.[19] Furthermore, in her pilgrimage from Kellynch Hall to Upper Cross and Lyme to Bath, the landscapes she encounters function as a kind of psychic geography of her development so that, when the withered hedgerows and tawny autumnal meadows are replaced by the invigorating breezes and flowing tides of Lyme, we are hardly surprised that Anne's bloom is restored (I, chap. 12). Similarly, when Anne gets to Bath, this woman who has heard and overheard others has trouble listening because she is filled with her own feelings, and she decides that "one half of her should not be always so much wiser than the other half, or always suspecting the other half of being worse than it was" (II, chap. 7). Therefore, in a room crowded with talking people, Anne manages to signal to Captain Wentworth her lack of interest in Mr. Elliot through her assertion that she has no pleasure in parties at her father's house. "She had spoken it," the narrator emphasizes; if "she trembled when it was done, conscious that her words were listened to" (II, chap. 10), this is because Anne has actually "never since the loss of her dear mother, known the happiness of being listened to, or encouraged" (I, chap. 6).

The fact that her mother's loss initiated her invisibility and silence is important in a book that so closely associates the heroine's felicity with her ability to articulate her sense of herself as a woman. Like Elinor Tilney, who feels that "A mother could have been always present. A mother would have been a constant friend; her influence would have been beyond all others" (NA, II, chap. 7), Anne misses the support of a loving female influence. It is then fitting that the powerful whispers of well-meaning Mrs. Musgrove and Mrs. Croft furnish Anne with the cover—the opportunity and the encouragement—to discuss with Captain Harville her sense of exclusion from patriarchal culture: "Men have had every advantage of us in telling their own story. . . . The pen has been in their hands" (II, chap. 11). Anne Elliot will "not allow books to prove anything" because they "were all written by men" (II, chap. 11); her contention that women love longest because their feelings are more tender directly contradicts the authorities on women's "fickleness" that Captain Harville cites. As we have already seen, her speech reminds us that the male charge of "inconstancy" is an attack on the irrepressible interiority of women who cannot be contained within the images provided by patriarchal culture. Though Anne remains inalterably inhibited by these images since she cannot express her sense of herself by "saying what should not be said" (II, chap. 11) and though she can only replace the *Baronetage* with the *Navy Lists*—a book in which women are conspicuously absent—still she is the best example of her own belief in female subjectivity. She has both deconstructed the dead selves created by all her friends to remain true to her own feelings, and she has continually reexamined and reassessed herself and her past.

Finally, Anne's fate seems to be a response to Austen's earlier stories in which girls are forced to renounce their romantic ambitions: Anne "had been forced into prudence in her youth, she learned romance as she grew older—the natural sequel of an unnatural beginning" (I, chap. 4). It is she who teaches Captain Wentworth the limits of masculine assertiveness. Placed in Anne's usual situation of silently overhearing, he discovers her true, strong feelings. Significantly, his first response is to drop his pen. Then, quietly, under the cover of doing some business for Captain Harville, Captain Wentworth writes her his proposal, which he can only silently hand to her before leaving the room. At work in the common sitting room of the White Hart Inn, alert for inauspicious interruptions, using his other letter as a kind of blotter to camouflage his designs, Captain Wentworth reminds us of Austen herself. While Anne's rebirth into "a second spring of youth and beauty" (II, chap. 1) takes place within the same corrupt city that fails to fulfill its baptismal promise of purification in *Northanger Abbey*, we are led to believe that her life with this man will escape the empty elegance of Bath society.

That the sea breezes of Lyme and the watery cures of Bath have revived Anne from her ghostly passivity furnishes some evidence that naval life may be an alternative to and an escape from the corruption of the land so closely associated with patrilineal descent. Sir Walter Elliot dismisses the navy because it raises "men to honours which their fathers and grandfathers never dreamt of" (I, chap. 3). And certainly Captain Wentworth seems almost miraculously to evade the hypocrisies and inequities of a rigid class system by making money on the water. But it is also true that naval life seems to justify Sir Walter's second objection that "it cuts up a man's youth and vigour most horribly." While he is thinking in his vanity only about the rapidity with which sailors lose their looks, we are given an instance of the sea cutting up a man's youth, a singularly unprepossessing man at that: when worthless Dick Musgrove is created by Austen only to be destroyed at sea, we are further reminded of her trust in the beneficence of nature, for only her anger against the unjust adulation of sons (over daughters) can explain the otherwise gratuitous cruelty of her remarks about Mrs. Musgrove's "large fat sighings over the destiny of a son, whom alive nobody had cared for" (I, chap. 8). Significantly, this happily lost son was recognized as a fool by Captain Wentworth, whose naval success closely associates him with a vocation that does not as entirely exclude women as most landlocked vocations do: his sister, Mrs. Croft, knows that the difference between "a fine gentleman" and a navy man is that the former treats women as if they were "all fine ladies, instead of rational creatures" (I, chap. 8). She herself believes that "any reasonable woman may be perfectly happy" on board ship, as she was when she crossed the Atlantic four times and traveled to and from the East Indies, more comfortably (she admits) than when she settled at Kellynch Hall, although her husband *did* take down Sir Walter's mirrors.

Naval men like Captain Wentworth and Admiral Croft are also closely associated, as is Captain Harville, with the ability to create "ingenious contrivances and nice arrangements . . . to turn the actual space to the best possible account" (I, chap. 11), a skill not unrelated to a "profession which is, if possible, more distinguished in its domestic virtue than in its national importance" (II, chap. 12). While Austen's dowagers try to gain power by exploiting traditionally male prerogatives, the heroine of the last novel discovers an egalitarian society in which men value and participate in domestic life, while women contribute to public events, a complementary ideal that presages the emergence of an egalitarian sexual ideology.[20] No longer confined to a female community of child-bearing and childrearing, activities portrayed as dreary and dangerous in both Austen's novels and her letters,[21] Anne triumphs in a marriage that represents the union of traditionally male and female spheres. If such a consummation can only be envisioned in the future, on the water, amid imminent threats of war, Austen nonetheless celebrates friendship between the sexes as her lovers progress down Bath streets with "smiles reined in and spirits dancing in private rapture" (II, chap. 11).

When Captain Wentworth accepts Anne's account of their story, he agrees with her highly ambivalent assessment of the woman who advised her to break off their engagement. Lady Russell is one of Austen's last pushy widows, but, in this novel which revises Austen's earlier endorsement of the necessity of taming the shrew, the cautionary monster is one of effacement rather than assertion. If the powerful origin of *Emma* is the psychologically coercive model of the woman as lady, in *Persuasion* Austen describes a heroine who refuses to become a lady. Anne Elliot listened to the persuasions of the powerful, wealthy, proper Lady Russell when she refrained from marrying the man she loved. But finally she rejects Lady Russell, who is shown to value rank and class over the dictates of the heart, in part because her own heart is perverted, capable of revelling "in angry pleasure, in pleased contempt" (II, chap. 1) at events sure to hurt Anne. Anne replaces this cruel stepmother with a different kind of mother surrogate, another widow, Mrs. Smith. Poor, confined, crippled by rheumatic fever, Mrs. Smith serves as an emblem of the dispossession of women in a patriarchal society, and she is, as Paul Zietlow has shown, also the embodiment of what Anne's future could have been under less fortunate circumstances.[22]

While Lady Russell persuaded Anne not to marry a poor man, Mrs. Smith explains why she should not marry a rich one. Robbed of all physical and economic liberty, with "no child . . . no relatives . . . no health . . . no possibility of moving" (II, chap. 5), Mrs. Smith is paralyzed, and, although she exerts herself to maintain good humor in her tight place, she is also maddened. She expresses her rage at the false forms of civility, specifically at the corrupt and selfish double-dealings of Mr. Elliot, the heir apparent and the epitome of patri-archal society. With fierce delight in her revengeful revelations, Mrs. Smith proclaims herself an "injured, angry woman" (II, chap. 9) and she articulates Anne's—and Austen's—unacknowledged fury at her own unnecessary and un-recognized paralysis and suffering. But although this widow is a voice of angry female revolt against the injustices of patriarchy, she is as much a resident of Bath as Lady Russell. This fashionable place for cures reminds us that society *is* sick. And Mrs. Smith participates in the moral degeneration of the place when she selfishly lies to Anne, placing her own advancement over Anne's potential marital happiness by withholding the truth about Mr. Elliot until she is quite sure Anne does not mean to marry him. Like Lady Russell, then, this other voice within Anne's psyche can also potentially victimize her.

It is Mrs. Smith's curious source of knowledge, her informant or her muse, who best reveals the corruption that has permeated and informs the social con-ventions of English society. A woman who nurses sick people back to health, wonderfully named nurse Rooke resembles in her absence from the novel many of Austen's most important avatars. Pictured perched on the side of a sickbed, nurse Rooke seems as much a vulture as a savior of the afflicted. Her freedom of movement in society resembles the movement of a chess piece which moves parallel to the edge of the board, thereby defining the limits of the game. And she "rooks" her patients, discovering their hidden hoards.

Providing ears and eyes for the confined Mrs. Smith, this seemingly ubiqui-tous, omniscient nurse is privy to all the secrets of the sickbed. She has taught Mrs. Smith how to knit, and she sells "little thread-cases, pin-cushions and cardracks" not unlike Austen's "little bit (two Inches wide) of Ivory." What she brings as part of her services are volumes furnished from the sick chamber, stories of weakness and selfishness and impatience. A historian of private life, nurse Rooke communicates in typically female fashion as a gossip engaged in the seemingly trivial, charitable office of selling feminine handcrafts to the fashionable world. This and her gossip are, of course, a disguise for her sub-versive interest in uncovering the sordid realities behind the decorous appear-ances of high life. In this regard she is a wonderful portrait of Austen herself. While seemingly unreliable, dependent (as she is) for information upon many interactions which are subject to errors of misconception and ignorance, this uniquely female historian turns out to be accurate and revolutionary as she re-veals "the manoevers of selfishness and duplicity" (II, chap. 9) of one class to another. Finally, sensible nurse Rooke also resembles Austen in that, despite all her knowledge, she does not withdraw from society. Instead, acknowledg-ing herself a member of the community she nurses, she is a "favourer of matrimony" who has her own "flying visions" of social success (II, chap. 9). Although many of Austen's female characters seem inalterably locked inside Mr. Elton's riddle, nurse Rooke resembles the successful heroines of the author's works in making the best of this tight place.

That Austen was fascinated with the sickness of her social world, especially its effect on people excluded from a life of active exertion, is probably last illustrated through the Parker sisters in *Sanditon*, where officious Diane supervises the application of six leeches a day for ten days and the extraction of a number of teeth in order to cure her disabled sister Susan's poor health. One sister representing "activity run mad" (chap. 9), the other languishing on the sofa, the two remind us of lethargic Lady Bertram, crippled Mrs. Smith, ill Jane Fairfax, fever-stricken Marianne Dashwood, the infected Crawfords, hypochondriacal Mary Musgrove, ailing Louisa Musgrove, and pale, sickly Fanny Price. But, as nurse Rooke's healing arts imply, the diseased shrews and the dying fainters define the boundaries of the state in which Austen's most successful characters usually manage to settle. A few of her heroines do evade the culturally induced idiocy and impotence that domestic confinement and female socialization seem to breed. Neither fainting into silence nor self-destructing into verbosity, Elizabeth Bennet, Emma Woodhouse, and Anne Elliot echo their creator in their duplicitous ability to speak with the tact that saves them from suicidal somnambulism on the one hand and contaminating vulgarity on the other, as they exploit the evasions and reservations of feminine gentility.

NOTES

Epigraphs: Memoirs, vol. 3, 259, quoted by Marilyn Butler, *Maria Edgeworth* (Oxford: Clarendon Press, 1972), 9; *Poems*, J. 657; *The Girls' Book of Diversions*, quoted in C. Willett Cunnington, *Feminine Attitudes in the Nineteenth Century*, 124; From "Pro Femina," *Knock upon Silence* (Garden City, N.Y.: Doubleday, 1965), 41, lines 1–2.

1 Virginia Woolf, *A Room of One's Own*, 69–70. James Edward Austen-Leigh explains that Austen objected to having the creaking door fixed "because it gave her notice when anyone was coming," in *Memoir of Jane Austen*, ed. R. W. Chapman (Oxford: Clarendon Press, 1967), 102.

2 Sir William Blackstone, *Commentaries of the Laws of England, Book The First* (Oxford, 1765), 442.

3 Virginia Woolf, "Jane Austen," in *The Common Reader* (New York: Harcourt, Brace and World, 1925), 142, 146.

4 A. Walton Litz and Margaret Drabble, *Lady Susan/The Watsons/Sanditon* (London: Penguin, 1974), 13–14.

5 James Edward Austen-Leigh, *Memoir of Jane Austen*, 157.

6   Robin Lakoff, *Language and Woman's Place* (New York: Harper Colophon, 1975), 19.

7   Simone de Beauvoir, *The Second Sex*, (New York: Knopf, 1953), 315.

8   See, for example, the most recent presentation of this argument by Everett Zimmerman, "Admiring Pope no more than is Proper: *Sense and Sensibility*," in *Jane Austen: Bicentenary Essays*, ed. John Halperin (New York: Cambridge University Press, 1975), 112–22.

9   Fanny Price's love for Mansfield Park as a place of peace and tranquility is discussed by Tony Tanner, "Jane Austen and 'The Quiet Thing,'" in *Critical Essays on Jane Austen*, ed. B. C. Southam (New York: Barnes and Noble, 1968), 136–61. See also Alistair M. Duckworth, *The Improvement of the Estate: A Study of Jane Austen's Novels* (Baltimore, Md.: Johns Hopkins University Press, 1971), 71–80.

10 Irene Tayler and Gina Luria, "Gender and Genre: Women in British Romantic Literature," in *What Manner of Woman: Essays on English and American Life and Literature*, ed. Marlene Springer (New York: New York University Press, 1977) 113.

11 Leo Bersani, *A Future for Astyanax: Character and Desire in Literature* (Boston: Little, Brown, 1976), 77. That Fanny disavows the role of angel assigned her by Henry Crawford as "an office of high responsibility" (347) is no contradiction, for her very disavowal certifies her exemplary, Christian humility.

12 Lionel Trilling's influential essay, "*Mansfield Park*," in *Jane Austen: A Collection of Critical Essays*, ed. Ian Watt (Englewood Cliffs, N.J.: Prentice-Hall, 1963), 124–40, has been restated most effectively by Stuart M. Tave, *Some Words of Jane Austen* (Chicago: University of Chicago Press, 1973), 158–204.

13 Samuel Richardson, *Sir Charles Grandison*, 6 vols. (Oxford: Shakespeare Head, 1931), 4:302.

14 D. W. Harding, "Regulated Hatred: An Aspect of the Work of Jane Austen," *Scrutiny* 8 (March 1940): 346–62.

15 Wendy Kolmar at Indiana University has written a dissertation on these and lesser-known Victorian women novelists, entitled "Women Writing for Women: Victorian Middle-Class Fiction in the 1860s and 70s."

16 The most sustained discussion of Austen's ironic undercutting of her own endings appears in Lloyd W. Brown, *Bits of Ivory: Narrative Techniques in Jane Austen's Fiction* (Baton Rouge: Louisiana State University Press, 1973), 220–29.

17 Jane Austen's family were almost all delighted with Aunt Norris, as their collected opinions show. See *Jane Austen: A Casebook on "Sense and Sensibility," "Pride and Prejudice," "Mansfield Park,"* ed. B. C. Southam (New York: Macmillan, 1976), 200–03.

18 W. J. Harvey, "The Plot of *Emma*," in *Emma*, A Norton Critical Edition, ed. Stephen M. Parrish (New York: Norton, 1972), 456.

19 Stuart Tave, *Some Words of Jane Austen* (Chicago: University of Chicago Press, 1973), 256–87.

20 Michelle Zimbalist Rosaldo suggests that the most egalitarian societies are those in which men participate in domestic life. See "Women, Culture, and Society: A Theoretical Overview," in *Women, Culture, and Society*, ed. Michelle Zimbalist Rosaldo and Louise Lamphere (Princeton: Princeton University Press, 1974), 41.

21 From Mrs. Palmer's fear of red-gum in her newborn infant (*Sense and Sensibility*) to Mrs. Musgrove's noisy and selfish household of siblings (*Persuasion*), Austen portrays the dis-

comforts of motherhood. See also the letters in which she laments, "poor Woman! how can she be honestly breeding again?" (to Cassandra, 1 October 1808, *Letters*, 210); "poor Animal, she will be worn out before she is thirty" (to Fanny Knight, 23 March 1817, *Letters*, 488); "by not beginning the business of Mothering quite so early in life, you will be young in Constitution, spirits, figure & countenance, while Mrs. Wm Hammond is growing old by confinement & nursing" (to Fanny Knight, 13 March 1817, *Letters*, 483).

22 Paul Zietlow, "Luck and Fortuitous Circumstance in *Persuasion:* Two Interpretations," ELH 32 (1965): 179–95, argues that Mrs. Smith is a "goddess who descends on stage at a crucial moment to avert catastrophe" (193).

14. Jane Austen and the Masturbating Girl
EVE KOSOFSKY SEDGWICK

THE PHRASE ITSELF is already evidence. Roger Kimball in his treatise on educational "corruption," *Tenured Radicals*, cites the title "Jane Austen and the Masturbating Girl" from an MLA convention program quite as if he were Perry Mason, the six words a smoking gun.[1] The warm gun that, for the journalists who have adopted the phrase as an index of depravity in academe, is happiness—offering the squibby pop (fulmination? prurience? funniness?) that lets absolutely anyone, in the righteously exciting vicinity of the masturbating girl, feel a very pundit.[2]

There seems to be something self-evident—irresistably so, to judge from its gleeful propagation—about use of the phrase, "Jane Austen and the Masturbating Girl," as the QED of phobic narratives about the degeneracy of academic discourse in the humanities. But what? The narrative link between masturbation itself and degeneracy, though a staple of pre-1920s medical and racial science, no longer has any respectable currency. To the contrary: modern views of masturbation tend to place it firmly in the framework of optimistic, hygienic narratives of all-too-normative individual development. When Jane E. Brody, in a recent "Personal Health" column in the *New York Times*, reassures her readers that, according to experts, it is actually entirely possible for people to be healthy *without* masturbating; "that the practice is not essential to normal development and that no one who thinks it is wrong or sinful should feel he or she must try it"; and that even "those who have not masturbated . . . can have perfectly normal sex lives as adults," the all but perfectly normal Victorianist may be forgiven for feeling just a little—out of breath.[3] In this altered context, the self-evidence of a polemical link between autoeroticism and narratives of wholesale degeneracy (or, in one journalist's historically redolent term, "idiocy")[4] draws on a very widely discredited body of psychiatric and eugenic expertise whose only direct historical continuity with late twentieth-century thought has been routed straight through the rhetoric and practice of fascism. But it does so under the more acceptable gloss of the modern trivializing, hygienic developmental discourse, according to which autoeroticism not only is funny—any sexuality of any power is likely to hover near the threshold of hilarity—but must be relegated to the inarticulable space of (a barely superseded) infantility.

"Jane Austen and the Masturbating Girl"—the essay, not the phrase—began as a contribution to a Modern Language Association session that the three of us who proposed it entitled "The Muse of Masturbation." In spite of the half-century-long normalizing rehabilitation of this common form of isometric exercise, the proposal to begin an exploration of literary aspects of autoeroticism seemed to leave many people gasping. That could hardly be because literary pleasure, critical self-scrutiny, and autoeroticism have nothing in common. What seems likelier, indeed, is that the literal-minded and censorious metaphor that labels any criticism one doesn't like, or doesn't understand, with the would-be-damning epithet "mental masturbation," actually refers to a much vaster, indeed foundational open secret about how hard it is to circumscribe the vibrations of the highly relational but, in practical terms, solitary pleasure and adventure of writing itself.

As the historicization of sexuality, following the work of Foucault, becomes increasingly involved with issues of representation, different varieties of sexual experience and identity are being discovered both to possess a diachronic history—a history of significant change—and to be entangled in particularly indicative ways with aspects of epistemology and of literary creation and reception. This is no less true of autoeroticism than of other forms of sexuality. For example, the Aesthetic in Kant is both substantively indistinguishable from, and at the same time definitionally opposed against, autoerotic pleasure. Sensibility, too—even more tellingly for the example of Austen—named the locus of a similarly dangerous overlap. As John Mullan points out in *Sentiment and Sociability: The Language of Feeling in the Eighteenth Century,* the empathetic alloidentifications that were supposed to guarantee the sociable nature of sensibility could not finally be distinguished from an epistemological solipsism, a somatics of trembling self-absorption, and ultimately—in the durable medical code for autoeroticism and its supposed sequelae—"neurasthenia."[5] Similarly unstable dichotomies between art and masturbation have persisted, culminating in those recurrent indictments of self-reflexive art and critical theory themselves as forms of mental masturbation.

Masturbation itself, as we will see, like homosexuality and heterosexuality, is being demonstrated to have a complex history. Yet there are senses in which autoeroticism seems almost uniquely—or at least, distinctively—to challenge the historicizing impulse. It is unlike heterosexuality, whose history is difficult to construct because it masquerades so readily as History itself; it is unlike homosexuality, for centuries the *crimen nefandum* or "love that dare not speak its name," the compilation of whose history requires acculturation in a rhetoric of the most pointed preterition. Because it escapes both the narrative of reproduction and (when practiced solo) even the creation of any interpersonal trace, it seems to have an affinity with amnesia, repetition or the repetition compulsion, and ahistorical or history-rupturing rhetorics of sublimity. Neil Hertz has pointed out how much of the disciplinary discourse around masturbation has been aimed at discovering or inventing proprietary traces to attach to a practice which, itself relatively traceless, may seem distinctively to threaten the orders of propriety and property.[6] And in the context of hierarchically oppressive relations between genders and between sexualities, masturbation can seem to offer—not least as an analogy to writing—a reservoir of potentially utopian metaphors and energies for independence, self-possession, and a rapture that may owe relatively little to political or interpersonal abjection.

The three participants in "The Muse of Masturbation," like most of the other scholars I know of who think and write about masturbation, have been active in lesbian and gay as well as in feminist studies. This makes sense because thinking about autoeroticism is beginning to seem a productive and necessary switch-point in thinking about the relations—historical as well as intrapsychic—between homo- and heteroeroticism: a project that has not seemed engaging or necessary to scholars who do not register the antiheterosexist pressure of gay and lesbian interrogation. Additionally, it is through gay and lesbian studies that the skills for a project of historicizing any sexuality have developed, along with a tradition of valuing nonprocreative forms of creativity and pleasure; a history of being suspicious of the tendentious functioning of open secrets; and a politically urgent tropism toward the gaily and, if necessary, the defiantly explicit.

At the same time, part of the great interest of autoeroticism for lesbian and gay thought is that it is a long-execrated form of sexuality, intimately and invaluably entangled with the physical, emotional, and intellectual adventures of many, many people, that today completely *fails* to constitute anything remotely like a minority identity. The history of masturbation phobia—the astonishing range of legitimate institutions that so recently surveilled, punished, jawboned, imprisoned, terrorized, shackled, diagnosed, purged, and physically mutilated so many people, to prevent a behavior that those same institutions now consider innocuousness itself—has complex messages for sexual activism today. It seems to provide the most compelling possible exposure of the fraudulence of the scientistic claims of any discourse, *including medicine,* to say, in relation to human behavior, what constitutes disease. "The mass of 'self-defilement' literature," as Vernon A. Rosario II rather mildly points out, can "be read as a gross travesty of public health education"[7]—and queer people have recently needed every available tool of critical leverage, including travesty, against the crushing mass of legitimated discourses showing us to be moribund, mutant, pathetic, virulent, or impossible. Even as it demonstrates the absolutely discrediting inability of the "human sciences" to offer any effectual resistance to the most grossly, punitively inflictive moralistic hijacking, however, the same history of masturbation phobia can also seem to offer the heartening spectacle of a terrible oppression based on "fear" and "ignorance" that, ultimately, withered away from sheer transparent absurdity. The danger of this view is that the encouragement it offers—an encouragement we can hardly forgo, so much need do we have of courage—depends on an Enlightenment narrative that can only relegitimate the same institutions of knowledge by which the crime was in the first place done.

Today there is no corpus of law or of medicine about masturbation; it sways no electoral politics; institutional violence and street violence do not surround it, nor does an epistemology of accusation; people who have masturbated who may contract illnesses are treated as people who are sick with specific disease organisms, rather than as revelatory embodiments of sexual fatality. Yet when so many confident jeremiads are spontaneously launched at her explicit invocation, it seems that the power of the masturbator to guarantee a Truth from which she is herself excluded has not lessened in two centuries. To have so powerful a form of *sexuality* run so fully athwart the precious and embattled sexual *identities* whose meaning and outlines we always insist on thinking we know, is only part of the revelatory power of the Muse of masturbation.

Bedroom scenes are not so commonplace in Jane Austen's novels that readers get jaded with the chiaroscuro of sleep and passion, wan light, damp linen, physical abandon, naked dependency, and the imperfectly clothed body. *Sense and Sensibility* has a particularly devastating bedroom scene, which begins:

> Before the housemaid had lit their fire the next day, or the sun gained any power over a cold, gloomy morning in January, Marianne, only half-

dressed, was kneeling against one of the window seats for the sake of all the little light she could command from it, and writing as fast as a continual flow of tears would permit her. In this situation, Elinor, roused from sleep by her agitation and sobs, first perceived her; and after observing her for a few moments with silent anxiety, said, in a tone of the most considerate gentleness,

"Marianne, may I ask?—"

"No, Elinor," she replied, "ask nothing; you will soon know all."

The sort of desperate calmness with which this was said, lasted no longer than while she spoke, and was immediately followed by a return of the same excessive affliction. It was some minutes before she could go on with her letter, and the frequent bursts of grief which still obliged her, at intervals, to withhold her pen, were proofs enough of her feeling how more than probable it was that she was writing for the last time to Willoughby.[8]

We know well enough who is in this *bedroom:* two women. They are Elinor and Marianne Dashwood, they are sisters, and the passion and perturbation of their love for each other is, at the very least, the backbone of this powerful novel. But who is in this *bedroom scene?* And, to put it vulgarly, what's their scene? It is the naming of a man, the absent Willoughby, that both marks this as an unmistakably sexual scene, and by the same gesture seems to displace its "sexuality" from the depicted bedroom space of same-sex tenderness, secrecy, longing, and frustration. Is this, then, a hetero- or a homoerotic novel (or moment in a novel)? No doubt it must be said to be both, if love is vectored toward an object and Elinor's here flies toward Marianne, Marianne's in turn toward Willoughby. But what, if love is defined only by its gender of object-choice, are we to make of Marianne's terrible isolation in this scene; of her unstanchable emission, convulsive and intransitive; and of the writing activity with which it wrenchingly alternates?

Even before this, of course, the homo/hetero question is problematical for its anachronism: homosexual identities, and certainly female ones, are supposed not to have had a broad discursive circulation until later in the nineteenth century, so in what sense could heterosexual identities as against them?[9] And for that matter, if we are to trust Foucault, the conceptual amalgam represented in the very term "sexual identity," the cementing of every issue of individuality, filiation, truth, and utterance *to* some representational metonymy of the genital, was a process not supposed to have been perfected for another half-century or three-quarters of a century after Austen; so that the genital implication in either "homosexual" *or* "heterosexual," to the degree that it differs from a plot of the procreative or dynastic (as each woman's desire seems at least for the moment to do), may mark also the possibility of an anachronistic gap.[10]

In trying to make sense of these discursive transitions, I have most before me the model of recent work on Emily Dickinson, and in particular Paula Bennett's discussion of the relation between Dickinson's heteroerotic and her homoerotic poetics in *My Life a Loaded Gun* and *Emily Dickinson: Woman Poet*.[11] Briefly, Bennett's accomplishment is to have done justice, for the somewhat later, New England figure of Dickinson, to a complex range of intense female homosocial bonds, including genitally figured ones, in her life and writing—without denying the salience and power of the male-directed eros and expectation that also sound there; without palliating the tensions acted out between the two; and at the same time without imposing an anachronistically reified view of the feminist consistency of these tensions. For instance, the all-too-available rhetoric of the polymorphous, of a utopian bisexual erotic pluralism, has little place in Bennett's account. But neither does she romanticize the female-female bonds whose excitement, perturbation, and pain—including the pain of power struggle, of betrayal, of rejection—she shows to form so much of the primary level of Dickinson's emotional life. What her demanding account does enable her to do, however, is to offer a model for understanding the bedrock, quotidian, sometimes very sexually fraught female homosocial networks in relation to the more visible and spectacularized, more narratable, but less intimate, heterosexual plots of pre-twentieth-century Anglo-American culture.

I see this work on Dickinson as exemplary for understandings of such other, culturally central, homosocially embedded women authors as Austen and, for example, the Brontës. (Surely there are important generalizations yet to be made about the attachments of sisters, perhaps of any siblings, who live together as adults.) But as I have suggested, the first range of questions yet to be asked properly in this context concerns the emergence and cultural entailments of "sexual identity" itself during this period of the incipience of "sexual identity" in its (still incompletely interrogated) modern senses. Indeed, one of the motives for this project is to denaturalize any presumptive understanding of the relation of "hetero" to "homo" as modern sexual identities—the presumption, for instance, of their symmetry, their mutual impermeability, or even of their both functioning as "sexual identities" in the same sense; the presumption, as well, that "hetero" and "homo," even with the possible addition of "bi," do efficiently and additively divide up the universe of sexual orientation. It seems likely to me that in Austen's time, *as in our own*, the specification of any distinct "sexual identity" magnetized and reoriented in new ways the heterogeneous erotic and epistemological energies of everyone in its social vicinity, without at the same time either adequating or descriptively exhausting those energies.

One "sexual identity" that did exist as such in Austen's time, already bringing a specific genital practice into dense compaction with issues of consciousness, truth, pedagogy, and confession, was that of the onanist. Among the sexual dimensions overridden within the past century by the world-historical homo/hetero cleavage is the one that discriminates, in the first place, the autoerotic and the alloerotic. Its history has been illuminated by recent researches of a number of scholars.[12] According to their accounts, the European phobia over masturbation came early in the "sexualizing" process described by Foucault, beginning around 1700 with publication of *Onania,* and spreading virulently after the 1750s. Although originally applied with a relative impartiality to both sexes, antionanist discourse seems to have bifurcated in the nineteenth century, and the systems of surveillance and the rhetorics of "confession" for the two genders contributed to the emergence of disparate regulatory categories and techniques, even regulatory worlds. According to Ed Cohen, for example, anxiety about boys' masturbation motivated mechanisms of school discipline and surveillance that were to contribute so much to the late-nineteenth-century emergence of a widespread, class-inflected male homosexual identity and hence to the modern crisis of male homo/heterosexual definition. On the other hand, anxiety about girls' and women's masturbation contributed more to the emergence of gynecology, through an accumulated expertise in and demand for genital surgery; of such identities as that of the hysteric; and of such confession-inducing disciplinary discourses as psychoanalysis.

Far from there persisting a minority identity of "the masturbator" today, of course, autoeroticism per se in the twentieth century has been conclusively subsumed under that normalizing developmental model, differently but perhaps equally demeaning, according to which it represents a relatively innocuous way station on the road to a "full," in other words, alloerotic, adult genitality defined almost exclusively by gender of object choice. As Foucault and others have noted, a lush plurality of (proscribed and regulated) sexual identities had developed by the end of the nineteenth century: even the most canonical late-Victorian art and literature are full of sadomasochistic, pederastic and pedophilic, necrophilic, as well as autoerotic images and preoccupations; while Foucault mentions the hysterical woman and the masturbating child along with "entomologized" sexological categories such as zoophiles, zooerasts, automonosexualists, and gynecomasts, as typifying the new sexual taxonomies, the sexual "*specification of individuals,*" that he sees as inaugurating the twentieth-century regime of sexuality.[13] Although Foucault is concerned to demonstrate our own continuity with nineteenth-century sexual discourse, however (appealing to his readers as "we 'Other Victorians' "),[14] it makes a yet-to-be-explored difference that the Victorian multiplication of sexual species has today all but boiled down to a single, bare—and moreover fiercely invidious—dichotomy. Most of us now correctly understand a question about our "sexual orientation" to be a demand that we classify ourselves as a heterosexual or a homosexual, regardless of whether we may or may not individually be able or willing to perform that blank, binarized act of category assignment. We also understand that the two available categories are not symmetrically but hierarchically constituted in relation to each other. The identity of the masturbator was only one of the sexual identities subsumed, erased, or overridden in this triumph of the heterosexist homo/hetero calculus. But I want to argue here that the status of the masturbator among these many identities was uniquely formative. I would suggest that as one of the very earliest embodiments of "sexual identity" in the period of the progressive epistemological overloading of sexuality, the masturbator may have been at the cynosural center of a remapping of individual identity, will, attention, and privacy along modern lines that the reign of "sexuality," and its generic concomitant in the novel and in novelistic point of view, now lead us to take for granted. It is of more than chronological import if the (lost) identity of the masturbator was the protoform of modern sexual identity itself.

Thus it seems likely that in our reimaginings of the history of sexuality "as" (we vainly imagine) "we know it," through readings of classic texts, the dropping out of sight of the autoerotic term is also part of what falsely naturalizes the heterosexist imposition of these books, disguising both the rich, conflictual erotic complication of a homoerotic matrix not yet crystallized in terms of "sexual identity" and the violence of heterosexist definition finally carved out of these plots. I am taking *Sense and Sensibility* as my example here because of its odd position, at once germinal and abjected, in the Austen canon and hence in "the history of the novel"; and because its erotic axis is most obviously the unwavering but difficult love of a woman, Elinor Dashwood, for a woman, Marianne Dashwood. I don't think we can bring this desire into clear focus until we also see how Marianne's erotic identity, in turn, is not in the first place exactly either a same-sex-loving one or a cross-sex-loving one (though she loves both women and men), but rather the one that today no longer exists *as* an identity: that of the masturbating girl.

Reading the bedroom scenes of *Sense and Sensibility*, I find I have lodged in my mind a bedroom scene from another document, a narrative structured as a case history of "Onanism and Nervous Disorders in Two Little Girls" and dated "1881":

Sometimes [X . . .'s] face is flushed and she has a roving eye; at others she is pale and listless. Often she cannot keep still, pacing up and down the bedroom, or balancing on one foot after the other. . . . During these bouts X . . . is incapable of anything: reading, conversation, games, are equally odious. All at once her expression becomes cynical, her excitement mounts. X . . . is overcome by the desire to do it, she tries not to or someone tries to stop her. Her only dominating thought is to succeed. Her eyes dart in all directions, her lips never stop twitching, her nostrils flare! Later, she calms down and is herself again. "If only I had never been born," she says to her little sister, "we would not have been a disgrace to the family!" And Y . . . replies: "Why did you teach me all these horrors then?" Upset by the reproach, X . . . says: "If someone would only kill me! What joy. I could die without committing suicide."[15]

If what defines "sexual identity" is the impaction of epistemological issues around the core of a particular genital possibility, then the compulsive attention paid by antionanist discourse to disorders *of* attention makes it a suitable point of inauguration for modern sexuality. Marianne Dashwood, though highly intelligent, exhibits the classic consciousness symptoms noted by Tissot in 1758, including "the impairment of memory and the senses," "inability to confine the attention," and "an air of distraction, embarrassment and stupidity."[16] A surprising amount of the narrative tension of *Sense and Sensibility* comes from the bent bow of the absentation of Marianne's attention from wherever she is. "Great," at one characteristic moment, "was the perturbation of her spirits and her impatience to be gone" (174); once out on the urban scene, on the other hand, "her eyes were in constant inquiry; and in whatever shop the party were engaged, her mind was equally abstracted from every thing actually before them, from all that interested and occupied the others. Restless and dissatisfied every where . . . she received no pleasure from any thing; was only impatient to be at home again . . ." (180). Yet when at home, her "agitation increased as the evening drew on. She could scarcely eat any dinner, and when they afterwards returned to the drawing room, seemed anxiously listening to the sound of every carriage" (177).

Marianne incarnates physical as well as perceptual irritability, to both pleasurable and painful effect. Addicted to "rapidity" (75) and "requiring at once solitude and continual change of place" (193), she responds to anything more sedentary with the characteristic ejaculation: "I could hardly keep my seat" (51). Sitting is the most painful and exciting thing for her. Her impatience keeps her "moving from one chair to another" (266) or "[getting] up, and walk[ing] about the room" (269). At the happiest moments, she frankly pursues the locomotor pleasures of her own body, "running with all possible speed down the steep side of the hill" (74) (and spraining her ankle in a tumble), eager for "the delight of a gallop" when Willoughby offers her a horse (88). To quote again from the document dated 1881,

> In addition to the practises already cited, X . . . provoked the voluptuous spasm by rubbing herself on the angles of furniture, by pressing her thighs together, or rocking backwards and forwards on a chair. Out walking she would begin to limp in an odd way as if she were lopsided, or kept lifting one of her feet. At other times she took little steps, walked quickly, or turned abruptly left. . . . If she saw some shrub she straddled it and rubbed herself back and forth. . . . She pretended to fall or stumble over something in order to rub against it. (DZ, 26–27)

Exactly the overresponsive centrality of Marianne's tender "seat" as a node of delight, resistance, and surrender—and its crucial position, as well, between the homosocial and heterosocial avidities of the plot—is harnessed when Elinor manipulates Marianne into rejecting Willoughby's gift of the horse:

> Elinor thought it wisest to touch that point no more. . . . Opposition on so tender a subject would only attach her the more to her own opinion. But by an appeal to her affection for her mother . . . Marianne was shortly subdued. (89)

The vision of a certain autoerotic closure, absentation, self-sufficiency in Marianne is radiantly attractive to almost everyone, female and male, who views her; at the same time, the same autoerotic inaccessibility is legible to them through contemporaneous discourses as a horrifying staging of auto-consumption. As was typical until the end of the nineteenth century, Marianne's autoeroticism is not defined in opposition to her alloerotic bonds, whether with men or with women. Rather, it signifies an excess of sexuality altogether, an excess dangerous to others but chiefly to herself: the chastening illness that ultimately wastes her physical substance is both the image and the punishment of the "distracted" sexuality that, continually "forgetting itself," threatens, in her person, to subvert the novel's boundaries between the public and the private.

More from the manuscript dated 1881:

> The 19th [September]. Third cauterisation of little Y . . . who sobs and vociferates.

In the days that followed Y . . . fought successfully against temptation. She became a child again, playing with her doll, amusing herself and laughing gaily. She begs to have her hands tied each time she is not sure of herself. . . . Often she is seen to make an effort at control. Nonetheless she does it two or three times every twenty-four hours. . . . But X . . . more and more drops all pretense of modesty. One night she succeeds in rubbing herself till the blood comes on the straps that bind her. Another time, caught in the act by the governess and unable to satisfy herself, she has one of her terrible fits of rage, during which she yells: "I want to, oh how I want to! You can't understand, Mademoiselle, how I want to do it!" Her memory begins to fail. She can no longer keep up with lessons. She has hallucinations all the time. . . .

The 23rd, she repeats: "I deserve to be burnt and I will be. I will be brave during the operation, I won't cry." From ten at night until six in the morning, she has a terrible attack, falling several times into a swoon that lasted about a quarter of an hour. At times she had visual hallucinations. At other times she became delirious, wild eyed, saying: "Turn the page, who is hitting me, etc."

The 25th I apply a hot point to X's clitoris. She submits to the operation without wincing, and for twenty-four hours after the operation she is perfectly good. But then she returns with renewed frenzy to her old habits. (DZ, 33)

As undisciplined as Marianne Dashwood's "abstracted" attention is, the farouche, absent presence of this figure compellingly reorganizes the attention of others: Elinor's rapt attention to her, to begin with, but also, through Elinor's, the reader's. *Sense and Sensibility* is unusual among Austen novels not for the (fair but unrigorous) consistency with which its narrative point of view is routed through a single character, Elinor; but rather for the undeviating consistency with which Elinor's regard in turn is vectored in the direction of her beloved. Elinor's self-imposed obligation to offer social countenance to the restless, insulting, magnetic, and dangerous abstraction of her sister constitutes most of the plot of the novel.

It constitutes more than plot, in fact; it creates both the consciousness and the privacy of the novel. The projectile of surveillance, epistemological demand, and remediation that both desire and "responsibility" constrain Elinor to level at Marianne, immobilized or turned back on herself by the always-newly-summoned-up delicacy of her refusal to press Marianne toward confession, make an internal space—internal, that is, to Elinor, hence to the reader hovering somewhere behind her eyes—from which there is no escape but more silent watching. About the engagement she is said to assume to exist between Marianne and Willoughby, for example, her "wonder"

> was engrossed by the extraordinary silence of her sister and Willoughby on the subject. . . . Why they should not openly acknowledge to her mother and herself, what their constant behaviour to each other declared to have taken place, Elinor could not imagine.
>
> . . . For this strange kind of secrecy maintained by them relative to their engagement, which in fact concealed nothing at all, she could not account; and it was so wholly contradictory to their general opinions and practice, that a doubt sometimes entered her mind of their being really engaged, and this doubt was enough to prevent her making any enquiry of Marianne. (100)

To Marianne, on the other hand, the question of an engagement seems simply not to have arisen.

The insulation of Marianne from Elinor's own unhappiness, when Elinor is unhappy; the buffering of Marianne's impulsiveness, and the absorption or, where that is impossible, coverture of her terrible sufferings; the constant, reparative concealment of Marianne's elopements of attention from their present company: these activities hollow out a subjectivity for Elinor and the novel that might best be described in the 1980s jargon of codependency, were not the pathologizing stigma of that term belied by the fact that, at least as far as this novel is concerned, the codependent subjectivity simply *is subjectivity*. Even Elinor's heterosexual plot with Edward Ferrars merely divides her remedial solicitude (that distinctive amalgam of "tenderness, pity, approbation, censure, and doubt" [129]) between the sister who remains her first concern, and a second sufferer from *mauvaise honte*, the telltale "embarrassment," "settled" "absence of mind" (123), unsocializable shyness, "want of spirits, of openness, and of consistency," "the same fettered inclination, the same inevitable necessity of temporizing with his mother" (126), and a "desponding turn of mind" (128), all consequent on his own servitude to an erotic habit formed in the idleness and isolation of an improperly supervised youth.

The codependency model is the less anachronistic as Marianne's and Edward's disorders share with the pre-twentieth-century version of masturbation the property of being structured as addictions. (Here, of course, I'm inviting a meditation on the history of the term "self-abuse," which referred to masturbation from the eighteenth century until very recently—when it's come, perhaps by analogy to "child abuse," to refer to battering or mutilation of oneself.

Where that older sense of "abuse" has resurfaced on the other hand, is in the also very recent coinage, "substance abuse.") Back to 1881:

> The afternoon of the 14th of September X . . . is in a terribly overexcited state. She walks about restlessly, grinding her teeth. . . . There is foam on her lips, she gasps, repeating, "I don't want to, I don't want to, I can't stop myself, I must do it! Stop me, hold my hands, tie my feet!" A few moments later she falls into a state of prostration, becomes sweet and gentle, begging to be given another chance. "I know I'm killing myself," she says. "Save me." (DZ, 30)

Although *the addict,* as a medicalized personal identity, was (as Virginia Berridge and Griffith Edwards demonstrate in *Opium and the People*) another product of the latter nineteenth century, the hypostatization of the notion of "will" that would soon give rise to the "addict" identity, and that by the late twentieth century would leave no issue of voluntarity untinged by the concept of addiction, is already in place in *Sense and Sensibility.*[17] A concept of addiction involves understanding something called "the will" as a muscle that can strengthen with exercise or atrophy with disuse; the particular muscle on which "will" is modeled in this novel is a sphincter, which, when properly toned, defines an internal space of private identity by holding some kinds of material inside, even while guarding against the admission of others. Marianne's unpracticed muscle lets her privacy dribble away, giving her "neither courage to speak of, nor fortitude to conceal" (333) the anguish she experiences. By contrast, in the moment of Elinor's profoundest happiness, when Marianne is restored from a grave illness, Elinor's well-exercised muscle guarantees that what expands with her joy is the private space that, constituting her self, constitutes it also as the space of narrative self-reflection (not to say hoarding):

> Elinor could not be cheerful. Her joy was of a different kind, and led to anything rather than to gaiety. Marianne restored to life, health, friends, and to her doating mother, was an idea to fill her heart with sensations of exquisite comfort, and expand it in fervent gratitude;—but it led to no outward demonstrations of joy, no words, no smiles. All within Elinor's breast was satisfaction, silent and strong. (310)

Such an apparently generalizable ideal of individual integrity, the unitary self-containment of the strong, silent type, can never be stable, of course. Elinor has constructed herself in this way around an original lack: the absentation of her sister, and perhaps in the first place the withholding from herself of the love of their mother, whom she then compulsively unites with Marianne, the favorite, in the love-drenched tableaux of her imagination. In the inappropriately pathologizing but descriptively acute language of self-help, Marianne's addiction has mobilized in her sister a discipline that, posed as against addiction, nonetheless also is one. Elinor's pupils, those less tractable sphincters of the soul, won't close against the hapless hemorrhaging of her visual attention flow toward Marianne; it is this, indeed, that renders her consciousness, in turn, habitable, inviting, and formative to readers as "point of view."

But that hypostatization of "will" had always anyway contained the potential for the infinite regress enacted in the uncircumscribable twentieth-century epidemic of addiction attribution: the degenerative problem of where, if not in some further compulsion, one looks for the will *to* will. As when Marianne, comparing herself with the more continent Elinor,

> felt all the force of that comparison, but not as her sister had hoped, to urge her to exertion now; she felt it with all the pain of continual self-reproach, regretted most bitterly that she had never exerted herself before; but it brought only the torture of penitence, without the hope of amendment. Her mind was so much weakened that she still fancied present exertion impossible, and therefore it only dispirited her the more. (270)

In addition, the concept of addiction involves a degenerative perceptual narrative of progressively deadened receptiveness to a stimulus that therefore requires to be steadily increased—as when Marianne's and her mother's "agony of grief" over the death of the father, at first overpowering, was then "voluntarily renewed, was sought for, was created again and again" (42). Paradoxically afflicted, as Marianne is, by both hyperesthesia and an emboldening and addiction-producing absent-mindedness ("an heart hardened against [her friends'] merits, and a temper irritated by their very attention" [337]), the species of the masturbating girl was described by Augustus Kinsley Gardner in 1860 as one

> in whom the least impression is redoubled like that of a "tam-tam," [yet who seeks] for emotions still more violent and more varied. It is this necessity which nothing can appease, which took the Roman women to the spectacles where men were devoured by ferocious beasts. . . . It is the emptiness of an unquiet and sombre soul seeking some activity, which clings to the slightest incident of life, to elicit from it some emotion which forever escapes; in short, it is the deception and disgust of existence.[18]

The subjectivity hollowed out by *Sense and Sensibility*, then, and made available *as* subjectivity for heterosexual expropriation, is not Marianne's but

Elinor's; the novel's achievement of a modern psychological interiority fit for the heterosexual romance plot is created for Elinor through her completely one-directional visual fixation on her sister's specularized, desired, envied, and punished autoeroticism. This also offers, however, a useful model for the chains of reader relations constructed by the punishing, girl-centered moral pedagogy and erotics of Austen's novels more generally. Austen criticism is notable mostly, not just for its timidity and banality, but for its unresting exaction of the spectacle of a Girl Being Taught a Lesson—for the vengefulness it vents on the heroines whom it purports to love, and whom, perhaps, it does. Thus Tony Tanner, the ultimate normal and normalizing reader of Austen, structures sentence after sentence: "Emma . . . *has to be tutored* . . . into correct vision and responsible speech. Anne Elliot *has to move*, painfully, from an excessive prudence."[19] "Some Jane Austen heroines *have to learn* their true 'duties.' They all *have to find* their proper homes" (TT, 33). Catherine "quite literally is in danger of perverting reality, and one of the things she *has to learn* is to break out of quotations" (TT, 44–45); she "*has to be disabused* of her naive and foolish 'Gothic' expectations" (TT, 48). "[Elizabeth and Darcy] *have to learn to see* that their novel is more properly called . . ." (TT, 105). A lot of Austen criticism sounds hilariously like the leering school prospectuses or governess manifestoes brandished like so many birch rods in Victorian s-m pornography. Thus Jane Nardin:

> The discipline that helps create the moral adult need not necessarily be administered in early childhood. Frequently, as we have seen, it is not—for its absence is useful in helping to create the problems with which the novel deals. But if adequate discipline is lacking in childhood, it must be supplied later, and this happens only when the character learns "the lessons of affliction" (*Mansfield Park*, 459). Only after immaturity, selfishness, and excessive self-confidence have produced error, trouble, and real suffering, can the adult begin to teach himself or herself the habits of criticism and self-control which should have been inculcated in childhood.[20]

How can it have taken this long to see that when Colonel Brandon and Marianne finally get together, their first granddaughter will be Lesbia Brandon?

Even readings of Austen that are not so frankly repressive have tended to be structured by what Foucault calls "the repressive hypothesis"—especially so, indeed, to the degree that their project is avowedly *anti*repressive. And these antirepressive readings have their own way of re-creating the spectacle of the girl being taught a lesson. Call her, in this case, "Jane Austen." The sight to be relished here is, as in psychoanalysis, the forcible exaction from her manifest text of what can only be the barest confession of a self-pleasuring sexuality, a disorder or subversion, seeping out at the edges of a policial conservatism always presumed and therefore always available for violation. That virginal figure "Jane Austen," in these narratives, is herself the punishable girl who "has to learn," "has to be tutored"—in truths with which, though derived from a reading of Austen, the figure of "Jane Austen" can no more be credited than can, for their lessons, the figures "Marianne," "Emma," or, shall we say, "Dora" or "Anna O."

It is partly to interrupt this seemingly interminable scene of punitive/pedagogical reading, interminably structured as it is by the concept of repression, that I want to make available the sense of an alternative, passionate sexual ecology—one fully available to Austen for her exciting, productive, and deliberate use, in a way it no longer is to us.

That is to say, it is no longer available to us *as passion*; even as its cynosural figure, the masturbating girl, is no longer visible as possessing a sexual identity capable of redefining and reorganizing her surround. We inherit it only in the residual forms of perception itself, of subjectivity itself, of institution itself. The last time I taught *Sense and Sensibility*, I handed out to my graduate class copies of some pages from the 1981 "Polysexuality" issue of *Semiotext(e)*, pages that reproduce without historical annotation what appears to be a late-nineteenth-century medical case history in French, from which I have also been quoting here. I handed it out then for reasons no more transparent than those that have induced me to quote from it here—beyond the true but inadequate notation that even eight years after reading it, my memory of the piece wouldn't let up its pressure on the gaze I was capable of levelling at the Austen novel. I hadn't even the New Historicists' positivist alibi for perpetuating and disseminating the shock of the violent narratives in which they trade: "Deal," don't they seem tacitly but moralistically to enjoin, "deal with your own terror, your own arousal, your disavowals, in your own way, on your own time, in your own [thereby reconstituted as invisible] privacy; it's not our responsibility, because *these awful things are real*." Surely I did want to spread around to a group of other readers, as if that would ground or diffuse it, the inadmissibly, inabsorbably complex shock of this document. But the pretext of the real was austerely withheld by the informal, perhaps only superficially sensationalistic *Semiotext(e)* format, which refused to proffer the legitimating scholarly apparatus that would give any reader the assurance of "knowing" whether the original of this document was to be looked for in an actual nineteenth-century psychiatric archive or, alternatively and every bit as credibly, in a manuscript of pornographic fiction dating from any time—any time including the present—in the intervening century. Certainly plenty of the other pieces in that issue of *Semio-*

text(e) are, whatever else they are, freshly minted and joltingly potent pornography; just as certainly, nothing in the "1881" document exceeds in any detail the known practices of late-nineteenth-century medicine. And wasn't that part of the shock?—the total plausibility either way of the same masturbatory narrative, the same pruriently cool clinical gaze at it and violating hands and instruments on it, even (one might add) further along the chain, the same assimilability of it to the pseudo-distantiating relish of sophisticated contemporary projects of critique. Toward the site of the absent, distracted, and embarrassed attention of the masturbatory subject, the directing of a less accountable flood of discursive attention has continued. What is most astonishing is its continuing entirely unabated by the dissolution of its object, the sexual identity of "the masturbator" herself.

Through the frame of 1881/1981 it becomes easier to see how most of the love story of *Sense and Sensibility*, no simple one, has been rendered all but invisible to most readers, leaving a dryly static tableau of discrete moralized portraits, posed antitheses, and exemplary, deplorable, or regrettably necessary punishments, in an ascetic heterosexualizing context.[21] This tableau is what we now know as "Jane Austen"; fossilized residue of the now subtracted autoerotic spectacle, "Jane Austen" is the name whose uncanny fit with the phrase "masturbating girl" today makes a ne plus ultra of the incongruous.

This history of impoverished "Jane Austen" readings is not the result of a failure by readers to "contextualize historically": a New Historicizing point that you can't understand *Sense and Sensibility* without entering into the alterity of a bygone masturbation phobia is hardly the one I am making. What alterity? I am more struck by how profoundly, how destructively twentieth-century readings are already shaped by the discourse of masturbation and its sequelae: *more* destructively than the novel is, even though onanism per se, and the phobia against it, are living issues in the novel as they no longer are today.

We can be the less surprised by the congruence as we see masturbation and the relations surrounding it as the proto-form of any modern "sexual identity"; thus as lending their structure to many vantages of subjectivity that have survived the definitional atrophy of the masturbator as an identity: pedagogic surveillance, as we have mentioned, homo-hetero divides, psychiatry, psychoanalysis, gynecology. The interpretive habits that make it so hard to register the erotics of *Sense and Sensibility* are deeply and familiarly encoded in the therapeutic or mock-therapeutic rhetoric of the "1881" document. They involve the immobilizing framing of an isolated sexual subject (a subject, that is, whose isolation is decreed by her identification with a nameable sexual identity); and her staging as a challenge or question addressed to an audience whose erotic invisibility is guaranteed by the same definitional stroke as their entitlement to intervene on the sexuality attributed to her. That it was this particular, apparently unitary and in some ways self-contained, autoerotic sexual identity that crystallized as the prototype *of* "sexual identity" made that isolating embodiment of "the sexual" easier, and made easier as well a radical naturalization and erotic dematerialization of narrative point of view concerning it.

And the dropping out of sight in this century of the masturbatory identity has only, it seems, given more the authority of self-evidence to the scientific, therapeutic, institutional, and narrative relations originally organized around it. *Sense and Sensibility* resists such "progress" only insofar as we can succeed in making narratively palpable again, under the pressure of our own needs, the great and estranging force of the homoerotic longing magnetized in it by that radiant and inattentive presence—the female figure of the love that keeps forgetting its name.

NOTES

"Jane Austen and the Masturbating Girl" was written in 1990, based on a paper delivered at the Modern Language Association in 1989. What I refer to as the "1881" document from *Semiotext(e)* (see n. 15) was later published, under less equivocal scholarly auspices, in Jeffrey Mousaieff Masson's collection, *A Dark Science: Women, Sexuality, and Psychiatry in the Nineteenth Century* (New York: Farrar, Straus, and Giroux, 1986); Démétrius Alexandre Zambaco, "Masturbation and Psychological Problems in Two Little Girls," 61–89, trans. Masson and Marianne Loring from "Onanisme avec troubles nerveux chez deux petites filles," *L'Encéphale*, vol. 2 (1882), 88–95, 260–74.

The project sketched out in this chapter has evoked, not only the foreclosing and disavowing responses mentioned in its first paragraph, but help, encouragement, and fellowship as well: from Michael Moon, Paula Bennett, Vernon Rosario, Ed Cohen, Barbara Herrnstein Smith, and Jonathan Goldberg, among others.

1 Kimball, *Tenured Radicals: How Politics Has Corrupted Our Higher Education* (New York: Harper and Row, 1990), 145–46.

2 See, for a few examples of the phrase's career in journalism, Roger Rosenblatt, "The Universities: A Bitter Attack . . . ," *New York Times Book Review*, 22 April 1990, 3; letters in the *Book Review*, 20 May 1990, 54, including one from Catharine R. Stimpson disputing the evidential status of the phrase; Richard Bernstein, "The Rising Hegemony of the Politically Correct: America's Fashionable Orthodoxy," *New York Times*, 28 October 1990, sec. 4 (Week in Review), 1, 4.

3 Jane E. Brody, "Personal Health," *New York Times*, 4 November 1987.

4 Rosenblatt, "The Universities," 3.

5 John Mullan, *Sentiment and Sociability: The Language of Feeling in the Eighteenth Century* (New York: Oxford University Press, 1988), 201–40.

6 Neil Hertz, *The End of the Line* (New York: Columbia University Press, 1985), 148–49.

7 Vernon A. Rosario II, "The Nineteenth-Century Medical Politics of Self-Defilement and Seminal Economy," presented at the Center for Literary and Cultural Studies, Harvard University, "Nationalisms and Sexualities" conference, June 1989, 18.

8 Jane Austen, *Sense and Sensibility* (Harmondsworth, Middlesex: Penguin Books, 1967), 193. Further citations from this edition are incorporated in the text.

9 This is (in relation to women) the argument of, most influentially, Lilian Faderman in *Surpassing the Love of Men: Romantic Friendship and Love between Women from the Renaissance to the Present* (New York: William Morrow, 1981), and Smith-Rosenberg in "The Female World of Love and Ritual" in *Disorderly Conduct: Visions of Gender in Victorian America* (New York: Oxford University Press, 1985), A recently discovered journal, published as *I Know My Own Heart: The Diaries of Anne Lister* (1791–1840), ed. Helena Whitbread (London: Virago, 1988), suggests that revisions of this narrative may, however, be necessary. It is the diary (for 1817–23) of a young, cultured, religious, socially conservative, self-aware, landowning rural Englishwoman—an almost archetypal Jane Austen heroine—who formed her sense of self around the pursuit and enjoyment of genital contact and short- and long-term intimacies with other women of various classes.

10 Foucault, *The History of Sexuality: An Introduction*, trans. by Robert Harley (New York: Pantheon Books, 1978), 1.

11 Paula Bennett, *My Life A Loaded Gun: Female Creativity and Feminist Poetics* (Boston: Beacon Press, 1986), 13–94; *Emily Dickinson: Woman Poet* (Iowa City: University of Iowa Press, 1990).

12 Useful historical work touching on masturbation and masturbation phobia includes G. J. Barker-Benfield, *The Horrors of the Half-Known Life: Male Attitudes Toward Women and Sexuality in Nineteenth-Century America* (New York: Harper and Row, 1976); Ed Cohen, *Talk on the Wilde Side* (New York: Routledge, 1993); John D'Emilio and Estelle B. Freedman, *Intimate Matters: A History of Sexuality in America* (New York: Harper and Row, 1988); E. H. Hare, "Masturbatory Insanity: The History of an Idea," *Journal of the Mental Sciences* 108 (1962): 1–25; Robert H. MacDonald, "The Frightful Consequences of Onanism: Notes on the History of a Delusion," *Journal of the History of Ideas* 28 (1967): 423–31; John Money, *The Destroying Angel: Sex, Fitness and Food in the Legacy of Degeneracy Theory, Graham Crackers, Kellogg's Corn Flakes and the American Health History* (Buffalo, N.Y.: Prometheus, 1985); George L. Mosse, *Nationalism and Sexuality: Respectability and Abnormal Sexuality in Modern Europe* (New York: Fertig, 1985); Robert P. Neuman, "Masturbation, Madness, and the Modern Concept of Childhood and Adolescence," *Journal of Social History* 8 (1975): 1–22; Elaine Showalter, *The Female Malady: Women, Madness, and English Culture, 1830–1980* (New York: Pantheon Books, 1985); Smith-Rosenberg, *Disorderly Conduct;* and Jean Stengers and Anne van Neck, *Histoire d'une grande peur: la masturbation* (Brussels: Editions de l'Université de Bruxelles, 1984).

13 Foucault, *History of Sexuality*, 1: 105, 43.

14 Ibid., 1:1.

15 Démétrius Zambaco, "Onanism and Nervous Disorders in Two Little Girls," trans. Catherine Duncan, *Semiotext(e)* 4 ("Polysexuality") (1981): 30; further citations are incor-

porated in the text as DZ. The letters standing in place of the girls' names are followed by ellipses in the original; other ellipses are mine. In quoting from this piece I have silently corrected some obvious typographical errors; since this issue of *Semiotext(e)* is printed entirely in capital letters, and with commas and periods of indistinguishable shape, I have also had to make some guesses about sentence division and punctuation.

16 Quoted and discussed in Cohen, *Talk on the Wilde Side,* 89–90.

17 Virginia Berridge and Griffith Edwards, *Opium and the People: Opiate Use in Nineteenth-Century England,* 2d ed. (New Haven, Conn.: Yale University Press, 1987). For more on the epistemology of addiction, codependency, and addiction attribution, see my chapter "Epidemics of the Will," in *Tendencies* (Durham, N.C.: Duke University Press, 1993).

18 Augustus Kinsley Gardner, "Physical Decline of American Women" (1860), quoted in Barker-Benfield, *Horrors of the Half-Known Life,* 273–74.

19 Tony Tanner, *Jane Austen* (Cambridge, Mass.: Harvard University Press, 1986), 6; page numbers of remaining quotations cited in the text with TT; emphasis, in each case, added.

20 She is remarkably unworried about any possible excess of severity: "In this group of characters [in *Mansfield Park*], lack of discipline has the expected effect, while excessive discipline, though it causes suffering and creates some problems for Fanny and Susan Price, does indeed make them into hard-working, extremely conscientious women. The timidity and self-doubt which characterize Fanny, and which are a response to continual censure, seem a reasonable price to pay for the strong conscience that even the unfair discipline she received has nurtured in her." Jane Nardin, "Children and Their Families," *Jane Austen: New Perspectives,* ed. Janet Todd, Women and Literature, New Series, vol. 3 (New York: Holmes and Meier, 1983), 73–87; both passages quoted are from 83.

21 As Mullan's *Sentiment and Sociability* suggests—and not only through the evocation of Austen's novel in its title—the eponymous antithesis "sense" vs. "sensibility" is undone by, quite specifically, the way sensibility itself functions as a point of pivotal intersection, and potentially of mutual coverture, between alloerotic and autoerotic investments. Mullan would refer to these as "sociability" vs. "isolation," "solipsism," or "hypochondria." He ignores specifically antimasturbatory medical campaigns in his discussion of late eighteenth-century medicine, but their relevance is clear enough in, for example, the discussion he does offer of the contemporary medical phenomenology of menstruation. "Menstruation is represented as an irregularity which takes the guise of a regularity; it is especially likely to signify a precarious condition in the bodies of those for whom womanhood does not mean the life of the fertile, domesticated, married female. Those particularly at risk are the unmarried, the ageing, and the sexually precocious" (226). "The paradox, of course, is that to concentrate upon the palpitating, sensitized body of the woman caught in the difficult area between childhood and marriage is also to concede the dangers of this condition—those dangers which feature, in another form, in writings on hysteria" (228). In *Epistemology of the Closet* (Berkeley: University of California Press, 1990), especially 141–81, I discuss at some length the strange historical career of the epithets "sentimentality" and "sensibility," in terms of the inflammatory and scapegoating mechanics of vicariation: of the coverture offered by these apparently static nouns to the most volatile readerly interchanges between the allo- and the auto-.

15. Ulysses *and the Twentieth Century*

FRANCO MORETTI

J OYCE AND ZOLA, Joyce and the advertising poster, Joyce and Musil . . .
And Joyce and Proust, of course: from Edmund Wilson to Joseph Frank and
Giacomo Debenedetti, a parallel that by now is a little classic of contemporary criticism. But is it really so certain that what is of most interest is the
similarity between *Ulysses* and *À la recherche?* Think of Molly's monologue,
and of the Guermantes reception: two episodes, at first sight, quite similar—
two finales, swollen and arched back to recover time past. But if the starting
point is the same, the episodes develop quite differently. In Molly's vigil, Iser
writes, the past recovers that openness that it had long ago lost: time is regained
because it is *reopened:* freed from all fixity, all certainty.[1] By contrast, the happiness pervading Marcel has quite another origin. It consists in recognizing with
certainty: discovering "the permanent essence of things." Time regained is time
fixed: carved once and for all—immobile.

Instead of Joyce "and" Proust, in the following pages I shall therefore speak
of Joyce "against" Proust. It is not a matter of hierarchies (even if I have my own
preferences, of course). It is that I want to highlight a feature of literary evolution: the fact that creative moments (such as the time of Proust and Joyce)
are characterized by radical splits—and *for that very reason* are creative moments. What I have in mind is a bush-like history, with unequal, asymmetrical
branches growing as best they can—and even, perhaps, trying to get the better
of one another. A long way from Hegel's spirit of the times, in the singular, recurring in every picture, every novel, and every symphony! Literary history is a
battlefield—and especially, as we shall see, in the years of modernism. For now,
however, a bit of stylistics:

Proust takes particular delight—writes Spitzer—in dependent clauses, because they illustrate the dependence (and this is not just a play on words) of man upon chance, of the individual upon the whole and so on, in a kind of acoustic and architectonic imitation.[2]

Chance—but translated into an architectonic form. "This tightening and condensation," we read at another point in the essay, "and this ability to accumulate the sentence, seem to me to spring above all from Proust's ability to see connections between the most disparate things. In these complex representations there is an enormous mastery and dominion over things, which knows all about precedence and subordination, and can put important and trivial things in their appropriate places . . ."[3] Total dominion over the most disparate things: a splendid metaphor. Could we possibly apply it to *Ulysses?*

> *One of those chaps would make short work of a fellow. Pick the bones clean no matter who it was. Ordinary meat for them. A corpse is meat gone bad.* Well and what's cheese? Corpse of milk. *I read in this* Voyages in China *that the Chinese say a white man smells like a corpse.* Cremation better. Priests dead against it. Devilling for the other firm. Wholesale burners and Dutch oven dealers. Time of the plague. Quicklime feverpits to eat them. Lethal chamber. Ashes to ashes. Or bury at sea. Where is that Parsee tower of silence? Eaten by birds. Earth, fire, water. Drowning they say is the pleasantest. See your whole life in a flash. But being brought back to life no. Can't bury in the air however. Out of a flying machine. *Wonder does the news go about whenever a fresh one is let down.* Underground communication. We learned that from them. *Wouldn't be surprised. Regular square feed for them.* Flies come before he's well dead. *Got wind of Dignam. They wouldn't care about the smell of it. Saltwhite crumbling mush of corpse: smell, taste like raw white turnips.* (*Ulysses,* Gabler edition VI, 980–94)

The sentences in italics constitute the first draft of the paragraph, published in *Little Review,* in September 1918; all the rest is added later, between 1918 and 1921, actually doubling the original length. Great is Joyce's delight, we might repeat with Spitzer, in multiplying dependent clauses—except that those clauses are clearly *not* dependent. Even where a degree of subordination can be glimpsed ("If a corpse is meat gone bad, *then* cheese is corpse of milk"), Joyce's parataxis functions to the opposite effect: it constructs separate, independent sentences. Nothing is "in its appropriate place," here: or rather, the appropriate place for things and thoughts is no longer, as in Proust, a matter of "precedence or subordination," but always equal and independent.[4]

No dominion over things, here. Every sentence, and almost every word, of the stream of consciousness is a world in itself: complete, independent. Every paragraph, a digression in miniature—which continues to expand, like the one we have just read, because there exists no "organic" fetter to hold it in check. It is the logic of mechanical form: the potentially infinite addition of Goethe, Flaubert, Kraus, Pound, Dos Passos, Musil . . . And indeed, for Joyce, "to work" at *Ulysses* basically means *to extend Ulysses,* until the day when the printer loses patience, and sends the proofs—scribbled over for the nth time—back to him: "*trop tard.*" Too late, time has run out, an astrological idiocy wants the Book to be born on the same day as the Author, and an extrinsic fact (like death, more seriously, for others) thus assumes responsibility for putting an end to the infinite form.

But if even *Ulysses* comes to a halt, one question still remains. In this universe entirely made up of independent sentences, where everything is in the foreground and every working day adds new details, what meaning can the individual page, or the individual sentence, have? Indeed—does it still have one?

In realist texts, Roland Barthes has written, "residues of functional analysis" are often encountered:

> The irreducible residues of functional analysis have this in common: they denote what is ordinarily called 'concrete reality' (insignificant gestures, transitory attitudes, insignificant objects, redundant words). The pure and simple 'representation' of the 'real,' the naked relation of 'what is' (or has been), thus appears as a resistance to meaning.[5]

Insignificant gestures, transitory attitudes, redundant words . . . No doubt about it, it is the world of Leopold Bloom. And if Barthes is right, it is a world extraordinarily *poor in meaning.* Quite the opposite, in fact, from the one foreseen by the poetics of "epiphany." Here is Joyce, twenty years before *Ulysses:*

> [The object's] soul, its whatness, leaps to us from the vestment of its appearance. The soul of the commonest object, the structure of which is so adjusted, seems to us radiant. The object achieves its epiphany. (*Stephen Hero,* 25)

The soul of objects—"their essential secret, their meaning . . . the second reality that is the only quality which makes things worth representing"[6]—is this what we find in *Ulysses?* The *claritas,* the "radiance" of the young Joyce? On the contrary, the great novelty of the stream of consciousness consists in its proceeding for pages and pages *without the slightest revelation.* It is the true world of prose: detailed, regular, rather banal. The view is determinedly earthbound, with nothing taking flight—as in the grand vision of the *Portrait*—towards a higher reality. And as in space, so too in time. Parataxis offers a reliable, mechanical grid, where each present is at once followed by another—different, but no more important. No instant ever stands out from the others, unrepeatable (Proust: "and suddenly the memory revealed itself"), to fix the meaning of the story once and for all.

In short, a *Ulysses* without epiphanies. It is a point over which the mature Joyce parts company with his own early work, and with most of his contemporaries. It is not Dublin, the city of revelations: it is Paris. The Paris of *Nadja,* all "sudden parallels, petrifying coincidences, . . . flashes of light that would make you see, really *see* . . ."; where people go for a walk always hoping to come across the "event from which each of us is entitled to expect the revelation of his own life's meaning." Or the Paris of Aragon, who senses "the wonder inherent in commonplace things," and in his *Paysan de Paris* aims precisely to show "the places where the divine manifests itself."[7] And even before the surrealists, of course, Proust's Paris: where, one unforgettable day, "the souls held captive in some inferior being . . . start and tremble, they call us by our name, and as soon as we have recognized their voice the spell is broken."

The *madeleine:* that is a true epiphany—soul, death, summons, resurrection, miracle . . . But it is precisely the sacred connotations of the episode, so akin to the language of the *Portrait,* that underline the distance of *Ulysses* from every form of revelation. For memory to reemerge, Proust writes, "I shut out every obstacle, every extraneous idea, I stop my ears and inhibit all attention against the sounds from the next room . . . I clear an empty space in front of it." An empty space: quite right, the formula of the sacred, precisely what epiphany needs. But empty space is also completely impossible in the crowded world of *Ulysses,* all noise and interference. It is as if the stream of consciousness never managed to extricate itself from the close-knit fabric of metonymy, whereas the *madeleine,* and the epiphany of *Portrait,* can always leap from the latter into metaphor. From prose, to poetry:

And soon, mechanically, dispirited after a dreary day with the prospect of a depressing morrow, I raised to my lips a spoonful of the tea in which I had soaked a morsel of the cake. No sooner had the warm liquid mixed with the crumbs touched my palate . . .

So far, we are in the world of prose, of metonymic details—lips, spoonful, cake, crumbs, palate . . . All things that are also in Joyce. But then, the symbolic continuity is broken:

then a shudder ran through me and I stopped, intent upon the extraordinary thing that was happening to me. *An exquisite pleasure* had invaded my senses . . . having had on me *the effect which love has* of filling me with *a precious essence;* or rather this essence was not in me, it was me. . . . What did it mean?[8]

Que signifiait-elle? "What did it mean?" (*Portrait of the Artist as a Young Man,* 4). "What does it mean then, what can it all mean?" (*To the Lighthouse,* III, 1). A question that is like an alarm bell: we are leaving the world of mimesis, to enter that of meaning. But it is also the question that Bloom, for all his curiosity, never asks himself. Because Bloom really speaks a one-dimensional language: made up of simple additions, where things coexist without strain and without secrets. Around him, only the "insignificant gestures" of Roland Barthes: the "insignificant objects" and "redundant words" of his essay on "The Reality Effect." Superficial, resistant to meaning. Very well—but why? What can be the meaning of this absence of meaning?

A bit of vulgar materialism. In the Gabler edition, the fourth chapter of *Ulysses* (Bloom's first) numbers about 550 lines; the fifth, 570; the sixth, 1030. In all, some fifty pages, and two thousand odd lines. Well, in this space, Bloom receives more than *three thousand* assorted stimuli, of which around two-thirds are internal (memories, reflections, emotions), and one-third external (visual, verbal, olfactory and tactile stimuli). To pile vulgarity upon vulgarity: more than sixty heterogeneous elements per page, or one and a half per line. In short: one stimulus every ten words.[9]

There it is, Simmel's metropolis. At last, it has taken linguistic form. But it has also created a far from simple problem: is it really possible to make those three thousand stimuli *meaningful?* Yes, of course—if you are willing to *reduce them.* If you make an "empty space" in front of them, as in front of Proust's crumbs, and restrict the field of observation:

When suddenly, in she came, stood for a moment silent (as if she had been pretending up there, and for a moment let herself be now), stood quite motionless for a moment against a picture of Queen Victoria wearing the blue ribbon of the Garter; and all at once he realized that it was this: it was this:—she was the most beautiful person he had ever seen. (*To the Lighthouse,* 1, 1)

. . . it was this: it was this. A revealing stylistic feature, this syncopated and almost feverish use of the deictic. One colon, then another, then a dash: a triple focusing, which brings things closer, and squeezes out their meaning. But the meaning is precisely the result of exclusion: of a field that contracts and again contracts—this: this—and relegates everything else to the background. But in the stream of consciousness there is really no background: all sentences are main, all is foreground. And where all is in the foreground, nothing is ever really close—never a "this." It is a broad perception, but unfocused: able only to slide over things.

Well then, what is the meaning of this absence of meaning? Simple—it helps Bloom to live. It helps him to live *in the metropolis:* a place that requires more intelligence, to be sure—but also more stupidity. Where he must learn to see and not see, to understand and not understand. "Unfocused interaction," as Erving Goffman has called it: "civil inattention."[10] A neutrality, opacity, and emotional mediocrity, that enable millions of human beings to live side by side without exterminating each other. If on that June day everything were meaningful, Bloom's head would burst—and so would the reader's. Consequently, when we read *Ulysses* we learn to accept the fact that thousands of things gradually become familiar to us, but never more than familiar. We see them again, and know they are there; but are never sure of their meaning, or why they are there.

Such are the "themes" of the stream of consciousness, which recur innumerable times without ever being fixed in a sure form. Here, too, we are at the antipodes to Proust: "This time he [Swann] had distinguished quite clearly a phrase which emerged for a few moments above the waves of sound . . ." He had distinguished quite clearly—well, in *Ulysses* there is never such sureness of identity: "I saw that picture somewhere I forget now old master or faked for money. He is sitting in their house, talking. Mysterious" (*Ulysses*, V, 289–91). Or again:

> Yet they say, who was it told me, there is no carnal. You would imagine that would get played out pretty quick. Yes, it was Crofton met him one evening bringing her a pound of rumpsteak. What is this she was? Barmaid in Jury's. Or the Moira, was it? (*Ulysses*, VI, 245–8)

Yet they say, who was it told me . . . Adorno's Mahler comes to mind:

> The concept of the theme as a given, then to be modified, is inadequate to Mahler. Rather, the nucleus undergoes a treatment similar to that of a narrative element in oral tradition; at each telling it becomes slightly different. . . . To this extent the variants are the countervailing force to fulfillment. They divest the theme of its identity [whereas] the fulfillment is the positive manifestation of what the theme has not yet become.[11]

326   Franco Moretti

The last sentence more or less sums up what I have been trying to say. On the one hand, "fulfillment" of the theme, the "positive manifestation" of the *madeleine,* the epiphany of meaning. On the other, the "variants" in Mahler and Joyce, the "oral tradition" of the stream of consciousness: themes that "become slightly different at each telling." But that in the meantime, as I was saying, become familiar. And here a second musical analogy is called for:

> Wagner's work [is endowed] with an enigmatic quality and even today, in contrast with almost all other music, the listener is left with the sense of a blind spot, of something unresolved—notwithstanding his familiarity with the music. Wagner denies the listener who accompanies him the satisfaction of a thing clearly defined and it is left in doubt whether the formal meaning of a given moment has been rightly apprehended. Sachs's words— "I can't hold on to it—but nor can I forget it"—are an allusion to this.[12]

It is the paradox of the *Leitmotiv:* you recognize it without ever perhaps having known it. Armed with Max Chop's booklets, Wagnerian audiences are bewitched from the outset by the urge to identify it, and thrilled by its reappearance. But this pleasure relegates musical understanding to the background. Adorno again:

> Among the functions of the *Leitmotiv* can be found, alongside the aesthetic one, a commodity-function, rather like that of an advertisement: anticipating the universal practice of mass culture later on, the music is designed to be remembered, it is intended for the forgetful.[13]

Learning by heart replacing comprehension: for Adorno, it is an unforgivable regression. But in the context of our discourse, something else comes into play as well. Staiger:

> [In Homer] the happiness that the return of the familiar brings, the triumph of knowing that now life no longer flows on without stopping but is something lasting, and that objects have a firm, stable existence and can be identified—all this is so powerful that even today every unspoiled reader experiences in it an inspired feeling for the early days of mankind.[14]

Perhaps it is not just a feeling for the earliest days. In so far as the metropolis is itself a world—vast, complicated, dangerous—then the happiness conveyed by the return of the familiar is by no means inappropriate to the twentieth century. In the unending melody of *Ulysses,* for example (which surpasses even the *Ring* in the number and variety of its themes), the return of the *Leitmotiv* is the only thing that helps us, if not actually to understand—what is there to *understand,* in a stream of consciousness paragraph? — at least to get our bearings. When things and individuals from the city of Dublin, places and gestures and words, begin to reappear — always overdetermined by their new contexts, but also, just like the Wagnerian *Leitmotiv,* always clearly recognizable — well, their return makes *Ulysses* feel like a world you can live in. Its extent remains vast, and its laws almost incomprehensible. At the same time, however — just as in a big foreign city — here and there the first fixed points are established: a bee sting, a cake of soap, a phrase from Mozart . . .

Not much? True enough, not much — from the point of view of *meaning.* But in a different perspective, it is truly *a world of things.* It is the language of the big city.

WORLD TEXTS

So warm. His right hand once more slowly went over his brow and hair. Then he puts on his hat again, relieved: and read again: choice blend, made of the finest Ceylon brands. The far east. *Lovely spot it must be: the garden of the world, big lazy leaves* to float about on, cactuses, flowery meads, *snaky lianas they call them. Wonder is it like that. Those Cinghalese lobbing about in the sun* in dolce far niente, not doing a hand's turn all day. Sleep six months out of the twelve. Too hot to quarrel. *Influence of the climate.* Lethargy. Flowers of idleness. The air feeds most. Azotes. Hothouse in Botanic gardens. Sensitive plants. Waterlilies. Petals too tired to. Sleeping sickness in the air. Walk on roseleaves. Imagine trying to eat tripe and cowheel. *Where was the chap I saw in that picture somewhere? Ah yes, in the dead sea floating on his back, reading a book with a parasol open. Couldn't sink if you tried, so thick with salt. Because the weight of the water, no, the weight of the body in the water is equal to the weight of the what? Or is it the volume is equal to the weight? It's a law something like that.* Vance in High school cracking his fingerjoints, teaching. The college curriculum. Cracking curriculum. *What is weight really when you say the weight? Thirty two feet per second per second. Law of falling bodies: per second per second. They all fall to the ground. The earth. It's the force of gravity of the earth is the weight.* (*Ulysses,* v, 27–46: the phrases in italics are those originally published in *Little Review,* July 1918)

Leopold Bloom, and a shop window: an ideal situation for the stream of consciousness. In this case, moreover, in front of the Belfast Oriental Tea Company, the device really does function as Mephistopheles's cloak: it makes it possible to fly through space, into those "other worlds"—here, the Orient—of which epic digressions are made. It is a situation recalling Faust's reverie on the seashore—but with one important difference. At the time of *Ulysses*, the conquest of extra-European space is a fait accompli, and Bloom's geographical stereotypes—"secondhand abstractions," as Edward Said has called them[15]—are the proof of it: testimony to a dominion so self-confident that it parades its very ignorance as indisputable knowledge. It is as if, in *Ulysses*, the grand world were suddenly shrunk. Let us take a closer look.

London, late nineteenth century. The reading room of the Reform Club, seen by a French novelist:

> "Well, but where can he [the thief] fly to? . . . No country is safe for him."
> "Pshaw!"
> "Where could he go, then?"
> "Oh, I don't know that. The world is big enough."
> "It was once . . ."
> "What do you mean by 'once'? Has the world grown smaller?"
> "Certainly . . ."

Smaller, because you can travel round it more quickly, of course ("That is true, gentlemen, only eighty days, now that the section between Rothal and Allahabad, on the Great Indian Peninsular Railway, has been opened"). But there is something that shrinks the world even more than speed, and that is *predictability*:

> "Yes, in eighty days! But that doesn't take into account bad weather, contrary winds, shipwrecks, railway accidents, and so on."
> "All included," returned Phileas Fogg, continuing to play . . .
> "But suppose the Hindus or Indians pull up the rails? Suppose they stop the trains, pillage the luggage vans, and scalp the passengers!"
> "All included. . . ." (Jules Verne, *Around the World in Eighty Days*, 3)

Tout compris: Phileas Fogg does not know it, but he has just christened modern tourism. For that clause with its glorious future promises a journey that can be calculated in advance, like every other economic investment: twenty thousand pounds, exactly; eighty days, and not a second more.[16] And that is not all. For material security is very soon supplemented by a semiotic protection that enables the tourist to encounter signs, and nothing but signs, everywhere—and signs that he already knows. Thus Mark Twain, in a book entitled—how perfect—*Innocents Abroad*:

In a little while we were speeding through the streets of Paris and delight-
fully recognizing certain names and places with which books had long ago
made us familiar. It was like meeting an old friend when we read "Rue de
Rivoli" on the street corner; we knew the genuine vast palace of the Louvre
as well as we knew its picture. . . . (*Innocents Abroad*, 12)

Re-cognition. It is the tourist's supreme wish. A desire so strong that the journey becomes truly complete only when, with photography, it is in turn fixed in
a sign: into a good—and if possible perfect—likeness of the original signs. A person travels, here, not in order to see the world, but in order to see once more—
through the world—his own encyclopaedia. On the semiotic level, Jonathan
Culler has written: "Tourism reveals the difficulties of appreciating otherness
except through signifying structures that mark and reduce it."[17]

Reducing otherness . . . These are the right words with which to return
to Leopold Bloom, and his thoughts on the Orient: garden of the world . . .
sleep six months out of twelve . . . influence of the climate . . . walk on roseleaves . . . Sound familiar, these phrases? Of course, they are old acquaintances:
they are the *idées reçues* of Bouvard and Pécuchet—who had themselves traveled around culture in (just over) eighty days. And, in one way, Joyce's commonplaces still function like Flaubert's: they reduce the unknown to the known;
they know everything, they *close* everything. They shrink the world, as I was
saying earlier: they bring the distant closer, and make it familiar.[18] But to this
old function the commonplaces of *Ulysses* have added a new one. They have become the scaffolding for Bloom's random associations: the support for the new
metropolitan perception. In more radical terms, they are the *extremely banal*
basis, without which the *extremely audacious* technique of the stream of consciousness could not exist.

It is the same interweaving of regression and development (simplified plot,
complex score) already encountered in the *Ring*, where it was facilitated by the
presence of two different languages. In Joyce, of course, there is only one language, but the twofold level survives, to be exploited with equal intelligence.
What, after all, is the stream of consciousness for? As I have said (only too often):
for opening up to the stimuli of modernity; and for keeping them all present, in
the foreground, without losing a single one of them. But such an endeavour has
its cost. Arnold Gehlen: "Man's world-openness might appear to be a great burden. He is flooded with stimulation, with an abundance of impressions, which
he must somehow learn to cope with. . . . Man must find *relief* from the burden of overwhelming stimulation."[19] Relief and coping: this is what Bloom's
commonplaces are for. A technical detail reveals it to us: their position in the

Joycean paragraph. Almost never at the beginning—which is the moment of world-openness, when it would be absurd to have a closed mind. Often at the end, in order to file away what has happened with a formula, as in *Bouvard and Pécuchet*. And almost always around the middle of the paragraph: in order to hold together the associative galaxy of the stream of consciousness. A "banality rate" is thus established in Bloom's mind: a regular, constant rhythm—two or three stimuli, one commonplace, two or three stimuli, one commonplace—that accompanies him throughout the day, offering firm support amid the throng of external and internal impulses. These are Bloom's certitudes. The moments in which the meaning of things is revealed to him: clear, indisputable.

The moments in which the meaning of things . . . Yes, indeed, commonplaces are *Bloom's epiphanies.* The only ones appropriate for *Ulysses:* metaphors, yes—but dead metaphors, covering the metonymic fabric with a blanket of obviousness that makes it still more opaque.[20] But this is quite all right, as we have seen: the world-city requires more lucidity *and more stupidity.* Or rather, a new kind of stupidity: curiosity, plus the impersonal; the anomie of *disparate* stimuli, and the standardization of *common*places. The expanse of epic space is here welded to the novelistic theme of malleability, and the project initiated with *Faust* is finally accomplished: an epic of socialization. For this is the meaning of that day in 1904. What does Bloom do—from when he gets up to when he finally goes to sleep? Nothing. He walks, he looks round, he remembers, he dreams, he thinks. But in this *dolce far niente,* Bloom reviews his own receptive apparatus, and refurbishes his own imaginary. He harmonizes with the social that is outside him, and with the social that is inside him.

But where, inside?

FREE ASSOCIATION

Where, inside? As usual, that famous label—stream of consciousness—offers no help: it is not a stream, and it is not consciousness. What, then? "The Depth Approach" is the title of Chapter 1 of *The Hidden Persuaders;* and one of Wenders's characters, at the end of *Kings of The Road,* says: "The Americans have colonized our subconscious." The link with the world of *Ulysses* seems self-evident. But is it really the *subconscious* speaking, in Bloom's "stream of consciousness"?

Let us begin with a technical detail. The similarity has often been noted between the stream of consciousness and the psychoanalytic technique of "free association." Well, Freud writes, the "higher degree of freedom of association" is achieved when:

> I may, for instance, require the experimenter to allow a proper name or a number to occur to him freely. What then occurs to him would presumably be even more arbitrary and more indeterminable than with our own technique. It can be shown, however, that it is *always strictly determined* by important internal attitudes of mind . . . The associations to numbers chosen at random are perhaps the most convincing; they run off so quickly and *proceed with such incredible certainty to a hidden goal* that the effect is really staggering.[21]

"Free" associations? Certainly, free from any conscious selection. But the italics (added by me) make it clear that for Freud the really staggering thing is the *lack of freedom* of the associative process. The true protagonist, here, is not freedom, but psychological determinism: the "important internal"—or subconscious—"attitudes of mind" that steer the associations to their necessary conclusion. "Psychical events are determined. There is nothing arbitrary about them," writes Freud in *The Interpretation of Dreams*; and a few years later, *The Psychopathology of Everyday Life* (which examines phenomena that are indeed very Joycean) aims precisely to eliminate chance from even the tiniest behavioral and linguistic mishaps.[22]

Very well. And here is Joyce:

> Makes them feel more important to be prayed over in Latin. Requiem mass. Crape weepers. Blackedged notepaper. Your name on the altarlist. Chilly place this. Want to feed well, sitting in there all the morning in the gloom kicking his heels waiting for the next please. Eyes of a toad too. What swells him up that way? Molly gets swelled after cabbage. Air of the place maybe. Looks full up of bad gas. Must be an infernal lot of bad gas round the place. Butchers, for instance: they get like raw beefsteaks. Who was telling me? Mervyn Browne. Down in the vaults of saint Werburgh's lovely old organ hundred and fifty they have to bore a hole in the coffins sometimes to let out the bad gas and burn it. Out it rushes blue. One whiff of that and you're a doner. (*Ulysses*, VI, 602–12)

Latin, mourning, food, the priest's face, Molly, gas, butchers, the organ in the crypt . . . These really are free associations: they move in ten different directions, without any objective or logic. And why are they so free? Because there is no "hidden goal": no force that intervenes to deflect their course; no "important internal attitude of mind" that "strictly determines" their direction. Because, in other words, in the course of the associative process *the subconscious never comes into play.*

But if the stream of consciousness has nothing to do with consciousness, then, nor yet with the subconscious, who the devil *is* speaking in Bloom's stream of consciousness?

It is the "preconscious": a "system" to which Freud, after some initial interest, attributes rather little importance. Within it, we find quite different wishes from those that belong "to the suppressed part of the mind and become active in us at night."[23] No, the wishes of the preconscious are always daytime, waking, acknowledged ones: if they remain "not dealt with," Freud adds with uncharacteristic vagueness, it is always because of "external reasons." *External:* implying that conflict with other psychological forces is not involved here. And twenty years later, in *The Ego and the Id:* "The latent, which is unconscious only descriptively, not in the dynamic sense, we call *preconscious.*"[24]

Descriptive, not dynamic. It was undoubtedly this symbolic neutrality of the preconscious that very quickly made it boring to Freud (but not to us, who have had plenty of practice with boring things). I am thinking of one word in particular, the abracadabra of the stream of consciousness and of *Ulysses:* "Yes." The first and last word of Molly's monologue: the last in the book, then, but also the one that reopens it, carrying us back to the beginning of the chapter — or even to the beginning of the beginning, seeing that the last letter of "Yes" is likewise the first letter of "Stately," which is the first word of the first chapter . . . And since we are on the subject, let me add that "Yes" is the opposite of "No," and it places the Joycean stream of consciousness at the opposite pole from Freud's "negation." As Francesco Orlando would say, it makes it into a world with a "low figurality rate":[25] one in which nothing is forbidden, and there is therefore no need to mask anything. The prevalence of metonymy over metaphor is the rhetorical consequence of this state of affairs, supplemented — to complete the picture — by the role of the "insignificant" within the stream of consciousness.[26]

Lack of dynamism. Neutrality. Meaninglessness. Low figurality rate. Defects? I do not know. Perhaps so, for a symbolist aesthetics. But to a sociology of literary forms, this opaque limbo appears to be the ideal instrument for surviving in the big city. Therein, finally, lies the whole difference between Bloom and Biberkopf. Biberkopf is the man of the Id and the Superego: he takes everything dreadfully seriously, and so eventually snaps amid all the complications of Berlin. Bloom is the man of the preconscious, and he survives: receptive, tolerant, always able to recover. His rather banal wishes, with nothing illicit about them, will be boring for psychoanalysis, but not for advertising: which thrives precisely upon such lawful desires, which have nevertheless—due to "external reasons": lack of money, or time, or whatever—remained as yet "not dealt with." And finally the preconscious—ever open, and extendable at will—is the ideal space for the category that has underpinned this whole chapter: the space of the possible—*as possible.*

Stadtluft macht frei, runs an old German proverb: city air makes you free. Free from your own lord, it used to mean in its day. But today it seems instead to suggest: free as a breath of air, or a fantasy, can be. The billions of human beings who have ended up in big cities—have they really lived better? Hard to say. But they have *dreamed* better, of that I am sure. And the credit, if credit it is, goes to these: advertising, the stream of consciousness, the preconscious.

NOTES

1 "The past now is liberated from all restrictions of time and space, and so situations flow into one another elliptically, regaining the openness of outcome which they had been deprived of long ago in the past . . . Thus the past remembered suggests completely new combinations, and Molly's own life comes back to her with a surplus of possibilities . . ." (Wolfgang Iser, *The Implied Reader: Patterns of Communication in Prose Fiction from Bunyan to Beckett* [Baltimore: Johns Hopkins University Press, 1974], 224).

2 L. Spitzer, "Zum Stil Marcel Proust's" (1944), in *Stilstudien* 2 (Munich: Max Hueber Verlag, 1928), 420.

3 Ibid., 368.

4 The two different syntactical choices produce also two opposite representations of possibility. In Proust, possibility is expressed in the weakening of the main sentence by the subordinate clauses: it is an attenuation of certainty, a specification that branches out and relativizes. It is a possibility that speaks in the subjunctive: the verbal form that "limits the validity of assertions" (Weinrich), and evokes "insecurity and negation" (Vossler); that tends to "interiorize and sentimentalize sentences, burdening them with nostalgia, fear, doubt, and desire" (Spitzer). In Joyce, by contrast, the world of the possible is wholly in the indicative. Each clause is a direct assertion: perhaps mistaken, because Bloom makes every kind of blunder, but never weakened by doubt. The sense of the possible here relies upon a quantitative, even crude, fact: that the things mentioned are constantly increasing, in a never-ending addition in which everything is equivalent, clearly visible, in the foreground . . .

5 R. Barthes, "The Reality Effect," in *The Rustle of Language* (Berkeley: University of California Press, 1989), 146.

6 G. Debenedetti, *Il romanzo del Novecento* (Milan: Garzanti, 1981), 427, 295, 303 (notebooks dating from 1962–63 and 1963–64).

7 This idea of the ordinary/marvellous is very widespread at the beginning of the twenti-

eth century, from Rilke ("[Mother and I] had a different conception of the wonderful. To us, things that happened naturally would always be the most wonderful," *Notebooks of Malte Laurids Brigge*, Part One) to Woolf ("To be on a level with ordinary experience, to feel simply that's a chair, that's a table, and yet at the same time, It's a miracle, it's an ecstasy," *To the Lighthouse*, III, II). In the terms of Erich Heller's great hypothesis on modern poetry, it is as though all these authors harboured a very intense nostalgia for the miracle of the Eucharist—daily bread, divine presence—which is, moreover, the fairly obvious model for Proust's *madeleine*.

8   The first draft of this episode (the planned preface to *Contre Sainte-Beuve*) presents a far more homogeneous symbolic fabric—and perhaps this is just why Proust modified it. For the divergence between metonymy and metaphor is not just a sign of epiphany, it actually *is* epiphany: it accomplishes the vertical emergence of meaning from the horizontal world of prose.

9   I extrapolate these results from nine samplings which seem to me representative of the chapters as a whole (IV: lines 1–30, 111–39, 369–96; V: lines 27–59, 279–310, 510–41; VI: lines 1–28, 229–59; 995–1026). It should be added that while the internal stimuli remain fairly constant from one chapter to the next, the external ones change considerably in both quantity and quality (as is only logical, given their dependence upon the context). One of the most surprising facts about the survey is the minimal quantity (about one per cent) of stimuli connected with strong emotions: sign of an emotional neutrality that distinguishes the Joycean stream of consciousness from that of his contemporaries, and to which I shall return in the Excursus appended to this chapter. At the other extreme, the commonest datum (around thirty per cent of the total) is represented by miniature encyclopaedic "entries" crossing Bloom's mind, which indicate the close kinship between *Ulysses* and *Bouvard and Pécuchet*.

    In general, quantitative analysis might be an appropriate interpretive key for the "mechanical form" of the stream of consciousness. Where the whole is (almost only) the sum of the individual parts, doing the sum is always a good start.

10   E. Goffman, *Behaviour in Public Places* (Glencoe, N.Y.: Free Press, 1963).

11   T. W. Adorno, *Mahler*, trans. Edmund Jephcott (Chicago: University of Chicago Press, 1992), 88.

12   T. W. Adorno, *In Search of Wagner* (London: NLB, 1981), 43.

13   Ibid., 31. The fact that the advertising slogan remains engraved "like a Wagnerian *Leitmotiv*" had already been observed in 1911 by P. Raveau, "La Guerre à l'affiche," in *La Publicité*, May 1911 (quoted in Varnedoe and Gopnik, *High and Low*, 249).

14   E. Staiger, *Basic Concepts of Poetics*, trans. J. Hudson and L. Frank (Philadelphia: Pennsylvania State University Press, 1991), 102–3.

15   E. Said, *Orientalism* (Harmondsworth, U.K.: Penguin Books, 1985), 252.

16   In general, *Around the World in Eighty Days*, trans. Jacqueline Rogers (Harmondsworth, U.K.: Penguin Books, 1994) is a wonderful allegory of the nineteenth century: on the one hand, the economy and technology (or, more accurately, the pound sterling and the railway train), which help Fogg to complete his journey; on the other hand, politics and religion, which create every kind of obstacle for him. (The most perilous adventures, incidentally,

take place on the site of the 1857 Indian Mutiny, and in the central United States: in both cases, Englishmen against Indians, in the vicinity of a railway line.)

17 J. Culler, "The Semiotics of Tourism," in *Framing the Sign* (Oxford: Basil Blackwell, 1988), 167.

18 While checking the geographical references in the fifth and eighth chapters of *Ulysses*, I realized that commonplaces are more frequent in so far as the place mentioned is *more distant*—and, indeed, in so far as it is *more unknown*. The maximum scores are registered by Asia, of which we saw an example in the passage on the Belfast Tea Company, and Africa, which almost automatically evokes the thought of cannibals. The minimum scores are registered by Dublin and Ireland, to which Bloom usually reacts in a rather personalized way.

19 A. Gehlen, *Man: His Nature and Place in the World* 1950: reprint, (New York: Columbia University Press, 1988), 28.

20 That epiphany should be revealed by the *in*-significant had been Joyce's original insight, at the end of *Stephen Hero*; but it was probably too paradoxical an idea, and Joyce beat a rapid retreat, to devote himself (like Proust, or the surrealists) to the "deeply deep" epiphanies of *Portrait*. It is only with *Ulysses* that the meaningless returns to the centre of his work, to be represented *as meaningless*. An idea that critics have never much appreciated, nor perhaps understood: whence their vain attempts to save Joyce from himself, by attributing to *Ulysses* all manner of deep messages. But there are so many deep novels already, and the beauty of *Ulysses* is just the opposite . . .

21 S. Freud, *Introductory Lectures on Psychoanalysis*, trans. James Strachey (Harmondsworth, U.K.: Penguin Books, 1974), 136–7 (italics are mine).

22 S. Freud, *The Interpretation of Dreams*, trans. James Strachey (Harmondsworth, U.K.: Penguin Books, 1976), 659; *The Psychopathology of Everyday Life*, trans. Alan Tyson (Harmondsworth, U.K.: Penguin Books, 1975), 300–344.

23 Freud, *Interpretation of Dreams*, 702.

24 S. Freud, "The Ego and the Id," in *On Metapsychology: the Theory of Psychoanalysis*, trans. under the editorship of James Strachey (Harmondsworth, U.K.: Penguin Books, 1984), 353.

25 F. Orlando, *Towards a Freudian Theory of Literature*, trans. Charmaine Lee (Baltimore: Johns Hopkins University Press, 1978), 164.

26 When salvation appears on the horizon, I find myself confronted by a metaphor, and *I must* interpret it in a figurative sense, otherwise I shall fail to comprehend the phrase. But when a sail appears on the horizon, *I can* interpret the expression in a figurative sense (synechdoche for a ship), but I can also content myself with the literal sense of "sail." Texts dominated by metonymy thus usually possess a lower figurality rate than those dominated by metaphor.

16. To Move Without Moving:
An Analysis of Creativity and Commerce in
Ralph Ellison's Trueblood Episode
HOUSTON A. BAKER JR.

> Them boss quails is like a good man, what he got to do he *do.*
> —Trueblood

IN HIS ESSAY "Richard Wright's Blues," Ralph Ellison states one of his cherished distinctions: "The function, the psychology, of artistic selectivity is to eliminate from art form all those elements of experience which contain no compelling significance. Life is as the sea, art a ship in which man conquers life's crushing formlessness, reducing it to a course, a series of swells, tides and wind currents inscribed on a chart" (94).[1] The distinction between nonsignificant life experiences and their inscribed, artistic significance (i.e., the meaning induced by form) leads Ellison to concur with André Malraux that artistic significance alone "enables man to conquer chaos and to master destiny" (94).

Artistic "technique," according to Ellison, is the agency through which artistic meaning and form are achieved. In "Hidden Name and Complex Fate" he writes:

> It is a matter of outrageous irony, perhaps, but in literature the great social clashes of history no less than the painful experience of the individual are secondary to the meaning which they take on through the skill, the talent, the imagination and personal vision of the writer who transforms them into art. Here they are reduced to more manageable proportions; here they are imbued with humane value; here, injustice and catastrophe become less important in themselves than what the writer makes of them (148–49).

Even the thing-in-itself of lived, historical experience is thus seen as devoid of "humane value" before its sea change under the artist's transforming technique.

Since Ellison focuses his interest on the literary, the inscribed, work of art, he regards even folklore as part of that realm of life "elements . . . which contain no compelling significance" in themselves. In "Change the Joke and Slip the Yoke," he asserts:

> . . . the Negro American writer is also an heir to the human experience which is literature, and this might well be more important to him than his living folk tradition. For me, at least, in the discontinuous, swiftly changing and diverse American culture, the stability of the Negro folk tradition became precious as a result of an act of literary discovery. . . . For those who are able to translate [the folk tradition's] meanings into wider, more precise vocabularies it has much to offer indeed. (72–73)

During a BBC program recorded in May 1982 and entitled "Garrulous Ghosts: The Literature of the American South," Ellison stated that the fiction writer, to achieve proper resonance, must go beyond the blues—a primary and tragically eloquent form of American expression:

> The blues are very important to me. I think of them as the closest approach to tragedy that we have in American art forms. And I'm not talking about black or white, I mean just American. Because they do combine the tragic and the comic in a very subtle way and, yes, they are very important to me. But they are also limited. And if you are going to write fiction there is a level of consciousness which you move toward which I would think transcends the blues.

Thus Ellison seems to regard Afro-American folklore, before its translation into "more precise vocabularies," as part of lived experience. Art and chaos appear to be homologous with literature and folklore.

To infer such a homology from one or two critical remarks, however, is to risk the abyss of "false distinction," especially when one is faced with a canon as rich as Ralph Ellison's. For it is certainly true that the disparagement of folk expression suggested by these remarks can be qualified by the praise of folklore implicit in Ellison's assertion that Afro-American expressive folk projections are a group's symbolically "profound" attempts to "humanize" the world ("The Art of Fiction: An Interview," 172). Such projections, even in their crudest forms, constitute the "humble base" on which "great literature" is erected (172).

It does seem accurate, however, to say that Ellison's criticism repeatedly implies an extant, identifiable tradition of Western literary art—a tradition consisting of masters of form and technique who must be read, studied, emulated, and (if one is lucky and eloquent) equaled. This tradition stands as the signal, vital repository of "humane value." And for Ellison the sphere that it describes is equivalent to the primum mobile, lending force and significance to all actions of the descending heavens and earth.

Hence, while the division between folk and artistic may be only discursive, having no more factual reality than any other such division, it seems to matter to Ellison, who, as far as I know, never refers to himself as a folk artist. Moreover, in our era of sophisticated "folkloristics," it seems mere evasion to shy from the assertion that Ellison's criticism ranks folklore below literary art on a total scale of value. What I argue is that the distinction between folklore and literary art evident in Ellison's critical practice collapses in his creative practice in the *Invisible Man's* Trueblood episode. Further, I suggest that an exacting analysis of this episode illuminates the relation not only between Ellison's critical and creative practices but also between what might be called the public and private commerce of black art in America.

The main character in the Trueblood episode, which occupies chapter two of *Invisible Man*, is both a country blues singer (a tenor of "crude, high, plaintively animal sounds") and a virtuoso prose narrator. To understand the disjunctiveness between Ellison's somewhat disparaging critical pronouncements on "raw" folklore and his striking fictional representation of the folk character, one must first comprehend, I think, the sharecropper Trueblood's dual manifestation as trickster and merchant, as creative and commercial man. Blues and narration, as modes of expression, conjoin and divide in harmony with these dichotomies. And the episode in its entirety is—as I demonstrate—a metaexpressive commentary on the incumbencies of Afro-American artists and the effects of their distinctive modes of expression.

In an essay that gives a brilliant ethnographic "reading" of the Balinese cockfight, the symbolic anthropologist Clifford Geertz asserts:

Like any art form—for that, finally, is what we are dealing with—the cockfight renders ordinary, everyday experience comprehensible by presenting it in terms of acts and objects which have had their practical consequences removed and been reduced (or, if you prefer, raised) to the level of sheer appearances, where their meaning can be more powerfully articulated and more exactly perceived. (443)

Catching up the themes of Balinese society in symbolic form, the cockfight thus represents, in Geertz's words, "a metasocial commentary . . . a Balinese reading of Balinese experience, a story they tell themselves about themselves" (448).

The anthropologist's claims imply that the various symbolic (or "semiotic") systems of a culture—religion, politics, economics—can themselves be "raised" to a metasymbolic level by the orderings and processes of "ritual interactions" like the Balinese cockfight.

The coming together of semiotic systems in ways that enlarge and enhance the world of human meanings is the subject of Barbara Babcock-Abrahams's insightful essay "The Novel and the Carnival World." Following the lead of Julia Kristeva, Babcock-Abrahams asserts that a "metalanguage" is a symbolic system that treats of symbolic systems; for example, *Don Quixote* "openly discusses other works of literature and takes the writing and reading of literature as its subject" (912). Both social rituals and novels, since they "embed" other semiotic systems within their "texture," are "multivocal," "polyvalent," or "polysemous"—that is, capable of speaking in a variety of mutually reflexive voices at once.

The multiple narrative frames and voices operative in Ellison's Trueblood episode include the novel *Invisible Man*, the protagonist's fictive autobiographical account, Norton's story recalled as part of the fictive autobiography, Trueblood's story as framed by the fictive autobiography, the sharecropper's own autobiographical recall, and the dream narrative within that autobiographical recall. All these stories reflect, or "objectify," one another in ways that complicate their individual and composite meanings. Further, the symbolic systems suggested by the stories are not confined to (though they may implicitly comment on) such familiar social configurations as education, economics, politics, and religion. Subsuming these manifestations is the outer symbolic enterprise constituted by the novel itself. Moreover, the Trueblood episode heightens the multivocalic character of the novel from within, acting as a metacommentary on the literary and artistic system out of which the work is generated. Further enriching the burden of meanings in the episode is the Christian myth of the Fall and Sigmund Freud's mythic "narrative" concerning incest, which are both connoted (summoned as signifiers, in Babcock-Abrahams's terms) and parodied, or inverted. I analyze the text's play on these myths later in my discussion.

For the moment, I am primarily interested in suggesting that the Trueblood episode, like other systematic symbolic phenomena, gains and generates its meanings in a dialogic relation with various systems of signs. The sharecropper chapter as a text derives its logic from its intertextual relation with surrounding and encompassing texts and, in turn, complicates their meanings. The Balinese cockfight, according to Geertz, can only tell a "metastory" because it is intertextually implicated in a world that is itself constituted by a repertoire of "stories" (e.g., those of economics and politics) that the Balinese tell themselves.

As a story that the author of *Invisible Man* tells himself about his own practice, the Trueblood episode clarifies distinctions that must be made between Ellison as critic and Ellison as artist. To elucidate its metaexpressive function, one must summon analytical instruments from areas that Ellison sharply debunks in his own criticism.

For example, at the outset of "The World and the Jug," a masterfully instructive essay on the criticism of Afro-American creativity, Ellison asks:

> Why is it so often true that when critics confront the American as *Negro* they suddenly drop their advanced critical armament and revert with an air of confident superiority to quite primitive modes of analysis? Why is it that sociology-oriented critics seem to rate literature so far below politics and ideology that they would rather kill a novel than modify their presumptions concerning a given reality which it seeks in its own terms to project? (115–16)

What I take these questions to imply is that a given artistic reality designed to represent "Negro American" experience should not be analyzed by "primitive" methods, which Ellison leaves unspecified but seems to associate with sociological, ideological, and political modes of analysis. In the following discussion I hope to demonstrate that sociology, anthropology, economics, politics, and ideology all provide models essential for the explication of the Trueblood episode. The first step, however, is to evoke the theater of Trueblood's performance.

Trueblood's narration has an unusual audience, but to the farmer and his Afro-American cohorts the physical setting is as familiar as train whistles in the Alabama night. The sharecropper, a white millionaire, and a naive undergraduate from a nearby black college have arranged themselves in a semicircle of camp chairs in the sharecropper's yard. They occupy a swath of shade cast by the porch of a log cabin that has survived since the days of slavery, enduring hard times and the ravages of climate. The millionaire asks, "How are you faring now? . . . Perhaps I could help." The sharecropper responds, "We ain't doing so bad, suh. 'Fore they heard 'bout what happen to us out here I couldn't get no help from nobody. Now lotta folks is curious and go outta their way to help" (52). What has occurred "out here"—in what the millionaire Mr. Norton refers to as "new territory for me" (45) and what the narrator describes as "a desert" that "almost took [his] breath away" (45)—is Jim Trueblood's impregnation of both his wife and his daughter. The event has brought disgrace on the sharecropper and has mightily embarrassed officials at the nearby black college.

The whites in the neighboring town and countryside, however, are scarcely outraged or perturbed by Trueblood's situation. Rather, they want to keep the sharecropper among them; they warn the college officials not to harass him or his family, and they provide money, provisions, and abundant work. "White folks," says Trueblood, even "took to coming out here to see us and talk with us. Some of 'em was big white folks, too, from the big school way cross the State. Asked me lots 'bout what I thought 'bout things, and 'bout my folks and the kids, and wrote it all down in a book" (53). Hence, when the farmer begins to recount the story of his incestuous act with his daughter Matty Lou, he does so as a man who has thoroughly rehearsed his tale and who has carefully refined his knowledge of his audience: "He cleared his throat, his eyes gleaming and his voice taking on a deep, incantatory quality, as though he had told the story many, many times" (53).

The art of storytelling is not a gift that Trueblood has acquired recently. He is introduced in *Invisible Man* as one who "told the old stories with a sense of humor and a magic that made them come alive" (46). A master storyteller, then, he recounts his provocative exploits to an audience that is by turns shamed, indignant, envious, humiliated, and enthralled.

The tale begins on a cold winter evening in the sharecropper's cabin. The smell of fat meat hangs in the air, and the last kindling crackles in the dying flames of the stove. Trueblood's daughter, in bed between her father and mother, sleepily whispers, "Daddy." At the story's close, the sharecropper reports his resolution to prevent Aunt Cloe the midwife from aborting his incestuous issue. At the conclusion of his tale, he reiterates his judgment that he and his family "ain't doing so bad" in the wake of their ordeal.

Certainly the content and mode of narration the sharecropper chooses reflect his knowledge of what a white audience expects of the Afro-American. Mr. Norton is not only a "teller of polite Negro stories" (37) but also a man who sees nothing unusual about the pregnant Matty Lou's not having a husband. "But that shouldn't be so strange," he remarks (49). The white man's belief in the promiscuity of blacks is further suggested by Mr. Broadnax, the figure in Trueblood's dream who looks at the sharecropper and his daughter engaged in incest and says, "They just nigguhs, leave 'em do it" (58). In conformity with audience expectations, the sharecropper's narrative is aggressively sexual in its representations.

Beginning with an account of the feel of his daughter's naked arm pressed against him in bed, the farmer proceeds to reminisce about bygone days in Mobile when he would lie in bed in the evenings with a woman named Margaret and listen to the music from steamboats passing on the river. Next, he introduces the metaphor of the woman in a red dress "goin' past you down a lane . . . and kinda switchin' her tail 'cause she knows you watchin'" (56). From this evocative picture, he turns to a detailed account of his dream on the night of his incestuous act.

The dream is a parodic allegory in which Trueblood goes in quest of "fat meat." In this episode the name "Mr. Broadnax" (Mr. Broad-in-acts) captures the general concepts that mark any narrative as allegory. The man whose house is on the hill is a philanthropist who gives poor blacks (true bloods) sustaining gifts as "fat meat." The model implied by this conceptualization certainly fits one turn-of-the-century American typology, recalling the structural arrangement by which black southern colleges were able to sustain themselves. In one sense, the entire Trueblood episode can be read as a pejorative commentary on the castrating effects of white philanthropy. Trueblood's dream narrative is parodic because it reveals the crippling assumptions (the castrating import) of the philanthropic model suggested in "Broadnax." The man who is broad-in-acts in the dream is the one who refers to the sharecropper and his daughter as "just nigguhs." Further, his philanthropy—like Mr. Norton's—has a carnal undercurrent: it is dangerously and confusingly connected with the sexuality of Mrs. Broadnax. What he dispenses as sustaining "fat meat" may only be the temporarily satisfying thrill of sexual gratification. The "pilgrim," or quester, in Trueblood's dream allegory flees from the dangers and limitations of such deceptive philanthropy. And the general exposé effected by the narrative offers a devastating critique of that typography which saw white men on the hill (northern industrialists) as genuinely and philanthropically responsive to the needs of those in the valley (southern blacks).

Instructed to inquire at Mr. Broadnax's house, Trueblood finds himself violating a series of southern taboos and fleeing for his life. He enters the front door of the home, wanders into a woman's bedroom, and winds up trapped in the embraces of a scantily clad white woman. The gastronomic and sexual appetites surely converge at this juncture, and the phrase "fat meat" takes on a dangerous burden of significance. The dreamer breaks free, however, and escapes into the darkness and machinery of a grandfather clock. He runs until a bright electric light bursts over him, and he awakens to find himself engaged in sexual intercourse with his daughter.

In *Totem and Taboo*, Freud advances the hypothesis that the two taboos of totemism—the interdictions against slaying the totem animal and against incest—result from events in human prehistory (141–46).[2] Following Darwin's speculations, Freud claims that human beings first lived in small hordes in which one strong, jealous man took all women to himself, exiling the sons to protect his own exclusive sexual privileges. On one occasion, however, Freud suggests, the exiled sons arose, slew, and ate the father, and then, in remorse, established the taboo against such slaughter. To prevent discord among themselves and to ensure their newly achieved form of social organization, they also established a taboo against sexual intercourse with the women of their own clan. Exogamy, Freud concludes, is based on a prehistorical advance from a lower to a higher stage of social organization.

From Freud's point of view, Trueblood's dream and subsequent incest seem to represent a historical regression. The sharecropper's dreamed violations of southern social and sexual taboos are equivalent to a slaughter of the white patriarch represented by Mr. Broadnax, who does, indeed, control the "fat" and "fat meat" of the land. To eat fat meat is to partake of the totemic animal. And having run backward in time through the grandfather clock, Trueblood becomes the primal father, assuming all sexual prerogatives unto himself. He has warned away "the boy" (representing the tumultuous mob of exiled sons) who wanted to take away his daughter, and as the sexual partner of both Matty Lou and Kate, he reveals his own firm possession of all his "womenfolks"—his status, that is to say, as a sexual producer secure against the wrath of his displaced "sons." Insofar as Freud's notions of totemism represent a myth of progressive social evolution, the farmer's story acts as a countermyth of inversive social dissolution. It breaks society down into components and reveals man in what might be called his presocial and unaccommodated state.

One reason for the sharecropper's singular sexual prerogatives is that the other Afro-Americans in his area are either so constrained or so battered by their encounters with society that they are incapable of a legitimate and productive sexuality. The sharecropper's territory is bounded on one side by the black college where the "sons" are indoctrinated in a course of instruction that leaves them impotent. On the other side lie the insane asylum and the veterans' home, residences of black men driven mad—or at least rendered psychologically and physically crippled—by their encounters with America. These "disabled veterans" are scarcely "family men" like Trueblood. Rather, they are listless souls who visit the whores in "the sun-shrunk shacks at the railroad crossing . . . hobbling down the tracks on crutches and canes; sometimes pushing the legless, thighless one in a red wheelchair" (35). In such male company Trueblood seems the only person capable of ensuring an authentic Afro-American lineage. When he finds himself atop Matty Lou, therefore, both the survival of the clan and the sharecropper's aversion to pain require him to reject the fate that has been physically or psychologically imposed on his male cohorts. He says, "There was only one way I can figger that I could git out: that was with a knife. But I didn't have no knife, and if you'all ever seen them geld them young boar pigs in the fall, you know I knowed that was too much to pay to keep from sinnin'" (59). In this reflection, he brings forward one of the dominant themes of *Invisible Man*. This theme—one frequently slighted, or omitted, in discussions of the novel— is black male sexuality.

Perhaps critical prudery prevents commentators from acknowledging the black male phallus as a dominant symbol in much of the ritual interaction of *Invisible Man*. In *The Forest of Symbols: Aspects of Ndembu Ritual*, the symbolic anthropologist Victor Turner provides suggestive definitions for both "ritual" and "dominant symbols." He describes ritual as "prescribed formal behavior for occasions not given over to technological routine, having reference to beliefs in mystical beings or powers. The symbol is the smallest unit of ritual which still retains the specific properties of ritual behavior; it is the ultimate unit of specific structure in a ritual context" (19). For Turner, the most prominent—the "senior," as it were—symbols in any ritual are dominant symbols (20); they fall into a class of their own. The important characteristic of such symbols is that they bring together disparate meanings, serving as a kind of condensed semiotic shorthand. Further, they can have both ideological and sensuous associations; the mudyi tree of Ndembu ritual, for example, refers both to the breast milk of the mother and to the axiomatic values of the matrilineal Ndembu society (28).

Ellison's *Invisible Man* is certainly an instance of "prescribed formal behavior" insofar as the novel is governed by the conventions of the artistic system in which it is situated, a system that resides ludically outside "technological routine" and promotes the cognitive exploration of all systems of "being" and "power," whether mystical or not. The black phallus is a dominant symbol in the novel's formal patterns of behavior, as its manifold recurrence attests. In "The Art of Fiction: An Interview," Ellison writes, "People rationalize what they shun or are incapable of dealing with; these superstitions and their rationalizations become rituals as they govern behavior. The rituals become social forms, and it is one of the functions of the artist to recognize them and raise them to the level of art" (175).

Stated in slightly different terms, Ellison's comment suggests an intertextual (indeed, a connoted) relation between the prescribed formal social behaviors of American racial interaction and the text of the novel. Insofar as Jim Crow social laws and the desperate mob exorcism of lynchings (with their attendant castrations) describe a formal pattern of Anglo-American behavior toward black men, this pattern offers an instance of ritual in which the black phallus gathers an extraordinary burden of disparate connotations, both sensuous and ideological. It should come as no surprise that an artist as perceptive as Ellison recognizes the black phallus as a dominant symbol of the sometimes bizarre social rituals of America and incorporates it into the text of a novel. In "The Art of Fiction," in fact, Ellison calls the battle-royal episode of *Invisible Man* "a ritual in preservation of caste lines, a keeping of taboo to appease the gods and ward off bad luck" (175). He did not have to invent the ritual, he says; all he had to do was to provide "a broader context of meaning" for the patterns the episode represents.

The black phallus, then, does seem an implicit major symbol in Ellison's text, and, prudery aside, there are venerable precedents for the discussion of male sexual symbols in ritual. For example, in "Deep Play" Geertz writes:

> To anyone who has been in Bali any length of time, the deep psychological identification of Balinese men with their cocks is unmistakable. The double entendre here is deliberate. It works in exactly the same way in Balinese as it does in English, even to producing the same tired jokes, strained puns, and uninventive obscenities. [Gregory] Bateson and [Margaret] Mead have even suggested that, in line with the Balinese conception of the body as a set of separately animated parts, cocks are viewed as detachable, self-operating penises, ambulent genitals with a life of their own. (417)

Certainly the notion of "ambulent genitals" figures in the tales of the roguish trickster recorded in Paul Radin's classic work *The Trickster*. In tale 16 of the Winnebago trickster cycle, Wakdjunkaga the trickster sends his penis across the waters of a lake to have intercourse with a chief's daughter.

The black phallus as a symbol of unconstrained force that white men contradictorily envy and seek to destroy appears first in the opening chapter of *Invisible Man*. The influential white men of a small southern town force the protagonist and his fellow black boxers in the battle royal to gaze on "a magnificent blonde—stark naked" (18). The boys are threatened both for looking and for not looking, and the white men smile at their obvious fear and discomfiture. The boys know the bizarre consequences that accompany the white men's ascription of an animallike and voracious sexuality to black males. Hence, they respond in biologically normal but socially fearful (and justifiably embarrassed) ways. One boy strives to hide his erection with his boxing gloves, pleading desperately to go home. In this opening scene, the white woman as a parodic version of American ideals ("a small American flag tattooed upon her belly" [19]) is forced into tantalizing interaction with the mythically potent force of the black phallus. But because the town's white males exercise total control of the situation, the scene is akin to a castration, excision, or lynching.

Castration is one function of the elaborate electrically wired glass box that incarcerates the protagonist in the factory-hospital episode: "'Why not castration, doctor?' a voice asked waggishly" (231). In the Brotherhood, the class struggle is rather devastatingly transformed into the "ass struggle" when the protagonist's penis displaces his oratory as ideological agent. A white woman who hears him deliver a speech and invites him home seizes his biceps passionately and says, "Teach me, talk to me. Teach me the beautiful ideology of Brotherhood" (405). And the protagonist admits that suddenly he "was lost" as "the conflict between the ideological and the biological, duty and desire," became too subtly confused (406). Finally, in the nightmare that concludes the novel, the invisible man sees his own bloody testes, like those of the castrated Uranus of Greek myth, floating above the waters underneath a bridge's high arc (557). In the dream, he tells his inquisitors that his testes dripping blood on the black waters are not only his "generations wasting upon the water" but also the "sun" and the "moon"—and, indeed, the very "world"—of his own human existence (558). The black phallus—in its creative, ambulent, generative power, even when castrated—is like the cosmos itself, a self-sustaining and self-renewing source of life, provoking both envy and fear in Anglo-American society.

While a number of episodes in *Invisible Man* (including Trueblood's dream) suggest the illusory freedoms and taboo-induced fears accompanying interaction between the black phallus and white women, only the Trueblood encounter reveals the phallus as indeed producing Afro-American generations rather than wasting its seed upon the waters. The cosmic force of the phallus thus becomes, in the ritual action of the Trueblood episode, symbolic of a type of royal paternity, an aristocratic procreativity turned inward to ensure the royalty (the truth, legitimacy, or authenticity) of an enduring black line of descent. In his outgoing phallic energy, therefore, the sharecropper is (as we learn on his first appearance in *Invisible Man*) indeed a "hard worker" who takes care of "his family's needs" (46). His family may, in a very real sense, be construed as the entire clan, or tribe, of Afro-America.

As cosmic creator, Trueblood is not bound by ordinary codes of restraint. He ventures chaos in an outrageously sexual manner—and survives. Like the Winnebago trickster Wakdjunkaga, he offers an inversive play on social norms. He is the violator of boundaries who—unlike the scapegoat—eludes banishment.[3] Indeed, he is so essential to whites in his sexual role that, after demonstrating his enviable ability to survive chaos, he and his family acquire new clothes and shoes, abundant food and work, long-needed eyeglasses, and even the means to reshingle their cabin. "I looks up at the mornin' sun," says the farmer, describing the aftermath of his incestuous act, "and expects somehow for it to thunder. But it's already bright and clear. . . . I yells, 'Have mercy, Lawd!'" and waits. And there's nothin' but the clear bright mornin' sun" (64–65).

Noting that most tricksters "have an uncertain sexual status," Victor Turner points out that on some occasions "tricksters appear with exaggerated phallic characteristics: Hermes is symbolized by the herm or pillar, the club, and the ithyphallic statue; Wakdjunkaga has a very long penis which has to be wrapped around him and put over his shoulder in a box; Eshu is represented in sculpture as having a long curved hairdress carved as a phallus" ("Myth," 580). Such phallic figures are, for Turner, representatives par excellence of what he calls "liminality" (*Forest*, 93–112). Liminality describes that "betwixt and between" phase of rites of passage when an individual has left one fixed social status and has not yet been incorporated into another. When African boys are secluded in the forest during circumcision rites, for example, they are in a liminal phase between childhood and adulthood. They receive, during this seclusion, mythic instruction in the origin and structures of their society. And this instruction serves not only to "deconstruct" the components of the ordered social world they have left behind but also to reveal these elements recombined into new and powerful composites. The phallic trickster aptly represents the duality of this process. In his radically antinomian activities—incest, murder, and the destruction of sacred property—he symbolically captures what Turner describes as the "amoral and nonlogical" rhythms and outcomes of human biology and of meteorological climate: that is, the uncontrollable rhythms of nature ("Myth," 577). But the trickster is also a cultural gift bearer. Turner emphasizes that "the Winnebago trickster transforms the pieces of his broken phallus into plants and flowers for men" ("Myth," 580). Hermes enriches human culture with dreams and music. In a sense, therefore, the phallic trickster is a force that is, paradoxically, both anticonventional and culturally benevolent. The paradox is dissolved in the definition of the trickster as the "*prima materia*—as undifferentiated raw material" from which all things derive (*Forest*, 98). Trueblood's sexual energies, antinomian acts, productive issue, and resonant expressivity make him—in his incestuous, liminal moments and their immediate aftermath—the quintessential trickster.

In his sexual manifestation, Ellison's sharecropper challenges not only the mundane restraints of his environment but also the fundamental Judeo-Christian categories on which they are founded. As I have already noted, he quickly abandons the notion of the knife—of casting out, in Mr. Norton's indignant (and wonderfully ironic) phrase, "the offending eye." His virtual parodies

of the notions of sin and sacrifice lend comic point to his latitudinarian challenge to Christian orthodoxy. When his wife brings the sharpened ax down on
his head, Trueblood recalls, "I sees it, Lawd, yes! I sees it and seein' it it twists
my head aside. Couldn't help it . . . I moves. Though I meant to keep still, I
moves! Anybody but Jesus Christ hisself woulda moved" (63). So much for re-
pentance and salvation through the bloody sacrifice of one's life. But Trueblood
goes on to indicate why such sacrifice may not have been required of him: with
the skill of a revisionist theologian, he distinguishes between "blood-sin" and
"dream-sin" (62) and claims, with unshakable certainty, that only the dream of
his encounter at the Broadnax household led to his sexual arousal and subsequent incest.

But while this casuistic claim suffices in the farmer's interaction with the
social world, his earlier appraisal of the event suggests his role as a cosmically
rebellious trickster. He says that when he awoke to discover himself atop Matty
Lou, he felt that the act might not be sinful, because it happened in his sleep.
But then he adds, ". . . although maybe sometimes a man can look at a little
old pigtail gal and see him a whore" (59). The naturalness, and the natural unpredictability, of sexual arousal implied by "although" seems more in keeping
with the sharecropper's manifestation as black phallic energy.

Trueblood's sexual energies are not without complement in the arid regions where the sharecropper and his family eke out their existence. His wife,
Kate, is an awesome force of both new life and outgoing socioreligious fury. His
yard is filled with the children she has borne, and his oldest child, Matty Lou,
is Kate's double—a woman fully grown and sexually mature who looks just like
her mother. Kate and Matty Lou—both moving with the "full-fronted motions
of far-gone pregnancy" (47)—are the first human figures that Mr. Norton sees
as he approaches the Trueblood property. The two bearers of new black life are
engaged in a rite of purification, a workaday ritual of washing clothes in a huge
boiling cauldron, which takes on significance as the men situate themselves in
a semicircle near the porch where the "earth . . . was hard and white from where
wash water had long been thrown" (51). In a sense the women (who flee behind
the house at Norton's approach) are present, by ironic implication, as the sharecropper once more confessionally purges himself—as he, in vernacular terms,
again "washes his dirty linen" before a white audience. Further, Matty Lou, as
the object of Trueblood's incestuous desire, and Kate, as the irate agent of his
punishment for fulfilling his desire, assume significant roles in his narrative.

The reversal of a traditional Freudian typology represented by Trueblood's
dream encounter at the Broadnax Big House is reinforced by an implied parody of the Christian myth of the Fall.[4] For if the white Mrs. Broadnax serves

as the temptress Eve in the dream, then Matty Lou becomes an ersatz Eve, the paradoxical recipient of the farmer's lust. Similarly, if Mr. Broadnax—an inhabitant of the sanctuary-like precincts of a house of "lighted candles and shiny furniture, and pictures on the walls, and soft stuff on the floor"—is the avenging father, or patriarch, of the dream, then the matriarchal Kate replaces him in exacting vengeance. The "fall" of Trueblood is thus enacted on two planes—on a dream level of Christian myth and on a quotidian level of southern black actuality. In its most intensely conscious and secular interpretation, the incestuous act is a rank violation that drives Kate to blind and murderous rage: "I heard Kate scream. It was a scream to make your blood run cold. It sounds like a woman who was watching a team of wild horses run down her baby chile and she caint move. . . . She screams and starts to pickin' up the first thing that comes to her hand and throwin' it" (61).

The "doubleness" of Kate and Matty Lou is felt in the older woman's destructive and avenging energies, which elevate her to almost legendary proportions. Her woman's wrath at the sharecropper's illicit violation of "my chile!" spirals, inflating Kate to the metaphorical stature of an implacable executioner: "Then I sees her right up on me, big. She's swingin' her arms like a man swingin' a ten-pound sledge and I sees the knuckles of her hand is bruised and bleedin . . . and I sees her swing and I smells her sweat and . . . I sees that ax" (63). Trueblood tries to forestall Kate's punishing blow but, he says, he "might as well been pleadin' with a switch engine" (63). The ax falls, and the farmer receives the wound whose blood spills on Matty Lou. The wound becomes the "raw and moist" scar the protagonist notices when he first moves "up close" on the sharecropper (50).

Kate becomes not only an awesome agent of vengeance in the sharecropper's account but also the prime mover of the parodic ritual drama enacted in the chilly southern cabin. It is Kate's secular rage that results in the substitute castration-crucifixion represented by Trueblood's wound. She is the priestess who bestows the scarifying lines of passage, of initiation—the marks that forever brand the farmer as a "dirty lowdown wicked dog" (66). At her most severe, she is the moral, or socioreligious, agent of both Trueblood's "marking" and his exile. She banishes him from the community that rallies to support her in her sorrow. In keeping with her role as purifier—as supervisor of the wash—she cleans up the pollution, and dirt and danger, represented by Trueblood's taboo act.

It is important to bear in mind, however, that while Kate is a figure of moral outrage, she is also a fertile woman who, like her husband, provides "cultural gifts" in the form of new life. In her family manifestation, she is less a secular agent of moral justice than a sensitive, practical parent who turns away in sick disgust at the wound she inflicts on Trueblood. And though she first banishes the farmer, she also accepts his return, obeys his interdiction against abortions for herself and Matty Lou, and welcomes the material gains that ironically accrue after Trueblood's fall from grace. The sharecropper says, "Except that my wife an' daughter won't speak to me, I'm better off than I ever been before. And even if Kate won't speak to me she took the new clothes I brought her from up in town and now she's gettin' some eyeglasses made what she been needin' for so long" (67).

As a woman possessed of a practical (one might say a "blues") sensibility, Kate knows that men are, indeed, sometimes "dirty lowdown wicked" dogs who can perceive a whore in a pigtailed girl. She is scarcely resigned to such a state of affairs where her own daughter is concerned, but like the black mother so aptly described in Carolyn Rodgers's poem "It Is Deep," Kate knows that being "religiously girdled in her god" (11) will not pay the bills. She thus brings together the sacred and the secular, the moral and the practical, in a manner that makes her both a complement for Trueblood and (again in the words of Rodgers) a woman who "having waded through a storm, is very obviously, a sturdy Black bridge" (12).

To freight Trueblood's sexual manifestation and its complement in Kate with more significance than they can legitimately bear would be as much a critical disservice as were previous failures, or refusals, even to acknowledge these aspects. For while it is true that sexuality burdens the content of his narrative, it is also true that Trueblood himself metaphorically transforms his incestuous act into a single, symbolic instance of his total life situation: "There I was [atop Matty Lou] trying to git away with all my might, yet having to move *without* movin'. I flew in but I had to walk out. I had to move without movin'. I done thought 'bout it since a heap, and when you think right hard you see that that's the way things is always been with me. That's just about been my life" (59).

Like the formidable task of the invisible man's grandfather, who gave up his gun during the Reconstruction but still had to fight a war, Trueblood's problem is that of getting out of a tight spot without undue motion—without perceptibly moving. The grandfather adopted a strategy of extrication by indirection, pretending to affirm the designs of the dominant white society around him. Having relinquished his gun, he became "a spy in the enemy's country," a man overcoming his adversaries with yeses. He represents the trickster as subtle deceiver. Trueblood, in contrast, claims that to "move without movin'" means to take a refractory situation uncompromisingly in hand: "You got holt to it," he says, "and you caint let go even though you want to" (60). He conceives of himself in the throes of his incestuous ecstasies as "like that fellow . . . down in Birmingham. That one what locked hisself in his house and shot [with a gun that he had *refused to give up*] at them police until they set fire to the house and burned him up. I was lost" (60). An energetic, compulsive, even ecstatically expressive response is required:

> Like that fellow [in Birmingham], I stayed . . . He mighta died, but I suspects now that he got a heapa satisfaction before he went. I *know* there ain't nothin' like what I went through, I caint tell how it was. It's like when a real drinkin' man gets drunk, or like a real sanctified religious woman gits so worked up she jumps outta her clothes, or when a real gamblin' man keeps on gamblin' when he's losing. (60)

In his energetic response, Trueblood says a resounding no to all the castratingly tight spots of his existence as a poor black farmer in the undemocratic South.[5]

The most discursively developed *expressive* form of this no is, of course, the narrative that Trueblood relates. But he has come to this narrative by way of music. He has fasted and reflected on his guilt or innocence until he thinks his "brain go'n bust," and then, he recalls, "one night, way early in the mornin', I looks up and sees the stars and I starts singin'. I don't know what it was, some kinda church song, I guess. All I know is I *ends up* singin' the blues. I sings me some blues that night ain't never been sang before" (65–66). The first unpremeditated expression that Trueblood summons is a religious song. But the religious system that gives birth to the song is, presumably, one in which the term "incest" carries pejorative force. Hence, the sharecropper moves on, spontaneously, to the blues.

In *The Legacy of the Blues*, Samuel Charters writes: "Whatever else the blues was it was a language: a rich, vital, expressive language that stripped away the misconception that the black society in the United States was simply a poor, discouraged version of the white. It was impossible not to hear the differences. No one could listen to the blues without realizing that there are two Americas" (22). On the origins of this blues language, Giles Oakley quotes the blues singer Booker White: "You want to know where did the blues come from. The blues come from behind the mule. Well now, you can have the blues sitting at the table eating. But the foundation of the blues is walking behind the mule way back in slavery time" (7). The language that Trueblood summons to contain his act grows out of the soil he works, a soil that has witnessed the unrecompensed labor of many thousand blacks walking "behind the mule," realizing, as they negotiated the long furrows, the absurdity of working from "can-to-caint" for the profit of others.

Born on a farm in Alabama and working, at the time of his incestuous act, as an impoverished, cold, poorly provisioned sharecropper, Trueblood has the inherent blues capacity of a songster like Lightnin' Hopkins, who asserts, "I had the one thing you need to be a blues singer. I was born with the blues" (Charters 183). Originating in the field hollers and work songs of the agrarian South and becoming codified as stable forms by the second decade of the twentieth century, the blues offer a language that connotes a world of transience, instability, hard luck, brutalizing work, lost love, minimal security, and enduring human wit and resourcefulness in the face of disaster. The blues enjoin one to accept hard luck because, without it, there is "no luck at all." The lyrics are often charged with a surreal humor that wonders if "a match box will hold my clothes." In short, the "other America" that they signal is a world of common labor, spare circumstances, and grimly lusty lyrical challenges to a bleak fate.

In the system of the blues Trueblood finds the meet symbolic code for expressing the negativity of his own act. Since he is both a magical storyteller and a blues singer par excellence, he can incorporate the lean economics and fateful intransience of the blues world into his autobiographical narrative. His metaphorical talent, which transforms a steamboat's musicians into a boss quail's whistle and then likens the actions of the quail to those of a good man who "do" what he "got to do," reflects a basic understanding of the earthy resonances of blues. He says of his evenings listening to boats in Mobile:

> They used to have musicianers on them boats, and sometimes I used to wake her [Margaret] up to hear the music when they come up the river. I'd be layin' there and it would be quiet and I could hear it comin' from way, way off. Like when you quail huntin' and it's getting dark and you can hear the boss bird whistlin' tryin' to get the covey together again, and he's coming toward you slow and whistlin' soft, 'cause he knows you somewhere around with your gun. Still he got to round them up, so he keeps on comin'. Them boss quails is like a good man, what he got to do he *do*. (55)

Further, the farmer begins his story by describing his desperate economic straits, like those frequently recorded in blues—that is, no wood for fuel and no work or aid to be found (53)—and then traces the outcome of his plight. Matty Lou is in bed with her mother and father because it is freezing: "It was so cold all of us had to sleep together; me, the ole lady and the gal. That's how it started" (53). It seems appropriate—even natural—that blues should expressively frame the act resulting from such bitter black agrarian circumstances.

And it is, in fact, blues affirmation of human identity in the face of dehumanizing circumstance that resonates through the sharecropper's triumphant penultimate utterance: "I make up my mind that I ain't nobody but myself and ain't nothin' I can do but let whatever is gonna happen, happen" (66).

The farmer's statement is not an expression of transcendence. It is, instead, an affirmation of a still recognizable humanity by a singer who has incorporated his personal disaster into a code of blues meanings emanating from an unpredictably chaotic world. In translating his tragedy into the vocabulary and semantics of the blues and, subsequently, into the electrifying expression of his narrative, Trueblood realizes that he is not so changed by catastrophe that he must condemn, mortify, or redefine his essential self. This self, as the preceding discussion indicates, is in many ways the obverse of the stable, predictable, puritanical, productive, law-abiding ideal self of the American industrial-capitalist society.

The words the sharecropper issues from "behind the mule" provide a moral opposition (if not a moral corrective) to the confident expressions of control emanating from Mr. Norton's technological world. From a pluralistic perspective, the counteractive patterns represented by the sharecropper and the millionaire point to a positive homeostasis in American life. In the southern regions represented by Trueblood, an oppositional model might suggest, the duty-bound but enfeebled rationalist of northern industry can always achieve renewal and a kind of shamanistic cure for the ills of civilization. But the millionaire in the narrative episode hardly appears to represent a rejuvenated Fisher King. At the close of the sharecropper's story, in fact, he seems paralyzed by the ghostly torpor of a stunned Benito Cereno or a horrified Mr. Kurtz. Thus a pluralistic model that projects revivifying opposition as the relation between sharecropper and millionaire does not adequately explain the Norton-Trueblood interaction. Some of the more significant implications of the episode, in fact, seem to reside not in the opposition between industrial technocrat and agrarian farmer but in the two sectors' commercial consensus on Afro-American expressive culture. Eshu and Hermes are not only figures of powerful creative instinct. They are also gods of the marketplace. Two analytical reflections on the study of literature and ideology, one by Fredric Jameson and the other by Hayden White, elucidate the commercial consensus achieved by Trueblood and his millionaire auditor.

Fredric Jameson writes:

The term "ideology" stands as the sign for a problem yet to be solved, a mental operation which remains to be executed. It does not presuppose cut-and-dried sociological stereotypes like the notion of the "bourgeois" or the "petty bourgeois" but is rather a mediatory concept: that is, it is an imperative to re-invent a relationship between the linguistic or aesthetic or conceptual fact in question and its social ground. . . . Ideological analysis may . . . be described as the rewriting of a particular narrative trait or seme as a function of its social, historical, or political context. (510–11)

Jameson's interest in a reinvented relation between linguistic fact and social ground is a function of his conviction that all acts of narration inscribe social ideologies. In other words, there is always a historical, or ideological, subtext in a literary work of art. For, since history is accessible to us only through texts, the literary work of art either has to "rewrite" the historical texts of its time or "textualize" the uninscribed events of its day in order to "contextualize" itself. What Jameson calls the "ideology of form" White calls "reflection theory." If literary art can indeed be said to reflect, through inscription, the social ground from which it originates, at what level of a specifically social domain, asks White, does such reflection occur? How can we most appropriately view literary works of art as distinctively "social" entities?

White's answer is that ideological analysis must begin with a society's exchange system and must regard the literary work as "merely one commodity among others and moreover as a commodity that has to be considered as not different in kind from any other" (376–77). To adopt such an analytical strategy, according to White, is to comprehend "not only the alienation of the artist which the representation of the value of his product in terms of money alone might foster, but also the tendency of the artist to fetishize his own produce as being itself the universal sign and incarnation of value in a given social system" (378). White could justifiably summon Ellison's previously quoted remarks on the transformative powers of art to illustrate the "fetishizing" of art as the incarnation of value. In Ellison's view, however, artistic value is not a sign or incarnation in a given social system but, rather, a sign of humane value in toto. What is pertinent about White's remarks for the present discussion, however, is that the relation Jameson would reinvent is for White an economic one involving challenging questions of axiology.

To apply Jameson's and White's reflections in analyzing the Trueblood episode, one can begin by recognizing that the sharecropper's achievement of expressive narrative form is immediately bracketed by the exchange system of Anglo-American society. Recalling his first narration of his story to a group of whites, the sharecropper remembers that Sheriff Barbour asked him to tell what happened:

... and I tole him and he called in some more men and they made me tell it again. They wanted to hear about the gal lots of times and they gimme somethin' to eat and drink and some tobacco. Surprised me, 'cause I was scared and spectin' somethin' different. Why, I guess there ain't a colored man in the county who ever got to take so much of the white folkses' time as I did. (52)

Food, drink, tobacco, and audience time are commodities the sharecropper receives in barter for the commodity he delivers—his story. The narrative of incest, after its first telling, accrues an ever-spiraling exchange value. The Truebloods receive all the items enumerated earlier, as well as a one hundred dollar bill from Mr. Norton's Moroccan-leather wallet. The exchange value of the story thus moves from a system of barter to a money economy overseen by northern industrialists. The status of the farmer's story as a commodity cannot be ignored.

As an artistic form incorporating the historical and ideological subtext of American industrial society, the sharecropper's tale represents a supreme capitalist fantasy. The family, as the fundamental social unit of middle-class society, is governed by the property concept. A man marries—takes a wife as his exclusive "property"—to produce legitimate heirs who will keep their father's wealth (in other words, his property) in the family. Among royalty or the aristocracy such marriages may describe an exclusive circle of exchange. Only certain women are eligible as royal or aristocratic wives. And in the tightest of all circumstances, incest may be justified as the sole available means of preserving intact the family heritage—the nobleman's or aristocrat's property. An unfettered, incestuous procreativity that results not only in new and legitimate heirs but also in a marked increase in property (e.g., Trueblood's situation) can be viewed as a capitalist dream. And if such results can be achieved without fear of holy sanction, then procreation becomes a secular feat of human engineering.

Mr. Norton reflects that his "real life's work" has been, not his banking or his researches, but his "first-hand organizing of human life" (42). What more exacting control could this millionaire New Englander have exercised than the incestuous domination of his own human family as a productive unit, eternally giving birth to new profits? Only terror of dreadful heavenly retribution (of punishment for "impropriety") had prevented him from attempting such a construction of life with his pathetically idealized only child, now deceased. Part of his stupefaction at the conclusion of the sharecropper's narrative results from his realization that he might have safely effected such a productive arrangement of life. One need not belabor the capitalist-fantasy aspect of Trueblood's narrative, however, to comprehend his story's commodity status in an industrial-capitalist system of exchange. What the farmer is ultimately merchandising is an image of himself that is itself a product—a bizarre product—of the slave trade that made industrial America possible.

Africans became slaves through what the West Indian novelist George Lamming describes as an act of "commercial deportation" overseen by the white West (93). In America, Africans were classified as "chattel personal" and turned into commodities. To forestall the moral guilt associated with this aberrant, mercantile transformation, white Americans conceptualized a degraded, subhuman animal as a substitute for the actual African. This categorical parody found its public, physical embodiment in the mask of the minstrel theatrical. As Ellison writes in "Change the Joke and Slip the Yoke," the African in America was thus reduced to a "negative sign" (63): "The [minstrel] mask was the thing (the 'thing' in more ways than one) and its function was to veil the humanity of Negroes thus reduced to a sign, and to repress the white audience's awareness of its moral identification with its own acts and with the human ambiguities pushed behind the mask" (64). Following the lead of Constance Rourke, Ellison asserts that the minstrel show is, in fact, a "ritual of exorcism" (64). But what of the minstrel performance given by the Afro-American who dons the mask? In such performances, writes Ellison:

> Motives of race, status, economics and guilt are always clustered. . . . The comic point is inseparable from the racial identity of the performer . . . who by assuming the group-debasing role for gain not only substantiates the audience's belief in the "blackness" of things black, but relieves it, with dreamlike efficiency, of its guilt by accepting the very profit motive that was involved in the designation of the Negro as national scapegoat in the first place. There are all kinds of comedy; here one is reminded of the tribesman in *Green Hills of Africa* who hid his laughing face in shame at the sight of a gut-shot hyena jerking out its own intestines and eating them, in Hemingway's words, "with relish." (64–65)

Trueblood, who assumes the minstrel mask to the utter chagrin of the invisible man ("How can he tell this to white men, I thought, when he knows they'll say that all Negroes do such things?"), has indeed accepted the profit motive that gave birth to that mask in the first place. He tells his tale with relish: "He talked willingly now, with a kind of satisfaction and no trace of hesitancy or shame" (53). The firm lines of capitalist economics are, therefore, not the only ideological inscriptions in the sharecropper's narrative. The story also contains the distorting contours of that mask constructed by the directors of the economic system to subsume their guilt. The rambunctiously sexual, lyrical, and sin-adoring "darky" is an image dear to the hearts of white America.

Ideologically, then, there is every reason to regard the sharecropper's story as a commodity in harmony with its social ground—with the system of exchange sanctioned by the dominant Anglo-American society. For though Trueblood has been denied "book learning" by the nearby black college, he has not failed to garner some knowledge of marketing. Just as the college officials peddle the sharecropper's "primitive spirituals" to spring's seasonally descended white millionaires, so Trueblood sells his own expressive product—a carefully constructed narrative, framed to fit market demands. His actions as a merchant seem to compromise his status as a blues artist, as a character of undeniable folk authenticity. And his delineation as an untrammeled and energetic prime mover singing a deep blues no to social constraints appears to collapse under the impress of ideological analysis. The complexities of American culture, however, enable him to reconcile a merchandising role as oral storyteller with his position as an antinomian trickster. For the Afro-American blues manifest an effective, expressive duality that Samuel Charters captures as follows:

> The blues has always had a duality to it. One of its sides is its personal creativity—the consciousness of a creative individual using it as a form of expression. The other side is the blues as entertainment. Someone like Memphis Slim is a professional blues entertainer. But the blues is a style of music that emphasizes integrity—so how does a singer change his style without losing his credibility as a blues artist? (168)

As entertainment, the blues, whether classic or country, were sung professionally in theaters.[6] And their public theatricality is analogous to the Afro-American's donning of the minstrel mask. There is, perhaps, something obscenely—though profitably—gut-wrenching about Afro-Americans delivering up carefully modified versions of their essential expressive selves for the entertainment of their Anglo-American oppressors. And, as Charters implies, the question of integrity looms large. But the most appropriate inquiry in the wake of his comment is, Integrity, *as what?*

To deliver the blues as entertainment—if one is an entertainer—is to maintain a fidelity to one's role. Again, if the performance required is that of a minstrel and one is a genuine performer, then donning the mask is an act consistent with one's stature. There are always fundamental economic questions involved in such uneasy Afro-American public postures. As Ellison suggests, Afro-Americans, in their guise as entertainers, season the possum of black expressive culture to the taste of their Anglo-American audience, maintaining, in the process, their integrity as performers. But in private sessions—in the closed circle of their own community—everybody knows that the punch line to the recipe (and the proper response to the performer's constrictive dilemma) is, "Damn the possum! That sho' is some good gravy!" It is just possible that the "gravy" is the inimitable technique of the Afro-American artist, a technique (derived from lived blues experience) as capable of "playing possum" as of presenting one.

A further question, however, has to do with the artist's affective response to being treated as a commodity. And with this query, White's and Jameson's global formulations prove less valuable than a closer inspection of the self-reflexive expressivity of Afro-American spokespersons in general. Ellison's Trueblood episode, for example, suggests that the angst assumed to accompany commodity status is greatly alleviated when that status constitutes a sole means of securing power in a hegemonic system.

In the Trueblood episode, blacks who inhabit the southern college's terrain assume that they have transcended the peasant rank of sharecroppers and their cohorts. In fact, both the college's inhabitants and Trueblood's agrarian fellows are but constituencies of a single underclass. When the college authorities threaten the farmer with exile or arrest, he has only to turn to the white Mr. Buchanan, "the boss man," to secure immunity and a favorable audience before Sheriff Barbour, "the white law" (52). The imperious fiats of whites relegate all blacks to an underclass. In Trueblood's words, "no matter how biggity a nigguh gits, the white folks can always cut him down" (53). For those in this underclass, Ellison's episode implies, expressive representation is the only means of prevailing.

Dr. Bledsoe, for example, endorses lying as an effective strategy in interacting with Mr. Norton and the other college trustees. And Trueblood himself adopts tale telling (which is often conflated with lying in black oral tradition) as a mode of expression that allows him a degree of dignity and freedom within the confines of a severe white hegemony. The expressive "mask," one might say, is as indispensable for college blacks as it is for those beyond the school's boundaries. Describing the initial meeting between Mr. Norton and the sharecropper, the protagonist says, "I hurried behind him [Mr. Norton], seeing him stop when he reached the man and the children. They became silent, their faces clouding over, their features becoming soft and negative, their eyes bland and deceptive. They were crouching behind their eyes waiting for him to speak—just as I recognized that I was trembling behind my own" (50). The evasive silence of these blacks is as expressive of power relations in the South as the mendacious strategy advocated by Dr. Bledsoe.

When the protagonist returns from his ill-fated encounters with Trueblood and the crew at the Golden Day, the school's principal asks him if he is unaware that blacks have "lied enough decent homes and drives [got enough material advantage by lying] for you to show him [Mr. Norton]" (136). When the protagonist responds that he was obeying Mr. Norton's orders by showing the millionaire the "slum" regions of Trueblood rather than "decent homes and drives," Bledsoe exclaims, "He *ordered* you. Dammit, white folk are always giving orders, it's a habit with them. . . . My God, boy! You're black and living in the South—did you forget how to lie?" (136).

Artful evasion and expressive illusion are equally traditional black expressive modes in interracial exchange in America. Such modes, the Trueblood episode implies, are the only resources that blacks at any level can barter for a semblance of decency and control in their lives. Making black expressiveness a commodity, therefore, is not simply a gesture in a bourgeois economics of art. Rather, it is a crucial move in a repertoire of black survival motions in the United States. To examine the status of Afro-American expressiveness as a commodity, then, is to do more than observe, within the constraints of an institutional theory of art, that the art world is a function of economics. In a very real sense, Afro-America's exchange power has always been coextensive with its stock of expressive resources. What is implicit in an analysis of black expressiveness as a commodity is not a limited history of the "clerks" but a total history of Afro-American cultural interaction in America.

In *When Harlem Was in Vogue*—a brilliant study that treats the black artistic awakening of the 1920s known as the "Harlem Renaissance"—David Levering Lewis captures the essential juxtaposition between white hegemony and black creativity as a negotiable power of exchange. Writing of Charles Johnson, the energetic black editor of *Opportunity* magazine during this period, Lewis says:

> [Johnson] gauged more accurately than perhaps any other Afro-American intellectual the scope and depth of the national drive to "put the nigger in his place" after the war, to keep him out of the officer corps, out of labor unions and skilled jobs, out of the North and quaking for his very existence in the South—and out of politics everywhere. Johnson found that one area alone—probably because of its very implausibility—had not been pro-

scribed. No exclusionary rules had been laid down regarding a place in the arts. Here was a small crack in the wall of racism, a fissure that was worth trying to widen. (48).

"Exclusionary rules" were certainly implicit in the arts during the 1920s, but what Lewis suggests is that they were far less rigid and explicit than they were in other domains. Blacks thus sought to widen the "fissure," to gain what power they could to determine their own lives, through a renaissance of black expressiveness.

An ideological analysis of expressiveness as a commodity should take adequate account of the defining variables in the culture where this commercialization occurs. In Afro-American culture, exchanging words for safety and profit is scarcely an alienating act. It is, instead, a defining act in aesthetics. Further, it is an act that lies at the heart of Afro-American politics conceived in terms of who gets what and when and how. Making a commodity of black expressiveness, as I try to make clear in my concluding section, does entail inscription of an identifying economics. But aggressively positive manifestations of this process (despite the dualism it presupposes) result from a self-reflexive acknowledgment that only the "economics of slavery" gives valuable and specifically black resonance to Afro-American works of art.

The critic George Kent observes a "mathematical consistency between Ellison's critical pronouncements and his creative performance" (161). Insofar as Ellison provides insightful critical interpretations of his own novel and its characters, Kent's judgment is correct. But the "critical pronouncements" in Ellison's canon that suggest a devaluing of Afro-American folklore hardly seem consistent with the implications of his Trueblood episode. Such statements are properly regarded, I believe, as public remarks by Ellison the merchant rather than as incisive, affective comments by Ellison the creative genius.

Trueblood's duality is, finally, also that of his creator. For Ellison knows that his work as an Afro-American artist derives from those "economics of slavery" that provided conditions of existence for Afro-American folklore. Black folk expression is a product of the impoverishment of blacks in America. The blues, as a case in point, are unthinkable for those happy with their lot.

Yet, if folk artists are to turn a profit from their monumental creative energies (which are often counteractive, or inversive, vis-à-vis Anglo-American culture), they must take a lesson from the boss quail and "move without moving." They must, in essence, sufficiently modify their folk forms (and amply advertise themselves) to merchandise such forms as commodities in the artistic market.

To make their products commensurate with a capitalistic marketplace, folk artists may even have to don masks that distort their genuine selves. Ralph Ellison is a master of such strategies.

Ellison reconciles the trickster's manifestations as untrammeled creator and as god of the marketplace by providing critical advertisements for himself as a novelist that carefully bracket the impoverishing economics of Afro-America. For example, in "Change the Joke and Slip the Yoke" he writes, "I use folklore in my work not because I am a Negro, but because writers like Eliot and Joyce made me conscious of the literary value of my folk inheritance. My cultural background, like that of most Americans, is dual (my middle name, sadly enough, is Waldo)" (72).[7] What is designated in this quotation as "literary value" is in reality market value. Joyce and Eliot taught Ellison that if he was a skillful enough strategist and spokesman he could market his own folklore. What is bracketed, of course, is the economics that required Ellison, if he wished to be an Afro-American artist, to turn to Afro-American folklore as a traditional, authenticating source for his art. Like his sharecropper, Ellison is wont to make literary value out of socioeconomic necessity. But he is also an artist who recognizes that Afro-American folk forms have value in *themselves*; they "have named human situations so well," he suggests in "The Art of Fiction," "that a whole corps of writers could not exhaust their universality" (173). What Ellison achieves in the Trueblood episode is a dizzying hall of mirrors, a redundancy of structure, that enables him to extend the value of Afro-American folk forms by combining them with an array of Western narrative forms and tropes. Written novel and sung blues, polysyllabic autobiography and vernacular personal narrative, a Christian Fall and an inversive triumph of the black trickster—all are conjoined in a magnificently embedded manner.

The foregoing analysis suggests that it is in such creative instances that one discovers Ellison's artistic genius, a genius that links him inextricably and positively to his invented sharecropper. For in the Trueblood episode conceived as a chapter in a novel, one finds not only the same kind of metaexpressive commentary that marks the character's narration to Norton but also the same type of self-reflexive artist that the sharecropper's recitation implies—an artist who is fully aware of the contours and limitations, the rewards and dilemmas, of the Afro-American's uniquely expressive craft.

In the expository, critical moment, by contrast, one often finds a quite different Ralph Ellison. Instead of the *reflexive* artist, one finds the *reflective* spokesman. Paraphrasing Barbara Babcock-Abrahams, who uses a "failed" Narcissus to illustrate the difference between the "reflective" and the "reflexive," one might say that in his criticism Ralph Ellison is not narcissistic enough ("Reflexivity," 4). His reflections in *Shadow and Act* seem to define Afro-American folk expressiveness in art as a sign of identity, a sign that marks the creator as unequivocally Afro-American and, hence, other. I have sought to demonstrate, however, that Ellison's folk expressiveness is, in fact, "identity within difference." While critics experience alienation, artists can detach themselves from, survive, and even laugh at their initial experiences of otherness. Like Velázquez in his *Las Meninas* or the Van Eyck of *Giovanni Arnolfini and His Bride*, the creator of Trueblood is "conscious of being self-conscious of himself" as artist (Babcock-Abrahams, "Reflexivity," 4).[8] Instead of solacing himself with critical distinctions, he employs reflexively mirroring narratives to multiply distinctions and move playfully across categorical boundaries. Like his sharecropper, he knows indisputably that his most meaningful identity is his Afro-American self imaged in acts of expressive creativity.

Ralph Ellison's bracketings as a public critic, therefore, do not forestall his private artistic recognition that he "ain't nobody but himself." And it is out of this realization that a magnificent folk creation such as Trueblood emerges. Both the creator and his agrarian folk storyteller have the wisdom to know that they are resourceful "whistlers" for the tribe. They know that their primary matrix as artists is coextensive not with a capitalistic society but with material circumstances like those implied by the blues singer Howling Wolf:

> Well I'm a po' boy, long way from home.
> Well I'm a po' boy, long way from home.
> No spendin' money in my pocket, no spare meat on my bone.
> (Nicholas 85)

One might say that in the brilliant reflexivity of the Trueblood encounter, we hear the blues whistle among the high-comic thickets. We glimpse Ellison's creative genius beneath his Western critical mask. And while we stand awaiting the next high-cultural pronouncement from the critic, we are startled by a captivating sound of flattened thirds and sevenths—the private artist's blues-filled flight.

NOTES

1   All parenthetical page citations to Ellison's critical essays refer to his *Shadow and Act*, which comprises the bulk of his critical canon.

2   One of the general questions provoking Freud's inquiry into totemism is, "What is the ultimate source of the horror of incest which must be recognized as the root of exogamy?" (122).

3   For a stimulating discussion of the trickster in his various literary and nonliterary guises,

consult Barbara Babcock-Abrahams's provocative essay " 'A Tolerated Margin of Mess': The Trickster and His Tales Reconsidered." The author writes, "In contrast to the scapegoat or tragic victim, trickster belongs to the comic modality or marginality where violation is generally the precondition for laughter and communitas, and there tends to be an incorporation of the outsider, a leveling of hierarchy, a reversal of statuses" (153).

4   I had enlightening conversations with Kimberly Benston on the Trueblood episode's parodic representation of the Fall. I am grateful for his generous help.

5   The significance of the sharecropper's incestuous progeny may be analogous to that of the broken link of leg chain given to the invisible man during his early days in the Brotherhood. Presenting the link, Brother Tarp says, "I don't think of it in terms of but two words, *yes* and *no*; but it signifies a heap more" (379).

6   Ellison introduces this claim, which contradicts LeRoi Jones's assertions on blues, in a review of Jones's book *Blues People* (*Shadow* 249).

7   The implicit "trickiness" of Ellison's claim—its use of words to "signify" quite other than what they seem to intend on the surface—is an aspect of the Afro-American "critic as trickster." In a 1981 paper Henry Louis Gates, Jr., began an analysis—in quite suggestive terms— of the trickster's "semiotic" manifestation. For Gates the Afro-American folk figure of the "signifying monkey" is an archetype of the Afro-American critic. In the essays "Change the Joke and Slip the Yoke" and "The World in a Jug," Ellison demonstrates, one can certainly conclude, an elegant mastery of what might be termed the "exacerbating strategies" of the monkey. Perhaps one also hears his low Afro-American voice directing a sotto voce "Yo' Mamma!" at heavyweights of the Anglo-American critical establishment.

8   One of the most intriguing recent discussions of the Velázquez painting is Michel Foucault's in *The Order of Things* (3–16). Jay Ruby briefly discusses the Van Eyck in the introduction to his anthology (12–13).

WORKS CITED

Babcock-Abrahams, Barbara. "The Novel and the Carnival World." *Modern Language Notes* 89 (1974): 911–37.

——. "Reflexivity: Definitions and Discriminations." *Semiotica* 30 (1980): 1–11.

——. " 'A Tolerated Margin of Mess': The Trickster and His Tales Reconsidered." *Journal of the Folklore Institute* 11 (1974): 147–86.

Charters, Samuel. *The Legacy of the Blues.* New York: Da Capo, 1977.

Ellison, Ralph. *Invisible Man.* 1952. Reprint, New York: Vintage-Random, 1972.

——. *Shadow and Act.* New York: Signet-NAL, 1966.

Foucault, Michel. *The Order of Things.* New York: Random, 1973.

Freud, Sigmund. *Totem and Taboo.* Trans. James Strachey. New York: Norton, 1950.

Gates, Henry Louis Jr. "The 'Blackness of Blackness': A Critique of the Sign and the Signifying Monkey." MLA Convention, New York, 30 December 1981.

Geertz, Clifford. "Deep Play: Notes on the Balinese Cockfight." In his *The Interpretation of Cultures.* New York: Basic, 1973.

Jameson, Fredric. "The Symbolic Inference; or, Kenneth Burke and Ideological Analysis." *Critical Inquiry* 4 (1978): 507–23.

Kent, George. *Blackness and the Adventure of Western Culture.* Chicago: Third World, 1972.

Lamming, George. *Season of Adventure.* London: Allison and Busby, 1979.

Lewis, David Levering. *When Harlem Was in Vogue.* New York: Knopf, 1981.

Nicholas, A. S., ed. *Woke Up This Mornin': Poetry of the Blues.* New York: Bantam, 1973.

Oakley, Giles. *The Devil's Music: A History of the Blues.* New York: Harvest, 1976.

Radin, Paul. *The Trickster.* London: Routledge and Kegan Paul, 1955.

Rodgers, Carolyn. *How I Got Ovah: New and Selected Poems.* New York: Doubleday, 1975.

Ruby, Jay. Introduction to *A Crack in the Mirror: Reflexive Perspectives in Anthropology.* Ed. Jay Ruby. Philadelphia: University of Pennsylvania Press, 1982.

Turner, Victor. *The Forest of Symbols: Aspects of Ndembu Ritual.* Ithaca, N.Y.: Cornell Univ. Press, 1967.

——. "Myth and Symbol." In *International Encyclopedia of the Social Sciences,* Vol. 10. New York: Free Press, 1968.

White, Hayden. "Literature and Social Action: Reflections on the Reflection Theory of Literary Art." *New Literary History* 12 (1980): 363–80.

17. The World and the Home

Homi Bhabha

IN THE HOUSE OF FICTION you can hear, today, the deep stirring of the "unhomely." You must permit me this awkward word—the unhomely—because it captures something of the estranging sense of the relocation of the home and the world in an unhallowed place. To be unhomed is not to be homeless, nor can the "unhomely" be easily accommodated in that familiar division of social life into private and the public spheres. The unhomely moment creeps up on you stealthily as your own shadow and suddenly you find yourself with Henry James's Isabel Archer "taking the measure of your dwelling" in a state of "incredulous terror."[1] And it is at this point that the world first shrinks for Isabel and then expands enormously. As she struggles to survive the fathomless waters, the rushing torrents, James introduces us to the "unhomeliness" inherent in that rite of "extra-territorial" initiation—the relations between the innocent American, the deep, dissembling European, the masked emigré—that a generation of critics have named his "international theme." In a feverish stillness, the intimate recesses of the domestic space become sites for history's most intricate invasions. In that displacement the border between home and world becomes confused; and, uncannily, the private and the public become part of each other, forcing upon us a vision that is as divided as it is disorienting.

In the stirrings of the unhomely, another world becomes visible. It has less to do with forcible eviction and more to do with the uncanny literary and social effects of enforced social accommodation, or historical migrations and cultural relocations. The home does not remain the domain of domestic life, nor does the world simply become its social or historical counterpart. The unhomely is the shock of recognition of the world-in-the-home, the home-in-the-world. In a song called "Whose House is This?" Toni Morrison gives this problem of "unhomely" dwelling a lyric clarity:

> Whose house is this? Whose night keeps out the light in here? Say who owns this house? It is not mine. I had another sweeter. . . . The House is strange. Its shadows lie. Say, tell me, why does its lock fit my key?[2]

My earliest sense of the unhomely occurred in a prosaic house in Oxford, in a narrow street reserved for college servants and research fellows. It was a noisy red-brick terraced house haunted by the hydraulic regurgitations of the Victorian plumbing system, yet strangely appropriate to the task at hand, a thesis on V. S. Naipaul. I was writing about a small-time Trinidadian journalist, the son of an Indian indentured laborer, a devotee of Samuel Smiles and Charles Dickens, who was afflicted with the most noisy and public bouts of nervous dyspepsia. As I contemplated his tragic-comic failure to create a dwelling place, to ever find *A House for Mr. Biswas*, I wrestled with the wisdom of Iris Murdoch's laudable pronouncement, "A novel must be a house for free people to live in." Must the novel be a house? What kind of narrative can house unfree people? Is the novel also a house where the unhomely can live? I was straining nervously at the edges of Iris Murdoch's combination of liberalism and "catholic" existentialism, while Mr. Biswas's gastric juices ran amok. The cistern churned and burped, and I thought of some of the great homes of English Literature— Mansfield Park, Thrushcross Grange, Gardencourt, Brideshead, Howard's End, Fawlty Towers. Suddenly, I knew I had found, in the ruins of the Biswas bungalows and their unlikely, unsettled lives, my small corner of the world of letters— a postcolonial place.

Working on *A House for Mr. Biswas*, I found that I couldn't fit the political, cultural or chronological experience of that text into the traditions of Anglo-American liberal novel criticism. The sovereignty of the concept of character, grounded as it is in the aesthetic discourse of cultural authenticity and the practical ethics of individual freedom, bore little resemblance to the overdetermined, unaccommodated postcolonial figure of Mr. Biswas. The image of the house has always been used to talk about the expansive, mimetic nature of the novel; but in *Biswas* you have a form of realism that is unable to contain the anguish of cultural displacement and diasporic movement. Although the "unhomely" is a paradigmatic postcolonial experience, it has a resonance that can be heard distinctly, if erratically, in fictions that negotiate the powers of cultural difference in a range of historical conditions and social contradictions.

You can hear the shrill alarm of the unhomely at the moment when Isabel

Archer, in *The Portrait of A Lady*, realizes that her world has been reduced to one, high mean window, as her house of fiction becomes "the house of darkness, the house of dumbness, the house of suffocation."[3] If you hear it thus at the Palazzo Roccanera in the late 1870s, then a little earlier in 1873 on the outskirts of Cincinnati, in mumbling houses like 124 Bluestone Road you hear the undecipherable language of the black and angry dead; the voice of Toni Morrison's *Beloved*, "the thoughts of the women of 124, unspeakable thoughts, unspoken."[4] More than a quarter century later, in 1905, Bengal is ablaze with the Swadeshi or Home Rule movement when "homemade Bimala, the product of the confined space," as Tagore describes her in *The Home and the World*, is aroused by "a running undertone of melody, low down in the bass . . . the true manly note, the note of power." Bimala is possessed and drawn forever from the zenana, the secluded women's quarters, as she crosses that fated verandah into the world of public affairs . . . "over to another shore and the ferry had ceased to ply."[5] Much closer to our own times in contemporary South Africa, Nadine Gordimer's latest heroine, Aila, emanates a stilling atmosphere as she makes her diminished domesticity into the perfect cover for gun-running: suddenly the home turns into another world, and the narrator notices that "it was as if everyone found that he had unnoticingly entered a strange house, *and it was hers.*"

Gordimer's awkward sentence, with its rapid shift of genders and subjects —everyone, he, hers, provides the estranging syntax of the unhomely experience. Gordimer's sign of the woman's sense of possession and self-possession ("it was hers"), her ethical or historical transformation of the world, emerges retroactively, belatedly, *at the end of the sentence, towards the end of the book.* The historical or fictional subject is conscious of the "meaning" or intention of the act; but its transformation into a "public" symbolic or ethical realm demands a *narrative* agency that emerges after the event, often alienating "intent," and disturbing "causal" determinism. In *The Human Condition,*[6] Hannah Arendt meditates on just such a perplexity in signifying the social sphere as a narrative process. "In any series of events that together form a story with a unique meaning," she writes, "we can at best isolate the agent who set the whole process into motion; and although this agent frequently remains the subject, the hero of the story, we can *never point unequivocally to [the agent] as the author of the outcome*" (185).

In order to appear as material or empirical reality, the historical or social process must pass through an "aesthetic" alienation, or "privatization" of its public visibility. The discourse of "the social" then finds its means of representation in a kind of *unconsciousness* that obscures the immediacy of meaning,

darkens the public event with an "unhomely" glow. There is, I want to hazard, an incommunicability that shapes the public moment; a psychic obscurity that is formative for public memory. Then the house of fiction speaks in
tongues; in those undecipherable mumbling enunciations that emanate from
Beloved's "124," or the strange still silence that surrounds Nadine Gordimer's
Aila whether she inhabits a house in the colored ghetto of Benoni (son of sorrow), or in a "grey area" of the Cape. And suddenly, literature asks questions
at the very borders of its historical and disciplinary being: Can historical time
be thought outside fictional space, or do they lie uncannily beside each other?
Does the passage of power turn the agent of history into a stranger, a double-
agent living between the lines?

The process of the aesthetic that I am proposing for the grounds of historical "re-cognition," and as a reckoning with the historical event, must be
clarified. The aesthetic as the "obscuring" of the historical event that refigures
it through a temporal distancing or "lag," as I've described it, must be distinguished from two familiar genealogies of the aesthetic. It must not be confused
with the Kantian aesthetic, which is a mediatory process that brings existence
to its fullest being in a revelation of self-reflection. Nor do I subscribe to that tradition of a materialist aesthetic that sees art as the displaced or overdetermined
symptom of social reification—a fetishism of phenomenal forms that conceals
"real" ideological contradictions. Both these approaches to the aesthetic involve
transcendent schemes of thought and art where the progressive movement of
the dialectic at once poses the problem of difference, alienation, negation—at
the ontological or epistemological level—and sublates or disavows it in the process of representation. For instance, although Louis Althusser is fully aware
of the differential sites of the social formation, and the displaced or overdetermined nature of ideology more generally, the "subject" of cultural discourse is
caught within the relatively homogenous, totalizing confines of the Lacanian
Imaginary.

In contrast to this homogenous or transcendent temporality of the "aesthetic," I want to suggest that the aesthetic process introduces into our reading
of social reality not another reified form of mediation—the art object—but another temporality in which to signify the "event" of history. I take my lead from
what Walter Benjamin describes as the "constructive principle" of materialist
historiography, where the "historical materialist cannot do without the present
which is not a transition, but in which time stands still and has to come to
a stop. For this notion defines the present in which he himself is writing history."[7] I locate the aesthetic in this time of inscription whose stillness is not
stasis but a shock that Benjamin goes on to describe as "blasting a specific era

out of the homogeneous course of history." The present that informs the aesthetic process is not a transcendental passage but a moment of "transit," a form of temporality that is open to disjunction and discontinuity and sees the process of history engaged, rather like art, in a negotiation of the framing and naming of social reality—not what lies inside or outside reality, but where to draw (or inscribe) the "meaningful" line between them.

The unhomely moment relates the traumatic ambivalences of a personal, psychic history to the wider disjunctions of political existence. Beloved, the child murdered by her own mother, Sethe, is a daemonic, belated repetition of the violent history of black infant deaths, during slavery, in many parts of the South, less than a decade after the haunting of 124 Bluestone Road. (Between 1882 and 1895 from one-third to one-half of the annual black mortality rate was accounted for by children under five.) But the memory of Sethe's act of infanticide emerges through "the holes—the things the fugitives did not say; the questions they did not ask . . . the unnamed, the unmentioned." As we reconstruct the narrative of child murder through Sethe, the slave mother, who is herself the victim of social death, the very historical basis of our ethical judgments undergoes a radical revision.

In the denouement of her novel Gordimer provides another example of the complexity of the "unhomely" when she describes what she calls "the freak displacement" that has afflicted the world of her characters. "The biological drive of Sonny's life which belonged to his wife was diverted to his white lover [Hannah]. . . . He and Hannah had begot no child. . . . The revolutionary movement was to be their survivor. . . . But Aila, his wife, was the revolutionary now."[8] In the freak displacements of these novels, the profound divisions of an enslaved or apartheid society—negrification, denigration, classification, violence, incarceration—are relocated in the midst of the ambivalence of psychic identification—that space where love and hate can be projected or inverted; where the relation of "object" to identity is always split and doubled.

Such forms of social and psychic existence can best be represented in that tenuous survival of literary language itself which allows memory to speak:

> while knowing Speech can (be) at best, a shadow echoing
> the silent light, bear witness
> To the truth, it is not. . . .

Auden wrote those lines on the powers of *poesis*, in *The Cave of Making*, aspiring to be as he put it "a minor Atlantic Goethe." And it is to an intriguing suggestion in Goethe's final note on World Literature (1830) that I now turn to find a comparative method that would speak to the "unhomely" condition of the modern world. Goethe suggests that the possibility of a world literature arises from the cultural confusion wrought by terrible wars and mutual conflicts. Nations "could not return to their settled and independent life again without noticing that they had learned many foreign ideas and ways, which they had unconsciously adopted, and come to feel here and there previously unrecognized spiritual and intellectual needs."[9] Goethe's immediate reference is, of course, to the Napoleonic wars and his concept of "the feeling of neighborly relations" is profoundly Eurocentric, extending as far as England and France. However, as an Orientalist who read Shakuntala at seventeen, and who writes in his autobiography of the "unformed and overformed"[10] monkey God Hanuman, Goethe's speculations are open to another line of thought.

What of the more complex cultural situation where "previously unrecognized spiritual and intellectual needs" emerge from the imposition of "foreign" ideas, cultural representations, and structures of power? Goethe suggests that the inner nature of the whole nation as well as the individual man works all "unconsciously." When this is placed alongside his idea that the cultural life of the nation is "unconsciously" lived, then there may be a sense in which world literature could be an emergent, prefigurative category that is concerned with a form of cultural dissensus and alterity, where nonconsensual terms of affiliation and articulation may be established on the grounds of historical trauma. The study of world literature might be the study of the way in which cultures recognize themselves through their projections of "otherness." Where the transmission of "national" traditions was once the major theme of a world literature, perhaps we can now suggest that transnational histories of migrants, the colonized, or political refugees—these border and frontier conditions—may be the terrains of World Literature. The center of such a study would neither be the "sovereignty" of national cultures, nor the "universalism" of human culture, but a focus on those "freak displacements"—such as Morrison and Gordimer display—that have been caused within cultural lives of postcolonial societies. If these were considered the paradigm cases of a world literature based on the trauma of history and the conflict of nations, then Walter Benjamin's homeless modern novelist would be the representative figure of an "unhomely" world literature. For he "carries the incommensurable to extremes in the representation of human life and in the midst of life's fullness, gives evidence of the perplexity of living."[11] Which leads us to ask: Can the perplexity of the unhomely, intrapersonal world lead to an international theme?

Gordimer places this very question at the center of literary narrative: "Love, love/hate are the most common and universal of experiences. But no two are alike, each is a fingerprint of life. That's the miracle that makes literature and links it with creation in the biological sense" (275). To put Gordimer's point another way: the fingerprint of literature—its imagistic impulse, its tropic topos, its metaphoric medium, its allegorical voice—these forms of narrative created from contingency and indeterminacy—may provide historical discourse with its powers of narrative "beginning." For it was Michel de Certeau who suggested, in *The Writing of History*,[12] that "beginnings" require an "originary non-place," something "unspoken" which then produces a chronology of events. Beginnings can, in this sense, be the narrative limits of the knowable, the margins of the meaningful. In what she calls her "in medias res" openings, Morrison stages such a narrative "nonspace" and turns it into the performative time of the experience of slavery—no native informant, she writes, "the reader snatched as the slaves were from one place to another . . . without preparation or defense."[13] Her opening sign—"124 was spiteful"—offers no respite, no immediate meaning, because the house of slave-memory is not a resting place, not a Wordsworthian "spot of time." "124" is the unhomely, haunted site of the circulation of an event not as fact or fiction but as an "enunciation," a discourse of "unspeakable thoughts unspoken"—a phrase that circulates in the work and comes closest to defining its mode of utterance, the uncanny voice of memory.

To "un"-speak is both to release from erasure and repression, and to reconstruct, reinscribe the elements of the known. "In this case too," we may say with Freud, "the *Unheimlich* is what was once *heimisch*, homelike, familiar; the prefix 'un' is the token of repression." Morrison turns her narrative to just such an "affect" of distancing, obscuring the "referent," repeating and revising the "un-spoken" in order to make the act of narration an ethical act. "A few words have to be read before it is clear that 124 refers to a house . . . a few more . . . to discover why it is spiteful. . . . *By then it is clear that something is beyond control, but it is not beyond understanding since it is not beyond accommodation by both the women and the children*. . . . The fully realized haunting . . . is a sleight of hand. One of its purposes is to keep the reader preoccupied with the nature of the incredible spirit world while being supplied a controlled diet of the incredible political world."[14]

If we are seeking a "worlding" of literature, then perhaps it lies in a critical act that attempts to grasp the sleight of hand with which literature conjures with historical specificity, using the medium of *psychic uncertainty, aesthetic distancing, or the obscure signs of the spirit-world, the sublime and the subliminal*. As literary creatures and political animals we ought to concern ourselves with the understanding of human action and the social world as a moment when *something is beyond control, but it is not beyond accommodation*. This act of writing the world, of taking the measure of its dwelling, is magically caught in Morrison's description of her house of fiction—art as "the fully realized presence of a haunting" of history. Read as an image that describes the relation of art to social reality, my translation of Morrison's phrase becomes a statement on the political responsibility of the critic. For the critic must attempt to fully realize, and take responsibility for, the un-spoken, unrepresented pasts that haunt the historical present.

Our task remains, however, to show how historical understanding is transformed through the signifying process, represented in a language that is *somehow beyond control*. This is in keeping with Hannah Arendt's suggestion that the author of social action may be the initiator of its unique meaning, but as agent he or she cannot control its outcome.

It is not simply what the house of fiction contains or "controls" as *content*. What is just as important is the metaphoricity of the houses of racial memory that both Morrison and Gordimer construct, those subjects of the narrative that mutter or mumble like 124, or keep a still silence in a "grey" Cape Town suburb. Each of the houses in Gordimer's *My Son's Story* is invested with a specific secret or a conspiracy, an unhomely stirring. The house in the ghetto is the house of "colored" collusion; the lying house is the house of Sonny's adultery; then there is the silent house of Aila's revolutionary camouflage; there is also the nocturnal house of Will's, the narrator's, writing of the narrative that charts the phoenix rising in his home, while the words must turn to ashes in his mouth. But each house marks a deeper historical displacement. And that is the condition of being colored in South Africa, or as Will describes it, "halfway between . . . being not defined—and it was this lack of definition in itself that was never to be questioned, but observed like a taboo, something which no-one, while following, could ever admit to" (21–22).

This halfway house of racial and cultural origins bridges the "in-between" diasporic origins of the colored South African and turns it into the symbol for the disjunctive, displaced everyday life of the liberation struggle: "like so many others of this kind, whose families are fragmented in the diaspora of exile, code names, underground activity, people for whom a real home and attachments are something for others who will come after." Private and public, past and present, the psyche and the social develop an interstial intimacy. It is an intimacy that questions binary divisions through which such spheres of social experience are often spatially opposed. These spheres of life are linked through an "in-between" temporality that takes the measure of dwelling at home, while producing an image of the world of history. This is the moment of aesthetic distance that provides the narrative with a double edge which like the colored South African subject represents a hybridity, a difference "within," a subject

that inhabits the rim of an "in-between" reality. And the inscription of this border existence inhabits a stillness of time and a strangeness of framing that creates the discursive "image" at the crossroads of history and literature, bridging
the home and the world.

Such a strange stillness is visible in the portrait of Aila. Her husband Sonny,
now past his political prime, his affair with his white "revolutionary lover" in
abeyance, makes his first prison visit to see his wife. The wardress stands back,
the policeman fades, and Aila emerges as an unhomely presence, on the opposite side from her husband and son: "but through the familiar beauty there was
a vivid strangeness. . . . It was as if some chosen experience had seen in her,
as a painter will in his subject, what she was, what was there to be discovered.
In Lusaka, in secret, in prison—who knows where?—she had sat for her hidden
face. *They had to recognise her*" (230).

Through this painterly distance a vivid strangeness emerges; a partial or
double "self" is framed in a climactic political moment that is also a contingent historical event—"some chosen experience . . . who knows where? . . . or
what there was to be discovered." They had to recognize her, but *what* do they
recognize in her?

The history of Aila's hidden face emerges at the moment of her framing.
She begins to speak, "like someone telling a story," but soon we find it "difficult to follow. . . . You leave so much out." In her inability to articulate her
intention, to demonstrate a clear causality of commitment, or even a rational,
responsible political ideology we are confronted with the novel's poignant and
ambivalent interrogation of agency: "*Aila, Aila a revolutionary responsible for
her acts*" (239). There is no giddy suggestion that Aila's revolution is instinctive, part of her gendered "jouissance"; nor that it is the displaced symptom
of her domestic oppression; or some fatal return of the repressed knowledge
of Sonny's adultery. The political lesson Aila has to teach speaks through her
narrative refusal to "name" her choice. With a certain obduracy and greater obscurity, she herself becomes the "image" of historical agency that the narrative
is trying to wrench from her as an intention for her actions, an origin for her
events, a "cause" for her consciousness. Literature, through its "distancing" act,
frames this stillness, this enigmatic historical event. "The necessity for what
I've done—She placed the outer edge of each hand, fingers extended and close
together, as a frame on either sides of the sheets of testimony in front of her.
And she placed herself before him, to be judged by him" (241). Words will not
speak and the silence freezes into the images of apartheid: identity cards, police
frame-ups, prison mug shots, the grainy press pictures of terrorists. Of course,
Aila is not judged, nor is she judgmental. Her revenge is much wiser and more

complete. In her silence she becomes the un-spoken "totem" of the taboo of the colored South African. She displays the unhomely world, "the halfway between, not defined" world of the colored as the "distorted place and time in which they—all of them—Sonny, Aila, Hannah—lived" (241). The silence that doggedly follows Aila's dwelling now turns into an image of the "interstices," the in-between hybridity of the history of sexuality and race.

Aila's hidden face, the outer edge of each hand, these small gestures through which she speaks describe another dimension of "dwelling" in the social world. Aila, as colored woman, defines a boundary that is at once inside and outside, the insider's-outsideness. The stillness that surrounds her, the gaps in her story, her hesitation and passion that speak between the self and its acts— these are moments where the private and public touch in contingency. They do not simply transform the content of political ideas; the very "place" from which the political is spoken—the "public sphere" itself, becomes an experience of liminality which questions, in Sonny's words, what it means to speak "from the center of life."

The central political preoccupation of the novel—till Aila's emergence— focuses on the "loss of absolutes," the meltdown of the cold war, the fear "that if we can't offer the old socialist paradise in exchange for the capitalist hell here, we'll have turned traitor to our brothers" (214). The lesson Aila teaches requires a movement away from a world conceived in binary terms, away from a notion of the peoples' aspirations sketched in simple black and white. It also requires a shift of attention from the political as a theory to politics as the activity of everyday life. Aila leads us to the homely world where, Gordimer writes, the banalities are enacted—"the fuss over births, marriages, family affairs with their survival rituals of food and clothing" (243). But it is precisely in these banalities that the unhomely stirs, as the violence of a racialised society falls most enduringly on the details of life: where you can sit, or not; how you can live, or not; what you can learn, or not; who you can love, or not. Between the banal act of freedom and its historic denial rises the silence: "Aila emanated a stilling atmosphere; the parting jabber stopped. It was as if everyone found he had unnoticingly entered a strange house, and it was hers; she stood there."

In Aila's stillness, its obscure necessity, we have glimpsed what Emmanuel Levinas has magically described as the twilight existence of the aesthetic image —art's image as "the very event of obscuring, a descent into night, an invasion of the shadow."[15] The "completion" of the aesthetic, the distancing of the world in the "image," is precisely not a transcendental activity. The image—or the metaphoric, "fictional" activity of language—makes visible "an interruption of time by a movement going on the hither side of time, in its interstices." The complexity of this statement will become clearer when I remind you of the "stillness" of time through which Aila surreptitiously and subversively interrupts the ongoing presence of political activity, using her interstitial role in the domestic world to both "obscure" her political role and to articulate it the better.

The continual eruption of "undecipherable languages" of slave-memory in *Beloved* obscures the historical narrative of infanticide only to articulate the "unspoken"—that ghostly discourse which enters the world of 124 "from the outside" in order to reveal the profound temporal liminality of the transitional world of the aftermath of slavery in the 1870s—its private and public faces, its historical past and its narrative present. The aesthetic image discloses an ethical time of narration because, Levinas writes, "the real world appears in the image as it were between parenthesis." Like the outer edges of Aila's hands holding her enigmatic testimony; like 124, which is a fully realized presence haunted by undecipherable languages, Levinas's parenthetical perspective is also an ethical view. It effects an "externality of the inward" as the very enunciative position of the historical and narrative subject, "introducing into the heart of subjectivity a radical and an-archical reference to the other which in fact constitutes the inwardness of the subject."[16] Is it not uncanny that Levinas's metaphors for this unique "obscurity" of the image should come from those unhomely places in Dickens—those dusty boarding schools, the pale light of London offices, the dark, dank secondhand clothes shops?

For Levinas the "art-magic" of the contemporary novel lies in its way of "seeing inwardness from the outside," and for us, it is this ethical-aesthetic positioning that returns us, finally, to the community of the unhomely: "124 was spiteful. . . . The house on the veld was silent. The women in the house knew it and so did the children."

Why, in particular, the women? Carole Pateman argues that the continual "forgetting" of domestic life in the definition of the private/public distinction introduces a negation at the very center of social contract theory. Domestic life becomes, by virtue of its disavowal, a problematic boundary of civil society. It can be reoccupied by those who have taken up the position of the "inwardness from the outside." Which has indeed happened in the work of black American theorists like Patricia Hill Collins, who names the experience "the outsider-within status," and Patricia Williams, who sees the possibility of deploying this status to describe an ambivalent, transgressive, fluid positioning—of herself and her work—"that moves back and forth across a boundary which acknowledges that I can be black and good and black and bad and that I can also be black and white. . . ."

It is Toni Morrison, however, who takes this ethical and aesthetic project of "seeing inwardness from the outside" furthest or deepest—right into Beloved's naming of her desire for identity: "I want you to touch me on my inside part and call me my name." There is an obvious reason why a ghost should want to be so realized. What is more obscure—and to the point—is how such an inward and intimate desire would provide an "inscape" of the memory of slavery. For Morrison, it is precisely the historical and discursive boundaries of slavery that are the issue. Racial violence is invoked by historical dates—1876, for instance—but Morrison is just a little hasty with the events in-themselves: "the true meaning of the Fugitive Bill, the Settlement Fee, God's Ways, antislavery, manumission, skin voting. . . ." What has to be endured is the knowledge of doubt that comes from Sethe's eighteen years of disapproval and a solitary life in the unhomely world of 124 Bluestone Road. What finally causes the thoughts of the women of 124, "unspeakable thoughts to be unspoken," is the understanding that the victims of violence are themselves "signified upon": they are the victims of projected fears, anxieties and dominations that do not originate within the oppressed and will not fix them in the circle of pain. The stirring of emancipation comes with the knowledge that the belief "that under every dark skin there was a jungle" was a belief that grew, spread, touched every perpetrator of the racist myth, and was then expelled from 124.

With this knowledge comes a kind of self-love that is also the love of the "other." Eros and Agape together. This knowledge is visible in those intriguing "interstitial" chapters which lay over each other, where Sethe, Beloved and Denver perform a ceremony of claiming and naming: "Beloved, she my daughter"; "Beloved is my sister;" "I am beloved and she is mine." The women speak in tongues, from a space "in-between each other" which is a communal space. They explore an "inter-personal" reality: a social reality that appears within the poetic image as if it were in parenthesis. It is difficult to convey the rhythm and the improvisation of those chapters, but it is impossible not to see in them, the healing of history, a community reclaimed in the making of a name:

Who is Beloved?

Now we understand: She is the daughter that returns to Sethe so that her mind will be homeless no more.

Who is Beloved?

Now we may say: She is the sister that returns to Denver, and brings hope of her father's return, the fugitive who died in his escape.

Who is Beloved?

Now we know: She is the daughter made of murderous love who returns to love and hate and free herself. Her words are broken, like the lynched people with broken necks; disembodied, like the dead children who lost their ribbons. But there is no mistaking what her live words say as they rise from the dead despite their lost syntax and their fragmented presence. "My face is coming I have to have it I am looking for the join I am loving my face so much I want to join I am loving my face so much my dark face is close to me I want to join."

My subject today has been the nest of the phoenix, not its pyre. I have attempted to show you the world forcibly entering the house of fiction in order to invade, alarm, divide, dispossess. But I have also tried to show how literature haunts history's more public face, forcing it to reflect on itself in the displacing, even distorting image of Art. When the publicity of the "event," or the certainty of "intention" encounters the silence of the Word or the stillness of art, it may lose control and coherence, but it provides a profound understanding of what constitutes human necessity and agency. I have focused this argument on the woman framed—Gordimer's Aila; and the woman, re-named—Morrison's Beloved. In both their houses great world events erupted—Apartheid and Slavery—and their coming was turned into that particular obscurity of Art. In that unhomely second coming, both Aila and Beloved embody the "freak displacements" of their times. It could be said of these moments that they are of the world but not fully in it; that they represent the outsideness of the inside that is too painful to remember. "This is not a story to pass on," Morrison insistently repeats at the end of *Beloved* in order to engrave the event in the deepest resources of our amnesia, of our unconsciousness. When historical visibility has faded, when the present tense of testimony loses its power to arrest, then the distortions of memory offer us the image of our solidarity and survival. This is a story to pass on; to pass through the world of literature on its thither side and discover those who live in the unhomely house of Fiction. In the House of Fiction, there is a stirring of the unspoken, of the unhomely . . . today.

NOTES

This is the transcript of a lecture given at Princeton University. A number of historical and theoretical elaborations which were inappropriate to the occasion and format of the lecture will be developed in an essay based on this lecture, which will be published in *The Location of Culture* (New York: Routledge, 1994).

1 Henry James, *The Portrait of a Lady* (New York: Norton, 1975), 360.
2 Toni Morrison, "Honey and Rue," from a song-cycle for Kathleen Battle, *Carnegie Hall Stagebill*, January 1992, 12c.
3 James, *Portrait*, 360.
4 Toni Morrison, *Beloved* (New York: Signet, 1987), 198–9.

5 Rabindranath Tagore, *The Home and the World* (London: Penguin, 1985), 70–71.

6 Hannah Arendt, *The Human Condition* (Chicago: Univ. of Chicago Press, 1958).

7 Walter Benjamin, *Illuminations* (New York: Shocken Books, 1969), 262.

8 Nadine Gordimer, *My Son's Story* (London: Bloomsbury, 1990), 241–2.

9 J. E. Spingarin, ed., *Goethe's Literary Essays* (New York: Harcourt, Brace and Co., 1921), 98–9.

10 John Oxenford, ed., *The Autobiography of Goethe* (London: Henry G. Bohn, 1948), 467.

11 Walter Benjamin, *Illuminations*, 86.

12 Michel de Certeau, *The Writing of History* (New York: Columbia Univ. Press, 1988), 90–91.

13 Toni Morrison, "Unspeakable Thoughts Unspoken," *Michigan Quarterly Review* (fall 1990): 32.

14 Ibid., 32.

15 Emmanuel Levinas, "Reality and Its Shadow," in *Collected Philosophical Papers*, (Dordrecht: Martinus Nijhoff, 1987), 1–13.

16 Robert Bernasconi in "Levinas's Ethical Discourse, Between Individuation and Universality," in *Re-Reading Levinas*, ed. Bernasconi and Critchley, (Bloomington: Indiana Univ. Press, 1991), 90.

CONTRIBUTORS

HOUSTON A. BAKER Jr. is Susan Fox and George D. Beischer Arts and Sciences Professor of English and African and African American Studies at Duke University. He is the author and editor of numerous books, including *Modernism and the Harlem Renaissance* (1987); *Black Studies, Rap and the Academy* (1993); and most recently, *Critical Memory: Public Spheres, African American Writing, and Black Fathers and Sons in America* (2001); and *Turning South Again: Rethinking Modernism/Rereading Booker T.* (Duke, 2001). As a poet, his books include *Blues Journeys Home* (1985) and *Passing Over* (2000).

ROLAND BARTHES (1915–1980) taught off and on for a number of years in Bayonne, Paris, Biarritz, and Bucharest before he became a teaching fellow at the Centre National de Recherche Scientifique. In 1960, he joined the faculty at the École Pratique des Hautes Études, serving as a director of studies from 1962 until 1977, when he was elected to the chair of literary semiology at the Collège de France. His many books include *Writing Degree Zero* (1953); *Mythologies* (1957); *S/Z* (1970); *The Pleasure of the Text* (1973); *A Lover's Discourse* (1977); and *Camera Lucida: Reflections on Photography* (1980).

HOMI BHABHA is Professor of English and American Literature and Language at Harvard University. He is the author of *The Location of Culture* (1994) and the editor of *Nation and Narration* (1990).

R. P. BLACKMUR (1904–1965), poet and critic, taught in the English Department at Princeton University from 1940 until his death. He traveled worldwide as a cultural critic and American ambassador of the intellect under the auspices of the Rockefeller Foundation and from 1961 to 1962, he lectured as the Pitt Professor of American History and Institutions at Cambridge University. His books include *The Expense of Greatness* (1940); *Language as Gesture: Essays in Poetry* (1952); *New Criticism in the United States* (1959); *Eleven Essays in the European Novel* (1964); *Poems of R. P. Blackmur* (1977); and *Studies in Henry James* (1980).

CLEANTH BROOKS (1906–1994) taught at Louisiana State University, University of Texas, and University of Michigan, before he accepted a post in the English Department at Yale University, where he taught until his retirement in 1975. He is the author or editor of several books, including *Modern Poetry and the Tradition* (1939); *The Well-Wrought Urn* (1947); *Literary Criticism: A Short History* (1957); and *The Hidden God: Studies in Hemingway, Faulkner, Yeats, Eliot, and Warren* (1963).

KENNETH BURKE (1897–1995), reviewer, editor, translator, poet, and short fiction writer, was the author of many books. He accepted several part-time teaching positions, including one at the New School for Social Research in New York, at the University of Chicago and at Bennington College in Vermont. His critical books include *Counter-Statement* (1931); *Attitudes toward History* (1937); *Grammar of Motives* (1945); and *Language as Symbolic Action: Essays on Life, Literature, and Method* (1966).

PAUL DE MAN (1919–1983) taught at Bard College and later became Sterling Professor of English at Yale University. His books include *Blindness and Insight: Essays in the Rhetoric of Contemporary Criticism* (1971, rev. ed. 1983); *Allegories of Reading: Figural Language in Rousseau, Nietzsche, Rilke, and Proust* (1979); and *The Rhetoric of Romanticism* (1984).

ANDREW DuBois is a graduate student in the Department of English and American Literature and Language at Harvard University. His works include "Modernist Lyric in the Culture of Capital" (with Frank Lentricchia) in the *Cambridge History of American Literature*. He has also published in the *Harvard Review, Publisher's Weekly*, and the encyclopedia *Africana*.

STANLEY FISH is Dean of the College of Liberal Arts and Sciences at the University of Illinois at Chicago and Distinguished Visiting Professor at John Marshall Law School. He is the author and editor of several books, including *Surprised By Sin: The Reader in* Paradise Lost (1967, 2nd ed. 1998); *Is There a Text in This Class?: The Authority of Interpretive Communities* (1980); *Doing What Comes Naturally: Change, Rhetoric, and the Practice of Theory in Literary and Legal Studies* (1989); *Professional Correctness: Literary Studies and Political Change* (1995); and most recently, *How Milton Works* (2001).

CATHERINE GALLAGHER is Eggers Professor of English at the University of California, Berkeley, where she has taught since 1980. She is the author of *The Industrial Reformation of English Fiction: Social Discourse and Narrative Form, 1832–1867* (1985); *Nobody's Story: The Vanishing Acts of Women Writers in the Marketplace, 1670–1820* (1994); and *Practicing New Historicism* (2000, with Stephen Greenblatt). Her work as editor includes *The Making of the Modern Body: Sexuality and Society in the Nineteenth Century* (1987) and Aphra Behn's *Oroonoko; or, The Royal Slave* (1999).

SANDRA M. GILBERT is Professor of English at the University of California, Davis. She is the author and editor of several critical books and anthologies, including *The Madwoman in the Attic: The Woman Writer and the Nineteenth-Century Literary Imagination* (1979, 2nd ed. 2000); *The Norton Anthology of Literature by Women* (1985, rev. ed. 1996); *No Man's Land: The Place of the Woman Writer in the Twentieth Century* (1988); and *Masterpiece Theatre: An Academic Melodrama* (1995), all coauthored or coedited with Susan Gubar. She is also the author of several volumes of poetry, most recently *Kissing the Bread: New and Selected Poems, 1969–1999* (2000).

STEPHEN GREENBLATT is Cogan University Professor of English and Chair of the Concentration in History and Literature at Harvard University. His books include *Renaissance Self-Fashioning: From More to Shakespeare* (1980); *Shakespearean Negotiations* (1988); *Learning to Curse: Essays in Early Modern Culture* (1990); *Practicing New Historicism* (2000, with Catherine Gallagher); and, most recently, *Hamlet in Purgatory* (2001). Books he has edited include *Representing the English Renaissance* (1983); *The Norton Shakespeare* (1997); and *The Norton Anthology of English Literature* (7th ed., 2000).

SUSAN GUBAR is Distinguished Professor of English at Indiana University, Bloomington. She is the author and editor of numerous books, including *The Madwoman in the Attic: The Woman Writer and the Nineteenth-Century Literary Imagination* (1979, 2nd ed. 2000), *The Norton Anthology of Literature by Women* (1985, rev. ed., 1996); *No Man's Land: The Place of the Woman Writer in the Twentieth Century* (1988); and *Masterpiece Theatre: An Academic Melodrama* (1995), all coauthored or coedited with Sandra M. Gilbert; *Race Changes: White Skin, Black Face in American Culture* (1997); and most recently, *Critical Condition: Feminism at the Turn of the Century* (2000).

FREDRIC JAMESON is William A. Lane Jr., Professor of Comparative Literature, Professor of Romance Studies, and Chair of the Literature Program at Duke University. He is the author and editor of many books, including *Marxism and Form* (1972), *The Prison-House of Language* (1972); *The Political Unconscious* (1981); *Postmodernism, or, The Cultural Logic of Late Capitalism* (Duke, 1990); *Brecht and Method* (1998); and *The Cultural Turn* (1998).

MURRAY KRIEGER (1923–2000) was University Professor of English, Emeritus, at the University of California, Irvine, where he was the founding Director of the University of California Humanities Research Institute. He was also the founding Director of the School of Criticism and Theory at the University of California, Irvine. His numerous books include *The New Apologists for Poetry* (1956); *The Tragic Vision* (1960); *The Play and Place of Criticism* (1967); *The Classic Vision* (1971); *Theory of Criticism: A Tradition and its System* (1976); *Words About Words About Words: Theory, Criticism, and the Literary Text* (1988); and *The Institution of Theory* (1994).

FRANK LENTRICCHIA is Katherine Everett Gilbert Professor of Literature at Duke University. His critical books include *After the New Criticism* (1980); *Criticism and Social Change* (1983); *Ariel and the Police* (1988); and *Modernist Quartet* (1994). He is the author of a memoir, *The Edge of Night* (1994), and several novels, including *Johnny Critelli and The Knifemen: Two Novels* (1996); *The Music of the Inferno* (1999); and most recently *Lucchesi and The Whale* (Duke, 2001). His work as an editor includes *Critical Terms for Literary Study* (1988, rev. ed. 1995) and *Introducing Don DeLillo* (Duke, 1991).

FRANCO MORETTI is Professor of English and Director of the Center for the Study of the Novel at Stanford University. His books include *Signs Taken for Wonders: Essays in the Sociology of Literary Forms* (1983); *The Way of the World: The Bildungsroman in European Culture* (1987); *Modern Epic: The World-System from Goethe to García-Marquez* (1995); and *Atlas of the European Novel, 1800–1900* (1998).

JOHN CROWE RANSOM (1888–1974) taught in the English departments at Vanderbilt University and Kenyon College. The author of several books, his critical works include *The World's Body* (1938); *The New Criticism* (1941); and *Beating the Bushes: Selected Essays, 1941–1970* (1972). As a poet, his books include *Chills and Fever* (1924); *Two Gentlemen in Bonds* (1927); and *Selected Poems* (1945, rev. ed., 1963).

EVE KOSOFSKY SEDGWICK is Distinguished Professor at the City University of New York Graduate Center. She is the author of *Between Men: English Literature and Male Homosocial Desire* (1985, rev. ed. 1993); *Epistemology of the Closet* (1990); and *Tendencies* (1993). Her work as an editor includes *Performativity and Performance* (1995) and *Novel Gazing: Queer Readings in Fiction* (1997). Her most recent book is *A Dialogue on Love* (1999).

HELEN VENDLER began her academic career with an undergraduate degree in chemistry before deciding—while studying French and Italian on a Fulbright in Belgium—to devote her life to literature. She is now the A. Kingsley Porter Professor of English at Harvard University. Vendler has received sixteen honorary degrees and published numerous books, including *The Odes of John Keats* (1983); *Soul Says: On Recent Poetry* (1995); *The Art of Shakespeare's Sonnets* (1997); and *Seamus Heaney* (1998).

ACKNOWLEDGMENT OF COPYRIGHTS

John Crowe Ransom, "Poetry: A Note on Ontology," from *The World's Body*. Reprinted by permission of Simon and Schuster, Inc.

Cleanth Brooks, "Keats's Sylvan Historian: History Without Footnotes," from *The Well Wrought Urn: Studies in the Structure of Poetry*. Copyright ©1947 by Cleanth Brooks, renewed copyright ©1975 by Cleanth Brooks. Reprinted by permission of Harcourt, Inc.

Kenneth Burke, "Symbolic Action in a Poem by Keats," from *A Grammar of Motives* (Berkeley: University of California Press, 1969). Copyright ©1969 The Regents of the University of California. Reprinted by permission of University of California Press.

Krieger, Murray. "The Ekphrastic Principle and the Still Movement of Poetry; or, *Laokoön* Revisited," from *The Play and the Place of Criticism*, pp. 105–128. Copyright ©1967 The Johns Hopkins University Press. Reprinted with permission of The Johns Hopkins University Press.

R. P. Blackmur, "Examples of Wallace Stevens," from *Language as Gesture: Essays in Poetry*. Copyright ©1952 by Richard P. Blackmur and renewed 1980 by Elizabeth Blackmur. Reprinted by permission of Harcourt, Inc.

Helen Vendler, "Stevens and Keats's 'To Autumn.'" Copyright ©1980 by Helen Vendler. Reprinted by permission.

Fish, Stanley. " 'Lycidas': A Poem Finally Anonymous." *Glyph 8, Textual Studies*, edited by Walter Benn Michaels, pp. 1–18. Copyright ©1981 The Johns Hopkins University Press. Reprinted by permission of The Johns Hopkins University Press.

Paul de Man, "Literary History and Literary Modernity," from *Blindness and Insight: Essays in the Rhetoric of Contemporary Criticism*. Copyright ©1971 by Paul de Man. Used by permission of Oxford University Press, Inc.

Roland Barthes, "The Romans in Films," "Novels and Children," "Steak and Chips," and "The Great Family of Man," from *Mythologies*, translated by Annette Lavers. Translation copyright ©1972 by Jonathan Cape Ltd. Reprinted by permission of Hill and Wang, a division of Farrar, Straus and Giroux, LLC.

Catherine Gallagher and Stephen Greenblatt, "The Mousetrap," from *Practicing New Histori-cism*. Copyright © 2000 by The University of Chicago. Reprinted by permission of The Uni-versity of Chicago Press.

Sandra Gilbert and Susan Gubar, "Jane Austen's Cover Story (And Its Secret Agents)," from *The Madwoman in the Attic: The Woman Writer and the Nineteenth-Century Literary Imagina-tion*. Copyright © 1979 by Yale University Press. Reprinted by permission of Yale Univer-sity Press.

Eve Kosofsky Sedgwick, "Jane Austen and the Masturbating Girl." Copyright ©1991 by Eve Kosofsky Sedgwick. Reprinted by permission of author.

Franco Moretti, "*Ulysses* and the Twentieth Century," from *Modern Epic: The World-System from Goethe to García-Márquez*. Trans. Quintin Hoare (New York: Verso Books, 1996), pp. 149–167. Reprinted by permission of Verso Books.

Houston A. Baker Jr., "To Move without Moving: An Analysis of Creativity and Commerce in Ralph Ellison's Trueblood Episode." Reprinted by permission of the Modern Language Asso-ciation of America.

Bhabha, Homi, "The World and Home." *Social Text* 10, nos. 2–3 (1992): 141–153. Copyright © 1992 *Social Text*.

INDEX

Frank Lentricchia is the Katherine Everett Gilbert
Professor of Literature at Duke University. His critical
work includes *After the New Criticism* (1980), *Ariel and
the Police* (1988), and *Modernist Quartet* (1994). He is also
the author of numerous books and novels including *The
Edge of Night* (1994), and *Lucchesi and the Whale* (Duke,
2001).

Andrew DuBois is the coauthor, with Frank Lentricchia, of
"Modernist Lyric in the Culture of Capital," a book-length
section of the *Cambridge History of American Literature*.
He is currently a graduate student at Harvard University
and is writing a dissertation on John Ashbery.

Library of Congress Cataloging-in-Publication Data
Close reading : the reader / edited by Frank Lentricchia
and Andrew DuBois.
Includes bibliographical references and index.
ISBN 0–8223–3026–1 (cloth : alk. paper)
ISBN 0–8223–3039–3 (pbk. : alk. paper)
1. English literature—History and criticism—Theory, etc.
2. American literature—History and criticism—Theory,
etc.   I. Lentricchia, Frank.   II. DuBois, A. (Andrew)
PR21 .C58   2003   820.9—dc21   2002009198